COMPUTER SUPPORTED
COOPERATIVE WORK

Springer
London
Berlin
Heidelberg
New York
Barcelona
Budapest
Hong Kong
Milan
Paris
Santa Clara
Singapore
Tokyo

Stefan Kirn and
Gregory O'Hare (Eds)

Cooperative Knowledge Processing

The Key Technology for
Intelligent Organizations

 Springer

Stefan Kirn, Dr.rer.nat
Technische Universität
Ilmenau
Postfach 327, Max-Planck-
Ring 14, 98684 Ilmenau,
Germany

Gregory O'Hare, BSc, MSc,
CEng
Department of Computer
Science
University College Dublin,
Belfield, Dublin 4, Ireland

Series Editors

Dan Diaper
Department of Computer
Science, University of
Liverpool
PO Box 147, Liverpool L69
3BX, UK

Colston Sanger
GID Ltd, Little Shotters Ley,
Farnham Lane, Haselmere,
Surrey GU27 1HA, UK

ISBN 3-540-19951-9 Springer-Verlag Berlin Heidelberg New York

British Library Cataloguing in Publication Data
Cooperative Knowledge Processing: Key Technology for Intelligent
Organizations. – (Computer Supported Cooperative Work Series)
   I. Kirn, Stefan II. O'Hare, Greg
   III. Series
   658.4038011
   ISBN 3-540-19951-9

Library of Congress Cataloging-in-Publication Data
Cooperative knowledge processing: the key technology for intelligent organiza-
tions/Stefan Kirn and Greg O'Hare (eds)
   p. cm. -- (Computer supported cooperative work)
   Includes bibliographical references and index.
   ISBN 3-540-19951-9 (alk. paper)
   1. Work groups--Data processing. 2. Information technology-Management.
   I. Kirn, Stefan. II. O'Hare, G. M. P. (Greg M. P.) III. Series
   HD66.2   1996
   658.4'086'0285--dc20   96-9536

The use of registered names, trademarks etc. in this publication does not imply,
even in the absence of a specific statement, that such names are exempt from the
relevant laws and regulations and therefore free for general use.

The publisher makes no representation, express or implied, with regard to the
accuracy of the information contained in this book and cannot accept any legal
responsibility or liability for any errors or omissions that may be made.

Typeset by On-Screen Typography, Cheshunt, Herts
Printed and bound at the Athenæum Press Ltd., Gateshead, Tyne and Wear
34/3830-543210 Printed on acid-free paper

Contents Summary

The Contributors xvii

Preface xxi

1   Cooperative Knowledge Processing – Research
    Framework and Applications
    St. Kirn 1

2   Coordination in Organizations
    R. Müller 26

3   Communication-Oriented Approaches to Support
    Multi-User Processes in Office Work
    M. Syring and U. Hasenkamp 43

4   Coordinating Human and Software Agents through
    Electronic Mail
    *I. Finch, F. P. Coenen, T.J. M. Bench-Capon and
    M. J. R. Shave* 64

5   User Control over Coordination Mechanisms in
    Office Information Systems
    N. Mehandjiev, L. Bottaci and R. Phillips 79

6   Computational Support for the Management of
    Social Processes within Organizational Teams
    G. M. P. O'Hare, L. Macauley, P. Dongha and S. Viller 97

7   The Wolf in Sheep's Clothing: How Locks Can
    Gently Control Collaboration
    R. Unland 117

8   Enhancing Organizational Intelligence through
    Cooperative Problem Solving
    St. Kirn 139

9   Organizational Intelligence and Negotiation Based
    DAI Systems – Theoretical Foundations and
    Experimental Results
    R. Unland and St. Kirn 155

10 Incorporating Organizational Design Principles and
    Experiences into the Design and Implementation
    of Multi Agent Systems
    S. Abbas and G. M. P. O'Hare 173

11 Coordination Protocols
    K. Sundermeyer 196

12 Modeling Distributed Industrial Processes in a
    Multi-Agent Framework
    F. Brazier, B. Dunin-Keplicz, N. Jennings and J. Treur 212

13 Utilitarian Coalition Formation Between
    Autonomous Agents for Cooperative Information
    Gathering
    M. Klusch 230

Epilogue: Computers, Networks and the Corporation
T. Malone and J. Rockart 258

References 269

Name Index 289

Subject Index 293

Contents

The Contributors.. xvii

Preface xxi

1   Cooperative Knowledge Processing – Research
    Framework and Applications
    St. Kirn 1
    1.1   Introduction... 1
    1.2   Organizational Paradigms: Evolving Role of
           Information Technology 2
           1.2.1   Early Work.. 2
           1.2.2   Decision-Orientated Organization Theory.... 3
           1.2.3   Management of the 1990s Research
                   Program 4
           1.2.4   Integration of Human and Machine-Based
                   Problem Solving.. 7
    1.3   New Organizational Strategies: A Brief Review....... 7
           1.3.1   Business Process Orientation 8
           1.3.2   Fractalization 9
           1.3.3   Fractalization versus Business Process
                   Orientation: Conflicting Strategies? 9
    1.4   Technology of Cooperative Knowledge
           Processing 11
           1.4.1   Framework... 11
           1.4.2   Multi-Agent Decision Support Systems
                   (MA-DSS) 12
           1.4.3   Human Computer Cooperative Work
                   (HCCW)... 14
    1.5   Application Perspectives 16
           1.5.1   Attention Focusing Capabilities 17
           1.5.2   Knowledge Discovery 18

1.5.3   Business Process Orientation 19
1.5.4   Self-Organization Skills................................. 23
1.6   Summary... 24

2   **Coordination in Organizations**
R. Müller.. 26
2.1   Introduction... 26
2.2   Organizational Coordination............................. 27
2.2.1   Coordination Concepts 27
2.2.2   Types of Coordination.......................... 30
2.3   Computers and Coordination............................. 32
2.3.1   Possible Roles of the Computer.......... 32
2.3.2   Distributed Intelligence....................... 35
2.4   Design Issues and Applications 37
2.5   Example of a Strategy Related Coordination
System 38
2.5.1   Perception of Common Objects 40
2.5.2   Communication....................................... 41
2.5.3   Conflict Management (Group Decision
Making)... 42

√ 3   **Communication-Oriented Approaches to Support
Multi-User Processes in Office Work**
M. Syring and U. Hasenkamp 43
3.1   Introduction... 43
3.2   Office Work... 43
3.3   Requirements to Support Multi-User Processes in
Office Work... 45
3.3.1   Basic Requirements............................... 45
3.3.2   Formal Requirements 46
3.4   Communication Orientated Approaches for
Supporting Office Work 48
3.4.1   Decision Orientation vs. Communication
Orientation 48
3.4.2   Approaches and Systems for the Support
of Unstructured Communication 49
3.4.3   Approaches and Systems for the Support of
Structured Communication.................... 52
3.4.4   Other Approaches and Systems for the
Support of Office Group Work 59
3.5   Evaluation of the Approaches Presented................. 59
3.6   Summary... 63

4   Coordinating Human and Software Agents through Electronic Mail
*I. Finch, F. P. Coenen, T. J. M. Bench-Capon and
M. J. R. Shave* 64

4.1   Introduction... 64
4.2   Software Support Tools 65
   4.2.1   Simple Message Filtering.............................. 65
   4.2.2   Active Filtering...66
   4.2.3   Autonomous Agents....................................... 67
   4.2.4   Combining Simple Filters, Active Filters
         and Autonomous Agents.............................. 68
4.3   Modes of Interaction with Adcmail........................... 68
   4.3.1   Interactive Use of Adcmail............................ 69
   4.3.2   Filtering in Adcmail.. 69
   4.3.3   Adcmail Sub-systems 70
   4.3.4   The Task Scripting Language........................ 70
4.4   The Coordination Mechanism 71
   4.4.1   Human Agents 72
   4.4.2   Computer Supported Humans 74
   4.4.3   Autonomous Sub-systems............................. 75
4.5   Conclusions 76

5   User Control over Coordination Mechanisms in Office Information Systems
N. Mehandjiev, L. Bottaci and R. Phillips 79

5.1   Introduction... 79
5.2   Office Model in ECHOES 80
5.3   Collaborative Work Scenarios 82
   5.3.1   Scenario 1:Evolutionary Changes in the
         Processing of Application Forms................. 83
   5.3.2   Scenario 2: Answering a Nonroutine
         Enquiry 86
5.4   Modeling Coordination Mechanisms in
   ECHOES... 88
   5.4.1   Information Flow Aspect................................ 88
   5.4.2   Information Description Aspect 88
   5.4.3   Organizational Aspect.................................... 89
   5.4.4   Service Description Aspect............................ 89
   5.4.5   Degrees of Control over Coordination
         Mechanisms 92
5.5   Related Research.. 93
5.6   The ECHOES Project.. 95

5.6.1   Current State of the Prototype 95
5.6.2   Further Work Required................................. 95
5.7   Summary and Conclusion............................... 95

**6 Computational Support for the Management of Social
Processes within Organizational Teams**
G. M. P. O'Hare, L. Macauley, P. Dongha and S. Viller 97
6.1   Introduction.. 97
6.2   The Cooperative Requirements Capture (CRC)
        Project 98
6.3   The CRC Prototype 99
6.4   Description of the CRC User Interface.................. 103
        6.4.1   The Personal Communication Window 105
        6.4.2   The Group Communication Window........ 105
        6.4.3   The CRC Agenda Window.................... 105
        6.4.4   The Public Window 105
        6.4.5   Description Windows....................... 106
        6.4.6   The Brainstorming Window................. 106
        6.4.7   The CRC Group Members Window 106
6.5   Why Facilitation?...................................... 106
6.6   The Role of the Facilitator 107
6.7   CRC Support for the Social Process.................... 109
6.8   Facilitator Support within CRC Prototype 109
        6.8.1   Communication............................. 110
        6.8.2   Agenda Management....................... 110
        6.8.3   Monitoring Group Activity 110
        6.8.4   Monitoring Individual Activity 112
        6.8.5   Display Group Dynamics 112
        6.8.6   Recognising Problematic Social
                Syndromes................................. 112
        6.8.7   Retrospective Analysis 113
6.9   Future Work 114
6.10   Conclusions 114

**7 The Wolf in Sheep's Clothing: How Locks Can
Gently Control Collaboration**
R. Unland 117
7.1   Introduction... 117
7.2   Concurrency Control and Cooperative Work....... 120
        7.2.1   Extended Set of Lock Modes.............. 121
        7.2.2   The Two Effects of a Lock............... 122
        7.2.3   The Semantics of the Lock Modes........ 124

7.2.4 A Short Discussion of Consistency Aspects.................................. 124

7.2.5 Dynamic Assignment of an External Effect (Open Lock) 125

7.2.6 Upgrading a Lock 125

7.3 Locks in the Context of Nested Transactions........ 127

7.4 Rules on Locks and Notification Services.............. 129

7.5 Object-Related Locks.. 133

7.6 Subject-Related Locks 136

7.7 Conclusion... 137

8 **Enhancing Organizational Intelligence through Cooperative Problem Solving**
St. Kirn 139

8.1 Introduction... 139

8.2 Organisational Intelligence (OI)............................. 140

8.2.1 Organisational Process Intelligence 142

8.2.2 Organisational Product Intelligence........... 143

8.3 Incorporating Organizational Intelligence into Distributed AI Systems.. 143

8.3.1 Organisational Memory 143

8.3.2 Organisational Cognition............................ 146

8.3.3 Self Organisation, and Organisational Learning Skills... 147

8.3.4 Interactions between Multiagent Systems and their Environment................................ 149

8.3.5 Organisational Reasoning........................... 151

8.4 The Contribution of Distributed AI to the Intelligence of Computerized Enterprises 153

9 **Organizational Intelligence and Negotiation Based DAI Systems – Theoretical Foundations and Experimental Results**
R. Unland and St. Kirn 155

9.1 Introduction... 155

9.2 Theoretical Foundations 156

9.2.1 Matsuda's OI Approach – a Brief Introduction 156

9.2.2 The Capability to Learn from the Point of View of Organization Theory 157

9.3 Extension of Contract Net-Based Systems by OI Components... 160

9.4   Realization in a Scenario... 163
    9.4.1   Description of the Scenario......................... 163
    9.4.2   The Basic Structure of the System.............. 163
    9.4.3   Schematic Run of a Move in the
          OI-Scenario.. 165
9.5   Presentation and Evaluation of the Results........... 167
    9.5.1   Comparison Conventional ↔ Extended
          Contract Net... 168
    9.5.2.   Size of Organizational Memory................. 169
    9.5.3   Time Needed for Negotiated Moves.......... 170
9.6   Conclusion... 172

10   **Incorporating Organizational Design Principles and
Experiences into the Design and Implementation
of Multi Agent Systems**
S. Abbas and G. M. P. O'Hare.................................... 173
    10.1   Introduction... 173
    10.2   Distributed Artificial Intelligence (DAI)................ 174
    10.3   Organizational Theory (OT).................................... 176
    10.4   A DAI Perspective on Organisations..................... 178
    10.5   Synthesizing DAI & OT.. 179
        10.5.1   Social Ability.. 181
        10.5.2   Organizational Coherence........................... 181
        10.5.3   Task Decomposition..................................... 181
        10.5.4   Coordination.. 182
        10.5.5   Authority Relationships.............................. 182
        10.5.6   Decision Autonomy..................................... 183
        10.5.7   Communication.. 184
        10.5.8   Groups, Norms and Conformity................ 184
        10.5.9   Role... 185
        10.5.10 Environment.. 185
    10.6   Design Principles.. 186
    10.7   Agent Oriented Programming (AOP)..................... 187
    10.8   Warehouse World.. 189
    10.9   Design and Experimental Testing of Emergent
        Organizations.. 191
    10.10 Conclusions... 194

11   **Coordination Protocols**
K. Sundermeyer 196
    11.1   Introduction... 196
    11.2   From Speech Acts to Dialogs.................................. 197

11.2.1 Speech Acts and Message Types 198
11.2.2 Speech as Planned Action 200
11.2.3 Dialogs 201
11.3 Protocols 201
11.3.1 Task & Domain Specific Protocols 202
11.3.2 Generic Protocols 203
11.4 Conclusion 209

12 **Modeling Distributed Industrial Processes in a Multi-Agent Framework**
F. Brazier, B. Dunin-Keplicz, N. Jennings and J. Treur 212

12.1 Introduction 212
12.2 The Application Domain 213
12.3 A Specification Framework for Multi-Agent Systems 215
12.3.1 Task (De)composition 215
12.3.2 Information Exchange Between Tasks 217
12.3.3 Sequencing of Tasks 217
12.3.4 Delegation of Tasks 218
12.3.5 Knowledge Structures 219
12.4 Formal Model and Specification of a Multi-Agent System 219
12.4.1 Task Decomposition and Role Allocation. 219
12.4.2 Information Flow Within an Agent 220
12.4.3 Task Control Within an Agent 223
12.4.4 Control and Communication Between Agents 227
12.5 Discussion 228

13 **Utilitarian Coalition Formation Between Autonomous Agents for Cooperative Information Gathering**
M. Klusch 230

13.1 Introduction 230
13.2 A Brief Introduction to some Related Research Areas 231
13.2.1 Federated Database Systems 232
13.2.2 Terminological Knowledge Representation 236
13.3 The FCSI-Agent: Functionality and Architecture 237
13.3.1 Local Construction of Information Models 237

        13.3.2 Local Recognition of Interdatabase
                Dependencies... 241
13.4   Coalitions of FCSI Agents 244
        13.4.1 FCSI Coalition Types.................................... 245
        13.4.2 Decentralized Coalition Formation
                Between FCSI Agents 246
13.5   IDEAS – an Environment for the
        Implementation of FCSI Agents............................. 248
        13.5.1 A Brief Overview of IDEAS......................... 248
        13.5.2 Working with IDEAS.................................. 249
        13.5.3 Agent Execution 252
13.6   Conclusion and Discussion 254
13.7   Appendix 256

Epilogue: Computers, Networks and the Corporation
T. Malone and J. Rockart.. 258

References 269

Name Index...289

Subject Index.. 293

The Contributors

Shaheena Abbas

Department of Computation, University of Manchester Institute of Science and Technology (UMIST), PO Box 88, Manchester, M60 1QD, UK, abbas@sra.co.umist.ac.uk

Trevor Bench-Capon

Department of Computer Science, University of Liverpool, Liverpool, L69 3BX, UK, tbc@csc.liv.ac.uk

Leonardo Bottaci

Department of Computer Science, University of Hull, Hull HU6 7RX, UK, l.bottaci@dcs.hull.ac.uk

Frances Brazier

Artificial Intelligence Group, Department of Mathematics and Computer Science, Vrije Universiteit Amsterdam, De Boelelaan 1081a, 1081 HV Amsterdam, The Netherlands, frances@cs.vu.nl

Frans Coenen

Department of Computer Science, University of Liverpool, Liverpool, L69 3BX, UK, frans@csc.liv.ac.uk

Paul Dongha

Department of Computation, University of Manchester Institute of Science and Technology (UMIST), PO Box 88, Manchester, M60 1QD, UK, pauld@ccl.umist.ac.uk

Barbara Dunin-Keplicz

Institute of Informatics, University of Warsaw, ul. Banacha 2, 02-097 Warsaw, Poland, keplicz@mimuw.edu.pl

Ian Finch

Institute of Advanced Scientific Computation, University of Liverpool, Liverpool L69 3BX, UK, ian@csc.liv.ac.uk

Ulrich Hasenkamp

Fachbereich Wirtschaftswissenschaften, Phillips-Universität Marburg, Universitätsstr. 25, D-35037 Marburg, Germany, hasenkamp@wiwi.uni-marburg.de

Nick Jennings

Department of Electronic Engineering, Queen Mary and Westfield College, University of London, Mile End Road, London E1 4NS, UK, N.R.Jennings@qmw.ac.uk

Stefan Kirn

Technische Universität Ilmenau, Fakultät fur Wirtschaftswissenschaften, Institut für Wirtschaftsinformatik, PO Box 0565, D-98684 Ilmenau, Germany, Kirn@Wirtschaft.TU-Ilmenau.de

Matthias Klusch

Institut für Informatik, Christian-Albrechts-Universität Kiel, D-24118 Kiel, Germany, mkl@informatik.uni-kiel.de

Linda Macauley

Department of Computation, University of Manchester Institute of Science and Technology (UMIST), P.O. Box No. 88, Manchester, M60 1QD, UK, lindam@mac.co.umist.ac.uk

Thomas W. Malone

Center for Coordination Science, Massachusetts Institute of Technology (MIT), Cambridge, Massachusetts 02139, USA,

Nikolay Mehandjiev

Department of Management Systems and Sciences, University of Hull, Hull HU6 7RX, United Kingdom, N.D.MEHANDJIEV@msd.hull.ac.uk

Rolf Müller

Daimler Benz AG, Research and Technology, Organizational Computing, Alt-Moabit 96a, D-10559 Berlin, Germany, RMUELLER@DBresearch-berlin.de

Gregory O'Hare

Department of Computer Science, University College Dublin (UCD), Belfield, Dublin 4, Ireland, Gregory.OHare@ucd.ie

Roger Phillips

Department of Computer Science, University of Hull, Hull HU6 7RX, UK, r.phillips@dcs.hull.ac.uk

John F. Rockart

Center for Information Systems Research, Massachusetts Institute of Technology (MIT), Cambridge, Massachusetts 02139, USA

Michael Shave

Department of Computer Science, University of Liverpool, Liverpool, L69 3BX, UK, mshave@csc.liv.ac.uk

Kurt Sundermeyer

Forschung System Technik, Daimler Benz AG, Alt-Moabit 96a, D-10559 Berlin, Germany, sun@DBresearch-berlin.de

Michael Syring

MIT Gesellschaft für Management-Beratung, Informationssysteme und Technologie mbH, Lysegang 11, D-45139 Essen, Germany, michael.syring@MIT.rwe.de

Jan Treur

Artificial Intelligence Group, Department of Mathematics and Computer Science, Vrije Universiteit Amsterdam, De Boelelaan 1081a, 1081 HV Amsterdam, The Netherlands, treur@cs.vu.nl

Rainer Unland

University of Essen, Department of Mathematics and Computer Science, Database Management Systems and Knowledge Representation, D-45117 Essen, Germany, unlandr@informatik.uni-essen.de

Steve Viller

Computing Department, Lancaster University, Lancaster, LA1 4YR, UK, viller@comp.lancs.ac.uk

Preface

In the light of the challenges that face today's organizations, there is a growing recognition that future market success and long term survival of enterprises will increasingly depend upon the effective usage of information technology. Of late, a new generation of terminology has emerged to describe enterprises. This terminology draws heavily upon the virtual concept – virtual reality, virtual organization, virtual (working) environment, and indeed virtual product. However, developing computerized organisations for the 21st century demands serious thought with regard to the judicious integration of organizational theory, design and practice with research tools and methods from within information processing technology.

Within this book, we approach this aim from the perspective of a radically decentralized (possibly virtual) enterprise. We assume that organizations are becoming increasingly process-orientated, rather than adhering to the former more traditional organizational structures based upon task oriented models. This approach has proved illuminating in that, due to the inherent autonomy of organizational subunits any approach to coordinating decentralized activities (including workflows and business processes) necessitates a cooperative style of problem solving.

This book introduces the reader to a stimulating new field of interdisciplinary research in cooperative problem solving. In Chapter 1 Kirn presents a view of three central disciplines, namely those of Organizational Theory, Computer Supported Cooperative Work (CSCW) and Distributed Artificial Intelligence (DAI). The applications given here demonstrate how future enterprises will benefit from recent advances in the technological arena of cooperative knowledge processing.

Chapter 2 by Müller, reviews coordination concepts from organizational theory. It places special emphasis upon the availability of computerized instruments which may potentially facilitate the coordination task. Müller then introduces the concept of Distributed Intelligence. This chapter demonstrates that Distributed Intelligence provides a useful framework within which modern post-industrial organizations can be designed, even though it (still) relates to the human side of an enterprise.

In Chapter 3, Syring and Hasenkamp consider communication-oriented approaches to supporting office work, covering a wide range of applications from Message Handling Systems to Distributed Knowledge Based Systems. A common characteristic is the support of multi-user processes in small groups or organizations which primarily involves communication and coordination activities. However, one of the most important challenges, that of sufficient system flexibility remains, as yet, to be addressed. Syring and Hasenkamp focus on the most important system requirements within office applications and both present and evaluate the current state of existing approaches and applications including both commercial products and prototype systems.

In Chapter 4 Finch et al. explain how as organizations gravitate toward decentralized control structures software systems have evolved which both facilitate and mirror this new working metaphor. One important class of such software is termed Groupware. Groupware offers many benefits to decentralized organizations such as enabling coordination between geographically and/or temporally distributed team members and making available extra decision support facilities. There are however, disadvantages associated with groupware, most notably an increase in the sheer volume of information disseminated to users and the associated increase in tasks and responsibilities to the users' workload. A number of software techniques can be used in addressing these problems, but these techniques have associated advantages and disadvantages. Finch et al. thus advocate a mixture of techniques for maximum advantage, concentrating on the use of autonomous software agents.

Mehandjiev et al. in Chapter 5 discuss how if office information systems are to be more effective then users must be afforded a greater control over the coordination mechanisms present within such systems. The paper demonstrates how various high level coordination patterns could be user controlled in two ways: (i) modifying a coordination pattern to cope with evolving organizational practices and; (ii) overriding a coordination mechanism for exceptional cases. This user control is exercised through a multi paradigm visual language. Two collaborative work scenarios are used to demonstrate various user control techniques specifically an office system and a university application processing system. The different coordination mechanisms are then presented within that theoretical framework and are compared with similar mechanisms in other collaborative office systems.

O'Hare et al. examine the issue of collaborative activity which they believe to be the core ingredient of intelligent organizations of the future. In particular they describe the Cooperative Requirements Capture (CRC) project and their attempts within this project to support the social process associated with collaborative activity. The central component to such support is effective support for the facilitator. Chapter 6 considers the importance of facilitation and describes the computational support afforded within the CRC cooperative working platform. The overall design of this platform is presented together with the agent oriented metaphor embraced within its development.

Chapter 7 by Unland studies how the next generation of information systems can satisfy the constantly growing demand for an adequate and sufficient support for teamwork. Moreover, these systems must manage and provide access to large amounts of data and information. This calls for systems that, on the one hand guarantee the consistency of its data/information and provides its user with a consistent view of their data space, while on the other hand, are capable of supporting all aspects of synergistic work. These partially conflicting requirements place great demands upon the concurrent control components of such systems. Unland advocates a flexible and adaptable concurrency control scheme which is especially tailored to the needs of synergistic cooperative work. The proposed concepts must be interpreted as low level building blocks which provide a solid and uniform platform upon which application-specific semantics can be expressed in a comprehensive and natural manner.

In Chapter 8, Kirn reviews how the concept of organizations has emerged from non-organized "black-box" entities to so-called "computerized" organizations. Organizational researchers have started to redesign their models of intelligent organizations with respect to the availability of advanced computing technology. The recently emerged concept of Organizational Intelligence integrates these efforts to suggest five components of intelligent organizational skills (communication, memory, learning, cognition, and problem solving). The work presented aims to improve the integration of human and computer-based problem-solving capabilities, and it draws conclusions for the design of Distributed AI systems.

Based on the work presented in the previous chapter, Unland and Kirn in Chapter 9 introduce work on adding learning capabilities to multi agent systems. Based on a comprehensive review of theoretical work they show how learning skills can be incorporated into a negotiation-based cooperative problem solver. Experimental results are presented to demonstrate that the increased "intellectual" capabilities of the extended system substantially contributes to system performance as well as to the quality of solutions.

In Chapter 10 Abbas and O'Hare, discuss how the concept of an "organization" has emerged as central to the structuring of activities of both decentralized industrial and commercial conglomerates and collections of intelligent problem solvers within Distributed Artificial Intelligence (DAI) systems. They investigate the fields of organizational theory and DAI looking specifically at their respective concept of an organization. The result is a synthesis of this work, which identifies general design guidelines that ought to be incorporated into the design of Multi Agent Systems (MAS). A particular Multi Agent scenario is then considered, that of *Warehouse World*, from which an organizational workbench subsequently emerges in order to experiment with the form and structure of computational organizations. The development of this workbench is realized through the use of Agent Oriented Programming techniques. The authors strive to export these findings to organizational theory.

Sundermeyer in Chapter 11 makes contributions which deal with structured communication towards coordination of activities among artificial agents. A short survey is given of how and why speech act theory has been used for defining message types in order to describe dialogues in the form of protocols. Some domain dependent and generic protocols are presented in more detail before the state of the art is summed up and some requirements for future developments are formulated.

A declarative compositional modeling framework, DESIRE, which has been designed by Brazier et al. is discussed in Chapter 12. It models knowledge-intensive multi agent systems, and provides a means to model distributed industrial and business processes. An agent's knowledge, reasoning processes and interaction with other agents, and the world are explicitly specified within this framework. Electricity transportation management is used to illustrate the characteristic elements of the approach, in particular with respect to dynamic aspects of distributed industrial and business processes; aspects which are of importance to knowledge management and knowledge-engineering.

In Chapter 13, Klusch provides a novel approach, for the recognition of interdatabase dependencies (IDD) using a federative agent system FCSI. The architecture of the FCSI is designed as a set of coalition-based, cooperative, intelligent agents each of them uniquely assigned to one autonomous local database system. The FCSI aims for a cooperative solution for the problem of searching for semantically related information while strictly respecting the autonomy requirements of each individual database system. This approach is particularly interesting because it applies techniques from Distributed Artificial Intelligence with an important real-world problem, that of the integration of loosely coupled databases, that are under decentralized and, thus, more or less autonomous control.

The final chapter, contributed by Malone and Rockart, returns to the question as to how organizations in the future will be different from those of today. Referring to various examples that are already existing in the business world they demonstrate that, computer-based coordination and cooperation technology will change the way work is getting done. In that perspective, they depict the future of enterprises as that which was first discovered in the MIT's Management of the 1990s research program.

We gratefully acknowledge the kind and fruitful cooperation of many persons who have contributed ideas, spirit, and enthusiasm to the project of producing this book. First of all, we are indebted to Colston Sanger who introduced the idea of initiating a workshop at the Department of Trade and Industry (DTI) which subsequently took place in December 1993. Colston, together with Dan Diaper then promoted this book which includes a selection of the papers presented at the workshop, together with additional contributions from influential experts in the field. We gratefully acknowledge the readiness of all the contributors to produce high quality papers, and the gentle support of several reviewers spending their time and creativity to improve the readability, and the line of argumentation of the book. It was a pleasure to collaborate with them, in making it easy to produce a book that may be of interest to a broad readership in both academia and business. We further acknowledge the tremendous effort of all those people who have been involved in the technical production. Special thanks go to Beverley Ford, and Rosie Kemp at Springer who have permanently pushed this book over a long period of time. Finally, we are indebted to our friends and families, Peter and May who for so long provided an environment within which learning could take place, and in particular to two little girls named Jessica and Michelle who have learned a lot about how to produce small green books in a virtual publishing and editing environment.

Ilmenau and Dublin,   Stefan Kirn & Gregory O'Hare
August 1996

Chapter *1*

Cooperative Knowledge Processing – Research Framework and Application Perspectives

Stefan Kirn

1.1 Introduction

Global competition, dynamic markets, and rapidly decreasing cycles of technological innovations provide important challenges for organizations today. Worldwide (just in time) availability of information, and permanent changes in their cultural, social, and political settings requires enterprises to dramatically improve their flexibility, and their self organization capabilities. Two main organizational strategies have been developed, by which enterprises do address these challenges today: radical decentralization of hierarchical structures, and customer orientation through enterprise-wide business process (re-)engineering.

Both strategies, decentralization and business process orientation, apply to an organizational model which is increasingly penetrated through modern information technologies. More and more, organizational activities are going to be implemented by computational entities instead of involving human employees. Sequences of organizational activities (workflows, processes) are increasingly operated on a pure computational basis. It has further been argued that modern information technologies cause organizational disintegration. This has given rise to the idea of computerized, information-integrated enterprises as the model of future organizations.

Decentralization enforces the autonomy of organizational subunits. As a consequence, local decision procedures as well as the behavior of those organizational subunits turn out to be under decentralized control. This calls for a bottom-up approach to coordination. On the other hand, business process orientation requires a more centralized approach, or at least a global view from which a top down approach to business process (re-)engineering can be developed. As a result, any approach resolving the conflict between these two organizational strategies requires to sustain the autonomy of the organizational units involved. This, in turn, calls for a pluralistic, coopera-tive, knowledge-based approach to coordination and conflict resolution.

Drawing from these requirements – computerization, fractalization, process orientation – we argue that *Cooperative Knowledge Processing* is a key technology for computerized, process-driven organizations. For this purpose, we first review how the role of information technology in organi-zation theory has changed in the past. Then, fractalization, and business process orientation are evaluated in order to work out the inherent conflict that exists between these new organizational strategies. Building on this analysis we introduce the reader into the field of cooperative knowledge processing, and outline the most important subfields of this new area of interdisciplinary research. The chapter then proceeds with a study on appli-cation perspectives in business, organization, and management. Finally, the last section summarizes the results.

1.2 Organizational Paradigms: Evolving Role of Information Technology

Organizational design requires to shape organizational structures so that the resulting body can pursue the aims and objectives formally introduced, negotiated and decided upon by the owners of the organization, its members and participants. Thus, the description, analysis, and explanation of organi-zations is one of the most important areas in management science. Since long, a diversity of organizational models has been developed, each with a partic-ular focus, and with distinct applicability to theoretical and real-world prob-lems. From these, we have selected four models in order to demonstrate how the integration of information technology into organizational research has changed over the past 50 to 70 years. They are: (i) the black box model orig-inating from traditional macroeconomic theory, (ii) the production-orien-tated organizational model of Gutenberg, (iii) the decision-orientated approach to modeling organizations, and (iv) the organizational model orig-inating from the Management of the 1990s Research Program which has been conducted by the Massachusetts Institute of Technology (MIT). While the first two models introduce the historical roots, models (iii) and (iv) originate from contemporary organizational research that considers information tech-nology as a constitutive component of modern organizations.

1.2.1 Early Work

The *black box-model* emerged from traditional macroeconomic theory, it considers organizations as single atomic entities. This model is not concerned with why an organization behaves as it does, nor does it relate internal structures and activities of an enterprise to its success on the market. Thus, there is no need and even no means to investigate how organizational information processing should be operated in order to improve the behavior of an enterprise, or to contribute to the integration of the organization with its environment.

The *production-orientated* model has been developed as a part of Gutenberg's production theory (Gutenberg 1951). Gutenberg distinguished two subsystems of an enterprise, namely the physical subsystem (that is, the physical place of production) and the administrative subsystem which involves decision making, planning, organization, and the management of information. In that view, enterprises *have* an organization. Organization is *the tool* by which the results of planning can be set in place. The important contribution of Gutenberg was to reveal that the internal organizational structure affects the outcome of production. However, his model involves two important shortcomings: production workers are considered as machine-like components of manufacturing systems, a concept which draws from the theory of scientific management (Taylor 1919). Further, the model does not investigate how the management and processing of information can *actively* contribute to organizational aims and objectives.

1.2.2 Decision-Orientated Organization Theory

The next important step in organization theory turns the focus of interest to decision making. It had been recognized that any economic activity presupposes decision making which, in turn, requires extensive information processing capabilities (March and Simon 1958, Huber and McDaniel 1986). By this way, the human factor and models of decision making have been introduced into the organizational model. As a result, three distinct organizational subsystems have been identified that together constitute the decision-orientated organizational model. They are:

1. The *subsystem of organizational aims and objectives* integrates the aims and objectives of the persons, groups, and organizational bodies that are related to the organization.
2. The *information processing subsystem* stores, retrieves, and processes data, information and knowledge in order to enable decisions that fit with the organizational aims and objectives. The information processing subsystem may, or may not involve information processing technology.
3. In general, decision making involves more than one person. Thus, the results of decision making also depends upon the *social subsystem* of an organization, i.e. the social relationships, the balance of power, the availability of information, etc.

Together, these three subsystems constitute organizations as goal-driven socio-technical entities that acquire and process information. Enterprises *are* organizations involving *humans* who *collaborate* in order to *produce* commodities and services. The effectiveness of organizational processes is directly related to the capability of decision making. Information technology adds to decision making in that it speeds up decision processes, and that it improves the quality of decisions by involving more actual, and even more relevant information as before. In that view, information technology is a tool that facilitates the storage, accessibility, maintenance, and manipulation of data. Software systems are assumed to being more or less passive technical components that are not capable to apply to organizational roles. Thus, from the decision-orientated approach quite similar shortcomings may evolve as from the production-orientated model, which considered the organization as being a tool to implement decisions, and which involved a far too restrictive model of production workers.

1.2.3 Management of the 1990s Research Program

The Management of the 1990s program was charged with the task of investigating the impact of the new information technologies on organizations with the goal of determining how the organizations of the 1990s – and beyond – will differ from those of today (Thurow 1991). To this purpose, the program used a very broad definition of information technology including all types of hardware, communication networks, and software. It also addressed the impact of rapidly increasing availability of computing power, and the growing importance of information technology integration.

From our perspective, four implications from this research are particularily relevant (Morton 1991, p. 11–21):

1. *Information technology is enabling fundamental changes in the way work is done.*

The degree to which a person can be affected by changes in information technology depends on how much of the work is based on information. Morton writes that information technology will be able to radically change cost structures – production work, coordinative work, and management work – of at least 50% of the members of an organization. Information technology will affect the economics and functionality of the coordination process in three ways:

(a) Distance can be shrunk to zero. Thus, the location of work can be re-examined, as can potential partners.
(b) Time can be shrunk toward zero or, at least, be significantly reduced.

(c) The accessibility and, thus, the role of organizational memory will change radically, as will the definition and maintenance of organizational knowledge.

2. *Information technology causes a disintegration of traditional organizational forms.*

The Management of the 1990s research program "... has shown that information technology is a critical enabler of the re-creation (redefinition) of the organization" (Morton 1991, p. 17). It affects the distribution of power, function, and control, the definition of organizational aims and objectives, and organizational culture. In that view, information technology facilitates adhocracies, organizational networking, the creation of virtual enterprises, and other new forms of getting work more effectively done as it is possible today. In such organizational settings, horizontal and vertical structures can be created and modified within and across organizational borders, just depending on the current task, the availability of resources, and the actual situation on world-wide markets.

3. *Information technology is enabling the integration of business functions at all levels within and between organizations.*

Due to the continuing expansion of electronic networks and their integration into global networks, the ability to flexibly interconnect tasks and people is increasingly available and affordable. Recent successes of standardization efforts in information technology enable companies to easily exchange tasks, and even to exchange capabilities within and across enterprises. This enables enterprises to electronically integrate their structures and processes in four different forms: within the value chain, by creating end-to-end links between value chains of different organizations, through value chain substitution via subcontract or alliance, and through electronic markets. Thus, the relevance of the membership-criteria will dramatically be reduced, intra- and interorganizational structures will be intertwined, and organizational boundaries will become more permeable as they are today. In consequence, organizational strategies will no longer be defined in splendid isolation within single organizational units only (Figure 1.1).

However, one should note that organizations must have the right information technology infrastructure, i.e. communication networks, application programs, interconnecting software, and educated and empowered users before they can fully exploit any of these four forms of electronic integration.

4. *Information technology presents new strategic opportunities for organizations that reassess their missions and operations.*

According to Morton, the shifting competitive climate together with new ways of getting work done and the increased electronic integration requires organizations to step back and rethink their missions on the way they are going to conduct their operations. Here, two major stages need to be considered. Within the *automate stage* information technology, applications are designed to take the cost out of "production" (Morton 1991, p. 16). Automation often generates new information as a by-product. This involves the *informate stage* (Zuboff 1988). Its distinguished characteristic is that this new sort of information can require the persons concerned, to change their skills and management practices if this new information is to be used successfully in order to improve the performance of an organization. In other words: the "doer", or machine minder will become an "analyzer" who understands the overall process rather than just looking at the local task (Morton 1991, p. 17).

From the Management of the 1990s program we learn that computer technology does not only provide an infrastructure for communication and data management, but that it enables the implementation of new organizational strategies, and to initiate the development of completely new organizational solutions. This has already changed the internal structures of many existing enterprises, and has resulted in major modifications of world-wide market relationships (Morton 1991), too.

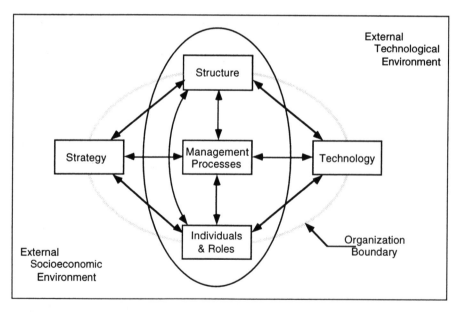

Figure 1.1   Framework of the management of the 1990s Program (Morton 1991)

1.2.4 Integration of Human and Machine-Based Problem Solving

The above discussion reveals that information technology is more and more penetrating our models, and our understanding of organizations. This requires us to rethink our current models of organizations. In future, we will see an increasing number of organizations that turn out to be pure computational entities collaborating in virtual environments in order to make monies for their owners. Such computational organizations are already well known in the financial services industry. For instance, a significant portion of today's business at the capital markets is operated by fully automated trading programs.

It thus has been recognized that it is quite unsatisfying to study such artificial enterprises from an organization theory perspective (Kirn *et al.* 1994). The only link left to traditional organization theory is that of humans are the owners of such computational organizations. The methods and tools provided by traditional organization theory are not suitable to deal with such computational organizations. Therefore, organization theory needs to be extended in that it can also be involved into describing, analyzing, explaining, and designing computerized, information integrated enterprises of the future. This raises the problem of how autonomous, self-contained computational agents (and, accordingly, computational organizations) can be incorporated into the organizational model. However, up to now there is little work in mainstream organizational research that really addresses this issue. Instead, it is left to related disciplines such as Operations Research (Matsuda 1992), Computer Supported Cooperative Work (Steiner *et al.* 1990), Coordination Theory (Malone and Crowston 1993; Kirn 1994), and Distributed Artificial Intelligence (Gasser 1992). Hence, up to now, the integration of human and artifical problem solving capabilities, which should be a topic of prior interest also to organization theory, is occupied by a cooperative effort of other scientific disciplines.

1.3 New Organizational Strategies: A Brief Review

In the past, a great deal of work has been devoted to develop new strategies by which organizations can meet the challenges of dynamic, and sometimes even unpredictable environments, rapidly decreasing cycles of innovation, and world-wide competition. Two different strategies can be identified: reengineering the *processes* of an organization, and radical decentralization (fractalization) of the *structure* of organizations. However, current approaches of business process orientation are, at least partially, incompatible with the strategy of radical decentralization. Applying to the

Management of the 1990s research program we suggest to resolve this inherent conflict through modern information technologies.

1.3.1 Business Process Orientation

According to Davenport a process may be defined as a structured measured set of activities, designed to produce a well-specified output for a single customer or market. Process orientation puts strong emphasis on *how* work is getting done, in contrast to a more product-orientated focus on *what*. Thus, business process orientation represents a revolutionary change in perspective: it turns the organization on its head, or at least on its side (Davenport 1993, p. 5).

The structure of business processes can clearly be distinguished from the more hierarchical forms of structure within an organization. While the latter is typically a snapshot which shows how responsibilities, resources, communication channels, and information flow are distributed across an organization, the former provides a dynamic view of how the organization delivers value. Further, while structures cannot be assessed or improved directly, processes involve cost, time, output quality and customer satisfaction, they relate to well known triggering events and they result in well defined final states. Thus, whenever one reduces cost or increases customer satisfaction processes are improved, and not the organizational hierarchy.

The key issues of process orientation can be summarized in five points (Davenport 1993, pp. 299–303):

1. Processes are the key elements to be addressed in order to transform organizations and to improve their performance.
2. An explicit – and holistic – approach to process orientation is necessary. This involves the description and analysis as well as the formal representation and the information technology-based management of business processes as the key factors for success.
3. Information technology provides a powerful tool for enabling and implementing processes.
4. How an enterprise approaches organization and human resources is critical to the enablement and implementation of smart business processes.
5. Process orientation must occur within a strategic context and must be guided by a vision of the future process states.

Since the pioneering work of Porter (Porter 1985), business process orientation has received an overwhelming attention by both academia and practitioners (Scheer 1994). Its most important contribution is that it provides for a systematic, intelligible approach to the modeling and (re-)engineering of organizations. Thus, for the rest of the chapter we assume that the design of future organizations will focus on processes, that is, that it will primarily be concerned with the modeling, management, and control of processes rather than applying to task decomposition, and to the modeling of static organizational structures.

1.3.2 Fractalization

The enterprise of the future will be radically decentralized, in order to meet the challenges of the increasing complexity of their environment, and the dynamics of world-wide competition. Decentralization involves the allocation of autonomy, resources, and responsibilities to deeper levels of the organizational hierarchy (Tapscott and Caston 1993, Warnecke 1991). This requires enterprises to replace the traditional approach of hierarchical planning by more decentralized concepts of coordination. In turn, autonomous organizational subunits need to exhibit a much greater degree of intelligence and self-referencing skills than they do today. This has given rise to the notion of organizational fractals (Warnecke 1991). These are equipped with self-organization skills thus enabling them not only to recursively form complex, highly organized entities but also to modify these entities, for instance with respect to dynamic environments or changing customer demands. Organizational fractals are provided with operational definitions of their local goals, and are capable to cooperatively creating global hierarchies of aims and objectives. They exhibit intelligent local and global coordination skills, and a benevolent style of cooperation. Accordingly, fractalization permits large organizations to exhibit greater flexibility and adaptivity, and also provides to them a medium through which they can effectively refresh their learning capabilities (Warnecke 1991).

1.3.3 Fractalization versus Business Process Orientation: Conflicting Strategies?

Organizational fractals involve a maximum degree of local autonomy, self-control, and self-organization skills. Aiming to maximize their local utility (for instance, in terms of profit), organizational fractals decide on their own, whether they are willing to cooperate, or to collaborate with other organizational units. There is no direct means, not even for the top management of an enterprise, by which fractals can be compelled to behave in a certain manner. The single acceptable way to control their behavior is through designing a globally consistent system of aims and objectives (Warnecke 1991).

However, due to bounded rationality, organizations are, in most cases, not able to establish consistent goal hierarchies. Instead, the different goals that exist within an organization are more or less inconsistent, the knowledge about goals and relationships between them remains necessarily incomplete, uncertain, fuzzy, and sometimes even false. Additional goal conflicts may arise between the goals of an organization and the preferences of its customers, between different organizations that wish to cooperate, and between the customers of distinct organizations that wish to pursue their aims in close cooperation.

On the other hand, current approaches to business process orientation presuppose that organizations have the time, knowledge and skills to precisely describe, analyze, and design enterprise-wide business processes. They further suppose that, through an iterative (not necessarily algorithmic) procedure of refinement, these descriptions can be augmented, or instantiated to more detailed descriptions of (partial) processes and fully expanded specifications of the respective workflows. This requires a centralized approach to business process engineering, or, at least, a global perspective (Hammer and Champy 1991) which, by definition, cannot exist within fractalized enterprises. Instead, organizational fractals must cooperate whenever they aim to create (bottom up!) an enterprise-wide business process. A similar conflict exists between the local autonomy of organizational fractals, and the need to tie them to an existing business process. These conflicts are directly related to the degree of autonomy of the fractals involved.

As a consequence, it is very difficult or may be even impossible in general to resolve these conflicts by standardized rules and decision criteria. Whenever one aims to introduce business process orientation into a system of organizational fractals one needs to apply to decentralized, cooperation-based concepts of process modeling and control (Kirn *et al.* 1994). Any coordination concept must sustain the individual autonomy of each single fractal, and it must provide appropriate knowledge processing techniques in order to cope with the epistemological issues of incompleteness, uncertainty, and fuzzyness.

These challenges can be addressed by recent advances in cooperative knowledge processing technology (Warnecke 1991, Kirn *et al.* 1994). This work aims to integrate decentralized but autonomously operating data and knowledge sources, and involves standard techniques from Artificial Intelligence in order to cope with the epistemological issues mentioned above. These techniques can help to bridge boundaries within and across organizations, and to flexibly exchange tasks, know how, and geographically distributed resources between distinct organizational units (Hastings 1993). By this way, they are quite well suited to reintegrate disintegrated organizational structures that have been replaced through "electronic" arm's-length relationships (Morton 1991, Hastings 1993).

1.4 Technology of Cooperative Knowledge Processing

1.4.1 Framework

Modern information technologies cause a disintegration of enterprises, which requires us to turn the attention to the (re-)integration of previously distributed organizational knowledge. This task requires a collaborative, interdisciplinary effort of different scientific disciplines, as there are organization theory, computer supported cooperative work, human computer interaction, and information processing technology (Simoudis and Adler 1992). With respect to such work, Figure 1.2 depicts some important topics in cooperative knowledge processing research. These are addressed by several ambitious research programs, for instance within ESPRIT (Europe), the Intelligent Manufacturing Systems initiative (Japan), and the DARPA Knowledge Sharing Effort (US).

We have argued, that any approach to coordinate decentralized activities needs to apply to cooperative styles of problem solving. For this purpose, and with respect to the number of humans and computational agents, six distinct types of cooperation can be identified. Each cooperation type refers to a distinguished area of research in cooperative knowledge processing (Table 1.1).

As far as knowledge processing is concerned, traditional Organization Theory and Groupware address cooperation is between *humans*. Thus, they both are concerned with supporting cooperative knowledge processing, but

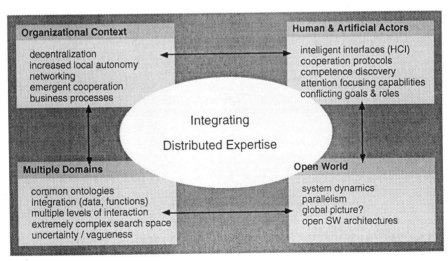

Figure 1.2   The challenges of cooperative knowledge processing

Table 1.1 Taxonomy of cooperation types in computerized organizations

multiple computational agents	Distributed Artificial Intelligence	Multi-Agent Decision Support Systems	Human Computer Cooperative Work
one computational agent		Personal Assistants (Assisting Computers, User Agents)	conventional Groupware
no computational agent involved			traditional Organization Theory
	no persons involved	one person	multiple persons

they do not provide any *cooperative knowledge processing technology*. Research in Personal Assistants (Hoschka 1991, Bocionek 1994) aims to develop hardware platforms and software agents in order to discharge humans from routine work. This has given rise to develop concepts of cooperation between one human expert and its intelligent assistant (Stolze 1991). Distributed Artificial Intelligence, on the other hand, is concerned with cooperative knowledge processing among pure computational entities, thus excluding humans from being involved (Bond and Gasser 1988a). Multi-Agent Decision Support Systems, and Human Computer Cooperative Work (Steiner *et al.* 1990a, Kirn 1993) refer to cooperation scenarios where a group of software agents either collaborate with one, or with several humans. Research in these areas involves perspectives from Distributed Artificial Intelligence (see also Chapters 8–13), (intelligent) Personal Assistants, Organization Theory (see also Chapters 2, 8, 9, 10) and Social Sciences.

Within this chapter, we are mainly interested in those subfields of cooperative knowledge processing, that involve two or more software agents, and at least one human expert. We further suppose that cooperation takes place in an organizational context. That is, the members of such Human Computer Teams are supposed to join the same organizational body, for instance the same company, organizational network, or virtual enterprise. We thus concentrate on Multi-Agent Decision Support Systems and Human Computer Cooperative Work, being primarily interested in the theoretical foundations, and organizational applications of these areas of cooperative knowledge processing.

1.4.2 Multi-Agent Decision Support Systems (MA-DSS)

Up to now, Multi-Agent Decision Support Systems are assumed being a subfield of Distributed Artificial Intelligence (Bond and Gasser 1988).

However, this classification is far too restrictive if one applies it to decision making in organizations, because of three reasons:

1. *Main Research Interest*: The main interest in doing research in Multi-Agent Decision Support Systems is on decision support. Thus, research in Multi-Agent Decision Support Systems addresses the integration of distributed expertise through information processing technology, in order to improve human decision making.
2. *Research Perspectives*: Research in Multi-Agent Decision Support Systems involves three distinct research perspectives:

   (a) The *decision support perspective* aims to improve (human) decision making through the integration of distributed expertise while at the same time preserving the local autonomy of "expertise-providers".
   (b) The *organization perspective* assumes that decision making is performed in organizations. Thus, any research approach is required to involve organizational structures and processes, hierarchies of aims and objectives, organizational behavior, etc.
   (c) The *technology perspective* supposes information technology support for cooperative knowledge processing. This involves a strong Distributed Artificial Intelligence Perspective, supplemented through advanced human computer interaction technology.

Thus, Multi-Agent Decision Support Systems have three main roots those of Decision Theory, Organization Theory, and Distributed Artificial Intelligence. Further, the development of Multi-Agent Decision Support Systems requires to involve deep knowledge from the respective application domains (for instance, financial consulting).

3. *Enabling Technology*: The design of attention (and, subsequently, knowledge) focusing capabilities of an organization is one of the hardest problems in organization theory in general (Blanning *et al.* 1992). From that perspective, Distributed Artificial Intelligence is an important enabling technology. However, it has been argued that Distributed Artificial Intelligence remains to be adapted more closely to the requirements of cooperation, and coordination in (human) organizations (Kirn 1994).

It is beyond the scope of this chapter to fully develop a research agenda in Multi-Agent Decision Support Systems. Although, Figure 1.3 depicts some of the most important questions that are currently approached by research in what one may call *organizational* Distributed Artificial Intelligence, and *information technology-oriented* Organization Theory. In the past, the major problem was to involve Distributed Artificial Intelligence technology into productive decision support applications. This, however, may have already

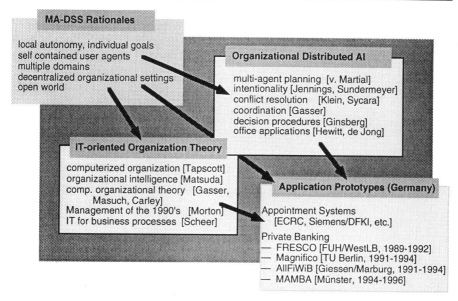

Figure 1.3   Multi-agent decision support systems: rationales, and ongoing research

begun to change. For instance, in 1992 a five-year national research program
has been launched in Germany that addresses distributed information
system applications in business and management (König *et al.* 1995). The
mission of this research program is to provide solutions, that meet the urgent
demand of industry for information *processing* technology in order to support
knowledge processing in loosely coupled organizations such as adhocracies,
virtual organizations, and strategic networks. Within that program, eight out
of 22 projects base their technical approach on Distributed Artificial
Intelligence. However, in contrast to earlier research in Distributed Artificial
Intelligence, these projects are strongly application-driven. Typically, the
research teams involve experts from management science and Distributed
Artificial Intelligence, working in close cooperation with industry.

1.4.3 Human Computer Cooperative Work (HCCW)

Evolving from the UK's mid-1980s Alvey Initiative Human-Computer
Cooperation (HCC) project (Smyth and Clarke 1990), the idea of integrating
computational agents with the human organization has gained great attention in literature (Steiner *et al.* 1990, de Greef *et al.* 1991, Kirn *et al.* 1994). The
goal of the HCC project "... was to develop a single-user cooperative mechanism where the generation of a satisfactory solution could be enhanced by
a machine having the ability to generate alternative and supplementary
information based on a solution proposed by the user" (Smyth 1994, p. 7).

While this early approach did never aim to develop software *agents*, recent work on human computer cooperation is being applied to scenarios which involve multiple humans cooperating with multiple software agents (Steiner et al. 1990). Within this context here, it seems fairly clear that the concept of human computer cooperation is of great interest to any research on computerized organizations. However, a brief review of recent work reveals important open problems, and it even identifies major research areas that remain to be addressed.

Research on Human Computer Cooperative Work is carried out in numerous disciplines, such as Computer Supported Cooperative Work, Office Information Systems, Intelligent User Interfaces, Artificial Intelligence, and, in particular, in Distributed Artificial Intelligence. Though there is a great awareness regarding the importance of interdisciplinary research, only little work has addressed so far on how to coordinate distinct research approaches, and how to integrate results that emerge from different fields of interest.

As part of the ESPRIT II project Imagine, first steps have been undertaken developing towards a framework of Human Computer Cooperative Work. By this work, Human Computer Cooperative Work has been loosely defined "… as cooperative work involving many human agents and many system agents" (de Greef *et al.* 1991). It first reviewed the respective theoretical foundations such as organization theory (Mintzberg 1979), Human-Computer Interaction, Structured Analysis (Yourdon 1989), linguistic approaches (Cohen and Perrault 1981, Levin and Moore 1977), mathematical game theory (Axelrod 1984), and Distributed Artificial Intelligence (Bond and Gasser 1988). On that basis, a set of research perspectives have been presented, as there are a task orientated perspective, a communicative and/or tool perspective, an ecological perspective, a democratic perspective, and a perspective on failure explanation and prevention. At the end, the approach identified three orthogonal design dimensions that span a space in which any system could be represented as a point (Figure 1.4).

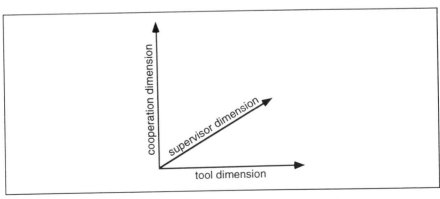

Figure 1.4   Human computer cooperative work design dimensions

The *cooperation dimension* refers to concepts of cooperation within software-based multi-agent systems emerging from Distributed Artificial Intelligence. This also involves the question how appropriate user interfaces can be developed that fit with the interaction requirements imposed by a Human Computer Cooperative Work scenario. The *supervisor dimension* points to the command and control agent(s) of a Human Computer Cooperative Work system. Finally, the *tool dimension* can be associated with support for human-human cooperative work, like as in the domain of Computer Supported Cooperative Work.

There has been a great deal of work in different scientific disciplines addressing issues that, in some way, relate to Human Computer Cooperative Work. Besides developing towards new information processing technologies, the basic motivation in doing such work is mainly to support humans being employed in more or less computerized enterprises. Among the most active disciplines are Computer Supported Cooperative Work (Chapter 6 seeks to apply DAI techniques within a CSCW context), Distributed Artificial Intelligence, and Human Computer Interaction. In contrast, there is only little (if any) work in organizational research that addresses how computational (knowledge-based) agents could be incorporated, on a human-like level, into organization theory. A more closer look reveals that software agents are subsumed under the information processing system, which is assumed to be a black box-like passive component of the organization. In the first view, this may be reasonable from the perspective of organizations in that it keeps the focus of work on relations among humans. However, this approach is a major drawback of current research, because it impedes information processing technology to becoming closely connected with organizational research.

1.5 Application Perspectives

Applying to the emergent relevance of information-integrated enterprises we are now going to discuss some applications of cooperative knowledge processing in computerized organizations. Most organizational activities require the selection, evaluation, and processing of individual and organizational knowledge. We thus apply to a decision-orientated approach (Kirn 1992) in order to classify knowledge processing activities according to the phases of decision making:

1. *Problem Identification*: The first phase requires organizations to focus their attention towards the most important tasks, and problems.
2. *Knowledge Discovery*: The second phase involves to identify, and select those capabilities that can effectively support solving the problem at hand.

3. *Planning*: The third phase develops an appropriate organizational problem solving strategy (plan), allocates the resources required, and identifies potential coordination tasks. Planning may be performed by one single member, or by a collaborative effort of several members of the organization.

4. *Plan Execution*: This requires the members of organization to process their individual tasks according to the plan to which they have applied.

5. *Evaluation of Results*: In the last phase, results are checked in order to terminate problem solving, or to trigger a new problem solving procedure.

To varying degrees, all these phases involve cooperative knowledge processing. We thus, examine in more detail the relevance of cooperative knowledge processing to organizational attention focusing capabilities, knowledge discovery, and process management. The latter integrates the tasks of planning, and plan (process) execution. Finally, it is discussed how self-organization skills can be introduced into process-orientated, computerized organizations.

1.5.1 Attention Focusing Capabilities

It has been argued that the real scarce organizational resource is the one of attention focusing capabilities (Blanning *et al.* 1992). The relevance of this problem is directly related to the degree of decentralization, the acceleration of information flow, and the ever increasing dynamics and complexity of the environment of organizations.

The capability of an organization to focus its attention on the most important problems and events depends, (i) upon the respective individual capabilities of its members, and (ii) upon the organizational capability to coordinate individual behaviors towards global goals. The capability of individuals to focus their attention involves two distinct issues:

1. *Taxonomy of local goals*: In an organizational context, individuals pursue informal (private), and formal (organizational) goals. In general, it is assumed that individuals aim at maximizing their utility which is supposed to being positively correlated to the degree to which they achieve their goals. However, there is an important limitation that of bounded rationality (March and Simon 1958).

2. *Information filtering*: In order to approach their local goals individuals need to filter, and to assess incoming information. Due to the increasing availability of electronic media, knowledge workers are suffering from information overload. Thus, information filtering mechanisms are required through which the limited information processing capabilities of humans can be allocated to the most important tasks and problems.

This has given rise to develop information filtering agents (ACM 1994). These are capable to evaluate information with respect to local goals, for instance through search for predefined keywords, role descriptions, deadlines, contextual information, or with respect to deep models of an application. Above all, information filtering agents relate to Personal Assistants.

In an organizational context, humans are cooperating, and collaborating with others of the same, and of other enterprises. Thus, attention focusing capabilites also involve an enterprise-wide perspective, which requires information filtering agents to collaborate in order to adapt their filtering work to their organizational environment. This, in turn, requires them to coordinate local goals towards global aims and objectives, to collaboratively identify important global problems, and to draw appropriate conclusions for those filtering criteria they are applying on their local level. In this view, cooperative information filtering agents either relate to Multi-Agent Decision Support Systems, or to Human Computer Cooperative Work.

1.5.2 Knowledge Discovery

The second phase of organizational problem solving requires to identify, and select those pieces of knowledge that can help to solve the problem at hand. In general, a diversity of knowledge sources will be able to contribute to a particular task. In our context here, knowledge sources are assumed to be under decentralized control, aiming to contribute to a maximum of global organizational productivity (benevolent agents).

This scenario inherently involves knowledge processing, and it necessarily requires a cooperative style of problem solving. Since long, Distributed Artificial Intelligence techniques have been employed to approach the problem of knowledge discovery in decentralized environments (Kirn 1992). More recently, the rapidly increasing availability of information within the Internet has attracted people to develop knowledge discovery agents that browse the Internet. Again, these agents firstly relate to the area of Personal Assistants. However, due to the complexity of the Internet (and similar knowledge sources) future knowledge discovery agents will perform their work in parallel, and cooperatively. This will transform the concept of knowledge discovery agents into that of a Multi-Agent Decision Suppport System, where the different knowledge discovery agents perform their search in close collaboration.

In Figure 1.5, each Knowledge Discovery Agent (KDA) represents a local search space as a part of the global space of knowledge. The search space of KDA 5 is partially covered by the search spaces of KDA 2 and KDA 4, respectively. Moreover, it has been demonstrated that, through a cooperative approach to problem solving, new knowledge can be generated (Kirn and Schlageter 1991). Thus, through a cooperative style of problem solving, the

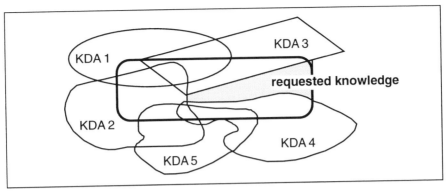

Figure 1.5 Collaborative search of knowledge discovery agents (KDAs)

agents may be able to generate knowledge that refers to the shadowed area in Figure 1.5.

1.5.3 Business Process Orientation

There is already a large body of literature originating from organization theory and management science as well as from Distributed AI, which argues that numerous problems in business and organizations could be quite naturally addressed by a multi-agent system approach. Some prominent examples are the virtual enterprise (Davidow and Malone 1992) and the fractalization of organizations (Warnecke 1991), the modeling and simulation of enterprises (Fox 1981), the efforts towards an integrated coordination theory (Malone 1987), support of business processes and workflows (Malone *et al.* 1993), and enterprise integration (Petrie Jr 1992).

1.5.3.1 Overview

The organizational model presented above, applied to a static and a dynamic perspective. The static organizational structure establishes durable relationships between humans, and computational members of an organization. The dynamic perspective is process-orientated, thus describing how humans and computational agents cooperate, and collaborate in order to achieve common goals. The question is, how this affects the concept of process orientation. With respect to the type of agents involved, three different process scenarios can be identified:

1. *Humans* only are involved. This scenario refers to the current discussion in the literature. Software systems may be involved also, supposed they do not apply to an organizational role (for instance text processors, electronic spreadsheets).

2. *Humans and computational* agents are involved. This provides for partially computerized processes and workflows. It requires us to integrate human and computer based problem solving (Human Computer Cooperative Work), to design intelligent user interfaces in order to enable humans collaborating with computational agents, and to provide coordination mechanisms being able to cope with interactions between humans and self-contained software agents.

3. *Computational agents* only are involved. Thus, processes and workflows are fully computerized. The main concern, thus, is on representation, management, and control of software-based processes (Kirn *et al.* 1994).

Referring to Table 1.1, the first point is a subfield of traditional organization theory. Due to the dominant role of human computer interfaces, the second point relates primarily to the field of Personal Assistants. Further research topics may relate either to Multi-Agent Decision Support Systems, or to Human Computer Cooperative Work. Finally, the third point refers to Distributed Artificial Intelligence. This area is of increasing relevance because of the evolving computerization of organizations. Two questions arise:

1. How can cooperation and collaboration between such *computational* agents be related to process-orientated models of organizations?
2. How can Distributed Artificial Intelligence contribute to the adaption and creation, coordination, and control of computerized processes that are embedded into an organizational context?

We have argued elsewhere that the first problem can be approached by taking advantage from the conceptual similarity between processes (and workflows), and multi-agent plans in Distributed Artificial Intelligence (Kirn *et al.* 1994). We are aware that, even on the conceptual level, there are still some differences between these two concepts. Nevertheless, multi-agent planning provides powerful techniques by which processes and workflows can be represented, evaluated, and controlled.

The second point involves three distinct topics: customization of processes, coordination of interacting processes, and organizational flexibility.

1.5.3.2 Customization of Business Processes

The basic idea behind the shift to business processes is that of enterprise-wide customer orientation. Customer orientation firstly requires enterprises to classify their customers with respect to the preferences they exhibit. They then, shape new (or redesign existing) products so that the preferences of a typical customer in such groups can best be addressed. Accordingly, the respective processes need to be (re-)designed with respect to the enterprises' aims and objectives.

However, in order to survive on dynamic markets enterprises need to be able to customize their products, and thus, their processes to new, or changing customer demands. Customization of a process can be achieved either by adapting a single process to the individual preferences of a particular customer, or by creating configurations of processes in order to meet more complex preference portfolios. This, in turn, requires organizations to provide a set of well-shaped processes representing elementary products (*lean processes*) together with a set of powerful operators by which customized process configurations (*smart process management*) can be provided. Further, process customization also includes to discover, evaluate and resolve interactions between distinct processes that perform in parallel. Process customization is performed on the operative layer of process management.

Figure 1.6 demonstrates the basic idea behind process customization: From a set of available scripts, workflows and processes are selected that can contribute to a task at hand. The second step involves to create (and optimize) a process configuration which can efficiently address a complex portfolio of preferences of a particular customer. The third step is to operate this process configuration. This in turn, involves coordination in order to detect, and to resolve inter- and intra-process relationships.

In contrast to traditional approaches (e.g. Gaitanides), process coordination is charged with adapting scripts, workflows and processes to the preferences of (a group of) customers, rather than dealing with interdependencies that exist between small subtasks being under the responsibility of distinct organizational units. This requires organizational fractals to exhibit

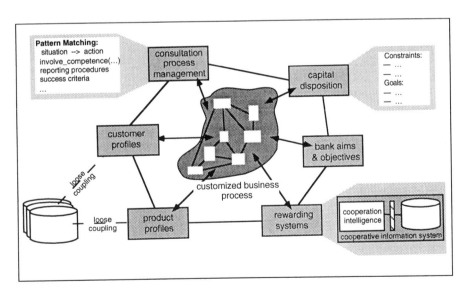

Figure 1.6   Customization of business processes

extensive coordinative capabilities. Thus, going far beyond today's concept of workflow management, future process management systems must be capable to efficiently support organizational flexibility through a diversity of methods of process customization. It has been argued recently, that this can efficiently be supported by methods of multi-agent planning. For more details, the reader is referred to recently published work (Kirn *et al.* 1994; v. Martial, 1992).

1.5.3.3 Coordination of Interacting Organizational Processes

Typically, within organizations a large number of processes are performing in parallel. Due to interacting goals, conflicting resource allocations, and the like, these processes cannot be operated in splendid isolation (see Chapter 2). Processes may further interact with their environments. Interactions between processes, or between a process and its environment, can be classified through three distinct dimensions:

First, process interactions may be classified with respect to the consequences that arise (v. Martial, 1992):

1. *Positive relationship*: There exists a positive relationship between two processes A and B, if and only if either the result of A, or the outcome of B, or the outcome of both processes *is being improved* through the interaction of process A with process B.
2. *Neutral relationship*: There exists a neutral relationship between two processes A and B, if and only if neither the result of A, nor the outcome of B, nor the outcome of both processes in combination will be affected by the interaction of process A with process B.
3. *Negative relationship*: There exists a negative relationship between two processes A and B, if and only if either the result of A, or the outcome of B, or the outcome of both processes *gets worse* through the interaction of process A with process B.

Second, four distinct process interaction types can be identified:

1. *Goal conflicts*: Goal conflicts arise from local autonomy. Resolving goal conflicts requires the agents (or organizational units) involved to apply sophisticated conflict resolution mechanisms, for instance negotiation-based approaches (Kuwabara and Lesser 1990), plan coordination (v. Martial 1992), or persuasion (Sycara 1985).
2. *Shared objects*: An object O is shared by two or more processes, if O is concurrently accessed (read, write, delete) through these processes. Shared objects are assumed to be non-consumable. However, they are bottlenecks within a system, in they require to sequentialize partial processes, workflows, and activities that are under decentralized control.

Chapter 7 considers the issue of locks and collaboration.

3. *Shared resources*: Shared resources are consumable. Thus, whenever a shared resource is accessed by a process, this process consumes a portion of that resource. As there is no unlimited availability of resources, the order in which processes have access to shared resources affects directly the efficiency of the whole system.
4. *Environment*: Each process is operated within a particular process environment. From the perspective of a single process, some parts of this environment are static while others are dynamic. It has been argued, that processes may also change their environments, which, in turn, may affect their own behavior in subsequent periods.

Third, interactions can also being classified with respect to the time dimension involved:

1. Static process interactions, that are detected, and resolved before execution time.
2. Dynamic process interactions, that are detected before, and resolved at execution time.
3. Dynamic process interactions, that are detected, and resolved at execution time.

Evolving from recent work in Distributed Artificial Intelligence, several coordination mechanisms have been suggested which all apply to widespread decentralization of the whole system, and which sustain the local autonomy of each agent involved. Examples are partial global planning (Decker and Lesser 1992), plan coordination (v. Martial 1992, Sycara 1989), or persuasion (Sycara 1985). Each of these coordination mechanisms has the potential to resolve the one, or the other of the interaction types described above.

1.5.4 Self-Organization Skills

According to recent discussions in the literature (Warnecke 1991), the ability to reorganize structure, and behavior is one of the most important skills of future organizations.

The organizational model presented above was built upon the concepts of computerization, radical decentralization, and process orientation. We have already mentioned that self-contained organizational units are process providers. While process customization referred to the ability of fractals to adapt their processes to changing customer demands, the ability of an enterprise to reorganize its structures, and (business) processes refers to its ability to integrate processes of different organizational units in order to

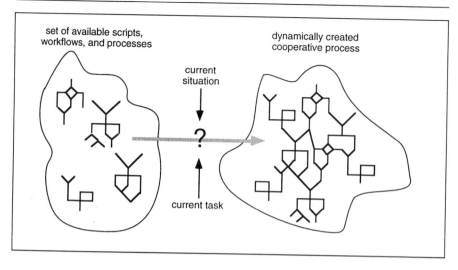

set of available scripts,
workflows, and processes

dynamically created
cooperative process

current
situation

?

current task

Figure 1.7   Integration of business processes

(re-)design its enterprise-wide organizational capabilities. Figure 1.7 demonstrates the basic idea that stands behind the idea of process integration.

Applying to computational agents, Distributed Artificial Intelligence has already addressed a great deal of work towards developing self-organization skills of multi-agent systems (Corkill 1982, Ishida 1992, Sugawara and Lesser 1993). This work was mainly concerned with self organization on the level of single atomic activities and (re-)design of organizational structures. Within our context, self organization primarily addresses processes, thus referring to the tactical level of process management. It has been demonstrated recently, that self organization of systems of computational agents can also be designed on the basis of processes (Kirn *et al.* 1994).

1.6 Summary

There is a growing understanding that today's organizations are seriously challenged by just-in-time availability of information, world-wide competition on dynamic markets and the ever increasing complexity of political, social and ecological settings. In order to cope with these challenges a variety of organizational strategies has been developed. Out of them, radical decentralization and business process orientation are the most prominent ones. The implementation of these strategies is accompanied by fundamental advances in information technology, and, in particular, in information *processing* technology. The Management of the 1990s program has revealed that these advances will have major impacts on the definition, structure, function, and capabilities of future organizations.

Drawing from these understandings, we assume that future organizations will be significantly computerized, and widespread decentralized. On this basis, we first reviewed how the integration of information processing into organization theory has evolved. This has revealed, that we still lack a comprehensive integration of research in information processing and organization theory. This impedes modern information *processing* technologies from efficiently contributing to meet the challenges today's organizations are faced with.

Drawing from this analysis it has been argued that the technology of cooperative knowledge may contribute significantly to solve these problems. According to the number of agents, cooperative knowledge processing can be classified into six distinct areas, out of which Multi-Agent Decision Support Systems and Human Computer Cooperative Work are of particular interest in organizational settings. Both fields utilize techniques developed within Distributed Artificial Intelligence, by which software agents are enabled to collaboratively work on common problems in order to achieve global aims.

Finally, several application perspectives have been developed. These perspectives involved important organizational issues such as attention focusing capabilities, knowledge discovery, customization and coordination of interacting business processes, and self organization skills of process-orientated, computerized enterprises.

The discussion has demonstrated that cooperative knowledge processing technologies exhibit quite a high potential for future organizations, for instance in that they enhance intellectual organizational skills, improve the responsiveness of enterprises to their environments, and efficiently coordinate decentralized activities towards global organizational aims.

Chapter *2*

Coordination in Organizations

Rolf Müller

2.1 Introduction

"Coordination" is a broad and colourful but not a well defined concept, though everybody has some idea of its meaning. For a long time questions of coordination played a role in many scientific fields, such as economics, cybernetics (Mesarovic *et al.* 1970) or organization theory (see Malone *et al.* 1991 for an overview). Physiologists speak of coordination in the context of body movements, while psychologists have in mind cognition or perception processes. Management science would refer to human work or decision processes. One of the main stimuli for drawing the attention of computer scientists to questions of coordination was the work of Winograd and Flores (Winograd and Flores 1986). Coordination as a research topic reached a culmination point with the establishment of the Center for Coordination Science, directed by Thomas W. Malone, at the MIT in 1990. Malone and Rockart within the Epilogue of this book access the impacts of IT and computer networking specifically on marketing and organizational strategies of large corporate organizations.

This paper aims to give a survey of organizational coordination with special emphasis of computerized coordination instruments. In Section 2 an introduction to coordination concepts in the context of management and organizational science will be given, and a typology integrating formerly independent views of coordination will be proposed. Section 3 is devoted to the role of computers within coordination and questions of coordination system design. The concept of Distributed Intelligence (DI) offers a useful framework for design. Some results of our own research work will be presented in Section 5, Our research refers to the coordination of important business processes, like innovation management, marketing and corporate strategy development, but only the latter is discussed in this paper.

2.2 Organizational Coordination

Organizations have evolved in order to manage complex tasks exceeding the abilities of individuals (see Chapter 3). But the combination of individual efforts has to be coordinated in order to suit a given purpose. The increasing complexity of highly developed forms of the division of labor call for coordination instruments of growing power. Thus, the general concept of coordination may be defined for human organizations as "the orderly arrangement of group effort, to provide unity of action in the pursuit of a common purpose" (Mooney 1947, p. 7). Since more differenciated forms of the division of labor on the other hand require more differenciated forms of coordination, many kinds of coordination instruments exist. These range from simple clocks combined with time schedules to more subtle means for exchanging goods (e.g. markets) or for forming a consensus, such as corporate cultures. The following examples taken from Poensgen (1980) illustrate the huge variety of coordination instruments: hierarchies, divisions, matrix organization, inventory buffers, standardization, project management, indoctrination, motivation, education, market mechanisms, negotiation and information.

2.2.1 Coordination Concepts

Coordination is a constituent of cooperation, the latter consisting of:

- goal orientated action,
- mutual benefits for the actors,
- division of labor,
- factual coordination and
- social coordination.

Whereas factual coordination refers to the tool level of work processes (e.g. coordination by a conveyor belt), social coordination is performed by direct personal interaction (e.g. by one person monitoring the behavior of another; Marwell and Schmitt 1975, p. 4ff).

Coordination is also a constituent of organizing the central management activity. After Kieser and Kubicek the interdependence between specialization and coordination is the key factor of organizing as a management function (Kieser 1993 p. 165). Staehle distinguishes three forms of specializations (he uses the term "differentiation") by

- task,
- information, and

● authority (power),

resulting for an organization in specific task, communication and authority structures respectively. Coordination is necessary because specialization, which usually leads to interdependent activities, performed by actors in different departments and divisions, breaks organizational coherence and produces new boundaries and discontinuities (Staehle 1987 p. 432). Coordination is the recovery of organizational coherence; therefore 'integration' is a synonym to 'coordination'. Further references on integration or process management, are e.g. Striening (1988) and Hansen (1992). 'Breakdown' is a central category in the coordination approach of Winograd and Flores (Winograd and Flores, 1986), where one instance of breakdown is related to organizations as networks of commitments (p. 150).

Conflicts belong to everyday life in organizations. Dealing with conflicts (e.g. by moderation) is an essential dimension of coordination (O'Hare *et al.* in Chapter 6 consider conflict within the context of computer supported meeting). There are different ways conflicts may arise, and how they are dealt with. An important aspect of conflicts, frequently overlooked, is uncertainty in the context of decision making. A conflict due to uncertainty exists, if for instance, the dependency between environmental outcomes and behavior choice is not known exactly in advance (March and Simon 1958, p. 113ff). Other examples for uncertainties are observation errors, unpredicted changes of the environment, or simply missing information. From another point of view, uncertainty is an important prerequisite for planning, since necessary room for manoeuvre also appears as uncertainty. This aspect will be deepened in Section 5, presenting a coordination approach for corporate strategy development.

Coordination is quite a universal concept since it almost seems everything can be coordinated. Within Chapter 11 Sundermeyer examines how coordination can be achieved within multi-agent communities through structured communication. The vagueness of the coordination concept is due to its high order semantics: coordination refers to special qualities of processes, not of objects. A simplified analysis based on Bunge's ontological framework (Bunge 1979) reveals its semantical structure:

event   = change (property (thing))
process   = time sequence (events)
coordination   = special property (process).

Inserting the equations into one another exhibits; why there is always some trouble using concepts of this family:

coordination = special property (time sequence (change (property (thing))).

The structure would be more complicated, if we take into account the system nature of "thing".

There have been some attempts to define the concept more exactly (see Section 2.2 below). The "coordination theoretic" approach of Malone and Crowston is one of the most prominent examples claiming coordination being of special importance for almost all branches of science and engineering. They define coordination as "the act of managing interdependencies between activities" (Malone and Crowston 1991, p. 3; p. 35 for further definitions) and identify the following four components of coordination:

Table 2.1 Components of Coordination (from Malone and Crowston 1991, p. 10)

Components of Coordination	Associated coordination process
Goals	Identifying goals (e.g., goal selection)
Activities	Mapping goals to activities (e.g., goal decomposition)
Actors	Mapping activities to actors (e.g., task assignment)
Interdependencies	"Managing" interdependencies (e.g., resource allocation, sequencing, and synchronizing)

These components of coordination are also part of the above mentioned cooperation concept, but the scope of coordination in their definition is not restricted to a special kind of activity. It includes both activities at the physical system level like the administration of computer memory or processes within electronic control devices and at the social system level as well. However, throughout this paper the scope of coordination will be used in a narrower way: it will be restricted to processes at the social system level, i.e. workgroups, departments and firms. Coordination will refer to human activities within such kinds of organizations.

Computer scientists are using the coordination concept in (at least) two completely different fields of application. One field is defined by the "management" or "organizational science" perspective, where coordination refers to social systems, and computers support living people in real organizations. This is the perspective of the current paper, of CSCW or Organizational Computing approaches, and a growing part of the AI community following Winograd and Flores (Winograd and Flores 1986). Another example of this view is Bobrow's statement opening the 1990 AAAI conference: "Our real challenge is not to build intelligent systems, but to help corporations and government build intelligent organizations" (*AAAI News*, Fall 1990, p. 25).

This point of view should not be confused with "coordination" in the context of Distributed Artificial Intelligence research (see Chapters 8 – 13). In particular, the Multi-Agent System (MAS) community (see Kirn and Klöfer 1993 for an overview) deals with model worlds of artificial agents, organizations and their coordination (see Chapter 11 specifically). MAS for real world coordination is merely a special case of MAS application. The relationship of both perspectives was discussed by Gioia (Gioia 1992) or Malone (Malone 1992) (Abbas and O'Hare in Chapter 10 consider how findings in Organizational theory can be used in the effective design of Multi-Agent Systems). Whether both concepts have anything in common apart from terminology is an interesting epistemic question not to be treated here.

2.2.2 Types of Coordination

Different types of coordination result from different kinds of interdependencies, which in turn are dependent upon different kinds of products, services, actors, work specializations, efforts, tasks and purposes. Organization theorists have proposed different taxonomies of coordination. Whereas some authors allow almost everything to be coordinated, e.g. Rühli defines coordination as mutual adjustment of system elements for the purpose of optimization (Rühli 1992, p. 1165); other authors restrict coordination to rather special processes like planning or decision making (e.g. Frese 1972, Laßmann 1992). Laßmann uses the term decision interdependency, whereby the decisions may concern three basic aspects: connected workflows, sharing limited resources, and environmental factors (e.g. markets).

For the purpose of this paper it seems adequate to adopt a "middle way" between those positions by referring coordination to interdependent human activities within work processes (in accordance with March and Simon 1958). The typologies given below may be used for classifying different approaches of coordination and system design. March and Simon distinguish two main types of coordination:

- coordination by plan and
- coordination by feedback.

The more a situation arises repeatedly the more "programmable" are the tasks and the appropriate individual activities. Related to the scheduling of such "subprograms" the *type of coordination ...* used in the organization is a function of the extent to which the situation is standardized ... We may label coordination based on pre-established schedules *coordination by plan*, and coordination that involves transmission of new information *coordination by feedback*. The more stable and predictable the situation, the greater the reliance on coordination by plan; the more variable and unpredictable the situation, the greater the reliance on coordination by feedback." (March and

Simon 1958 p. 160). Feedback involves communication among the employees in order to handle situations of unanticipated deviations from the plan. This communication may "give notice of deviations from planned or predicted conditions, or to give instructions for changes in activity to adjust to these deviations" (p. 160). Programmed tasks usually do not need communications through hierarchical channels (p. 161).

Both types of mechanisms can be further characterized (Staehle 1987, p. 436, Kieser 1993 p. 165) by coordination features:

- rules and programs,
- hierarchies,
- planning,
- self-adjustment.

The first three attributes are correlated to coordination by plan, whereas the latter is an instance of feedback coordination. They can control both levels of individual or departmental task execution.

Field of influence seems to be another rather important descriptor for coordination. Coordination may be divided by its field of influence into four categories (Rühli 1992, p. 1167):

- strategy,
- structure,
- culture,
- environment.

"Field of influence" refers both to what coordination affects and what it is affected by. Thus, there is coordination of strategy and coordination by strategy as well. For instance, corporate planning has a coordinating effect on the overall activities within the organization and, on the other hand, is subjected itself to coordination in the sense of plan adjustment and harmonization (metaplanning). Structure orientated coordination refers to formal or informal structures like hierarchies, staff management or team work. Corporate culture comprises mental images, normative or value systems. It serves as a coordination instrument by creating a consensus among people such as giving employees a corporate identity. Culture development itself needs to be coordinated by educational measures or incentives. Market relationships and instruments are like exchange processes, prices and competitive structures are among the most important environmental coordination methods. But there are also coordinating relationships beyond markets like public relation activities, societal strategies or mega-marketing (Rühli 1992 pp. 1170 ff). Further attributes of coordination may be preventive/reactive or formal/informal (Rühli 1992, pp. 1166ff).

A useful description of coordination processes may be obtained "in terms of successively deeper levels of underlying processes, each of which depend on the levels below it". (Malone and Crowston 1991, p. 16). The process level structure is exhibited in the following Table 2.2.

Table 2.2   Process level structure of coordination (from Malone and Crowston 1991, p. 16).

Process Level	*Components*	*Examples of Generic Process*
Coordination	goals, activities, actors, resources, interdependencies	identifying goals, ordering activities, assigning activities to actors, allocating resources, synchronizing activities
Group Decision Making	goals, actors, alternatives, evaluations, choices	proposing alternatives, evaluating alternatives, making choices (e.g. by authority, consensus or voting)
Communication	senders, receivers, messages, languages	establishing common languages, selecting receiver (routing), transporting message (delivering)
Perception of common objects	actors, objects	seeing same physical objects accessing shared databases

2.3   Computers and Coordination

Virtually all types of coordination mentioned above can be supported by computers with appropriately designed software. Software design for coordination and cooperation is a research area of increasing interest (e.g. Winograd and Flores 1986, Stefik 1986, Sandholzer 1990, Brauer and Hernandez 1991, Applegate *et al.* 1991, Greenberg 1991, Oberquelle 1991, Turoff 1991a, Barrett 1992, Masuch and Warglien 1992). After discussing possible roles for the computer and the design of coordination systems (Section 3.1) a Distributed Intelligence (DI) approach will be presented (Section 3.2), which we are using as a basis for our own research work and system design.

2.3.1   Possible Roles of the Computer

The computer is a machine with an unprecedented degree of universality. Based on appropriately designed software it can play very different roles, e.g. for arithmetic calculating, typewriting, equation or logical problem solving, pattern recognition, virtual reality simulation, optimizing. Everyone using a text system or a spreadsheet program knows from experience, that calculating or typewriting on a computer is not just doing the same thing on another medium; the computer adds qualitatively new functions such as spelling correction or checking for logical contradictions.

Fixing the role of the computer as a "problem solving" machine, and equating intelligent behavior with problem-solving behavior, is one of the main characteristics of mainstream AI. Moreover, in our opinion this design dogma is the main reason for AI's lack of applied success. Within the AI community this design idea has received far more attention than other alternatives; with almost no exceptions technical realization concepts follow the "problem solving" paradigm: to build machines simulating the problem-solving behavior of human (or at least animal) individuals.

Only in recent years, has there been a growing interest in alternative paradigms to the standard AI approach, partly stimulated by the neuronal net "revival", partly caused by AI research results not fulfilling the users expectations. A significant shift towards other paradigms like communication and coordination could be observed. One of the most radical attempts to develop a new approach by revising basic assumptions of traditional AI mainstream research, was provided by the work of Winograd and Flores (1986). The provoking character of their ideas for the AI community may well be estimated by the exceptional number of pages the editors of the AI Journal dedicated to reviews of their book by four different authors (AI 31 1987, pp. 213–261). Other concepts like "Society of Mind" (Minsky 1985), "Knowledge Medium" (Stefik 1986), "Intelligence without Representation" (Brooks 1991), "Ecology of Computation" (Hubermann 1988), or Varela's critizism on traditional views of cognition (Varela 1990), follow similar intentions. Further efforts may be found in a special issue of the *AI Journal* (vol. 47, 1991).

Since the begin of the 1980s it has become more and more recognized that computers can also play a role as communication media connecting people by exhibiting qualitatively new functions, compared to traditional mail and other forms of message exchange. Whereas science and engineering during the first phase of computer and software development concentrated on functions supporting isolated, individual, local work, we can observe during the last decade a significant rise towards design attributes for supporting global, distributed interdependent work, communication, coordination functions. Some of the well known examples are the Computer Supported Cooperative Work (CSCW) approaches (e.g. Greenberg 1991), Organizational Computing (Applegate *et al.* 1991), Coordination theory (Malone und Crowston 1991), Computer Mediated Communication (Hiltz and Turoff,1991). A useful study of design requirements for cooperative systems was given by Sandholzer (1990).

Within a company almost nothing happens without communication. People communicate with each other via a multitude of different media (voice, paper, fax, phone). The computer is an additional component in the existing landscape of electronic and non-electronic media. Electronic media are links of communicative chains constituting social systems, and enriching existing media with new qualities. Software design can be understood as media design. Computer integration is not the technical connection of computing machinery but integration of people (in the sense of Staehle, see Section 2.1) by new media. Purpose and efficiency of such media cannot be evaluated in terms of information technology but only in terms of human activities at the social systems level (improvement of and improvement by coordination). In this sense computers are coordination systems supporting the "communication" level (see Table 2.2 above, and also Chapter 3). This perspective was also stressed by Clark in the context of the research strategy at MIT: "Electronic mail, which has little to do with distributed computing but everything to do with distributed people, is a fundamental enhancement to options for human communication.... It is easy and tempting to think of networks as hooking computers together. They are better thought of as hooking people together, with a computer mediating the connection in an effective way. Whether the application is electronic mail or access to remote information, the motivation for communication is a human need, not internals of computer system design." (Clark 1991, S. 31f). Chapter 4 considers how software and human agents can be coordinated via electronic mail.

The history of media is a history of overcoming limits to communication and cooperation by surmounting barriers of space, time or language. Media can be classified by the kind of limits they help to overcome. Thus, electronic mail systems help to overcome space limits, databases time limits, translators language limits, virtual reality imagination limits, tutorial systems competence limits and future media limits, which we at present are unable even to recognize. Therefore, the notions "coordination system", "CSCW", "computer media", "lateral integration tool" can be used synonymously.

The basic question of how to design information systems in order to support coordination/cooperative work is of central concern in Winograd and Flores' work (Winograd and Flores 1986, p. 4ff). They argue that design questions are highly dependent on the designers view of an organization: What a person within a company "really" does, is not easily identified at all. They give the following example of a manager working in his office, in order to show how different views may result in very different descriptions of an activity (p. 144):

- sitting at a desk sipping coffee and moving a pencil over a piece of paper.
- writing English text.
- looking for the right word to finish a sentence.
- drafting an inter-office memo.
- reminding an administrative assistant about next week's meeting concerning the software contract.
- deciding whether the marketing manager should attend the meeting.
- working on preparations for the new contract.

- trying to increase the efficiency of how this office handles contracts.

There are at least as many alternatives for the design of a computer system as there are possible ways to describe the activities to be coordinated. Winograd and Flores regard activities as communication. Hence, organizations are "networks of conversations" (p. 150ff), and advocate the design of "tools for conversation" (p. 157) by arguing, that "new tools can be designed to operate in the domain of speech acts and conversation – the one in which terms like 'reminding', 'requesting', and 'agreeing' are relevant" and which "is the most fruitful domain for understanding and facilitating management" (p. 144). Thus, their approach can be allocated at the communication level of Table 2.3 above.

It is easy to agree with their general design assumption, which is shared by our own approach (see Chapters 3.2, 4. and 5.), of defining the computers role as a communication medium. But their theory is neither sufficient nor universal enough to provide design guidelines for a broad range of different applications; there are still too many degrees of freedom, and it becomes clear, that a lot research and experimental work still has to be done (Sandholzer 1990, p. 227). We strongly agree with Sandholzer's position, who stresses the primacy of organizational design over computer system design decisions (Sandholzer, 1990, p. VII and 4). The next chapter will introduce our approach as a further attempt towards the foundation of cooperative system design.

2.3.2 Distributed Intelligence

Just like many other practitioners, we had to face the difficulties of applying the classical AI approach in organizations such as our company (e.g. problems of "integration"). With time we became more and more convinced that new and fundamentally different theories for design had to be developed. We shared the experience of Winograd and Flores, that the limitations of AI (Coy and Bonsiepen 1989) and (at least some of the well known) difficulties of software design in general (Weltz and Ortmann,1992) had to be overcome. Our approach was to use the DI concept (Müller 1988, 1994) as a basis for our work.

A preliminary rough description of DI could be given as a property of a social system, consisting of interacting (human) individuals, which are connected by different kinds of media, including computers. Man–machine (human–computer) systems of this kind are also called sociotechnical systems.

But this definition is not the whole story since DI can also be regarded as a specific concept of intelligence in clear contrast to the traditional concept of local intelligence as used by the majority of psychologists and computer scientists, especially within the AI community. Most concepts of intelligence refer to properties of an individual, more precisely: the scope of these concepts subsumes abilities of a single and isolated individual rather than those of a collection of interacting entities. DI in our definition, is necessarily a property of a multitude of (at least two) interacting individuals (group, organization). The main feature of DI is its ability to combine existing components to a system with new qualities (not exhibited by the components). These qualities are emerging properties of the system structure (by mutual effects, interactions between the components). Such processes of self production are called "autopoiesis" (Maturana and Varela 1987) or "emergence".

Connecting individuals is performed by communication (in the sense of Maturana and Varela) using certain languages. "We call communication the coordinated behaviors mutually triggered among the members of a social unity. ... The particular feature of *communication*, therefore, is not that it results from a mechanism distinct from other behaviors, but that it takes place in a domain of social behaviors." (Maturana and Varela 1987, p. 193) (see Chapter 3). Within an organization different, more or less, formalized languages are used, e.g. in different kinds of documents; there are, for instance, graphical documents such as CAD representations, and text documents such as purchase orders, and technical reports. Numerical tables (spreadsheets) are the common documents for quantitative descriptions. Prices, wages, profit and interest rates can be regarded as elements of higher level languages occurring within monetary control and incentive systems, as well as symbol and activity regulations in the context of corporate identity.

A further key concept in the theory of Maturana and Varela perfectly fitting to our DI concept is that of "Operational Closure": "... the nervous system participates in the operation of a metacellular as a mechanism that maintains within certain limits the structural changes of the organism. This occurs through multiple circuits of neuronal activity structurally coupled to the medium. In this sense, the nervous system can be characterized as having *operational closure*. In other words, the nervous system's organization is a network of active components in which every change of relations of activity leads to further changes of relations of activity." (p. 164). This concept of operational closure also applies to living organizations on the communication level. Whereas within the framework of traditional computer science, it is merely the technical system level of databases and dataflows where operational closure is (implicitly) referred to, DI based design assumes operational closure on the social system level.

DI is similar to concepts of 'organizational intelligence' (Masuch and Warglien 1992, Blanning 1992) and "structural intelligence", whereby the latter may be defined as a system property determined only by the coupling of its elements, and not by a property of the elements themselves (except their coupling ability). Intelligent behavior of the system only emerges from purely structural system properties. Neural nets are the most prominent examples of this kind of systems. DI is less rigid than the structural intelligence concept by allowing arbitrary properties (even 'intelligence') of the elements. Huberman uses DI explicitly in the same sense as we do by stating "Intelligence is not restricted to single brains; it also appears, for example, in insect colonies, social and economic behavior in human societies, and scientific and professional communities." (Huberman 1992, p. 235). He follows a research strategy of observing living DI systems (economy, bee colony, or ant society), comparing them with technical systems (like computer networks), identifiying control and coordination mechanisms, possibly common to both of them and, finally using and adapting them for distributed computation procedures, which in turn may be used "to study issues of collective problem solving" (p. 236).

Critics of DI or organizational intelligence (Chapters 8 and 9 deal with Organizational Intelligence in more detail) concepts usually argue that intelligence may only be attributed to individuals, not to groups or organizations (e.g. Gioia 1992, p. 308). Besides the fact that any definition of intelligence is of purely axiomatic character, there is a common phenomenon well known to everybody working in large organizations supporting the DI perspective: Changes in the behavior of an organization as a whole more often than not are unforeseen or even not planned by the members of the organization.

2.4 Design Issues and Applications

This chapter refers to practical aspects of our own research work. We give a short description of the design issues derived from the DI perspective as discussed in the chapter before. In our research work we are especially focusing on the above mentioned

- communication structures of work (Section 2.1) and the
- feedback (self adjustment) type of coordination (Section 2.2),

This choice has been made for the following reason: Many companies are facing the challenge of increasing complexity of products, services, and production processes, combined with growing dynamics of the environment (e.g. market, technology). Therefore, they need new strategies and structures requiring deep transformations from sequential processing types (chains) to parallel forms (network structures like concurrent engineering), whereby formerly highly differenciated hierarchies have to be replaced by flat forms in order to reduce processing time and administration efforts and to ensure more flexibility. Successful companies in the future will become what Toffler called "adhocracies", "rapidly changing organizations with highly decentralized networks of shifting project teams" (Malone and Crowston 1991, p. 2). We do not assume that traditional organizations would be transformed completely into adhocracies but, instead take for granted a significant rise of adhocracies at different areas within existing organizations.

For this kind of organization, the planning type of coordination will lose its importance in favour of self adjustment, since adhocracies will deal mainly with unpredictable events triggered by market dynamics or internal communication processes. The vast majority of computer systems installed in companies do not fit the requirements of "spontaneous" group interaction support, because they were designed for supporting planning and sequential process types. Hence, there is a growing demand for computer systems suited for the self adjustment type of coordination, which at the moment are just in the beginning of their development. New kinds of such coordination systems in turn will allow for new and more efficient kinds of cooperation.

Self adjustment in the strong sense has far reaching consequences for the quality of worktools, especially computer systems: the computer system in order to be highly adaptable by interacting users to changing situations has to be designed by the users themselves. So, our system design approach is also part of the so-called "participatory design" field, which deals with a rich diversity of aspects concerning "the design of social systems including computer systems that are part of human work" (Comm. ACM vol. 36, June 1993, pp. 25ff).

We are working on coordination systems within two different fields of influence, namely strategy and structure (after the typology given in Section 2.2). We will give an illustration by a strategy orientated example in the next chapter.

2.5 Example of a Strategy Related Coordination System

Coordination within this example refers to processes of strategy development in organizations. The actors are all individuals (e.g. managers, staff members, analysts, marketing researchers) involved in activities like estimation of future demand, deciding and optimizing resource allocation. This kind of work takes place more or less independently at different areas of a company: top managers decide on the global long-term strategy (five and more years ahead) in terms of prices, wages, growth rates for sales, employees, profit, investments; departments decide similarly with respect to specific product lines, particular rentability goals. These planning and decision processes take place top down, bottom up, and across the entire organization at regular intervals – every year, every month.

Decisions on resource allocation, even those, concerning factors internally controllable by the organization itself, are always more or less risky, because of the dependency on environmental factors which cannot fully be controlled by the organization (e.g. new technologies, changing consumer behavior). This situation is characterized by a high degree of complexity and uncertainty. Complexity results from the large number of actors and conflicting goals in different departments. Uncertainty appears as two categories with different sources: one kind of uncertainty is due to missing information related to decisions of other actors and "forgotten" dependencies, side effects of one's own decisions on those of other departments; the other kind of uncertainty results from the above mentioned changes of the environment.

Summarizing the tool requirements: a strategy orientated tool should support

- the coordination of strategic planning, especially
- team orientated communication,
- management of conflicts, and
- account for uncertainties chances and risks.

We will restrict our scope to the quantitative aspects of planning. The most common tools used in this area are spreadsheets like Microsoft EXCEL or LOTUS 1-2-3. Already there are some initial attempts to accommodate uncertainty by allowing probability distributions and correlations for the spreadsheet variables (see, e.g. the RISK tool). Such add-ons incorporate risk assessment features into the calculations. But these tools do not exhibit any cooperative features which would support the coordination of group orientated strategy identification.

Our approach is an extension of these kinds of tools by providing cooperative functions in a generic way. This extension uses the method of "Quantitative Reasoning" (QR), based on Schmidt (Schmidt 1979, Müller 1993, Mehlmann 1993).

We would like to recall Winograd's and Flores' example quoted above (Section 2.1), by which they illustrate how much the design of computer tools depends on the perspective from which work processes are described. As long as planning is seen as a process of calculating, estimating and forecasting, the spreadsheet tools seem rather adequate; but regarding the same work processes from the cooperative perspective we notice a clear shortcoming of such tools, with respect, to the above mentioned process coordinating requirements. Just like Winograd and Flores, we also adopt the communication perspective for our design, by focusing on the conversational aspects of strategic planning processes and their integration company wide. The description of our strategy orientated coordination system design, will follow the process level structure of Table 2.2 (Section 2.2).

2.5.1 Perception of Common Objects

People occupied with planning in different areas of an organization refer to different objects: e.g. sales managers estimate sales figures, finance staff members intend to reduce production costs, and the number of employees to be hired is planned in the personnel department. Although the planners within one department do not have to know the plans of other departments in detail, they must have access to information on just those objects, which either are common to both, or are related to their "own" objects. So, for instance, the number of employees is related to labor costs by the average salary. As a first step of the system design, a complete list of objects as used across an organization has to be compiled and stored in a database. In a second step, this list has to be completed by defining the relationships between the objects. The QR-approach allows for a representation of different connections between these objects:

- part-whole relationships (class partition, like demand by class of goods),
- linear combinations, and
- quotients.

The following example of a financial model will illustrate the object representation as a semantical network. Class partitioning does not occur in this example.

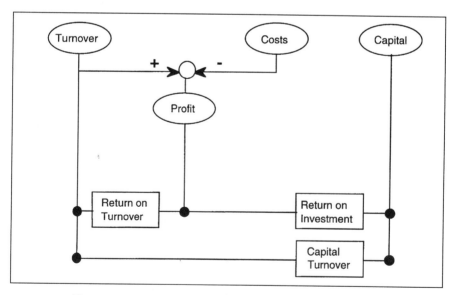

Figure 2.1   Financial model (Dupont system of business indicators)

Objects and relations of this model are defined as follows:

Object list: Turnover, Cost, Capital, Profit

Linear combination: Profit   = Turnover-Cost

Quotients: Return on Investment (ROI)   = Profit-Capital
                        Return on Turnover   = Profit-Turnover
                        Capital Turnover   = Turnover-Capital

The semantical network as illustrated by this example defines "empty" structures as purely relational definitions for numerical data to be provided in the next step by the user. Data for QR in general are real valued and always interval scaled. The interval represents the uncertainty and is interpreted as a range of confidence based on a given probability measure, e.g. "Profit = 10 (2) $ units" means that given a 99% confidence level the true value lies between 8 and 12 $ units. The bandwidth may be interpreted as measurement error, risk or range of fluctuation. QR uses a probabilistic interpretation of the intervals, whereby the values a and b' (b = confidence factor * b') are interpreted as mean and standard deviation of a random variable. A zero bandwidth is also possible as a special case.

A semantical network without data can be compared with a landscape consisting of as many white spots as there are nodes and relations. By successively putting one data element after the other into the network, a powerful inference process is able to calculate missing values by automatically reducing the uncertainty (bandwidth) of given values without any procedural programming by the user. There is no fixed and predetermined distinction between input and output variables. Any variable generally is input and output as well. The mechanism of forward and backward computation is only controlled by the meaning (network structure and bandwidth) of the variables. Within the QR tool there is a strict separation between the structural level of representation, the data level and the inference machine (for transforming and estimating data). This kind of architecture and information processing is very similar to rule based or constraint propagation methods of knowledge based approaches. Such architectures are of great advantage, since they are independent of any application: though QR is used in very different applications, its inference machine has never to be changed.

2.5.2 Communication

The object modeling step can also be regarded as language definition, whereby the concepts used by experts during the planning process have to be related explicitly within a broader context. So, for instance, the meaning of profit within the context of capital, cost and turnover is clearly defined by the semantical net model of Figure 2.1. Any practice of cooperative nature at least tacitly assumes a common language being used by the group members. But as our experience of building such models with different users shows, this assumption usually is not valid: even within the same department the term "cost" may be used in different meanings by different people, without being aware of any misunderstanding. The language definition step helps to avoid such hidden misunderstandings by clarifying the terminology used by the group members. Semantical models of real applications may comprise an arbitrary number of nodes. Typical networks have some hundreds of variables.

The variables provide a framework for specifying plans and communicate them among the different planning groups within an organization. This can either be done by just exchanging the sheets or by translating results from one sheet into another: a capital value of 10 (0) units specified by the financial department, combined with a rough ROI estimation of 20 (10) percent will be translated to the product department as "expected profit = 2 (1)". Each input value for a network variable will automatically be communicated to all other members using parts of the same network by transforming it similarly into values for all other network variables.

2.5.3 Conflict Management (Group Decision Making)

If the product department expects a profit outside this range, e.g. 4 (0) units, the plan is inconsistent. QR is able to identify all inconsistencies, even those which are hidden by the complexity of the network, and indicating the critical points for discussion to all members involved in the planning process. QR checks for such inconsistencies whether they can be solved by the computer. In certain types of conflicts QR is able to propose a solution. If the product department allows for profit a range, of (say) 4 (2) units, QR would generate the proposition "profit = 3 (2)" (approximately) as a compromise.

Acknowledgment

We thank Graham Wrightson, Alexander Mankowsky and Olaf Mehlmann for helpful suggestions and comments.

Chapter 3

Communication-Orientated Approaches to Support Multi-User Processes in Office Work

Michael Syring and Ulrich Hasenkamp

3.1 Introduction

While in the 1970s and 1980s the support of office work by end-user tools was focused on the individual workplace, there has been a tendency to support work more comprehensively during recent years. Systems called "groupware" directly support tasks based on division of labor either in small groups or in organization-wide processes. Workflow management can be viewed as part of the more comprehensive research area Computer Supported Cooperative Work (CSCW) (Hales 1991) that deals mainly with the support of processes based on predefined procedures, communication relations and competences.

From the viewpoint of "organizational computing" (Applegate 1991) we summarize and evaluate communication orientated approaches. We concentrate on the support of communication and coordination relations between human actors in organizations. Some approaches are new developments (e.g. semi-autonomous agents), while others have been used for a long time (e.g. conference systems). First we distinguish between types of office work and formulate requirements to support multi-user processes with respect to these types. On this basis the possibilities and limitations of different approaches for the support of multi-user office work are discussed.

3.2 Office Work

Office work can be viewed from several perspectives. Here we stress the communication and coordination tasks (see Chapters 2, 4 and 5). Many attempts have been made to systematize and categorize office work in order to establish determining factors for the optimal application of information and communication technology. For the purpose of this study, the categorization according to task types – as, e.g. developed by Panko and Sprague (1982) – is suitable. These task types cannot directly be related to job types, which are executives, managers and highly skilled persons, clerks, and assistants.

Table 3.1 shows three task types that differ in the criteria problem type, information need, cooperation partners, and solution type. Type 1 comprises one-time tasks that cannot be formalized and are characterized by improvisation. The actor must communicate quickly and case-orientated with differing partners, and social aspects play an important role. Type 2 represents tasks that are related to cases and can partly be formalized. These administrative tasks are on the one hand subject to certain rules, on the other hand they cannot be standardized because of possible variations in the solution, the partners, and the necessary information. Type 2 can further be divided in project tasks and regular tasks, the latter being characterized by a higher degree of repetition and structure. Type 3 finally represents routine tasks that can be formalized to a great extent.

Table 3.1   Types of office work (Picot)

Task type	Problem type	Information need	Cooperation partners	Solution type
Type 1 unstructured task	high complexity, low possibility to plan ahead	undetermined	differing, undetermined	undetermined
Type 2 semi-structured task	medium complexity and possibility to plan ahead	depends on case	changing, determined	determined to undetermined
Type 3 structured task	low complexity, high possibility to plan ahead	determined	determined	determined

The tasks that are assigned to or performed by individual actors in an organization are usually part of a more comprehensive task complex, that has to be accomplished by several actors working together. The individual tasks depend in general on each other in the sense, that the output of one task is input for another task. The resulting chain of tasks is called procedure or workflow. It can be viewed as an entity in the business process.

The range and the degree of the organizational regulation of workflows differ very much. While infrequent procedures are usually not formally defined and sometimes performed *ad hoc,* procedures with higher repetition frequencies are formalized, e.g. as part of an organization handbook.

The process orientation, which is increasingly being discussed as organizational design principle also for office work, leads to an integral view of workflows independent of department boundaries, and therefore to more comprehensive procedures. The enterprise is viewed as an ongoing process in the sense of an uninterrupted chain of outputs. The importance of an integral view can be demonstrated by the sectional character of information and communication systems in the context of the value chain (Porter 1985).

Organizational regulations can in this context be viewed as models that are given to the actors in an office as an official guideline for their work and can therefore serve as a basis for the control of multi-user processes. Organizational regulations, however, do not completely define the actions of the users. The regulations must be on a certain level of abstraction to be manageable and to avoid schematization. This may lead to the necessity of adaptations of organizational regulations to the conditions of individual situations (Suchman 1987), which are not covered by the abstract models. This situative dependency can be modeled only insufficiently in organizational regulations, so they cannot supply a complete picture of the actually performed multi-user processes. Even routine tasks afford to a certain extent problem solving processes and negotiations with other actors (Suchman 1983, Schmidt 1991, Schmidt 1993). This involves usually also informal structures. The political, social and psychological motivations for actions cannot acccurately be described and can certainly not be layed down in a deterministic model. They must, however, be considered by increased requirements regarding the flexibility of the coordinating system.

3.3 Requirements to Support Multi-User Processes in Office Work

3.3.1 Basic Requirements

Systems for the support of multi-user office work should perform actively, depending on the requirements of different task types: Structured tasks should be controlled actively based on predefined sequences. The system should determine who is the right person for the individual action, give administrative support for their work, supply the information and tools as needed, keep track of due dates and give reminders. Moreover, local actions should be performed automatically, as far as possible. Semi-structured tasks can partly be performed according to predefined sequences. For this task type there is a need for simple ways to alter existing procedure specifications. There must also be instruments for coordination support in those cases where an execution sequence has not been predefined. This means that besides the primary task execution also the accompanying coordination activities like finding relevant communication partners or delegating tasks have to be supported. For this purpose planning and negotiation mechanisms must be integrated, among others. In contrast to structured and semi-structured tasks the support of unstructured tasks cannot follow predefined sequences. It must be especially recognized that social aspects have more influence on communication and coordination processes in the execution of these activities than with structured or semi-structured tasks (see below).

Since multi-user processes normally comprise tasks with a varying degree of structuredness, there must be a smooth transition from one task type to another (Woo 1987) in order to have a full range support for multi-user processes. Furthermore, such a possibility for transition is necessary because structured tasks often require adaptations to individual situations, making deviations from predefined rules necessary. The resulting exception handling is a semi-structured or unstructured task.

3.3.2 Formal Requirements

- Efficiency requirements.

In general efficiency is expressed by productivity (ratio between quantitative output and input) or economic efficiency (ratio between assessed output and cost). Higher productivity by using communication orientated systems for the support of multi-user office work can be achieved by either reducing the input (especially personnel) or raising output. Cost improvements are possible mainly by reducing the overall time required for a given procedure. Improvements on the output side aim at raising the quality of the output, e.g. by unification of administrative practices or by improved quality of decisions. It is often very difficult to find operational definitions for productivity and economic efficiency of systems for the support of office work.

- Flexibility requirements.

Flexibility is understood to be the ability of a system to be adapted to changing conditions. Flexibility is generally contrary to the stability of an organizational system which can be expressed by the degree of general rules and regulations. Applying general rules instead of individual measures results in a permanent definition of decisions and procedures which may be more efficient in some environments. Organizational design has to find an optimum of flexibility and stability.

Since computerized communication systems are based on organizational regulations, there is always a danger of raising stability in a non-optimal way when subsystems are added. This aspect is especially important when semi-structured or unstructured tasks are to be supported because they tend to show less similarities and therefore afford specific rules. The support by a computerized system should in no case force a specific form of coordination between the actors. It should be possible to deviate from the rules and models underlying the system even though they provide the basis for active support. In this sense models should have a descriptive role in the overall system (Schmidt 1991).

Organizational regulations as well as the information and communication systems supporting them must be adapted to changing requirements on a continuing basis. The necessary changes can often not be done in the short term but require continuing processes regarding organizational and human resource development. The definition and alteration of organizational regulations should be possible through self organization, not necessarily involving a central institution. Systems for supporting office work must enhance this possibility and may not obstruct it: "Building computer systems where work is seen as simply being concerned with "information flow", and neglecting the [...] work needed to make the flow possible, can lead to serious problems. Computer support of cooperative work should aim at supporting self-organization [...]." (Schmidt 1992)

- Transparency requirements.

Since the responsibility for performing the tasks remains with the human actors, they must have the chance to control the actions supported or even executed automatically by the system. This means the system must be readily understandable in the sense that it delivers a useful picture of office work in terms of conventional business administration. In order to increase the transparency of multi-user processes in organizations and to achieve a direct connection with the actions to be taken we postulate an explicit representation of the organizational structures and processes. Moreover, the execution of ongoing processes must be subject to user control at any time.

- Openness and integration requirements.

A universal system for supporting all work being done in offices doesn't seem to be realistic due to the resulting complexity. Instead there is a need for cooperation with existing information and communication systems as well as with those under development.

The integration of coordination systems with corporate information systems can be viewed on several levels (Pedersen 1992). In this paper we do not specify the technical aspects of data processing. On the conceptual level there must be a significant independence from the underlying basic systems. Furthermore, the coordination instruments being used should be "open" in order to achieve a smooth transition also on the level of coordination processes (Rodden 1992).

- Requirements regarding human and social aspects.

Human and social needs of the organization members have to be considered when a system for the support of office work is designed, to avoid problems of acceptance and negative motivation which would endanger the expected benefits. There is especially a danger of overloading the members of an organization by too many complex application systems. The supporting systems must be characterized by a useful allocation of functions between man and machine. Active support should not be confused with patronizing the user.

In the design of a communication orientated system it must be recognized that communication between human actors does not only serve the immediate performance of multi-user tasks, but also is to a high degree necessary to foster social relations between the organization members. The portability of "social information", which determines the social presence of communication, is generally regarded to be highest in face-to-face interaction and lowest in asynchronous text orientated communication.

3.4 Communication Orientated Approaches for Supporting Office Work

Based on the discussion of decision orientated vs. communication orientated approaches for the support of multi-user processes we categorize communication orientated systems and evaluate them regarding their support potential.

3.4.1 Decision Orientation vs. Communication Orientation

A process orientated view, as followed in this paper, suggests a communication orientated view of office work. Communication between human actors – and machine agents – is the basis for coordination. The support of communication processes is therefore an important starting point for the support of multi-user office work.

A different starting point could be the decision process. Decision Support Systems (DSS) – systems that can support unstructured or semi-structured decision situations – have been augmented to become Group Decision Support Systems (GDSS) (DeSanctis 1985). If the support of multi-person decisions is not studied as isolated phenomenon, but rather in its organizational context, then the term Organizational Decision Support System (ODSS) is used (Watson 1990). Thus the focus has shifted from individual decisions via (small) group decisions to decisions in an organizational context (George 1991). Negotiation Support Systems (NSS) can be viewed as special GDSS (Foroughi 1990). While a GDSS supports decision makers who work together as a group, a NSS focuses especially on non-cooperative, competitive or antagonistic situations (Jelassi 1989).

GDSS differ from DSS not only by offering methods for collective decisions, but also by taking other work processes connected with the decision into consideration, including the communication between decision makers (Kraemer 1988). From this a need for differentiation between GDSS and the communication orientated systems arises. Pinneseault and Kraemer (1989) categorize GDSS approaches and differentiate between primarily communication orientated approaches and primarily decision orientated approaches. A definite distinction cannot be made, however. For example, the increasing consideration of semantic aspects in communication systems tends to support decisions. The distinction is therefore based on the perspective from which the multi-user process are viewed.

3.4.2 Approaches and Systems for the Support of Unstructured Communication

Communication orientated systems for the support of multi-user office work can be differentiated, whether or not they support certain patterns or structures of communication between actors ("structured communication"). These structures can roughly be interpreted as rules or limitations concerning the kinds of activities associated with communication, their sequence, and the involved parties. They form the basis for active support of multi-user processes and starting points for the realization of coordination instruments.

First we describe systems that do not support structured communication between actors. They are intended for pure transmission of information. Thus they provide a basic technical infrastructure for communication without any specific support for efficient coordination. Most of the systems described later in this paper build upon these communication mechanisms.

3.4.2.1 *Message-Handling Systems*

Message-Handling Systems (MHS) provide a service for computer based asynchronous transmission of documents, this includes electronic mail (see Chapters 4 and 5). Communication takes place not only between the sender and one recipient (1:1), but through mailing lists also between a sender and a defined group of recipients (1:n). The asynchronous mode relieves the participants to a great extent from spatial and temporal restrictions of collaboration.

The following arguments clarify the limitations regarding the support of multi-user processes:

- n:m communication is not supported.
- There is no common archive as an information pool for a work group or an organization.
- In mailing lists, group and organization structures can only be modeled insufficiently.
- All interpersonnel messages are of the same type (Tsichritzis 1987, Bogen 1988).
- The contents of the messages are not interpreted, except for a few header fields (Tsichritzis 1987).
- The communication context of a message is only faintly supported (Smith 1989) since messages are treated as isolated objects (Tsichritzis 1987).
- More complex activities within group processes are not sufficiently considered (Smith 1988, Bogen 1988).

MHS can aid substantially in speeding up communication processes. On the one hand, the systems are rather flexible because communication structures and semantics are hardly considered. On the other hand, the level of support is low. MHS can provide the basic technical communications infrastructure for systems that achieve a higher level of support by incorporating the communication structures of a group. An example is the project AMIGO MHS+ (Smith 1989): based on the existing services X.400 and X.500 a "group communication layer" is provided including information dissemination services, archiving services, and coordination services interacting with other services.

3.4.2.2 Synchronous Conference Systems

Conferences are a well-proven form of group work, which can contribute to many goals (Cook 1987). Depending on the distance of the participants meeting systems or remote synchronous conference systems are used.

Colab, developed at XEROX PARC (Stefik 1987a, Stefik 1987b), is one of the best known and most comprehensive systems for meeting support. It depends on installations in a specially equipped conference room. Besides a U-shaped table for up to six persons there are connected PCs for each person and a large display ("lifeboard") that can be seen by everybody. Also the individual screens have areas for common displays and workspaces. Within the project several specific tools for meetings have been developed. Similar systems are, e.g. GroupSystems/PLEXIS (Nunamaker 1991), CATeam (Lewe 1990, Lewe 1991) and Project Nick (Cook 1987). Capture Lab (Halonen 1990) supports group work not by special software ("groupware approach"), but rather mainly by shared access to a common computer ("shared hardware approach"). Co-oP (Bui 1987) finally is a more quantitatively orientated system ("decision conference" (Kraemer 1988)), which supports the decision process in a narrower sense.

Meeting systems are suitable for less structured and more complex tasks. They offer a relatively low level of communication support, while the level of decision support for specific situations is high:

- There are special tools for meeting support that suggest a meeting structure following certain phases.
- There is no differentiation of duties and rights of the participants.
- Personal participation fosters a confidential relationship.
- Flexibility is reduced by limitation to one place.

Synchronous communication between remote participants is supported by different forms of conference systems. The simplest and oldest form of audio-conference systems are telephone-conferences. If there are also ways for text and still-picture communication, they are called audiographic conferences. Video-conference systems can also transmit moving pictures, mostly between specially equipped conference studios. While these conferences must be planned ahead, the "Video-Wall" experiment by Xerox (Schooler 1991) aims at *ad hoc* communication between two places that are connected to each other by an audio and a video channel around the clock. At both places there are monitors in generally accessible spaces. Other projects even offer audio and video (AV) communications at the individual workplaces in order to foster unplanned and informal interaction (Buxton 1990).

By integrating telecommunications orientated AV conference systems with computer orientated meeting systems (Ishii 1990) it is possible to transmit and process information both computer readable and unreadable. MMConf (Crowley 1990) and MMC (Schooler 1991) are examples for wide-area multimedia conference systems.

In all, AV conference systems are useful for supporting weakly structured parts of groupwork. Especially with video conferencing it is possible to transmit gestures, miming and intonation. Communication is close to face-to-face conferences – even though it cannot be considered fully equivalent (Egido 1988). However, active support through information and communication technology is not provided:

- Special structures of the course of conferences are not supported.
- Group structures are not modelled.
- There is no common information pool for the group. The course of the conference can be recorded, but the storage media does not allow subsequent processing.

3.4.3 Approaches and Systems for the Support of Structured Communication

3.4.3.1 *Computer Conference Systems*

Asynchronous conference systems for participants in a local and wide area allow n:m communication in addition to message transmission between individuals. Contributions to a discussion on a common topic are stored and made available for every participant of the conference (Canning 1985). It is a form of indirect communication, where the recipients must not necessarily be defined by the author of the contribution. The contributions are usually stored in a central facility and can be queried by the participants. In comparison to the synchronous systems mentioned above, computer conference systems have more powerful ways of structuring the communication within the group (Turoff 1991a, Turoff 1989) (see also Chapter 6 this volume) :

- Information pool available to the whole group.
- Different types of contributions (answers, commentaries, etc.). The storage organization may be viewed as a specific hypertext structure.
- More than one conference for a given group is possible, e.g. for specific topics, or for better structuring of a problem solving process (sub-conferences).
- Roles reflecting specific duties and rights of participants.
- Application of special methods, e.g. the Delphi Method.

Computer conference systems are also suitable for less structured tasks. In this case, there is no active control of the status of the conference by the system. This may be different for some applications, because there is a potential for active support in the form of adaptation of conference structures and by incorporating other systems (Turoff 1989). In comparison to synchronous conference systems the participants are freed largely from spatial and temporal restrictions of collaboration, so that the systems can be integrated in the course of activities. On the other hand, the power of expression as in more direct, synchronous collaboration is lost.

3.4.3.2 *Administrative and Planning Systems*

Systems for planning and administration support strongly formalized tasks for mass data processing and programmable routine decisions (Mertens 1991). These typical commercial applications support not only isolated workplaces, but also model organizational flows. The support of multi-user processes can be illustrated by the concept "action orientated data processing", which has been put into effect in commercially available software products. The components of an action-orientated system notify the next actor by messages or they trigger automatic processes.

Most of today's administration and planning systems do not, however, provide active support for multi-user processes. Communication between the actors is achieved through the common data basis which is updated by different organizational units.

There is a number of limitations:

- The systems are limited to mass data processing.
- The contents of the communication are predefined by the data format or by the format of the action message.
- Cooperation relations are restricted to invariable partners.
- Systems are modeled following traditional function orientated organization forms with strong division of labor. The organizational context of the individual task is largely ignored.
- Exceptions can in most cases not satisfactorily be handled by the system.
- In spite of improved adaptability of standard software, the application systems are relatively unflexible.
- Construction and maintenance of implicitly specified cooperation relations causes relatively high cost.

Administration and planning systems offer a chance to efficiently support structured processes with a high degree of repetition. Weaker structured processes or those with fewer repetitions cannot at all or not efficiently be supported.

3.4.3.3 Office Procedure Systems

Office procedure systems aim at comprehensive support of office work, independent of specific application areas. The functionality of these systems includes the possibility to specify procedure types without the assistance of professional application developers. A special language or directly manipulated graphics is used to specify procedures in a form that can be interpreted by a machine and allows active control of multi-user processes. Main elements of the specification are actions (procedure elements), their sequence relations and the information exchanged between the actions (mostly in the form of documents). The allocation of actions to specific actors is done using a role concept. On this basis an application independent procedure control component controls the sequence and flow of procedure instances (instantiated procedure types). The systems find out who should be the next actor, sends him a message und supplies all necessary information. Usually it does not execute the actions done by the user – in most cases with the assistance of the usual tools for document processing.

The flexibility of an office procedure system is determined by the system architecture. In respect to centralization/decentralization the following basic variants can be identified: systems that have at least a centralized procedure control – e.g. SCOOP (Zisman 1977), DOMINO (Kreifelts 1991a, 1991b), or OfficeTalk-D (Ellis 1982). The formal definition for the internal representation of procedures is done using nets, expecially augmented Petri-Nets. In contrast, the prototype TLA (Tsichritizis 1982, Hogg 1985a) allows distributed procedures processing as well as control. Coordination between the actor-based processes is done solely by the exchange of structured messages. The systems PAGES (Mäntylä 1990) and email (Hogg 1985b) are based on intelligent forms that have been extended by processing and communication functions. All these systems rely on a message orientated communication model.

The systems mentioned are prototypes that have been developed since the late 1970s. For only a few years have there been commercial systems on the market. They are usually offered as components of integrated office information systems or of document management systems (Hales 1991). Most of these systems are not based on an email system, but on a database. In the system ProMInanD procedure types and status information are kept in a global database, and the procedure instances to be processed locally are stored in a local database. The propagation of procedure information is based on distributed transactions (Karbe 1991). The system for activity coordination, developed in the EuroCoOp project, may be viewed as an extension to procedure systems that can also support less structured activities. Based on a task model the execution of actions is controlled and monitored, just as in procedure systems. The facilities for specifying and revising activities have, however, been substantially improved by using hierarchical action definitions. One has to note though that the system does not support organization wide processes, but rather the work of small and medium sized groups (Kreifelts 1991c).

The critical review of office procedure systems addresses mainly problems of flexibility:

- It is not possible to model weakly structured tasks adequately as a predefined sequence of actions.
- Since the office is an open system (Hewitt 1986, Fikes 1980), it is not possible to specify the knowledge needed to carry out all office work (Barber 1983, Mazer 1987).
- Role and activity orientation is in contrast to a possible strong dependency from specific persons.
- The specification of communication structures as well as the mainly verbal asynchronous communication leads to a formal, task orientated style of interaction.
- Exception handling is not actively supported since procedure specifications only represent the normal flow of operations, but not the intentions behind a procedure. The user must interact manually by reversing

or forwarding actions, by resetting procedures to earlier recovery points, or by canceling the whole procedure (Kreifelts 1991a, Karbe 1991). This could result in inefficient non-standard procedures because the search for information takes much time and the regulations are not met.

The applicability of office procedure systems is mainly limited to structured office work. In comparison to administration and planning systems they provide more flexible support for less frequent procedures. This flexibility is due mainly to the problem-solving capabilities of the human actors. Compared to systems that do not consider communication structures, a more active support of group work and thus a higher degree of automation is possible.

3.4.3.4 Systems Based on the Speech Act Theory

Speech act theory systems (see Chapter 11) are based on the model that humans act by using language ("language/action perspective") (Winograd 1987a) (see also Chapter 2). This model is based on the linguistic speech act theory which deals mainly with the pragmatic dimension of language. Primarily illocutive acts are relevant that express an intention and imply commitments of the involved partners regarding their future behavior. Flores *et al.* (Flores 1980, Winograd 1987a, Winograd 1987b) describe an organization as a network of commitments.

Since a formal correlation of words and speech acts cannot be derived (Flores 1980, Winograd 1987b), the handling of conversations by natural language processing systems is not promising. The support must therefore rely on an explicit declaration of speech acts.

The Coordinator (Flores 1988) is the first system for the support of group work on the basis of speech act theory that is commercially available. It comprises typical email functions with the speciality that the messages represent different linguistic actions, which are determined by the message type selected by the user. The predetermined semi-structured message types are not interpreted by content. The selection of message types is the basis for the so-called conversation manager which determines what types of answer the recipient may use in an action-orientated conversation. The system manages the messages in archives individual to each user, including due-dates.

The systems Strudel (Shepherd 1990) and ConversationBuilder (Kaplan 1991, Kaplan 1992) can be seen as extensions to this approach. Both systems allow the definition of task-specific conversations. Elements of the speech act theory can also be found in the Structure Definition Language (SDL), which was developed as part of the COSMOS project for modeling all sorts of communication structures (Wilbur 1988, Bowers 1988a, Bowers 1988b). The conversation model is also used within the Business Design Technology (BDT) (Dunham 1991, Medina-Mora 1992). BDT comprises an analysis method, a design language and a software environment for implementing distributed business applications for supporting multi-user processes.

CHAOS (DeCindio 1988) is a more powerful prototype based on speech act theory. The system uses knowledge regarding the organization structure and the linguistic context of a group. The underlying knowledge bases are updated by completed conversations.

The conversation model can also be used for the description of task-specific forms of conversation. For example, the communication between the procedure control module and the user components of office procedure system DOMINO follow predefined conversation rules (Kreifelts 1988).

Common characteristic of these systems is the predefinition of a certain communication structure, and thus a prescriptive view of efficient communication (Nagasundaram 1990). It can be doubted, however, whether speech act theory can serve as a general basis for computerized communication:

- A problem seems to be the assumption that this structure is independent of the application area (Bowers 1988b, Nagasundaram 1990).
- Organizational regulations are not considered.
- Speech act theory was originally developed for face-to-face communication and spoken language. In the system mentioned above, however, it is used for ansynchronous, text orientated communication (Bowers 1988b).
- The predominance of "conversation for action" is not justified, since it will occur usually in conjunction with other conversation types.
- Systems based on speech act theory support only the pragmatic dimension of communication, whereas the contents of the messages are not considered.

The definition of message types – i.e. the definition of a protocol – can, however, in combination with application specific communication structures be regarded as a useful tool for computer-aided interpretation of messages.

3.4.3.5 Intelligent Filter Systems

Intelligent filter systems support sorting, priorities and further processing of information. In a communication system message, filter systems can support the handling of messages. In contrast to systems based on speech acts, these systems do not rely on a general conversation structure, but rather on an analysis of message characteristics.

Message filters can be seen as an ideal application area of natural language processing systems (Ram 1992, Thompson 1991). The performance is up to now limited, though. Alternative approaches are based on structuring of messages. Information Lens (Malone 1987) and its successor Object Lens (Lai 1988)/Oval (Malone 1992) are the best known systems of this type (Robinson 1991).

Information Lens defines semi-structured messages as objects in an inheritance network. A message type consists of a number of fields, some of them containing unstructured information. The user can specify rule based agents that apply their rules on a set of objects if certain events occur. For example, incoming messages can be prioritized automatically, sorted, filed, deleted or forwarded. There is also a mechanism for processing messages of a common mailbox. Information Lens requires certain agreements between sender and recipient in order to be able to interpret the messages – otherwise it assumes the most general type and the functionality is reduced to email.

For applications like processing of incoming mail, mail filters that allow unstructured messages and do not require agreements between communication partners are more suitable. While the message filter systems ISCREEN (Pollok 1988) and Mail-Man (Motiwalla 1992) have conditions concerning only few formal attributes of the messages, a more sophisticated filter system has been developed in the WISDOM project. It is based on a classification of unstructured messages into a defined hierarchy of message types (Lutz 1990). The filter rules relate to a semantic structure of the individual message that has to be built. In addition, the system can rely on an organization knowledge base.

The "semantic interpretation" of messages is the basis for action triggering and, therefore, also for the support or the automatization of task execution by message filter systems in the context of multi-user processes:

- Message filters that are applicable also for unstructured messages do not necessitate special agreements between the communication partners. On the other side, the error rate of these systems is relatively high.
- Message filter systems can be used in the context of office procedure systems: the filter specifications for the handling of incoming messages can provide for automatic initiation of office procedures. This makes sense especially in administrative applications with large message volumes.
- Not the procedures but only the message types to be used in multi-user processes are represented in filter systems. The filtering rules are not globally but rather locally defined by individual actors. These systems are mainly suitable for the support of semi-structured tasks.
- It must be generally criticized that a given message may have only one specific meaning in a filter system with relevance for further processing. This substance of a message must be explicated. In doing so part of the meaning of a message may be lost (Nagasundaram 1990).

3.4.3.6 Problem-Solving Approach

The starting point of the problem-solving approach is the idea to apply methods of artificial intelligence for the support of weakly structured tasks. An immense number of knowledge-based systems have been developed for office applications during the last few years – most of the systems aiming at an isolated support for the individual user.

The research conducted by Barber (1982, 1983) (OMEGA) at the beginning of the 1980s is regarded as the first contribution to the development of the problem-solving approach. The system served to support a single user, there was no explicit support for interactions between different users.

Systems based on the problem-solving approach comprise procedure planning and semi-autonomous agents who execute tasks for a user. In the WISDOM project there were two developments for procedure planning. The planning support system VIPS (Martial 1987) helps to specify procedures in a cooperative dialogue. First, the user classifies the problem area. The system then generates a skeleton that can be further refined. The WISDOM system LUPINO (Lutze 1988) in contrast, plans procedures and carries them out mostly automatically. The user states simply the initial state and the goal of the procedure. The system breaks the goal down in a hierarchical planning process, checks for consistency and carries the actions out, interlinked with the planning process. Ultimate control is up to human actors. The system can react to exceptions during the execution with plan revisions. LUPINO is based on a version of POLYMER (Croft 1988, Lefkowitz 1989), developed at the University of Massachusetts. Other systems to be mentioned here are ASPERA (Bena 1987) and COOKBOOK (Ishii 1988).

The second knowledge-based approach, namely "intelligent" or "semi-autonomous agents", has risen much attention. These system carry out many tasks for human users almost automatically, including communication and coordination. The problem-solving methods used are augmented as compared to procedure planning systems in order to cover the special aspects of distribution. Most systems use communication protocols, based on a structure similar to conversation for action. The systems D-POLYMER (Bhandaru 1990), Intelligent Workstation (Ader 1987), PAGES (Mäntylä 1990), MOAP/SACT (Woo 1990), KIK/TEAMWARE (Steiner 1990a 1990b), COMTRAC/CAP (Koo 1987, 1988), COKES (Kaye 1987) and OFFICE (Nierenburg 1986) are distributed knowledge-based approaches. Also the mail filters Information Lens and Object Lens/Oval (mentioned above) are semi-autonomous agents, but with a much lower level of support.

Systems based on the problem solving approach are much more complex than conventional office procedure systems. The representation of broad application knowledge opens new possibilities for supporting weakly structured work (Woo 1987):

- Active support for exception handling.
- Inclusion of non-standard procedures.
- Unified consideration of rules and regulations.
- Modeling of the inherent distribution of office work.

3.4.4 Other Approaches and Systems for the Support of Office Group Work

It is hardly possible to give a complete overview of groupware systems for office applications, although the development of these systems is still in the early stages. Therefore, in this section we can only mention a few approaches with limited application scope.

- Co-Authoring Systems (e.g. Ellis 1991, Fish 1988, Lewis 1988).
- "Issue-Based Information Systems" (Busch 1991, Conklin 1988, Rein 1990, Lee 1990).
- Calendar Management (Lauriston 1990, Woitass 1990).
- Organizational Memory Management (Steels 1985, Johansen 1987, Turoff 1991b, Ackerman 1990).
- Project Management.

Besides these specialized applications there are some approaches trying to integrate these applications in the sense of comprehensive support. Prototypes of that sort try to avoid the use of different media in the support of multi-user processes (e.g. Ishii 1990), or they aim at realizing a specific model (e.g. Intelligent Workstation (Ader 1987), COSMOS (Bowers 1988a, Wilbur 1988), Advanced Group Communication (part of AMIGO, (Prinz 1989)), Integrated Group Support Environment (Chen 1991), and Mocca (The Mocca Group 1992).

3.5 Evaluation of the Approaches Presented

The systems and approaches mentioned above are only partly really new; part of them are well-known concepts that are now viewed as an integral part of the organization, in order to foster multi-user processes *in toto*. We try to evaluate the approaches in the Summary with respect to the criteria mentioned above.

- Basic requirements.

Active support of structured tasks based on predefined procedures is best done with procedure systems. These systems are now coming into use. In most cases administrative and planning systems are used for the support of structured tasks; however, these systems do not provide active support of multi-user processes. Many of today's problems with information processing and communication support stem from the fact that the tasks being supported by these systems are not structured as strongly as it would be necessary for optimal application.

Semi-structured tasks can be supported especially by message filter systems and those following the problem-solving approach. The latter have the capability of considering organizational regulations in the planning process and of adapting them to specific situations. Most of the developments are in the prototype stadium however, and are based on unrealistic assumptions regarding the scope of the application areas, the willingness of human actors to cooperate, and the knowledge base available. Systems based on speech act theory that do not use organization specific knowledge are regarded as less suitable.

For unstructured tasks systems for the support of unstructured communication and computer conference systems would be the first choice; however, they provide only little or even no active support for coordination processes. The mechanisms for planning and negotiation support provided by systems based on the problem-solving approach can also be used for this task type; but because of the requirements of "social presence" associated with this task type this approach is less suitable.

Transitions between the different task types or mixtures are mostly unsatisfactorily dealt with. It is to be mentioned, however, that systems following the problem-solving approach support other coordination instruments beside organizational regulations and therefore provide a better potential for transitions between task types. However, the majority of these systems neglect structured tasks.

- Efficiency requirements.

In calculating an index for efficiency one usually discovers many problems of operationalization. This is also true in this case, as the concrete conditions of the application situation may differ substantially and are not known. Moreover, the systems cannot actually be compared because of different states of development. Therefore, the possible level of support is used as one criterion for efficiency here.

Figure 3.1 shows an estimated judgement about the approaches mentioned, regarding this criterion. Active support for multi-user processes can be achieved by mail filters, office procedure systems and knowledge-based systems. A relatively high level of support is also given by administrative and planning systems for routine tasks.

The other approaches support mainly the communication activities underlying the coordination task. Specific communication structures that might be used for achieving a higher level of support are, however, not at all or not intensively enough being used. Problem solving, coordination and tracking of ongoing processes are therefore left mainly to the human actor.

All approaches can help reduce the overall time of processes as compared to conventional paper-based office work by speeding up the communication.

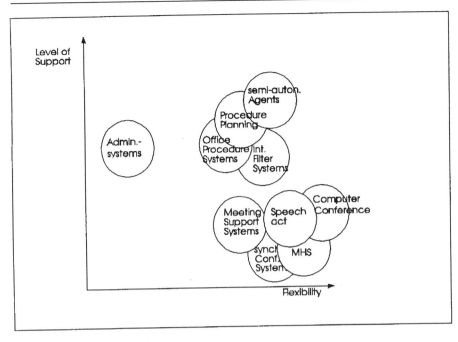

Figure 3.1 Level of Support and flexibility of communication-orientated approaches

Procedure systems as well as administration and planning systems can, moreover, reduce the overall time of processes through active monitoring. Time-consuming search, merge and match processes are reduced mainly by systems following the problem-solving approach.

A better quality of the results by unification of administrative practices and better tuning of task steps is also primarily possible with those systems that make organizational knowledge available to the user in the context of task execution.

● Flexibility requirements.

In communication-orientated systems efficiency is improved by general regulations, e.g. allocation of tasks, workflows, filter rules, etc., but at the same time this might result in reduced adaptability to changing environments and unexpected events. Figure 3.1 shows an estimated allocation of the approaches mentioned in this paper regarding this criterion.

It is obvious that flexible systems are available in the form of traditional communication systems.

Continuous change in organizations is especially supported by systems according to the problem solving approach – and to a lesser degree by procedure systems – as organizational regulations in these systems are not implicitly coded but explicitly represented.

Case orientated adaptation to specific situations is found to be good with systems following the problem solving approach because of the availability of planning and negotiation mechanisms. Some of the prototypes, however, use sophisticated methods for automatic planning that may hinder rather than enhance task execution in the case of simple problems that require much common sense. Systems providing cooperative problem solving are better suited.

● Transparency requirements.

Systems for the support of unstructured communication do not have a useful business orientated model of the work being done. They help with generating, disseminating, and managing information without any overview over the activities going on in the organization. They do not provide active support for the transition from abstract organizational requirements to concrete activities. This is also true for systems that rely solely on speech act theory.

Contrasted to the above, are systems following the problem-solving approach, procedure systems, and administration and planning systems. However, the latter do not generally provide an explicit representation of organizational regulations. Systems following the problem-solving approach represent – other than procedure systems – also the goals of actions and procedures. This is especially important with exception handling.

Control of ongoing processes is best being supported by procedure systems and systems following the problem-solving approach.

● Openness and integration requirements.

If one abstracts from technical DP problems and views the integration of systems for the support of office work on a conceptual level, then systems based on the problem solving approach, more than others, reveal a high potential for integrating coordination processes on a high semantic level, because they encompass an explicit representation of the tasks to be supported. They can also serve as integration tools for other systems – especially for those in use already. This aspect is mostly neglected in current prototypes, though.

● Requirements regarding human and social aspects.

Systems for the support of office work can help relieve the workload of human actors. This is especially true for systems supporting structured communication. These systems are, however, less apt for communicating "social information" than systems supporting face-to-face communication or synchronous communication between remote participants. Furthermore there is always the danger of patronizing the user with systems that control procedures actively. This is especially the case with those systems following the problem solving approach that are based on automatic planning.

3.6 Summary

Looking at the systems predominant today, namely administrative and planning systems on the one hand, and systems for supporting unstructured communication on the other, the opposition between flexibility and efficiency becomes apparent. This opposition can be overcome by "more intelligent" systems; the problem solving approach is most promising. Systems for the support of office work on this basis are still in the prototype state. The evaluation of the described, approaches helps with deducing important functional requirements for systems design that have, or have not sufficiently been considered so far:

- The office is an open system which cannot be modeled once and for all. The use of complex planning methods for realizing autonomous systems does not seem possible. Instead, the support of human actors in coordination and communication tasks is realistic. For this purpose semi-autonomous systems, realizing cooperative problem solving among man and machine, are best suited.
- The basis of these coordination processes are the communication relations between the actors. In order to allow machine agents to participate actively in coordination and communication processes, it is necessary to define communication protocols that allow machine interpretation of contents and intentions of the communication. It may not be forgotten that communication has a social function for human actors. The integration of communication between persons, between person and machine, and between machines as active participants in collaborative processes is a problem that is not sufficiently solved in the approaches developed to-date.
- There must be coordination instruments for tasks of different degrees of structuredness. Besides planning and negotiation mechanisms provided in problem-solving systems as their only mechanisms, organizational regulations – especially procedure specifications – have to be included. With organizational regulations we mean the enterprise view and not the technical view.
- Critical for future success is the possibility of integrating existing or emerging systems. A simple connection on a technical basis is not enough, but it is rather necessary to strive for a continuous active support of processes.

Chapter 4

Coordinating Human and Software Agents through Electronic Mail

Ian Finch, Frans Coenen, Trevor Bench-Capon and Michael Shave

4.1 Introduction

As organizations move towards decentralized control structures, software has evolved to facilitate this new style of working. Such software includes conferencing systems (Kerr *et al.* 1982, Flores *et al.* 1988), bulletin boards (Payes *et al.* 1987) and electronic mail collectively referred to as groupware (Greenberg 1991). Groupware offers many benefits:

- Distributed communication. Geographically distributed groups can communicate with one another, using a computer network. Cooperative tasks can thus be performed without group members having to meet, often a time and finance consuming operation.
- *Asynchronous communication.* Communication can be asynchronous, therefore individual group members can also be temporally distributed (which is often a side-effect of the geographic distribution of large organizations) (see Chapter 6).
- *External computer facilities.* Users can access additional computer facilities such as databases and information-gathering telemetry, so providing group members with more information on which to base their decisions.

There are also, however, a number of disadvantages associated with groupware, and networking in general:

- *Loss of support staff.* Tasks which were carried out by a number of support staff (for example secretaries or technical staff) become the responsibility of individual network users.

- *Added responsibility for users.* Frequently, individual users must take decisions which were previously taken by higher level managers in a centralized, hierarchical organization. There is thus more responsibility borne by the individual. This is exacerbated by the less formal nature of decentralized organizations, where person-to-person communication frequently replaces more formal, hierarchical communications.

- *Information overload.* The additional facilities supported by groupware make more information available to the user, but this is often excessive and results in *information overload.*

- *Administration of groupware supported tasks.* If many users work together using groupware tools, the team must be coordinated. It usually falls to one member of the team to fulfil this administrative role, increasing that person's workload (see Chapter 6).

To help alleviate these problems various software tools can be employed, for example filters to counteract information overload and autonomous agents to handle common requests. This paper examines the problems which arise when humans and such software agents need to cooperate. A communications management system, *adcmail*, which facilitates cooperation between humans and software agents using electronic mail, is also described.

Note that the work described has been carried out as part of the Aide de Camp project under the auspices of the SERC.

4.2 Software Support Tools

There are a number of software tools which can help alleviate the problems outlined in the introduction. These can be categorized as follows:

- Simple message filters.
- Active filters.
- Autonomous agents.

This last category is the most powerful, but to operate successfully we also need the first two. Each is described in the following subsections.

4.2.1 Simple Message Filtering

Filtering can have either a negative or a positive connotation. That is, a filter can either remove messages which are of no interest, or it can select and bring forward messages which match the filtering criteria. Both are termed *simple message filtering* (or just *simple filtering*). In general, positive filtering is much more important in information sharing systems than negative filtering, a fact which has been observed by a number of researchers, for example Malone *et al.* (1988).

The principal difficulty associated with message filtering is in determining the contents of the message. This can be achieved in various ways; typical options are:

- Natural language understanding of the message text.
- Word frequency searching.
- Keyword searching.
- Structured and semi-structured messages.
- Use of email headers.

These are arranged in order of sophistication (with natural language understanding being the ideal solution). Note that the less sophisticated the approach, the greater the involvement and responsibility of the sender. For a fuller discussion of mail filtering, the reader is directed to Coenen *et al.* (1992b).

The advantages of simple filters are that they can be created with minimal effort and greatly reduce the information presented to the user. The major disadvantage is that to filter messages effectively, some means of determining the contents of the message is necessary. This raises problems of either using expensive software technology or imposing rigid formatting on the message.

4.2.2 Active Filtering

It is possible to further alleviate information overload by introducing software which can respond to routine messages on behalf of the user. This is termed *active filtering*. Active filtering, as the name suggests, is a powerful variant on simple filtering where messages which match some criteria can be acted upon in many different ways. Whereas simple filters aid the user by simply removing messages which are of no interest, active filters can perform actions on the user's behalf in response to messages, obviating the need even to see the messages. The following examples illustrate the use of active filters:

- A message arrives requesting times when the recipient is free on a certain day. An active filter could intercept such a message and send the appropriate information by consulting the user's online diary.
- A message requests authorization from the user for purchasing some equipment. An active filter deduces that the user does not have the

status to grant such authorization and forwards it to the user's superior. Note that this counters the problem of less formal communications within an organization.

- A group of people are collaboratively producing a product document. One person is designated the *contact* and if any person outside the group wishes to see a copy of the document, it is the contact they must send a message to. If the contact receives a message asking for a copy of the document, an active filter can intercept the message, send messages to all the authors of the document, collate their responses and then send the collated document to the person who requested it. The process can be made even more efficient if the individual authors also have active filters which can send their sections of the message in response to the contact's request.

The main advantage of active filters is that they reduce the communication needs for the user, but once more there are problems in determining the contents of a message (with the same trade-off between sophistication and viability) and there may be a performance cost if there are a large number of complex filters in use.

4.2.3 Autonomous Agents

Simple and active filters, as described above, reduce information overload by intercepting messages and taking appropriate actions on behalf of the user. Another approach is to create *autonomous software agents* to which messages can be sent, instead of sending them to the user.

Autonomous agents are capable of initiating communication, as opposed to filters which can only respond to messages. Thus autonomous agents can be created to handle routine tasks such as:

- Automated report generation (for example collation of sales figures at the start of each month).
- Monitoring and accessing remote telemetry equipment.
- Interacting with and maintaining remote data sources.
- Coordinating cooperative tasks (for example stock monitoring).
- Generating automatic replies to standard request messages.

The use of autonomous agents offers several benefits, notably that complex programs can be used and the agents impose no performance load on the user (because they are running as independent processes). The disadvantage is in the development of autonomous agents. They will incur all the development costs normally associated with software, and additionally they will need to be able to communcicate with other agents.

4.2.4 Combining Simple Filters, Active Filters and Autonomous Agents

For greatest efficiency and flexibility, simple filters, active filters and autonomous agents must be available and able to interact with each other and with human users. To reap the greatest benefits from these software tools, we propose that a composite strategy be employed to show that not only will this enable the best tool to be employed for each job, but the disadvantages associated with each tool will be lessened by support from other tools.

For example, in the earlier product document example, the contact could be an autonomous agent which interacts with the individual authors' active filters. Furthermore, it ought not to matter which software agents are being used (indeed whether software agents are being used) for cooperation to take place. Thus, in some situations a user could be manually responding to messages, at other times active filters may be used due to an unusually high workload and in other instances the user may be away and, hence, an autonomous agent may handle all communication for the user. This must in no way compromise the cooperation within the organization.

The most significant problem in combining these three categories of agent is in coordinating their activities. The next section explores this problem.

4.3 Modes of Interaction with Adcmail

The remainder of this paper presents the Aide de Camp Communications Management System (*adcmail*) which has been specifically designed to coordinate human and software agents using electronic mail as the communication medium.

Adcmail is an X Windows based, mail user agent, capable of reading and sending messages using the RFC822 mail standard (Crocker 1982). There are three modes of interaction with adcmail:

- Interactive (for human agents).
- Filtering (for support of human agents).
- Sub-systems (for running autonomous agents).

Whilst the first two categories are well established as research areas, the third is a significant departure from previous work. It is, however, necessary to consider all three areas in some detail since, given the intertwined nature of the coordination mechanism, they are all related to each other.

4.3.1 Interactive Use of Adcmail

The human user of adcmail has full access to all standard mail functions through an X Windows interface. Thus, the user can read incoming mail, reply to, or forward messages, send messages and easily manage an hierarchy of mail folders. Furthermore, the user can maintain a list of aliases and customize the mail environment through a preferences window. For more demanding users, there are options for viewing all header fields, editing headers when sending email etc. For full information on adcmail, the interested reader is directed to Finch (1993).

4.3.2 Filtering in Adcmail

To help manage the user's messages, adcmail provides a filtering language called CFL (Cooperative Filtering Language). An important feature of CFL is that the filters facilitate cooperation with remote users; something not provided by other filtering languages (this is discussed briefly later and more fully in Coenen *et al.* (1992a). CFL can test conditions based on header fields (or other facts such as the date) to perform various actions such as:

● Sending a message.
● Replying to a message.
● Forwarding a message.
● Moving a message to another folder.
● Saving a message to a file.
● Printing a message.
● Deleting a message.

CFL was designed to be cognitively accessible to all potential users of adcmail, not just programmers. Thus, there is a great degree of flexibility in how a filter is written. As an example, the following filter moves messages from the mailing list "cscw-list@uk.co.gid" to a folder entitled "CSCW List":

```
# Move messages from the CSCW mailing list
cscw-list: if the to field is "cscw-list@uk.co.gid"
          then move message to "CSCW List"
```

The filter is divided into four parts; comment, label, condition and action list. In this example, the comment is the line starting with the hash character (#), the label is the word "cscw-list", the condition is the "if" clause and the action list is the "then" clause (consisting of only one action in this case).

Note that the filtering language ensures that addresses are compared in the same format etc., so the user need not be concerned with the exact format of incoming messages. For more information on the filtering language, the reader is directed to Finch (1993).

4.3.3 Adcmail Sub-systems

Whilst CFL is useful as support for the human user of adcmail, autonomous agents will usually require more powerful facilities, for example, the ability to interact with databases, expert systems or telemetry software. To cater for this need, adcmail can act as a communications facilitator for small dedicated programs (called sub-systems). These can either be specially written or adapted from existing programs and are triggered from CFL, acting as autonomous agents. Note that this completely removes one of the major problems in creating autonomous agents; the need to communicate with other agents. The autonomous agent need only be written to handle its specific task, whilst the communication is performed by adcmail.

A sub-system is sent input by adcmail, which will normally be the body of a message, with other information (such as headers or literal strings) prepended. This can be processed in an appropriate way, for example being used as the basis for a database query. The sub-system then generates output (incorporating the results of the processing if desired) which is sent back to adcmail, where it is interpreted and an appropriate action (or actions) taken. These actions can be any of those listed in the previous section.

As an example, suppose any mail sent to a user whilst they were on holiday was to be dealt with by a sub-system called "`holiday.script`". This could be accomplished using the following filter:

```
# Handle my email whilst I am on holiday
holiday: if today is in the list holidayDates
         and the to field is not in the list mailingLists
       then run "holiday.script"
```

Note the second part of the condition which ensures that no holiday messages are sent to mailing lists.

4.3.4 The Task Scripting Language

It was recognized during the Aide de Camp project, that a high proportion of the tasks which sub-systems would be needed for, would involve interaction with databases. To support this need, the *task scripting language* (TSL) was developed (Coenen 1992a, 1992b). TSL is a high-level language which allows Aide de Camp users to define tasks, in terms of task primitives, which are then compiled into adcmail sub-systems (referred to as TSL agents).

Each TSL script starts with a *read message task primitive* and ends with a *send message task primitive*. These are included automatically and are beyond the control of the TSL author. However, in between, the author is free to define whatever task they desire, using one or more of the currently available task primitives:

1. TRANSMIT – Complete a message template.
2. SELECT – Select an item from a database table (or tables) either for output, deletion or updating.
3. CALL – Invoke another function from the current function.
4. IF ... ELSE – Include a choice point.
5. CREATE-TABLE – Create a database table.
6. INSERT – Insert a row into a database table.
7. DELETE – Delete a row from a database table.

An example TSL script is given in Figure 4.1 and a detailed description of TSL is available in Coenen (1992). The example is taken from a working documents application (Coenen *et al.* 1992a). This allows Aide de Camp users to access a working papers database and retrieve information. The fragment given in Figure 4.1 is used to identify whether a particular document is held in the database. If so, an appropriate message is returned, otherwise an error message is sent.

```
RULE retrieve_doc THEN
    SELECT title
        FROM documents
        WHERE title = HEADER[2]
    IF title != NULL CALL message (title)
    ELSE CALL error (title)

RULE message (doc) THEN
    TRANSMIT "TRANSMIT" HEADER[0]
        "doc_database" (doc)

RULE error (doc) THEN
    TRANSMIT "TRANSMIT" HEADER[0]
        "\nERROR: Requested document "
    (doc) " not found"
```

Figure 4.1   A sample TSL script

4.4 The Coordination Mechanism

The coordination mechanism is the key requirement in allowing coordination of human and software agents. It was decided to use email header fields to coordinate agents, since this could be achieved within the current email standard (RFC822) providing compatibility with existing email systems. Furthermore, the header fields could also be used to describe the contents of messages, thus neatly combining solutions to determining message contents and coordinating agents. The message headers and body thus form a semi-structured message, which many researchers feel is a useful compromise between free text and a rigidly imposed format (Malone *et al.* 1988).

As an example of how this would work, consider the common problem of a meeting arrangement. Information such as the location, time and duration of the meeting must be exchanged. Furthermore, the messages must be synchronized so that deadlock or spinlock does not occur. The following headers could be used for this information:

X-AdC-Location: Seminar Room
X-AdC-Time: ?
X-AdC-Duration: 1?
X-AdC-Pass: 0

This would mean that the sender wishes the meeting to be in the "Seminar Room", has no preference for the time and suggests a one hour meeting. Furthermore, this is the first pass in the meeting arrangement process. There would also be a textual element to the message in the body, for human readers. Various agents (human and software) would then negotiate appropriate times, locations etc. setting the "X-AdC-Pass" header as appropriate.

Note that the actual headers used would have to be established by all involved participants. The responsibility for ensuring that adcmail was set up to handle these headers would fall to the site adcmail administrator.

The remainder of this section discusses how the three categories of agent can examine and modify these headers.

4.4.1 Human Agents

The human user of adcmail will compose messages in the "send" window (Figure 4.2). From the figure, it can be seen that this allows the user to supply various standard header fields and a textual message. However, by activating the "Forms" button, the user can select a standard form for messages from a scrolling list. For the meeting arrangement example, this is illustrated in Figure 4.3. Note that the "X-AdC-Pass" field is not displayed, but is instead initialised by the form. When the message is transmitted, the information is retrieved from the appropriate text regions and placed in the headers. Thus, forms provide a template for obtaining header field values.

In actual fact, forms provide more powerful facilities. In addition to indicating which header field values are required, forms indicate how replies to such messages should be formatted. A "reply form" is stored in the message

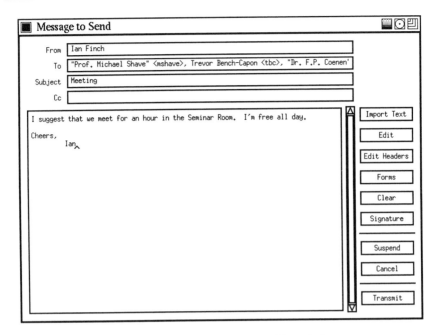

Figure 4.2   The message composition window

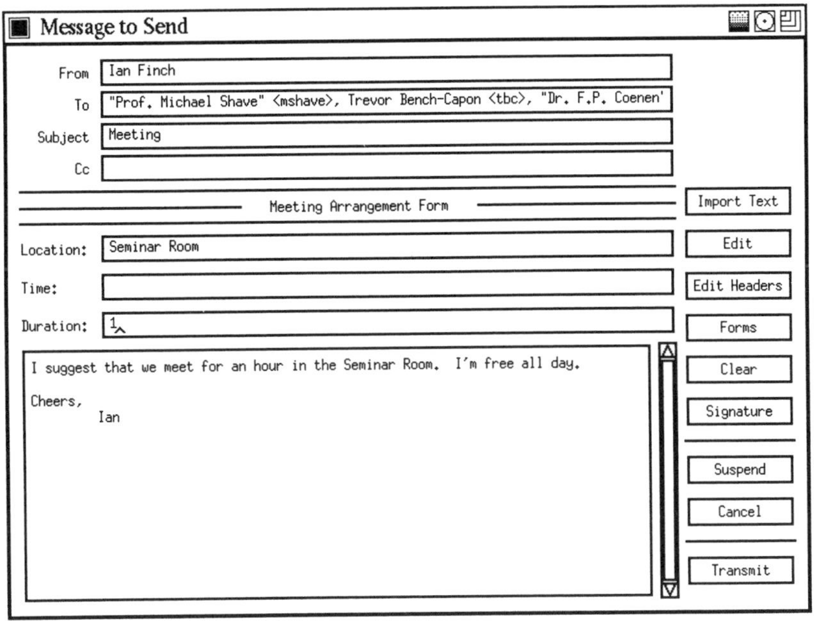

Figure 4.3   The meeting arrangement form

headers so that when a user replies to a message, they are presented with a template for their reply enabling them to compose their reply in a simple manner. Continuing with the meeting arrangement example, the reply window generated is illustrated in Figure 4.4. Note that some regions have been indicated as read-only (such as the room) whilst others can be altered. Furthermore, certain fields (such as the "X-AdC-Pass" field) are altered by the form itself (incremented in this case).

Thus human users can easily send and reply to messages using adcmail, accessing and setting the header fields through a simple interface. It must be briefly noted that users of other mail user agents will not be able to use the coordination facilities with this ease. They will have to alter the header fields manually. This should not be too difficult for simple activities (such as retrieving files) but will be cumbersome for more complex interactions.

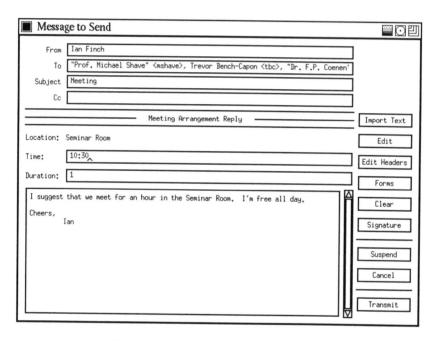

Figure 4.4   The meeting arrangement reply form

4.4.2 Computer Supported Humans

Computer supported humans will be using filters to help manage their mail folders. Thus, this section will indicate how headers can be accessed and modified from the filtering language (CFL).

Filters can access header fields in various ways (Finch 1993), but the general syntax is the <field name> field

Thus, to reference the location field a filter would use:

the X-AdC-Location field

If a reply were to be generated, this could be accomplished with the "reply" action which has the syntax:

reply [using] <file> [with <header> [, <header> ...]]

The filter can thus set header fields in a reply, enabling computer supported humans to communicate similarly as humans. To close this section, the following filter is triggered if no time is supplied and specifies a preferred time in reply:

```
# Supply a meeting time if none is given
specify-time: if the X-AdC-Time is "?"
            then reply using "standard.reply"
                    with the X-AdC-Time field containing "10:30",
                        the X-AdC-Pass field containing
                        the X-AdC-Pass field + 1
```

4.4.3 Autonomous Sub-systems

Although CFL provides powerful support facilities for network users, it is not well suited to the coordination of a complex task such as meeting arrangement. It is more likely that a sub-system will be responsible for the task. In this case, there are two parts to consider; the sub-system and the filter which triggers it. The following filter will trigger the meeting arrangement sub-system (called "meetings", passing it the relevant fields:

```
# Trigger the meetings arrangement sub-system
meetings: if the X-AdC-Pass is greater than 0
        then run "meetings" with the X-AdC-Location field
                    the X-AdC-Time field
                    the X-AdC-Duration field
                    the X-AdC-Pass field
```

The meetings sub-system will be passed all the information and can then decide on the best time, place, etc. for the meeting. The sub-system would probably be written using TSL, but since no restriction is placed on the language for developing sub-systems, the best language for the task can be chosen. Thus, if the sub-system needed to interact with telemetry equipment, it could be developed in C or assembly language, if a large amount of reasoning were required, PROLOG could be used or if there were already a suitable program written in FORTRAN it could simply be modified.

Having reached a conclusion, the sub-system may now wish to send a response. This is achieved simply by writing to the standard output stream with text in the appropriate format. In this case, it would be the keyword "reply" followed by header information, a blank line and the message body. For example:

reply X-AdC-Location: Seminar Room
    X-AdC-Time: 10:30
    X-AdC-Duration: 1:30
    X-AdC-Pass: 1

I suggest a meeting in Seminar Room from 10:30 to 12:00.

Full details of constructing sub-systems are given in Finch (1993).

As a further example, consider triggering a TSL agent. All TSL agents use an "X-AdC-Agent-Header" header to pass information to each other. This can be checked using a wildcard operator. If the header is found, the TSL sub-system can be activated to pass this header:

Trigger a TSL agent
tsl: if the X-AdC-Agent-Header is like "*"
    then run tsl with the X-AdC-Agent-Header

The first item of information in the "X-AdC-Agent-Header" field is the name of the TSL agent which is to be activated. The TSL sub-system checks for this agent's existence and activates it if found. The output from the agent is then picked up by the sub-system and passed back to adcmail to be interpreted, so appropriate actions can be taken.

This section has shown how headers can be used to summarize the contents of messages and coordinate agents in a cooperative task. This can be achieved with ease for any class of agent and with transparency of agents (the recipient need not know which class of agent sent the message and vice-versa). Furthermore, the coordination mechanism requires no extension to the existing email protocol and is thus compatible with existing mail agents.

4.5 Conclusions

To summarize the discussion of coordination using adcmail, it is worth examining various requirements for coordinating human and software agents, noting how they have been accommodated in adcmail:

- Determining the contents of a message. The contents of a message are indicated by appropriate header fields, the format of which are agreed by message sender and recipient.
- A coordination mechanism. Coordination is achieved through header fields in the message (agreed by message sender and recipient) which are then used to trigger appropriate actions.
- Transparency of agents. Since all categories of agent communicate in the same way (using the message headers and body), it is never necessary to know which type of agent sent the message. If, however, some coordination *does* need to know the class of agent which sent a message, this information can be supplied in a header field.
- No degradation of human–human communication. Human–human communication can proceed as normal, since the coordination system places no restriction on message formats.
- Compatibility with existing systems. Adcmail uses the existing RFC822 mail standard and does not adapt it in any way. This means that any existing mail agent (based on the RFC822 standard) can communicate with adcmail, although it may not be able to take advantage of the more powerful features.
- Networking existing applications. Existing applications can be easily converted into sub-systems and thus would have access to all mail facilities. Since sub-systems need only read from the standard input channel and write to the standard output channel, this is a relatively straightforward task accomplished either by modifying the original program or by adding a suitable "wrapper" to it.
- Interaction with external software systems. CFL can provide a mechanism to format messages appropriately for external software systems. This is related to the ability to communicate with existing systems.

In addition, it should be noted that the benefits of groupware listed in the introduction are also available through adcmail. Adcmail addressses the disadvantages of groupware as follows:

- *Loss of support staff.* To counteract the loss of support staff, specialized sub-systems can be added to the network. The network users can then pass specialized tasks on to these agents (either automatically or manually). It would also be possible to retain the services of the support staff and for appropriate work to be routed automatically from the network user to the support staff, thus reducing the load on the network user.
- *Added responsibility for users.* As with the specialists, there are two possibilities for combating added-user responsibility. The first is for

messages to be automatically passed to a user's superior if necessary. The second option is for the message to be delegated to a sub-system which can make the necessary decision.

- *Information overload.* The filtering aspect of adcmail (both simple and active) can greatly reduce information overload, by removing inappropriate messages without the user seeing them, storing messages until they are relevant and so forth. Further reductions in information overload are possible when autonomous agents are employed. A user may have a "secretary" sub-system which can perform tasks such as meeting arrangements and sending standard letters. Thus, if a message arrives requesting a meeting the secretary agent can arrange a time, place etc. and all the user receives is one message containing all the details, rather than the numerous messages which would be necessary to arrange the meetings. Such a scenario is discussed in more detail in Finch *et al.* (1992).

This paper has presented an overview of the Aide de Camp project, concentrating on the interaction between the various categories of agent. There is insufficient space here to describe other facets of the project, but the interested reader is directed to Coenen *et al.* (1992b) for a fuller discussion on how agents can access databases using TSL. More recent work has concentrated on the development of knowledge-based agents, which can respond to email messages on behalf of the user. A description of such an agent, which can answer student queries on behalf of a lecturer, can be found in Finch *et al.* (1994).

Chapter 5

User Control over Coordination Mechanisms in Office Information Systems

Nikolay Mehandjiev, Leonardo Bottaci and Roger Phillips

5.1 Introduction

Effective office systems must provide support for higher level organizational coordination patterns such as activity management, task scheduling and workload distribution. Such support, however, is more difficult to achieve than the more traditional processing support because coordination patterns have a "social" dimension, which makes them complex, irregular and dynamic and hence, difficult to formalize. They are also quite vulnerable to organizational change.

Some office systems avoid this problem by restricting the scope of the coordination support they provide. Examples of this approach are the mail filtering and rerouteing tools of Information Lens (Malone 1989). When viewed in the framework of the coordination theory of Malone and Crowston (Malone 1990), these systems offer support only for the communication process level and serve merely as tools to be used when coordinating. Explicit support for the other three process levels – coordination, group decision making and perception of common objects – is not provided by such systems (see Chapter 2).

This restricted support seems to be an appropriate solution for the "organic" (Lee 1988) type of offices (or "adhocracies" (Mintzberg 1979)), where the coordination and communication is typically performed by the office workers in an "ad hoc" manner. However, a higher level of coordination support might appear to be feasible for the "bureaucratic'" type of offices, where the coordination patterns appear easier to formalize. Two main problems, however, remain: firstly, the coordination patterns evolve too rapidly to be hard coded into the application; and secondly, there are always exceptions that have to be catered for.

We believe that user enhanceable office systems provide a good approach for tackling these two problems. Users of this type of system have access to the coordination rules and parameters, so they can either override them, in the exceptional cases, or modify them as they become obsolete. Such systems would be flexible enough to cater for the organizational dynamics and exceptions, while offering a comparatively high level support for the coordination activities in the target organization. Unfortunately, little has been done so far to develop this idea.

This paper describes how user enhanceability enables high level computer support for a range of coordination patterns. By a coordination pattern we mean the control aspect of any activity requiring nontrivial coordination. In particular, we do not restrict ourselves to activities that are concerned solely with coordination. One of the fundamental assumptions upon which the work of user-enhanceable systems is based, is that end-users are better able to modify systems in which the salient parameters are presented in concrete terms. It therefore seems inappropriate, for our goals, to factor out the coordination aspect of an activity because this presents coordination as an abstract notion divorced from any concrete instantiation. Given a coordination pattern, we define a coordination mechanism as a software mechanism that enacts this pattern. In other words, the work of a coordination mechanism results in coordination patterns.

As a test bed for our work, we are building a research tool for user enhanceable office systems, ECHOES (Easily CHangeable OfficE Systems). Key features of ECHOES are firstly, the visual language which enables nonprogrammers to modify application systems, and secondly, the underlying architecture that allows enhancements to the visual language. ECHOES belongs to the class of "radically tailorable systems" (Malone 1992), to which Oval also belongs.

In this paper we initially give a high-level description of the ECHOES office model. We use two collaborative work scenarios to illustrate "coordination in action". In particular, we see how coordination patterns can evolve to suit changing requirements and how exceptional coordination activities can be handled. Sections 4 gives a more general description of the coordination mechanisms in ECHOES and their mapping to the coordination theory framework offered by (Malone 1990). Sections 5 puts ECHOES in the context of the current research in the field. Sections 6 describes the implementation status of the system. A summary of the mechanisms is given in the final section.

5.2 Office Model in ECHOES

In ECHOES, the office is modeled as a set of "office clerks" that coordinate their activities by exchanging messages. Often these messages are embodied in artefacts of work such as electronic forms and so some coordination mechanisms are implemented as information flows. As an example, consider the processing of postgraduate student applications. The admissions officer initially reviews the application and collects associated documents such as references and publications. This information is then circulated to potential supervisors, who, upon receiving it, add comments and make requests for further information. The admissions officer responds to these requests and a decision may be made to interview the candidate. If this happens, further coordination through message exchange is required to arrange a date and so on.

The ECHOES office model belongs to the class of semi-formal agent-based office models which underlie systems such as Oval (Mintzberg 1979). These models have recently been widely used as a basis of the "workflow" systems. However, many workflow systems base their coordination mechanisms on variations of the control flow paradigm like flowcharts, petri nets or speech act modeling. Thus, in contrast to ECHOES, the coordination of activities in these systems is separated from the artefacts that are coordinated, which include electronic forms, office workers and so on. As we have argued earlier, this does not facilitate end-user comprehension of the mechanisms.

The coordination between the "office clerks" is complemented by coordination within each "office clerk", since each "office clerk" consist of two actors – an office worker and a computer-based software agent (see Figure 5.1). The office worker and software agent cooperate, the agent acting essentially as an "electronic secretary" to the office worker. The agent, which performs the routine portions of the office clerk's duties, is not intended to be intelligent. It also handles the communication with the rest of the system. A software agent may, on encountering exceptional cases, fail, in which case it will prompt the office worker for assistance. The office worker thus performs those portions of the processing activity that require judgement and substantive decision making. The agent may supply the office worker

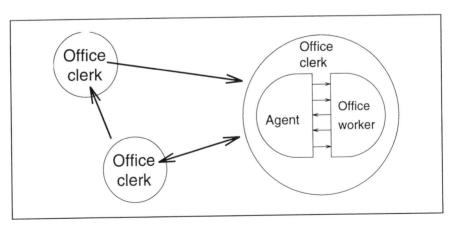

Figure 5.1   The structure of an abstract application system

with suggestions, checklists and other necessary information. The agent may also schedule activities for the office worker so that the office worker's attention may be directed at the most urgent task.

Each activity of an office clerk is presented in ECHOES by a service. The software implementation of a service would be responsible for the behavior of the software agent and for the coordination interface between the agent and the office worker.

Office functionality and structure are inherently complex and diverse and so ECHOES handles this complexity by abstracting the office model into four different aspects that complement each other. Each aspect of an office application is presented through a separate description within a multi-paradigm visual language. The four aspects are:

- information flow between the services. This aspect handles the ordering of activities that is necessary for handling the type of "prerequisite" coordination interdependencies (Malone 1990).
- organizational taxonomy where related services are grouped with job descriptions and assigned to actors in the organization. The organizational knowledge in this aspect is used for attention scheduling and workload redistributing – two examples of coordination mechanisms.
- information taxonomy where both information structures and messages are defined. This aspect handles the bottom level of coordination processes "Perception of common objects" from (Malone 1990).
- service description, where the bottom level functionality within each activity is described. It handles the conversions from asynchronous to synchronous communication, the human-computer coordination etc.

The four aspects are integrated through common elements. For example, an information flow will be directed to a service, that service will be present in the organizational taxonomy associated with office workers able to perform that service. The information flows in the model are typed with one of the entries in the information taxonomy, so the contents of each flow may be inspected by opening the relevant form or a set of forms. These integration links are the main navigation routes used by an application manager when enhancing a particular application system.

5.3 Collaborative Work Scenarios

ECHOES targets the mainly "bureaucratic" office that has some "organic" elements. A typical application would be a workflow application that was relatively small, constantly evolving and possibly with a short lifespan.

Examples of suitable workflow applications are systems for processing marketing promotions, a university's procedure for candidates' selection, and so on.

The departmental system for selecting university students will serve as a basis for our scenarios. In this system the applicants' forms are supplied to the department by the University Admissions Office. Within the department they undergo a quick check for inconsistencies and are then distributed to a number of selectors. Selected applicants are interviewed, after which a final decision on the application is made and the case is filed, the results being sent to the University Admissions Office and to the applicant.

5.3.1 Scenario 1: Evolutionary Changes in the Processing of Application Forms

The following scenario shows how the user-enhancement facilities within ECHOES can be used to modify the way in which office workers coordinate their activities. The example shows the sort of modification that would be part of the natural evolution of the office system. In this case the evolution is prompted by the need for new procedures arising from the introduction of new legislation, but the motivation could equally well have been generated internally, say from efficiency considerations.

For the purpose of this scenario, suppose that as a result of the introduction of new legislation concerning disabled students, the department must revise its admission procedures. A decision is made that a specific selector should be made responsible for admitting all disabled students into the department. In this way expertize and experience can be accumulated efficiently within a single individual. Since, in addition, the university must be aware of all disabled students to which an offer is made, this selector will also keep the university informed.

To implement the changes, the system must be modified in the following steps:

1. Since the processing of the disabled candidates will now differ from that of the other applicants, new activities will be required, hence the corresponding new services must be added to the system. In our case it is only necessary to add one new service to handle the selection activity.
2. An office worker who is the selector to be specialized must be associated with the new service.
3. All applications from disabled students must be routed through the new service.

These changes will involve changes in a number of coordination patterns as described below.

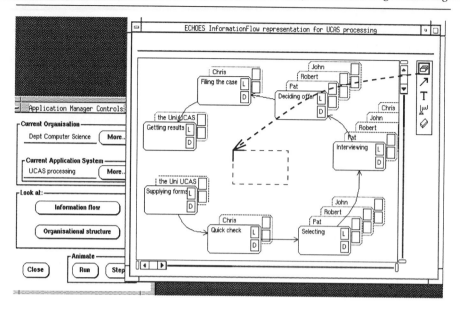

Figure 5.2 Adding a new service for admitting disabled students

In ECHOES, all modifications of an application system are performed by a particular office worker, called "the application manager". The application manager is a domain expert and is not expected to have a programming background. However, he or she is expected to be an advanced computer user.

In our scenario, the application manager will start modifying the system by adding a new service from the palette to the information flow diagram as shown in Figure 5.2.

As a result of adding the service to the diagram, ECHOES will try to allocate this service to a specific office clerk. And since the allocation information has to be elicited from the application manager, ECHOES will show the organizational taxonomy and will prompt the application manager to select the particular person or job description that will perform the new service. As shown on Figure 5.3, if the application manager selects a particular office worker, in this case Pat, ECHOES will ask the application manager to confirm that the new service will be the sole responsibility of Pat. This information will later be used to perform scheduling of the different activities and for distributing the workload among the selectors. In the case of a confirmation, ECHOES will automatically create a new job description `New Selector' that is a specialization of "Selector" (shown to the right on the same figure). Pat will be assigned this job description, and will now perform all services that the other two selectors perform plus the new service named "Selecting disabled applicants". The appropriate activity scheduling coordination mechanism will include this new service in Pat's "To do" list.

The ordering of the activities is based on their priority, therefore ECHOES will prompt the application manager to enter the priority of the new service. Scheduling the services ensures that the office worker's attention is directed to the most pressing activity at any given moment. This is an example of managing a shared resource, where the shared resource is the office worker's attention. Because the university needs to know as soon as possible about selected applicants who are disabled, the new service is given the highest possible priority. The priorities of the other services are then modified accordingly as shown on the second step on Figure 5.3.

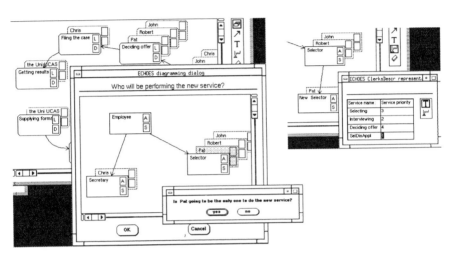

Figure 5.3　Assigning the new service to Pat

At this point in the scenario we have seen examples of modifying the behavior of two coordination mechanisms: assigning activities to actors and managing a shared resource by setting priorities. Note that in these examples we have not modified the coordination mechanisms, we have simply modified their input parameters.

Once the service is allocated, ECHOES will automatically indicate this on the information flow diagram. The application manager will then turn back to the information flow description to connect the new service with the rest of the diagram as shown on Figure 5.4.

The applications from disabled persons should pass through the new service rather than through the "Selecting" service. Since the routeing of forms either to the new or to the standard selecting service depends only on information supplied on the application form, the application manager may fork the relevant flow to the new service. Whenever an information flow is forked, ECHOES will ask for a routeing formula to be associated with each application. In our scenario, the application manager enters the following logical formula in the "Send to:" field of the application form:

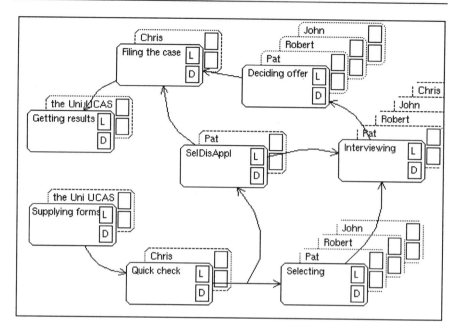

Figure 5.4   The new service is connected to the rest of the diagram

```
IF IsDisabledField=YES THEN SelDisAppl
                       ELSE Selecting
```

Program 5.1

After the application manager connects the new service with flows to the rest of the system, the processing inside this service should be described. Each service is created with a basic processing description. This can be overridden by copying the description of a similar service. In our case the application manager copies the description of "Selecting" and then modifies it to suit the new processing needs. Service descriptions have their own visual language.

5.3.2 Scenario 2: Answering a Nonroutine Enquiry

The following scenario illustrates how office workers can cooperate to deal with an exception to the routine office processes. An office worker, Chris, is busy working on a form with a particular service. At this moment, Chris is interrupted when an applicant, say Mr Brown, telephones. Mr Brown passed his interview a week ago. He urgently needs to know the result of his appli-

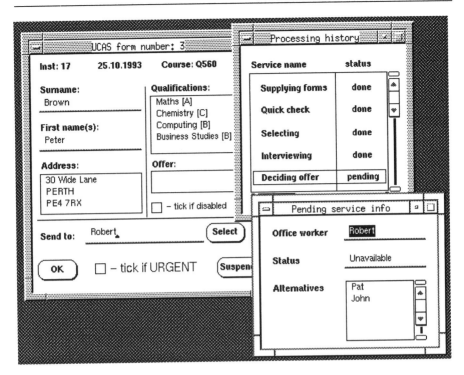

Figure 5.5 Mr Brown's application form and related information

cation, because on the next day he has to reply to an offer from another University. At this point the process embodied in the office system is inadequate and must be overridden.

Chris suspends her currently active service and retrieves Mr Brown's application by entering his details. She does not need to know where in the processing chain the form is at the moment. The application is then shown on the screen (see Figure 5.5). One of the outputs on the screen is the form's "Processing history". It shows that the form is about to enter "Deciding on offer" service. A click on the name of the service will show Chris the "Pending service info" (the bottom right corner of Figure 5.5), stating that the form is scheduled to be processed by Robert, since he is the selector who is responsible for Mr Brown's application. Robert is currently unavailable, but John and Pat are listed as available alternatives. Chris will then change the dynamic distribution address of the application by entering John as the value of the "Send to:" field. This will take the form out of Robert's queue and will put it on John's queue. In order that the form is not left waiting at the end of John's queue, Chris marks the application as "Urgent" by ticking the relevant box on the application. The queue control mechanism then puts the application in front of the queue and signals to John the arrival of the urgent application.

John suspends his current service and activates the "Deciding on offer" service, where the form is queued. John makes the decision required for Mr Brown's application. He does nothing else on the application, suspends the "Deciding on offer" service and resumes his former service.

Chris' view of Mr Brown's application form is now showing the new offer. She tells Mr Brown the outcome of his application, concludes her telephone conversation with him and resumes her previous activity. Mr Brown's application continues to the next service, which is "Filing the case". The processing of the application in this service is not urgent and the form was not marked "urgent" for this service.

5.4 Modeling Coordination Mechanisms in ECHOES

The following sections describe mechanisms for supporting coordination processes in each of the four aspects of the ECHOES model, and the facilities for user control embodied in them.

5.4.1 Information Flow Aspect

The information flow aspect of the model specifies the routes of communication between the clerks' services. Some of the routes may serve for describing the "prerequisite" interdependencies in the system (Malone 1990), where the result from one activity is needed as input to another activity. The set of all communication routes between the services constitutes the static part of the information flow aspect. Dynamic routeing, which was demonstrated in the first scenario, can serve to implement a "shared resource" type of interdependency, where an item of information has to be routed to only one of several consuming activities. The application manager can control these coordination mechanisms by either rearranging the information flows or by modifying the dynamic routeing formulae.

Electronic mail communication is also provided in order to handle exceptional communication patterns. In addition, the need for private communication channels for workers in a CSCW setting is mentioned by (CRC Project Team 1993) (see also Chapter 6).

5.4.2 Information Description Aspect

The information exchanged between the office clerks is modeled in terms of forms. A form models the information structure by a set of fields and offers a simple functional interface to the information contained in the fields. The layout of the form is controlled by the office manager through direct manipulation and the properties of the fields are specified by filling in tables. All different forms are represented in the information taxonomy.

The information taxonomy ensures that the data is recognizable in the right places throughout the system, thus handling the level of coordination patterns, known as "perception of common objects" (Malone 1990). The application manager can control this level by modifying the information taxonomy and the forms.

5.4.3 Organizational Aspect

Work allocation is an important coordination aspect. Various workload distribution decisions depend on responsibility and authority regulations. In order to facilitate or automate these decisions, we need information about the organizational structure and about the departmental affiliations of the personnel. This information is represented in the organizational taxonomy as an organizational structure chart and as departmental affiliation links. These affiliation links connect each particular office clerk with organizational elements. They also connect different organizational elements.

Each office clerk has a job description in terms of a set of services and priority information. This job description is the basis on which a coordination mechanism within each clerk schedules the different services for a clerk's attention. All office clerks are arranged in an organizational taxonomy according to these job descriptions.

Workflow coordination, workload distribution and attention scheduling correspond to generic coordination patterns from the highest coordination level in the framework of Malone and Crowston (Malone 1990). In general, this level contains ordering activities, assigning activities to actors and allocating resources. The application manager controls these patterns both by modifying control parameters such as the service priority and by modifying the job description taxonomy.

5.4.4 Service Description Aspect

A service is a relatively short and simple information processing activity such as checking an application form for completeness, customizing an enquiry letter, and so on. A service is a primitive in the information flow description. Several factors determine the approach taken to describe the relatively low-level information processing which takes place within a service. In particular, a service description has to:

- represent the mixture of event-driven and procedural elements that is inherent for this level of office practice;

- interface with the data-driven information flow aspect;
- provide a mechanism for emulating synchronous communications through the asynchronous message passing communication of the information flow aspect. Synchronous communication is required for ensuring that any urgent activity is dealt with immediately.
- integrate with the attention scheduling mechanism.

The underlying computational model for the description of services exploits the procedural semantics of rule-based behavior that is enclosed in an event-based control framework.

5.4.4.1 Underlying Computational Model

The computational model for the description of services exploits the procedural semantics of a rule-based behavior of the type:

```
rule IS
    IF        event
    THEN DO   action_1;
              action_2;
              ...
              action_n.
    REACHING new_state
```

Program 5.2

which is enclosed in a control framework of the type:

```
AT waiting-state
WAIT FOR AN EVENT TRIGGERING ANY OF
       rule_1 ... rule_m
```

or

```
AT transition-state
TRY IN ORDER
       rule_1 ... rule_m
ELSE DO default_rule
```

Program 5.3

where "default rule" has no triggering event. Only one rule can be active at a time. The events and the rule ordering determine which rule is to be activated. Note that the "waiting-states" implement the event-driven aspects of the processing, while the "transition-states" implement the procedural "if-elseif-elseif-...-else" or decision-tree type of control.

5.4.4.2 Events

The main coordination handling element in the service description is the event concept. An ECHOES event occurs when, for example, a form arrives at a service instance, a queue of forms exceeds a given length or a deadline arrives. More generally, an ECHOES event occurs when the logical expression describing it becomes true. The events generated by the arrival of a form at a service are the means by which service descriptions and the data-driven information flow descriptions are integrated.

An event can cause a variety of actions:

- an event can trigger processing actions;
- an event can reroute the flow of control;
- an event can be a synchronization signal between different services or between a service and its office worker.

5.4.4.3 Interaction with the Office Worker

The coordination and dialog between a service and its office worker is modeled by message exchange along interaction flows. Interaction flows are like information flows except that the interaction flows appear only on the relevant service description diagrams.

The application manager's knowledge of how to program by forms is exploited for "programming" the interactive dialog and thus controlling the coordination between a human and a computer. User input events are represented as forms in their own right, so for example, a click on a field will generate a form that contains the name of the field and send this form along an interaction flow to the service. When these forms enter the service they will activate corresponding service events. The system can thus support the spectrum of interaction styles between the user randomly filling a form and answering a strict sequence of questions, depending on the corresponding service description.

5.4.4.4 Attention Scheduling Mechanism

The aim of the attention scheduling mechanism is to support the office worker in the task of deciding what job to do next. In this respect it is a coordination mechanism that manages a shared resource, the office worker's attention. The attention scheduling mechanism presents activities in priority order and ongoing jobs can be interrupted by more important jobs. The control over this mechanism is performed on two levels:

- overriding the proposed order,
- changing the priorities of forms and services that serve as input for the attention scheduling mechanism

5.4.4.5 Visual Description

Services have their own visual language, which uses the metaphor of a ball bearing moving along pipes to represent the point of control and the underlying computational model. The events are shown to open and close valves on these pipes. Key factors that enable the application manager to understand service descriptions are the animation provided by the supporting tools and the the support of referential hypertext style links between the various elements of the description. More detailed description of this visual formalism is presented in (Mehandjiev 1994).

5.4.5 Degrees of Control over Coordination Mechanisms

In this paper we have seen two degrees of control over the coordination mechanisms. Firstly, users can override the mechanisms for exceptional cases, and secondly, the application manager can control them by modifying either their input parameters, such as service priorities, or by modifying aspects of the application as information flow, which can also be seen to form input data for the coordination mechanisms.

However, it is possible to have a third degree of control, in which the coordination mechanisms are themselves modified. For example, the algorithm of the workload distribution mechanism can be modified to take new parameters such as the lengths of the input queues into consideration.

Currently in ECHOES the application manager cannot make modifications at this third degree of control. This type of modifications should be performed by software professionals. There are two reasons for this:

- Such modifications should rarely be necessary for a well parametrized coordination mechanism. For example, the queue discipline could be based on a sorting algorithm, to be controlled by setting priorities on the forms, rather than by changing the algorithm itself.
- All coordination aspects are currently presented to the application manager as an integral part of an office aspect. Modifying the internals of any coordination mechanism would involve presenting the mechanism explicitly to the application manager. Therefore, another type of

description has to be added to the visual language, which may make comprehension difficult.

The underlying architecture of ECHOES does provide facilities for adding new types of visual descriptions, but this cannot be done by the application manager.

5.5 Related Research

In the area of computer supported collaborative work systems, the notion of user enhanceability is represented by the "radically tailorable" systems (Mintzberg 1979). Within this class, Oval (Mintzberg 1979 and Lai 1988) represents an agent-based cooperative system based on the mail filtering and routeing ideas in its predecessor, Information Lens (Malone 1989). It offers four types of building elements: objects, views, agents and links. The users of the system may use these elements to either build their system from scratch or to tailor a ready made system to suit their needs. The agents in Oval are independent, they communicate only asynchronously and the behavior of each of them is described by a set of production rules. While this architecture is certainly powerful enough to describe complex applications and coordination mechanisms through additional programming, its direct support for coordination techniques is at the "communication" process level.

ECHOES targets the more bureaucratic type of office, which enables it to enrich the semi-formal agent-based model of Oval with more complex organizational information as information flows, job descriptions, authority and departmental affiliation links. This additional information is structured according to techniques of frame knowledge representation and object-oriented analysis. This information enables higher level coordination mechanisms than in Oval, and the users can control these mechanisms through a visual multi-paradigm language.

The necessity for higher level coordination within a workgroup is a common problem for collaborative systems. One approach is to provide a "facilitator" for "effective management of the social process" (Macaulay 1993), that is for coordinating the focus, the goals and the activities of the participants. In the Cooperative Requirements Capture project (CRC Project Team 1993) the facilitator is a human being. The CRC prototype only offers support for its functions by providing group and activity monitoring and data representation. The CRC facilitator is somehow similar to the application manager in ECHOES. For example, both control the coordination patterns to optimize the work of the group. However, the major difference is that the applications manager is modifying coded coordination mechanisms in a comparatively static and "bureaucratic", environment, while the facilitator performs the coordination herself within an "organic" type of collaboration (see Chapter 6).

Two other agent-based systems that employ run time user-driven coordination mechanisms for "organic" activities are PAGES and OASIS. In PAGES (Hammainen 1990), all bottom level agents are associated with users in the same manner as in ECHOES, but the PAGES model is based on run time coordination and on local management. This makes the application systems flexible enough to immediately reflect new participants and forms. However, PAGES does not offer explicit support for workflow coordination and workload distribution, therefore restricting the efficiency of the applications in more static and bureaucratic environments.

In OASIS (Martens 1991) the coordination with the user is performed by a "task monitor" but no priorities and task interaction are involved. Thus the user remains the main coordinator in the system.

Unlike the user-driven coordination, the agent-driven coordination systems attempt to automate high level coordination patterns. In the ITX system (Lee 1993), a software agent, which supports a particular user, is the main vehicle of coordination. It interacts with other agents and with the system resources either on behalf of the user or on its own initiative. The agents enter into negotiations in order to achieve dynamically changing goals. These goals also control the intelligent behavior of the agents. This system belongs to the type of Distributed Artificial Intelligence systems (Gasser 1991). The difference between these systems and ECHOES is in the degree of intelligence of the software agents, and in the overall method for controlling the system (see Chapters 8 – 13).

A more restricted form of agent-driven coordination is described in (Bentley 1992). Each "User Display Agent" coordinates the user interaction with the system by composing a dynamic user specific view of the shared information space.

The agent like script environments in Cosmos (Dollimore 1991) support cooperating users, not only by providing contextual information, but also by offering context specific actions. The target type of applications are more structured so therefore a higher level of coordination support is possible. The model can be configured by using two text based languages – a scripting language and a communication structure definition language. The Cosmos team believe that making the system configurable by ordinary users could be achieved on a textual level with the help of good textual editors as opposed to developing diagrammatic versions of languages.

5.6 The ECHOES Project

5.6.1 Current State of the Prototype

The ECHOES prototype is implemented in Smalltalk-80 with VisualWorks and HotDraw – a generic drawing editor described in (Johnson 1992). It is based on the architecture of "pluggable visual descriptions", where the different visual descriptions are integrated through a common actor-based application model. The prototype uses direct manipulation, animation and hypertext like navigation techniques to achieve the required style of exploratory modifications and prototyping. Several scenarios, designed within a case study of a system for selecting university undergraduate applicants, are currently used to test ECHOES.

5.6.2 Further Work Required

Apart from testing the prototype, further work is required in investigating how the system would scale up, and how issues of version management and the consolidation of changes can be addressed. There are also many coordination issues raised when several applications run in a single office with a common set of office workers. A third direction is related to providing facilities for modifying the visual language by adding or substituting visual descriptions.

5.7 Summary and Conclusion

This paper has described how user enhanceability allows the implementation of high level coordination mechanisms:

- Agents can coordinate their activities through information flows. Email style message exchange may be used to override the standard communication patterns.
- Different activities within an agent are coordinated by a priority mechanism that bases its decision on explicitly represented and controlled properties and priorities of the activities. An office worker controls the mechanism by modifying these priorities.
- The distribution of the workload between identical processing activities of several different agents is done by another coordination mechanism. The mechanism is based on the dynamic addressing information that is

associated with the processed information. If none is specified, the distribution is based on information about the workload of the agents.

- The coordination between the application system and either human users of the system or other computer systems is performed identically to the inter-agent coordination, but the office worker has full control over the software agent that is servicing him/her. He or she can interrupt and suspend any activity of the agent and can choose different order of activities from the one suggested by the agent.

The users may exert control over the coordination mechanisms in two major ways: they can override the mechanisms in cases of exceptions (i.e. cases that were not foreseen when the application system was designed) or they can modify the action of the mechanisms when it becomes obsolete due to the natural evolution of the organization. The latter is normally done by modifying the organizational knowledge that serves as input data for the coordination mechanisms.

The structural model of the system and the organizational knowledge contained in it are presented to the users of the system in a visual way as a set of animated diagrams. The users explore it through its integration links and modify it through direct manipulation techniques.

We believe that realistic support of high level coordination processes in office application systems can be achieved through greater user control over the mechanisms that support these coordination processes.

Chapter 6

Computational Support for the Management of Social Processes within Organizational Teams

Gregory O'Hare, Linda Macauley, Paul Dongha and Steve Viller

6.1 Introduction

Organizations today need to adopt relevant technology in order to remain competitive. Staff time is a valuable resource and the judicious incorporation of technological advances can assist in improving their productivity, or indeed creativity. The tasks that organizations perform, the methods they adopt, and the quality thresholds that they must achieve, are becoming ever more complex and demanding (see Chapter 1).

We increasingly witness that the provision of today's services or the manufacture of today's products, demands the fusion of disparate skills within the company. Such fusion obliges collaborative activity to be performed and given that this frequently represents a source of potential acrimony, appropriate support should be given for this.

At the heart of any collaboration is the ability to communicate effectively, and to build up a working relationship and mutual understanding between team members (see Chapters 2, 3, 11). Disagreement and the resolution of conflict represent an alarming proportion of meeting time.

Of course the entities involved in such collaboration may not necessarily exist within the same location, city, country or continent. Thus, meetings may be both geographically distributed and perhaps, as a consequence temporally distributed. The entities need not necessarily be human and intelligent, "agents" are ever more prevalent within the corporate entity. Such computational entities can, for example, be responsible for such activities as, optimizing production scheduling routines, archiving and retrieving information from corporate databases and advising in such areas as "hedging" when contemplating share acquisitions.

Within the context of this chapter we look at the issue of collaborative activity which we believe to be a core ingredient to intelligent organizations of the future. We examine how the associated social process can be supported specifically within the context of the Cooperative Requirements Capture (CRC) project. Section 2 describes the CRC project whilst Section 3 describes the software prototype development. Section 4 outlines the user interface. Sections 5 and 6 consider facilitation, whilst Sections 7 and 8 describe the computational support provided for the facilitator within the CRC cooperative working platform. Finally, we conclude by briefly presenting some potential future work.

6.2 The Cooperative Requirements Capture (CRC) Project

The Cooperative Requirements Capture (CRC) Project was a collaborative project conducted between UMIST, ICL, Brameur Ltd and Human Technology. The main aim of the CRC project is to develop prototype tools which could be used to support a multidisciplinary team in the process of capturing requirements for computer-based systems.

All the members of the multidisciplinary team will have a stake in the decision taken concerning the proposed system. Four major categories of stakeholders have been identified:

1. Those who are responsible for its design and development, for example, the project manager, software designers, communications experts, technical authors.
2. Those with a financial interest, responsible for its sale, for example, the business analyst or in some situations the marketer, or those responsible for its purchase.
3. Those responsible for its introduction and maintenance within an organization, for example, training and user support staff, installation and maintenance engineers and users-managers.
4. Those who have an interest in its use, for example, users managers and all classes of users, i.e. primary (frequent hands-on users), secondary (occasional users or those who use the system through an intermediary) or tertiary (those affected by the introduction of the system).

Some of the stakeholders identified above, particularly in categories (1) and (3) have a direct responsibility for the design and development of the various system components and hence, have a major interest in being involved in the requirements capture process. Those in category (2) have a financial responsibility for the success of the computer system and therefore, may also need to be involved. The stakeholders in category (4) will be the recipients of the resulting computer system, who also have a major contribution to make in terms of specific task knowledge and the ability to assess the likely effects of the new system.

It is argued within the Cooperative Requirements Capture Project that requirements capture should be a collaborative and cooperative activity allowing the views, insights and needs of the representative stakeholders to be actively incorporated as part of the requirements capture process. However, whilst it is argued that requirements capture would be enriched by cooperation between representative stakeholders, it is by no means clear that interaction between people with such a diversity of motives would result in anything but chaos. By definition, the representative stakeholders all have different "stakes" in the resulting system and each "team member" will want to discuss those issues which are of interest to them. Thus, simply identifying the stakeholders is not sufficient.

Two further components are needed: firstly a mechanism for focusing the discussion of the "team" and encouraging the sharing of views and concerns; and secondly a structure is needed which will enable the team to address all the important issues and produce all the outputs needed by the commissioning organization within resources allocated. Within the CRC project the first component is provided through use of a meetings facilitator and the second component provided through the use of a user centered requirements capture method based on USTM (Macaulay et al. 1990).

Following the analysis of the target user population it was decided to develop a prototype system which was capable of supporting the stakeholders, the facilitator and the requirements capture method.

The next section outlines the CRC Prototype with subsequent sections specifically examining the provision for the management of the social process involved in the CRC methodology.

6.3 The CRC Prototype

The CRC prototype (or Cooperative Working Platform) supports a multidisciplinary, possibly geographically distributed team in undertaking a requirements capture task in a cooperative manner. There may be aspects of the requirements task which are performed synchronously, that is, all members of the team agree to hold a "meeting", while other aspects of the task will be asynchronous, with members monitoring and actively participating in the requirements evolution, as and when they can.

The prototype supports a representative subset of the whole of a requirements capture method, more specifically it supports object analysis. (see Macaulay 1993 for a fuller description of the object analysis). The users of the CRC prototype are able to hold a synchronous "brainstorming" session in which they generate a single pool of ideas for objects associated with the particular problem domain. The CRC prototype represents a generic tool in that it is not customized for any particular domain. The support offered is not based on any semantic understanding of the objects that are being brainstormed. The users are then able to discuss, evaluate, change and agree on these objects either synchronously or asynchronously, resulting in an accepted set of objects. We had initially intended that the prototype would support cooperative development of object structures, like those of whole-part or generalization-specialization structures. Whilst initial efforts to do this proved fruitful and offered considerable insight into how this support may be provided, it nevertheless became clear that this required further investigation in terms of how a group would undertake this task in a non-computer supported environment.

The prototype goes considerably beyond merely supporting communication between team members. A key feature of our approach to requirements capture is the recognition that not only does the requirements capture task need to be managed but additionally the social process taking place between the team members needs to be managed (Westley and Waters 1988). We believe that the effective management of both these processes is pivotal to any CSCW system and for this reason the CRC prototype explicitly provides support in both these "dimensions". The Cooperative Requirements Capture approach can be viewed as an integration of a requirements capture method that is collaborative in nature together with appropriate computational support for the management of the associated social process.

Cooperative Requirements =   *Requirements Capture Method +*
Capture   *Support for the Management of the Associated*
                                               Social Process

The primary objective of the CRC prototype, therefore, was to develop an integrated set of software tools that support a group in the solution of a common problem. To this end, key user operations were identified as follows:

- An ability to exchange both private and group messages.
- An ability to work within a private workspace.
- An ability to observe the efforts and contributions of other group members in a public shared workspace.
- An ability to recognize the receipt of messages.
- An ability to enter into some synchronous private communication with another group member.

Figure 6.1 below provides a schematic overview of the main features of the prototype showing several team members and a facilitator logged onto the prototype. The prototype has been designed using a client-server model from a distributed systems design, in which there is a central resource through which all communications are sent and data are redirected to their intended destination.

One advantage of this design is that it allows the system to store and organize data relating to messages or to requirements; all data are stored persistently as CLOS (Common Lisp Object System) objects, thus facilitating their subsequent analysis and interrogation.

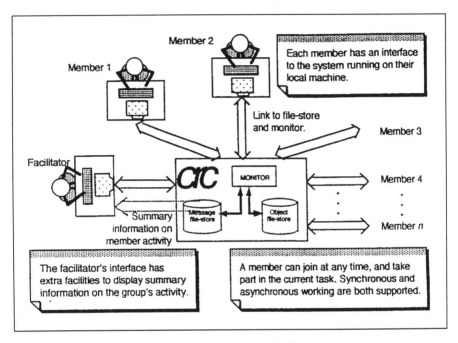

Figure 6.1   A schematic of the CRC prototype

A further feature of the design is that the user interfaces are designed as separate modules and hence, when running the CRC prototype on a team member's workstation only the user-interface module needs to be mounted. This will enable the user to simply open the "CRC Window" alongside other unrelated applications. In order to ensure maximum portability the design of the software was such that the interface modules could be realized in a variety of different languages and indeed mounted on heterogeneous host machines. For example, the user-interface module may be written in hypertext on the Apple Macintosh. The CRC prototype was implemented on SUN Workstations using the Common Lisp and the Common Lisp Object System (CLOS).

The design of the CRC prototype embraced an Agent-Oriented Design (AOD) philosophy (O'Hare (1995), O'Hare and Abbas (1994), O'Hare and Jennings (1996)). The reader is also referred to Chapter 10 in this volume for similar ideas on agency and agent-based design. Chapters 12 and 13 utilize similar metaphors within their design. The architecture of the Cooperative Working Platform is comprised of the following computational agents:

- Communication Agent.
- Listener Agent.
- Interface Agent.
- Facilitator Support Agent.
- Method Control Agent.

A computational agent has a particular set of capabilities and has an ability to communicate with other software agents with whom it is acquainted. Figure 6.2 diagrammatically presents a top-level description of the Cooperative Working Platform. Stakeholders communicate with each other via their SUN workstations over a local area network. Each stakeholder can communicate with those stakeholders with which it is acquainted by sending "messages". Each stakeholder has locally an Interface Agent which is responsible for enabling them to visualize the underlying software system and enabling their effective interaction. Messages are packaged to conform to a particular communication protocol prior to communication via the network. The associated encoding and decoding of messages transmitted along the network is the responsibility of a Communication (Comms) Agent. Upon decoding or encoding a message the Communication Agent forwards it to the appropriate agent. An agent in this sense can either be the Listener Agent, Conversation Analysis Agent, Method Control Agent or any of the Interface Agents associated with an individual stakeholder.

Whilst the messages are decoded by the Communication Agent the actions taken as a consequence of their receipt, are performed by the agent to whom the message is forwarded. The Listener Agent is responsible for recording all messages and generally archiving network traffic in the Message Base. The Facilitator Support Agent on the other hand, performs various analysis on the Message Base in an attempt either to diagnose a particular situation or to predict the likely occurrence of such a condition.

Finally, the Method Control Agent has direct responsibility for overseeing the particular requirements capture method being employed. It will maintain the evolution of the Object Base as the various discrete stages of the method are undergone. In order to regulate the progression of the method the Method Control Agent will necessarily have to communicate with the Facilitator Support Agent and the Listener Agent, together with interrogating the Object and Message Bases.

An overview of the CRC architecture and more details concerning its implementation are given in O'Hare et al. 1992. In order for the reader to visualize the operation of the CRC prototype we outline the CRC user interface in the subsequent section.

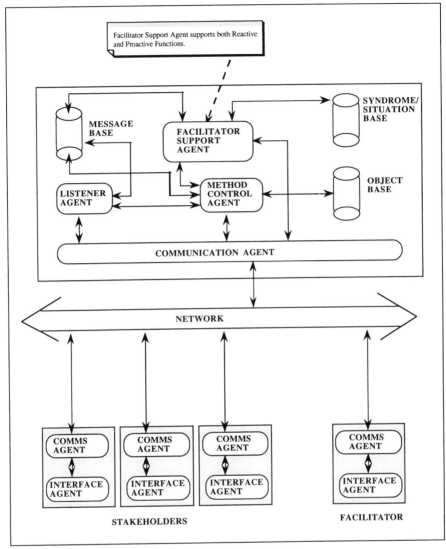

Figure 6.2   The structure of the cooperative working platform

6.4 Description of the CRC User Interface

The CRC prototype is depicted as a separate application and resides on the workstation desktop as a distinct window. It is advisable for this window to occupy the majority of the workstation screen since it contains a number of "child" windows. Figure 6.3 shows a typical group members screen at the point where the brainstorming session has finished and the discussion or evaluation of objects is underway.

Throughout the collaborative task all the windows are maintained in a consistent manner across each members workstation.

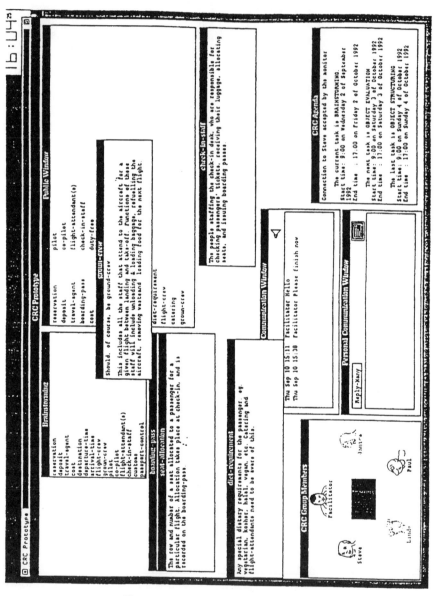

Figure 6.3   A group members interface

6.4.1 The Personal Communication Window

The personal communication window contains summary lines for the personal messages received by the individual in question. Each of the summary lines represents a separate "message summary" and constitutes an active region, which if selected, will activate a personal message viewer window enabling the entire message to be viewed. Linked to this window is the personal communication indicator, a small in-tray icon, which indicates the receipt of personal communications by placing addressed envelopes in the in-tray. Personal messages are only loaded into the personal communication window when this icon is clicked, thus explicitly demanding that the user acknowledges the receipt of such correspondence.

6.4.2 The Group Communication Window

The group communication window indicates the receipt of group messages and it exhibits the same functionality as the personal communication window, except that new messages are loaded automatically as and when they arrive. A separate message viewer window is provided for displaying the contents of messages.

6.4.3 The CRC Agenda Window

This window displays the current and future tasks to be performed within the currently adopted method. It may be the case that a method is commissioned other than that of the CRC method. The CRC prototype is implemented so as not to compromise this flexibility. In later versions of the system, the true generic nature of the platform could be demonstrated by enabling the facilitator or group, to select from a series of contrasting methods. The CRC agenda window also indicates the anticipated scheduling of each of the tasks which comprise the particular method utilized. This scheduling together with the ordering may be revised by the facilitator. Users have no need to interact with this window.

6.4.4 The Public Window

The public window displays items that are shared among the entire group. It therefore always displays the same information on each of the group members' screens. The items contained within the window are objects that have been generated as part of the brainstorming session, and are represented as "active regions" in the inner region of the window. Selection of such an object would result in a description window being viewed.

6.4.5 Description Windows

A description window is created for an object in the public window by selecting the object with the mouse. The windows are created in a "stack" on the
left-hand side of the main window, with the system providing a number of
functions to help managing them.

6.4.6 The Brainstorming Window

This window is used during the brainstorming phase of a group session to
allow group members to enter their ideas into the system, for subsequent
display on the Public Window. It maintains a private copy of all the objects
generated in a single session by that individual user.

6.4.7 The CRC Group Members Window

The CRC Group Members Window indicates those members who are part of
the group, and more importantly, those which are currently actively
connected to the application. The former is illustrated by representing the
members as uniquely labeled icons arranged around a meeting table with the
latter communicated by the given icon being highlighted at a given instance
in time. Each icon constitutes a separate subregion for each group member,
the facilitator, and the collective group as represented by the table.

   This section has briefly considered the general look and feel of the user
interface. In the forthcoming sections we will consider the role of facilitation
within computer-mediated meetings and how this role might be supported
in a computational sense. Specifically we look at those provisions made
within the context of the CRC prototype.

6.5 Why Facilitation?

The literature has come to recognize the central role of the facilitator in a
disparate social setting (see Chapter 5). The facilitator can take many forms,
but invariably they are bound by the common theme of rendering the task
of the social group that bit easier. In a learning environment the lecturer may
be thought of as facilitating the learning process (of course a counter view is
often held by students); in the manufacturing arena a supervisor may facilitate work on the shop floor whilst an inspector may facilitate quality, and in
a management context a chairperson may facilitate a meeting. It was this
latter social setting that is of interest to us within the context of the CRC
project.

Facilitation can generally be thought to achieve three things within a meeting context.

1. It helps both achieve, and subsequently maintain, a greater degree of group cohesion than would ordinarily be possible;
2. This group cohesion invariably has the causal effect of resulting in the group adopting a heightened degree of ownership to the collaborative tasks performed and the associated results and any intermediate decisions made;
3. As a result of (2) there typically emerges a greater commitment to group tasks and members will actively assist in the attainment of these tasks.

It is our conjecture within this paper that collaborative work necessitates facilitation. Consequently we have sought to embrace facilitation support within the design and development of the CRC prototype. We believe that collaborative activity conducted within a computer mediated environment makes the need for facilitation all the more acute.

It is clear even with the use of the most sophisticated multimedia interfaces that there is a significant reduction in the richness of the communication medium as compared to that experienced in a face-to- face setting. In the two-dimensional space time environment the ability of an individual member of the team to perceive, interpret and react to social cues is greatly inhibited.

This finding was certainly reflected in the experimentation performed within the CRC project. The details of the evaluation of the CRC prototype are reported elsewhere in the literature (Macaulay *et al.* 1994). Although this situation was anticipated, what surprised us was the extent to which the social cues were eroded and lost within the computer mediated environment. The problem that presented itself was how to address this "evaporation" of social cue content and specifically how to empower a facilitator to recognize possible social situations and react accordingly. One form of reaction may be merely ensuring that an individual or group had picked up on certain social cues.

6.6 The Role of the Facilitator

Within the CRC problem domain we examined the role of the facilitator and sought to identify the central tasks that they could reasonably be expected to perform. In the broadest sense the role of the facilitator can be considered to involve the creation and the establishment of the environment within which the meeting is to take place, the facilitation of the meeting, and the retrospective analysis of the social collaborative activity. Within the CRC project we merely concerned ourselves with the latter two tasks with a concentration on the penultimate. Meeting facilitation can be considered as comprising four subtasks identified as follows:

1. Agenda management;
2. Observing the social process;
3. Recognizing the occurrence or potential occurrence of social problems within the team and invoking potential solutions;
4. Making interventions in an opportunistic manner.

The support of such activities demanded that we broadened somewhat the remit of the functional specification of the cooperative working platform. Maintenance of social cohesion necessitates the ability to monitor the group dynamics with a view to recognizing potential problems, intervening if appropriate and suggesting strategies for the group to pursue when undertaking specific tasks (see Viller 1991 for further details of the role of the facilitator). Detailed task modeling of the facilitator tasks resulted in a task hierarchy depicted in Figure 6.4.

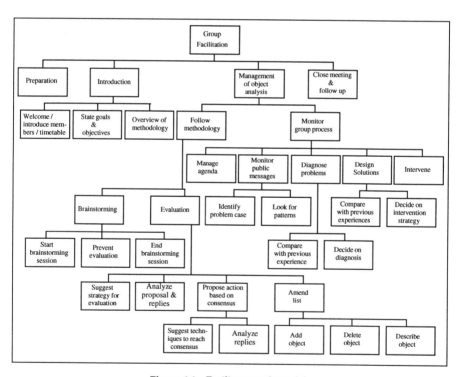

Figure 6.4   Facilitator task model

6.7 CRC Support for the Social Process

The CRC prototype sought to offer pragmatic support, not merely to the requirements capture method but also to the associated social process. This support was offered as a set of services that were available to both the users and the facilitator. As with the development of all such systems the set of services actually provided was necessarily a subset of those designed.

We can characterize these services as *General Services* available to all team members including the facilitator, *Facilitator Specific Services* and *Stakeholder Specific Services*. Within the context of this chapter we consider merely facilitator specific services.

These services can be categorized as

1. A communication service;
2. Agenda management;
3. Monitoring group activity;
4. Monitoring individual activity;
5. Displaying group dynamics;
6. Recognizing problematic social syndromes;
7. An ability to persistently store group interactions and perform retrospective analysis;

6.8 Facilitator Support within CRC Prototype

As discussed earlier it is difficult to assimilate the information regarding the communication within the CRC group, and based upon this, to infer the activities being performed let alone their effectiveness. The CRC prototype sought to address this. The facilitator can, like other group members monitor public group communications. They are aware of private communications which take place with the subject but not the specific message content.

The communication patterns which emerge are often confusing and hard to interpret in their own right. Frequently surges of activity were witnessed in our evaluations and during such times the facilitator frequently suffered from information overload. Furthermore, the form of the information was not particularly accessible and meaningful.

We will now consider each of the services identified above and outline the degree to which we were able to make provision within the CRC prototype.

6.8.1 Communication

The communication capabilities provided for the facilitator are directly comparable with those provided for each member of the CRC team. The facilitator can issue messages that are either private and dispatched to an individual, restricted and dispatched to a designated group or indeed broadcast in nature being transmitted to everyone. Figures 6.3 and 6.5 illustrate that messages destined for, and emanating from, the facilitator are handled in exactly the same manner by the system monitor.

This communication capability is, of course, the mechanism used by the facilitator when *inter alia* making interventions, announcing revisions to the agenda and advising ways of resolving social syndromes.

6.8.2 Agenda Management

The agenda is able to be influenced and updated by the facilitator. If the anticipated time allocated, *a priori*, to each task in the CRC process, proves inappropriate this can be revised by the facilitator. By monitoring group activity the facilitator for example, may deduce that it would be prudent to move from the brainstorming task to that of the object evaluation task. This deduction could simply be based upon the observation that a "steady state" has been reached in the list of objects identified. This proposal would need to be put to the group and upon acceptance the corresponding revision made to the agenda.

6.8.3 Monitoring Group Activity

The facilitator's interface to the CRC group members window differs from that for the group members in that additional information is available on individuals and group activity through selection of the appropriate icon. Figure 6.5 shows the facilitators interface at the same point in the session as the group members interface as shown in Figure 6.3.

Selecting the table icon will invoke the group statistics window, which contains information about the group members activity, and selecting an individual's icon will invoke an individual statistics window for that group member. The group statistics window provides a simple means for comparing the level of participation of the group members against each other. The number of messages sent by all the members can be displayed in a number of ways, being selectable from the frame menu. The textual view constitutes the default view, and gives the number of messages sent for each member. Three graphical views are available, which present the information as a number of horizontal bars with percentages: total gives the same information as the textual view, with the length of each bar displaying the member's

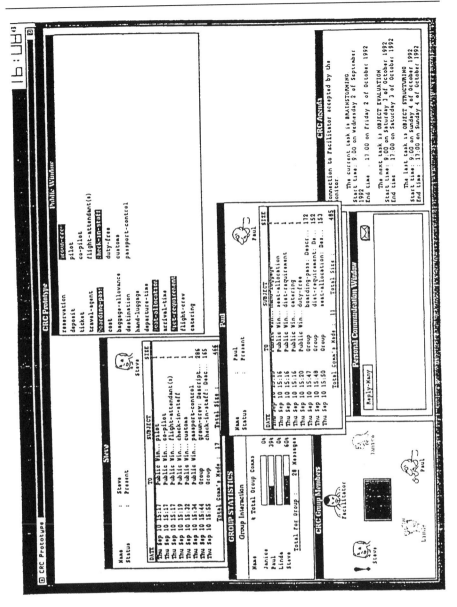

Figure 6.5 The facilitators interface

number of messages as a percentage of the total number of messages sent by the group; maximum displays each member's message count as a percentage of the member who sent the most; and average displays each member's message count relative to the average for the group.

6.8.4 Monitoring Individual Activity

An individual statistics window is available for each of the group members. When created, it has the name of the individual that it referred to in its title. These windows are very similar to the group and personal communication windows in that they contain a list of message summaries that, when selected, allow the contents of the relevant message to be viewed. The difference being the message summaries contained in these windows are for all the messages sent by the selected member during the current session. For reasons of privacy, you are only permitted to view the contents of messages that have been sent to the whole group, of which you could access anyway.

The summaries contain information about to whom each message was sent, its subject, and its length (number of characters). The latter piece of information provides a crude additional measure of member participation that may be considered along with the profile of the messages sent. The total length of all the messages sent, including personal messages, is given at the bottom of the list. The alternative, graphical view shows the distribution of the messages each member has sent among the rest of the group.

6.8.5 Display Group Dynamics

While the facilitator has got access to a set of *social meters* which offer a window on the social dynamics of the group, this does not enable them to gain any understanding of the current activity of group members. Experimentation demonstrated that this was an important characteristic and enabled the collaborative activity to be more easily tracked and understood. In recognition of this, the facilitator interface incorporates current activity icons displayed next to each group member's icon when logged on. The activity icons are: a light bulb, a pair of spectacles, a pen, and a question mark. They respectively indicate that the group member is: brainstorming, reading a message, composing a message, or the system has insufficient data to be able to identify exactly what each group member is doing.

Certain events are captured at each user interface and used as the basis for recognizing certain activities. This was achieved in the implementation with relative ease yet the added value that facilitators derived from such a simplistic addition was suprisingly quick. Of course a more sophisticated event handler could differentiate between a larger number of activities and thus provide a more finer grained view.

6.8.6 Recognizing Problematic Social Syndromes

Within meetings recurrent problems occur which can be characterized as social syndromes. Wesley and Watters (1988) referred to these as *Generic*

Problem Syndromes and categorized five such situations. These are described elsewhere in more detail Wesley and Watters (1988), Viller (1991). In brief they identified five such syndromes those of the multi-headed beast, feuding factions, dominant species, recycling (cyclic meeting) and sleeping meeting. Each of these could typically be characterized by observable symptoms. Considering each in turn, the multi-headed beast would be typified by multi-stranded discussion, digressions, interruptions, a lack of listening and generally a lack of integration of ideas. The feuding factions would involve anger, very direct forthright interactions between restricted subgroups within the team. The dominant species syndrome would be characterized by unequal air time in meetings, progressive withdrawal by other members, and increasing aggression or passiveness by group members. The recycling syndrome would involve a general lack of progress, irritation, confusion and recurrent themes in the discussion. Finally the sleeping meeting is probably the easiest syndrome to recognize with a lack of interaction, a gradual withdrawal and increasing lack of participation.

We sought to investigate the degree to which *social templates* could be created which could serve to identify the occurrence or potential onset of these syndromes. This proved more difficult than first envisaged. Whilst each syndrome was evident in face to face meetings finding the relevant and appropriate vocabulary and units of description proved very difficult. Nonetheless, significant strides were made in this direction although the discrimination of these templates proved inadequate.

The recognition represents only part of the problem. Having successfully recognized the complaint, a set of remedial actions needs to be activated. These could be involuntary system instigated actions or they could be advice tendered to the facilitator as to how to address the situation.

6.8.7 Retrospective Analysis

In addition to on-line support for the role of facilitation, we need to provide off-line support where the facilitator could look retrospectively at the evolution of the meeting and the progression of the collaborative task, while removed from the pressure of the meeting.

Within the CRC prototype partial provision exists for the automated delivery of graphical views of the meeting evolution. Since the monitor saves persistently all messages communicated then the interrogation of this raw data is supported. The subsequent presentation of this data in the appropriate graphical forms is as yet incomplete. In essence the message base serves as an enhanced transcript of the meeting. The normally laborious task of minute taking is performed automatically.

There are several prominent graphical views that are demanded two of these are a view of individual activity against time, including of course that of the facilitator and, a view of object evolution achieved by analyzing messages by object name. Figure 6.6 illustrates the latter view. These views are potentially very important in training or educating both the facilitator and team members as to their performance in meetings.

6.9 Future Work

The Cooperative Working Platform which we have used as a framework of reference within this chapter was very much a prototype. Nevertheless, it offered a very important medium within which we were able to experiment with regard to the support of collaborative tasks.

Clearly many of the ideas contained within the CRC prototype need to be developed and refined. In particular, the prototype needs to embrace multimedia technology and support, for example, the exchange of video and audio images of the members in the performance of their duties (or part of). Such enhancements would by definition change the manner within which the facilitator performs their duties.

The prototype would also need to be empowered with a greater degree of intelligence allowing it to perform more proactive functions in an opportunistic manner rather than reactive functions performed at the bequest of group members. Such intelligence would cause the previous delineation between personnel and technology to become blurred, thus enabling future organizations to be viewed as a synthesis of intelligence accrued from human and machine alike.

6.10 Conclusions

This paper has identified the importance of collaborative activity within intelligent organizations of the future. It has introduced the reader to one such system that seeks to provide computational support for such activity. In particular, we have focused upon the need to provide support for the social process. We have considered the role of the facilitator within the context of a computer- mediated environment and reflected upon their activities and how, if at all, this could be supported in a computational sense. We have presented the rudimentary support that we were able to provide within the context of the CRC prototype and identified potential future enhancements of this work.

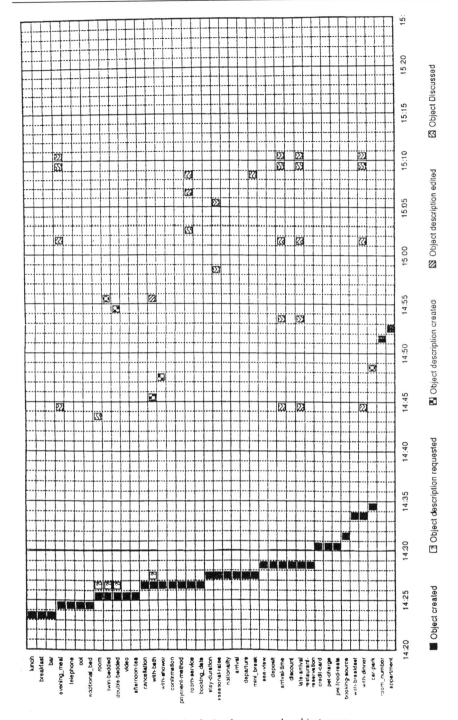

Figure 6.6   Analysis of messages by object name

Acknowledgments

The Cooperative Requirements Capture Project (CRC) was funded under the IED/DTI Advanced Technology Program (Project No. 1130) and was a collaborative project involving the participation of the Department of Computation UMIST, ICL, Brameur and Human Technology Ltd.

Chapter 7

The Wolf in Sheep's Clothing: How Locks Can Gently Control Collaboration

Rainer Unland

7.1 Introduction

A typical Cooperative Information System comprises a number of heterogeneous, autonomous, and distributed component software systems, like (multi)database systems, knowledge-based systems (especially expert systems) or multimedia systems. Each such system can be seen as an (information) agent which is capable of providing information and/or solving problems on its domain of expertise. In order to be able to solve a broad spectrum of complex, information-intensive problems, agents interact in different ways, often in an ad hoc manner; i.e. agents are capable of treating problems which can only be solved by selectively and individually fusing and combining problem-solving expertise and data/information sources from the various agents in the network. Such tasks may be executed autonomously, collaboratively or cooperatively, depending on the complexity and nature of the task. In general, if complex problems are to be solved they are subdivided into less complex subtasks which again are subdivided into subtasks and so on. In a similar way agents are sometimes arranged in higher-level coalitions or clusters, each coalition being grouped around some common domain of expertise. Coalitions can overlap in that agents can belong to more than one coalition (Haghjoo *et al.* 1993). This usually will result in a more cooperative style of work within such a coalition and a more isolated style of work between them.

Of immense importance for cooperative information systems are the features of communication (Chapter 3), collaboration, and coordination (Chapters 3 and 11). Following Ellis (Ellis *et al.* 1991), *communication* refers to the exchange of information/messages among (cooperating) agents. *Collaboration* demands that agents share common data/information (see Chapters 4, 12 and 13) . The effectiveness of communication and collaboration can be enhanced if the activities of agents are coordinated; i.e., *coordination* means the adjustment of the agents' work towards a common goal by structuring the flow of communication and the way of collaboration within a group.

From the above three features, especially collaboration, to be effective, demands that people share information. Unfortunately, current information systems – database systems in particular – contribute very little to a support of teamwork. Of course, they provide multiple access to shared objects, however, in a totally insufficient way. Basically, they isolate users from each other. For example, consider two designers working with a CAD database. Seldom are they able to simultaneously modify different parts of the same object and be aware of each other's changes; rather they have to check the object in and out and tell each other (usually personally or by email) what they have done. Techniques like conventional locking and transaction processing are not only inappropriate for cooperative work but can actually hinder tightly coupled teamwork. Long transactions are neither in their closed (Moss 1981) nor in their open nested variant (Beeri *et al.* 1988) well suited to interactive use, because changes made during a (sub)transaction are not visible to other users until the transaction commits. These problems point to a basic philosophical difference between database management and cooperative information systems. The former strives to give each user the illusion of being the system's only user, while cooperative information systems strive to make a user's actions visible to all other members of the given group (however, not necessarily to other users of the system). Shielding a user from seeing the intermediate states of other group members' transactions means to oppose creativity and true synergistic cooperation and therefore stands in direct opposition to the goals of cooperative information systems.

Experiences with groupware systems show that humans are very good at developing conflict resolution strategies rapidly (Ellis *et al.* 1990, 1991). However, they need support for conflict recognition (see Chapter 6), visualization, and administration ("to do" lists) (Jarke *et al.* 1992). Inconsistency and concurrent and conflicting access to objects can be handled by users as long as the system offers appropriate support.

This study clearly indicates that humans are prepared to accept some responsibility for the consistent processing of information. However, it nevertheless should not be misinterpreted as implying that a control and coordination of concurrent work is obsolete. Quite the reverse, control and coordination of teamwork will remain an extremely important and indispensable task. Without it a team will often engage in conflicting or repetitive actions.

A simple approach to coordination is the use of a warning mechanism. Users will typically be warned not to concurrently update the data checked out. In many systems of this kind, users do have the option of working concurrently by ignoring the warning, but they will (hopefully, at least mostly) do so with the full knowledge that they will have to deal with concurrent changes later. Another approach are *notify locks* (Greif and Sarin 1988). With notify locks changes are not locked out, but the system informs the reading transaction when the data item is changed. When users learn that the data they are looking at has changed, they can decide whether they want to continue or compensate for their actions, e.g. by bringing back old versions or performing further changes.

The above solutions, like most others, are applicable. But, they are still insufficient in that they essentially only support two extremes. Either complete isolation or no isolation (and, of course, no shelter) at all. Most of the responsibility for a consistent work on data is left to the user/application. What is needed is some finer-grained concept which allows the applications designer to capture and express at least most of the semantics of an application. This chapter concentrates on such a proposal. It presents a flexible and adaptable solution for a fine-grained control of concurrent and conflicting access to common data/information. Although the proposal is based on the locking approach, it is nevertheless especially tailored to the rather demanding needs of cooperative information systems. As will be shown, the approach is capable of supporting a wide spectrum of work profiles, e.g. highly cooperative synergistic work profiles as well as less cooperative or isolated ones. Such different styles of (team)work can even be realized within the same application environment. The proposed concepts must be interpreted as low level building blocks which provide a solid and uniform technical platform on the basis of which more application-specific operations can be realized; i.e. the proposed concepts are not meant to be directly applicable by the user or application. Instead, they provide the building blocks for the implementation of semantically richer high-level operations (as, e.g. methods within object-oriented systems).

The remainder of this chapter is organized as follows. Section 2 will introduce a set of flexible and adaptable lock modes. Moreover, it will be shown how these locks can be interpreted in a way that permits a far reaching support of cooperative environments. Section 3 shows how this technique can be profitably applied within nested environments. Section 4 adds to the proposed technique a trigger mechanism with integrated notification service to further improve the support of cooperative synergistic work. Section 5 presents a solution for the treatment of special objects (like standard or library objects). In Section 6 it will be shown how objects can safely be transferred from one application to the next. Finally, Section 7 concludes this chapter.

The solution presented in this chapter provides a vehicle for the design of all kinds of cooperative environments. Technically, however, our approach mainly relies on concepts and terms which were originally introduced in the database area. Not to confuse researchers from this area we will discuss our proposal in the database context. We will, for example, use the term transaction instead of activity/task or nested transaction instead of talking about general cooperative environments in which tasks are subdivided into subtask. However, our solutions can easily be adapted to such general cooperative environments.

7.2 Concurrency Control and Cooperative Work

One major reason why traditional concurrency control fails to adequately support cooperative work is that it cannot consider (application-)specific semantics of operations. If such semantics are exploited, the concurrency control scheme can provide higher degrees of concurrency. One necessary prerequisite for the expression of application-specific semantics is the provision of a rich set of fine-grained lock modes which can be individually adapted to the semantics of the operations of given applications. However, conventional database systems only provide two lock modes namely the *exclusive* or X- and the *shared* or S-lock mode (hierarchical locks are not considered here). Since transactions in these environments are usually short lived, these two modes are sufficient. More advanced applications, however, behave completely different. Transactions are typically interactive and of long duration which means that objects need to be locked for a substantially longer period of time. Therefore, it is essential that a lock mode fits as exactly as possible to the operations which will be executed on the object.

Example 1

Let us consider a CASE environment in which a number of software engineers work on the development of some software package. The following situations may occur. A programmer wants to implement a module from which he knows that a similar one was already implemented previously. He wants to use this module as a model. Moreover, he needs the currently valid specification of another module since he wants to use it in his program. In both cases the object has to be read, however, with different semantics. In the first case it is of minor relevance for the programmer whether the module is currently being modified by a concurrent transaction. In the second case, however, the read needs to be a consistent read.

Another situation may be a group of programmers that work cooperatively on the implementation of a program. Here it is rather desirable that a programmer of the group is allowed to read each of the commonly used modules even if this module is still under development. On the other hand, people who do not belong to the group should not be in a position to read modules which are still under development.

As the above example clearly indicates a proper lock technique needs to consider the intention (semantics) of an operation as well as the environment within which the operation is meant to be executed.

7.2.1 Extended Set of Lock Modes

In this section we will introduce an extended set of basic lock modes which can be regarded as inevitable in the context of most non-standard applications. We assume that updates are not directly performed on the data of the database but that some form of shadowing is realized.

Of course, the shared (S-) and exclusive (X-) lock will remain useful for all kinds of database applications.

- shared lock (S-lock): only permits reading of the object.
- exclusive lock (X-lock): permits reading, modification, and deletion of the object.

Sometimes an application or user is just interested in the existence of an object but not in its concrete realization. For example, if a programmer wants to integrate an already existing procedure into "his" software package he may only be interested in the existence of the procedure but not in its actual implementation. Therefore, from the user's point of view it is irrelevant whether the procedure will be modified concurrently (at least as long as the modification stays within some limits (for example, no modification of the interface of the procedure)). Such a demand can be satisfied if a lock mode is provided which permits the modification of an object but not its deletion. This leads to an update lock (U-lock):

- update lock (U-lock): permits reading and modification of the object.

Another often mentioned requirement is a "dirty read" (see example 1) or browse which allows the user to read an object irrespective of any lock currently granted for that object:

- browse lock (B-lock): permits browsing of the object (dirty read).

Especially design applications often want to handle several states of an object instead of one; i. e. in such environments an object is represented by its version graph. In (Klahold *et al.* 1985) it was shown that the conventional S-/X-lock scheme is not sufficient in such an environment, since the derivation of a new version corresponds not only to an insert operation (of the new version of the object) but also to an update operation (the version graph of the object is modified). Thus, it is desirable to enable a transaction to exclude others from simultaneously deriving a new version from a given version v; other transactions may only read v. Therefore, we include a further lock mode:

- derivation lock (D-lock): permits reading of the object and derivation of a new version.

Although this extended set of lock modes clearly allows the applications designer to capture more semantics it is still on a rather coarse level. Especially cooperative environments can hardly be supported. The next section presents a more flexible and convenient solution.

7.2.2 The Two Effects of a Lock

Since lock protocols rely on conflict avoidance they regulate access to data in a relatively rigid way. As a matter of principle, a transaction, first of all, has no rights at all on data of the database. Such privileges can only be acquired via an explicit request for and assignment of locks. In the remainder, we will distinguish between an owner of a lock (owner for short) and a competitor for a lock (competitor for short). An owner already possesses some lock on an object O, whereas a competitor is each a concurrent transaction, in particular each transaction that competes for a lock on O.

If we analyze the semantics of a lock, it becomes clear that a lock on an object O has always two effects:

1. it allows the owner to perform certain operations on O and
2. it restricts competitors in their possibilities to work on O.

This decomposition of the semantics of a lock makes it possible to differentiate between the rights which are assigned to the owner of a lock and the restrictions which are imposed on competitors. From now on, No. 1. will be called the internal effect of a lock request while No. 2. will be called its external effect.

Example 2

An X-lock has the internal effect in that it allows the owner to read, modify, and delete the locked object. The external effect ensures that competitors cannot lock the object in whatever mode.

An S-lock has the same internal and external effect since it allows the owner (internal effect) as well as competitors (external effect) to just read the object.

This distinction between the internal and the external effect of a lock makes it possible to establish the rights of an owner without simultaneously and automatically stipulating the limitations imposed on concurrent applications. We gain the freedom to determine the external effect of a lock individually.

The lock modes which were discussed in the previous section come with the following internal effects:

- exclusive lock (X-lock): permits reading, derivation of a new version,. modification, and deletion of the object.
- update lock (U-lock): permits reading, derivation of a new version, and modification of the object (not its deletion).
- derivation lock (D-lock): permits reading and derivation of a new version of the object (not its deletion or modification). This lock mode is only useful if the data model provides a version mechanism.
- shared lock (S-lock): permits reading of the object (neither its deletion or modification nor the derivation of a new version).
- browse lock (B-lock): same as S-lock.

The examination of the external effect leaves some leeway for further discussion. Conventional database systems enforce the operational integrity to be entirely ensured by the database management system. To be able to support the needs of advanced applications, however, it is inevitable to weaken this rigid view; i.e. to transmit some responsibility for the correct and consistent processing of data from the database system to the application. Especially, in design environments users want to work on data in a way which does not automatically guarantee serializability (cooperative work). But, of course, the database system has to ensure that concurrent work on data can preserve consistency as long as the applications take care of their part in consistency control. In this sense, an update and a read operation on the same object may be compatible as long as the reader is aware of the concurrent updater. A simultaneous modification of the same object by different transactions is usually prohibited, at least as long as the data is handled by the system as an atomic unit. However, if concurrent applications are capable of merging the different states of an object before it is checked in on the next higher level, concurrent updates can also be permitted.

In order to be able to precisely describe a lock mode in the remainder it is necessary to specify the internal and external effect. Therefore, X/Y denotes a lock which combines the internal effect X with the external effect Y.

Table 7.1 lays down which internal effect can be combined with which external effect. $\sqrt{}$ (—) indicates that the given internal effect can always (never) be combined with the corresponding external effect. $\bigcirc$ signifies that the validity of such a combination should depend on the design and abilities of the application. If the application is prepared to accept some responsibility for the consistent processing of data $\sqrt{}$ can be replaced by $\bigcirc$ (for example, to model cooperative environments). However, the sequence of $\sqrt{}$ in a row must be continuous; for example, in case an S/U lock is permitted S/D must be a possible lock, too. C corresponds to $\bigcirc$, but indicates that this combination should be used with care. It especially requires measures which assure that the concurrent modifications of the data cannot disturb the consistency of the data(base).

Table 7.1   Compatibility matrix internal/external effects

		external effect				
		B	**S**	**D**	**U**	**X**
B	√	√	√	√	√
S	√	√	O	O	—
D	√	√	O	C	—
U	√	O	C	C	—
X	√	—	—	—	—

(left margin labels reading vertically: i n t e r n a l   e f f e c t)

√	permitted
O	possible
—	prohibited
C	should be used with care

7.2.3 The Semantics of the Lock Modes

Since both, the B- and the S-lock mode allow the owner of the lock to read the locked object, it does not make any sense to keep both modes as internal effects. Whether a read is a consistent or a dirty one is decided by the corresponding external effect (does the owner allow his competitors to only read the object (external effect S) or to modify it (external effect U)). With respect to the external effect we want to lay down that B means that the appropriate object cannot be accessed by any competitor in whatever mode (corresponds to an exclusive mode).

An internal effect S when combined with the external effect S corresponds to the well known shared lock. Combined with a weaker external effect (U, X), it realizes a dirty read.

An internal effect U permits the modification of the object. A concurrent S-lock can be prohibited. An X-lock, additionally, grants the owner the right to delete the object. Since this is the only difference between these two lock modes, the X-lock is meant to be used only in case the object will be deleted. With this interpretation in mind it becomes clear why an X-lock prohibits a concurrent S-lock. Since the object will most probably be deleted, a read operation makes no sense.

7.2.4 A Short Discussion of Consistency Aspects

The main motive for the introduction of our approach is that we want to provide a basis for a skillful applications designer that allows him to satisfy the demands of "his" application in a proper way. This requirement can only be met if the tool kit enables a designer to transfer some of the responsibility for consistency from the system to the application. Only by such a transfer, for example, non-serializable cooperative work can be supported. On the other hand, our tool kit also supports consistency Level 3 (Gray *et al.* 1976) if all O (and C) are replaced by a —.

7.2.5 Dynamic Assignment of an External Effect (Open Lock)

In addition to the possibility of fixing the external effect when the lock is acquired, it is also possible to leave it open for the moment and fix it at a later time. In this case, the system assumes the strongest external effect, as a default. If, however, a conflict arises which can be solved by a weaker external effect the owner is asked whether he accepts this weaker external effect. This allows the owner to decide individually whether he wants to accept concurrent work on the object. Such a decision may depend on the competitor's profile or the current state of the object. A lock with a fixed external effect is called fixed lock, while a lock with an undecided external effect is called open lock.

7.2.6 Upgrading a Lock

In order to be able to decide whether a given lock is stronger than another one, we first need to define whether a given (internal/external) effect is stronger than another one.

Definition 1

An internal effect is stronger (weaker) than another one if it concedes *more* (*fewer*) rights on the locked object to the owner.

According to this definition, the internal effect B *is the weakest* one while X *is the strongest* one; i.e. the internal effects increase from B to X.

The external effect, however, lays down which lock modes can still be granted to competitors. Therefore, it works in reverse order.

Definition 2

An external effect is stronger (weaker) than another one if it concedes *fewer* (*more*) rights to a competitor.

Since the external effect X still allows a competitor to acquire each internal effect, it is the *weakest* one while B is the *strongest* one.

In the previous section it was said that √ in Table 7.1 indicates that the given internal effect can be combined with the external effect which goes with it without risk. However, in case of a new request X/Y it is not only necessary that X is compatible with each already granted external effect. Moreover, Y must be compatible with each already granted internal effect as the following example shows:

Example 3

A D/D-lock allows competitors to concurrently create their own new version of the given object. However, a conflict will arise if a competitor wants to acquire a D/S lock. Since this lock would exclude others from concurrently deriving a new version a D/S lock cannot be granted in case a D/D was already granted.

To avoid situations like the one in Example 3 we need to define the compatibility of locks:

Definition 3

Two locks are compatible,

1. If the owner's external effect permits the internal effect of the competitor.
2. If the competitor's external effect permits the internal effect of the owner.

Example 4

Let us assume that an S/U-lock was already granted to user P. If competitor Co wants to acquire a D/S-lock, this request can be granted. The external effect of P's lock permits the internal effect of Co's lock (condition 1: a D is weaker than a U). Moreover, the external effect of Co's lock permits the internal effect of P's lock (condition 2: an S is compatible with an S).

In order to support the upgrade of a lock mode we need to define under which circumstances a lock is stronger (weaker) than another one.

Definition 4

A lock L1 is stronger (weaker) than a lock L2, if

1. the *internal* effect of L1 is *at least* (*at most*) *as strong as* the *internal* effect of L2,
2. the *external* effect of L1 is *at least* (*at most*) *as strong as* the *external* effect of L2,
3. L1 is different from L2.

Example 5

Since the internal effect U is stronger than the internal effect D and the external effect B is stronger than the external effect S the U/B lock is weaker than the D/S lock.

For the following discussion we will assume that each C in Table 7.1 is replaced by a — since most applications will not be able to guarantee consistency in case of concurrent modifications on the same object. This assumption is no real restriction since the following discussion can easily be transferred to the extended compatibility matrix.

On the basis of the above definition, the different lock modes, which can be inferred from the (restricted) compatibility matrix (Table 7.1), can be arranged in a linear order (according to their strength):

$$(S/X) \rightarrow (S/U) \rightarrow (S/D) \rightarrow \quad (\begin{smallmatrix} S/S \\ D/D \end{smallmatrix}) \rightarrow (D/S) \rightarrow (U/S) \rightarrow (U/B) \rightarrow (X/B)$$

Exceptions are the exclusive read lock (S/S-lock) and the shared derivation lock (D/D-lock). The S/S-lock has a stronger external effect than the D/D-lock but a weaker internal effect. If an owner of an S/S lock wants to switch to a D/D lock (or vice versa) he needs to acquire the next stronger lock (the D/S-lock).

7.3 Locks in the Context of Nested Transactions

In this section it will be shown how the decomposition of a lock mode can be exploited by the concurrency control scheme in order to support a more cooperative style of work. Consider the transaction/application hierarchy of Figure 7.1. Let us assume that transaction T5 has acquired some object O in lock mode U/B from its parent (not visible in the figure). Now it wants some work on O be done by its child T10. To do so, T5 has to transmit the object/lock pair O/(U/B) to transaction T10. This leads to the following situation:

1. O is locked on the level of T5 in lock mode U/B.
2. O is available to the descendant tree of T10 in lock mode U/B.

Feature 1 is a necessary restriction, since it prevents other children of T5 (as well as T5 itself) from modifying O. Feature 2, however, is an unnecessary obstacle to the task of T10 for the following reason:

T5 is only interested in the results of the work of T10 on O, but not on how these results will be achieved. T10 needs O and the permission to work on O

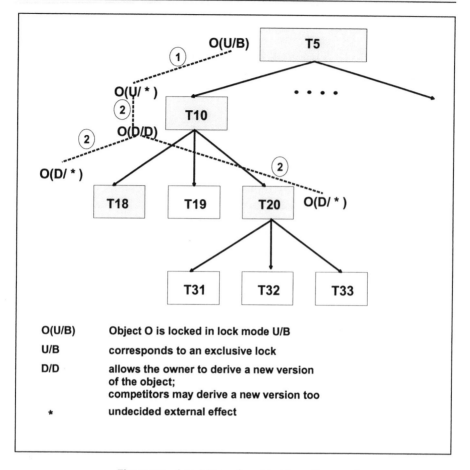

Figure 7.1   Acquisition of an object from the parent

in a way which corresponds to its task. However, it should be left to T10 to decide how the work on O can be performed best. For example, if T10 decides to develop several alternatives of O simultaneously, for example in T18 and T20, and to select afterwards the best alternative, such a proceeding should be permitted. In the scenario above this is prohibited, since the U/B lock on O prevents T18 and T20 from concurrently acquiring the necessary locks on O. If we take a closer look at the semantics of the subtask which T5 assigned to T10 it becomes clear that this task is sufficiently described by the object O and the internal effect of the lock on O.

However, the downward inheritance of the external effect of the lock is a useless obstacle, since it does not result in any advantage for T5. Instead, it unnecessarily restricts T10 in performing its task. Consequently we decided to transfer only the internal effect to the child transaction. Therefore, if T10 acquires an object O from T5 in mode U/B, this lock is set only on the level of T5 (see Figure 7.1). T10 simply inherits the internal effect of the lock. The external effect is left undecided (this results in U/* (1)). T10 may allow its children to acquire every lock on O with an internal effect equal to or weaker than U and every external effect which T10 wants to concede to its children. In Figure 7.1, T10 decides to allow its children to acquire concurrently O in D/D mode, therefore, to derive concurrently new versions from O (2) (a D/D lock allows the owner to derive a new version of the object; competitors may derive (concurrently) new versions, too). While this proceeding allows T10 to execute its work on O autonomously, it does not allow T10, for example, to transmit several alternatives of O to T5, since O is locked on the level of T5 in mode U/B (which does not permit the derivation of several alternatives).

7.4 Rules on Locks and Notification Services

Synergistic cooperative work can only be supported adequately if applications can actively *control* the preservation of the consistency of data/objects. This requires the concurrency control component to provide as much support to applications as possible. For example, our approach permits update operations to be compatible just by assigning the appropriate lock (U/U) to them. However, if concurrency control relied on pure locks, it would be too inflexible.

Example 6

Let us consider an abstract data type *PRICE-PRODUCT* on which the following four operations are defined (see Figure 7.2).

INCREASEVAT (op_1):   needs internal effect U
INCREASEPRICE (op_2):   needs internal effect U
COMPUTEPRICEINCLUSIVELYVAT (op_3):   needs internal effect S
COMPUTEPRICEEXCLUSIVELYVAT (op_4):   needs internal effect S

The compatibility of these operations (as shown in Figure 7.2) cannot be completely modeled yet. The problem is that we can define that op_1 and op_2 should acquire a U/U lock (which means that both update operations can be performed concurrently (which, of course, is desirable)). op_4, however, should be compatible to op_1 which means that we must assign an S/U lock to op_4. This implies that op_4 is compatible to op_2, too (which, of course, is incorrect).

The problem is that locks, as such, define compatibility still on a too global level. An S/U lock is compatible with a U/U lock regardless of whether the

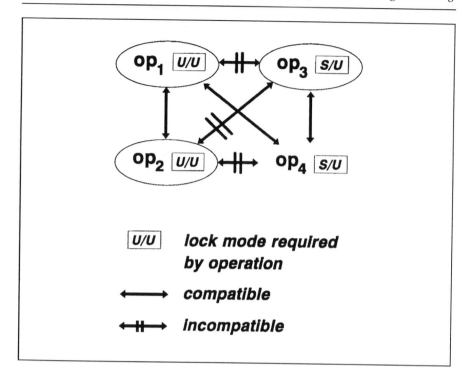

Figure 7.2 Relationship between operations

second lock is acquired by an operation op_1 or op_2. If we really want to exploit the semantics of applications, the *all-or-none principle* (a lock allows either all concurrent transactions to access the object in a given mode or none) must be replaced by a more expressive *yes-if principle*, i.e. concurrent transactions are allowed to access the object if certain conditions are fulfilled. For this reason, our approach supports the binding of rules to locks. The rule mechanism is similar to ECA rules (event – condition – action rules (Dayal *et al.* 1988).

on event {[case condition] do [action1] [action2]}*

An *event* can be an action which is triggered when an operation is performed on a(n):

- lock: request/release/up-/downgrade/transmission (lending, transfer, return)
- object: modification/transfer/deletion
- transaction: begin/end suspend/resume/(partial) rollback

Conditions can be

- special users: a certain user/application/transaction has triggered the event
- special operations: a certain operation has triggered the event
- object states: the object is in a certain state (for example, compiled/tested/etc.)

The condition specification is optional, which means that an event may directly trigger an action.

The *action* section can comprise two parts:

- In *action1* an exception can be expressed regarding the underlying lock. An exception can be *positive* or *negative*. With positive (negative) exception, a lock mode can be weakened (tightened) by explicitly declaring which event can cause which kind of weakening (tightening) and under which circumstances.
- *Action2* allows the system to react on events by (additionally) sending messages. To be able to do so the rule mechanism is accompanied by a *notification service* by which applications/users/agents can be informed about certain facts or can be asked to do certain things.

The system will react differently on an event if different conditions and actions are specified in the case do part.

Example 7

a. negative exception (optimistic version: everything that is not prohibited is permitted)

Given an S/U lock on object O. The following negative exception tightens the lock:

on lock-request
{[case <predicate P_m>] do [prohibit (U/*);] [notify-Request <t_m>]}*

This condition specifies that if a concurrent application wants to acquire some lock with internal effect U on object with OID O (would allow the requesting process to update O), the request will be rejected if predicate P_m is true. The notify-Request(ing process) clause specifies that the message t_m will be sent to the requesting process.

b. positive exception (pessimistic version: everything that is not explicitly permitted is prohibited)

Given an S/S lock on object O. The following positive exception weakens the lock:

on lock-request

{[case <predicate P_m>] do [permit (U/<B);] [notify-Self <t_m>]}

This condition specifies that if a concurrent application wants to acquire some lock with internal effect U, the request can be granted if the external effect of the requested lock is weaker than B (<B; for example, S or U) and predicate P_m is true. The notify-Self clause specifies that the message t_m will be sent to the owner of the S/S lock.

c. Solution for example 6

The scenario of Figure 7.2 can be modeled as follows (it is assumed that both op_3 and op_4 will acquire an S/S lock on instances of *PRICE-PRODUCT*):

When op_1 is executed it must bind the following rule to its lock on the object dealt with:

1. on lock-request

    case op_3 do prohibit (U/>B); notify-Request "VAT is being modi-
    fied"

When op_3 is executed it must bind the following rule to its lock on the object dealt with:

2. on lock-request

    case op_2 do permit (S/U)

Rule 1 assures that op_3 cannot acquire a lock on object O as long as op_1 holds its lock on O. However, if op_3 is the first operation to request a lock on O, then op_1 cannot concurrently acquire its lock on O, since the necessary U/U lock is not compatible with the already granted S/S lock (of operation op_3). Finally, if op_2 wants to acquire a lock on O, the lock can be granted since rule 2 permits this exception.

Similar rules must be installed for op_2 and op_4.

Another good example for the usefulness of rules is the open lock. An open lock was defined as a lock whose external effect is left undecided. Compatibility with other requests is decided individually each time a request is submitted. The decision may depend on the profile of the requesting process and the current state of the object, respectively. One possibility is that the owner of the lock himself makes the decision. A better solution would be to let the system automatically decide on the basis of predefined rules. This frees the owner from being (frequently) disturbed in his work by concurrent processes.

The extended lock concept can be used as a solid basis to implement higher-level concepts, like semantics-based concurrency control (Chrysanthis *et al.* 1991, Herlihy and Weihl 1988, Schwarz and Spector 1984, Weihl 1988).

7.5 Object-Related Locks

Usually, locks are bound to transactions. In cooperative environments it seems to be reasonable to think about an extension of this rule in a direction that locks can also be bound to objects. Similar to the life of a human being who is born single and who may, at some later time, acquire marriage status (which rules out a return to the status "unmarried"), objects may also go through several states in their lifetime. They may be "born" without any restrictions on the way in which they can be treated. However, during their lifetime, some restrictions may come into force (see Example 8).

Example 8

Especially in design applications the concept of versioning is of great relevance.

1. Version graph

In the context of version graphs it is commonly required that a nonleaf node (inner node) cannot be modified to prevent the successors of that node from being invalidated (since the predecessor is no longer the version from which they were created). Here an object is born without any restrictions (leaf) and, later, changes to an object which can no longer be modified (nonleaf node).

2. Time versions

Time versions only permit one version of an object to be valid at a given time. If the currently valid (latest) state of an object is to be modified, a new version is created. This results in a linear sequence of versions. In this case the object is born with the restriction not to be changeable. Later on, it will change to an object which can neither be modified nor used as a basis for the derivation of a new version (nonleaf node).

3. Standard or library objects

Many application classes, especially design environments, put standard or library objects at the users' disposal. Such objects can only be read. They are born with the restriction: *modification prohibited*.

Our idea is to link locks permanently to objects. This kind of lock will be called object-related lock (OR-lock for short). An OR-lock, once imposed on an object, can neither be weakened nor released, it can only be upgraded. The lock remains valid as long as the object exists. OR-locks behave like conventional locks (locks linked to transactions, called transaction-related locks or

TR-locks for short, which only have an internal effect). If an OR-lock is granted, the community of all (potential) transactions can be seen as the owner of the lock. All rights of the internal effect can still be acquired while all other rights are no longer "grantable". Since an OR-lock is persistent we will distinguish it from a transaction lock by placing a P in front of the signature.

The following OR-locks can directly be adopted from the set of conventional locks:

- PU-Lock: Prohibits deletion of the object. All other operations are permitted.
- PD-Lock: Prohibits deletion and modification of the object. All other operations are permitted.
- PS-Lock: Prohibits deletion, modification, and derivation of a new version of the object. It only permits the read operation.

It is particularly worthwhile taking a closer look at the PD-lock. This lock permits the derivation of a new version of the object locked. Unfortunately, it is not laid down whether only one derivation can be produced or more. But such a distinction is extremely useful, since it makes it possible to automatically control the observance of the rules of different version models (time versions and version graphs). Due to the great significance of version models, a distinction seems to be reasonable. Therefore, the PD-lock is split into two lock modes:

- PSD-lock: Only permits derivation of exactly one new version; i.e. after the first derivation of a new version the lock mode is converted to a PS-lock (forms a sequence of versions).
- PMD-lock: Permits derivation of any number of new versions (forms a version graph).

Finally, a PX-lock is introduced as the lock with which every object is "born":

- PX-lock: Is a pseudo lock which does not impose any restrictions on the object (needs not to be considered by the concurrency control component).

The introduction of a PB-lock does not make any sense, since it has the same effect as the PS-lock.

Table 7.2 describes the compatibility between an OR-lock and (the internal effect of) a conventional lock:

Similar to the external effect of conventional locks, OR-locks increase from PX to PS since each step on this way concedes fewer rights on the object.

Table 7.2 Compatibility matrix object/transaction-related locks

			internal effect of the transaction lock			
o			S	D	U	X
b	l	PX	√	√	√	√
j	o	PU	√	√	√	—
e	c	PMD	√	√	—	—
c	k	PSD	√	O	—	—
t		PS	√	—	—	—

√   permitted
O   single derivation only
—   prohibited

As already mentioned, with the help of OR-locks concurrency control overhead can be reduced. For instance, with a PS-lock the object has no longer to be considered by the concurrency control component, since the only applicable operation is the read operation. A PS-lock is especially favorable if standard objects need to be handled.

Let us consider Figure 7.3, in which the standard object O2 is a shared subcomponent of several complex objects (CO1, CO2, CO3). If, for example, some application T locks CO1 in an exclusive mode (U/B-lock), this lock

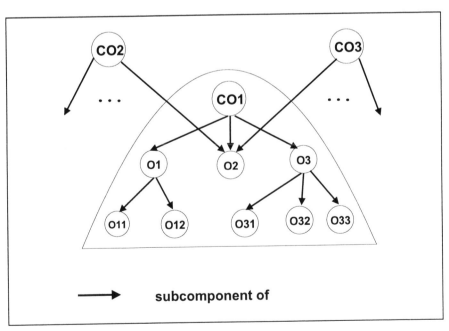

Figure 7.3 Standard object O2 as subcomponent of several complex objects

prevents each competitor Co from locking any of the other complex objects which also include O2 (here CO2 and CO3). However, if a PS-lock is imposed on O2, the lock manager no longer has to consider O2. Therefore, the concurrent access can be granted. Situations like this are frequent, especially in design environments.

7.6 Subject-Related Locks

Non-standard applications are usually extremely complex in comparison with traditional applications. One frequently finds complex tasks which need to be split into several units of work, each of which, nevertheless, may still be complex and of long duration. Since these units of work represent *one* complex task, they often have a complex control flow; i.e. some units can be executed concurrently while others need to be executed in succession. Each unit of work accesses a (large) number of objects. Some of them are only used within *one* given unit. However, the more central objects with respect to the task are often used in (nearly) all subtasks. Consequently, we must be able to safely transfer objects from one unit of work to the next. If units of work correspond to (sub)transactions, we need a mechanism which allows an object to be safely transferred from one transaction to the next (see also Wächter and Reuter 1992). Consider, for example, an administration department. If someone makes an application (for example, a business trip), he has to fill in the application form. The application form usually has to pass through several stages; it has to be countersigned by a manager, registered and checked for correctness, some computations have to be performed etc. Often each subtask is performed by a different person/department. This means that we need to control the correct flow of the application form; i.e. a safe transfer from one subtask (transaction) to the next has to be ensured. For this reason we provide subject-related locks. A subject-related lock (SR-lock for short) again is defined by an internal/external effect pair. It is bound to a subject for some time. During this period, the subject is the owner of the lock and can decide autonomously how to use the locked object (for example, in which application). A subject can be anything identified as such by the concurrency control component, for example, an application, a user (group), an agent, a named sequence of actions (transactions) etc.

A subject-related lock corresponds to a transaction-related lock (TR-lock) in that it is defined by an internal/external effect pair. It is bound *temporarily*, however, to a *subject* and not to a transaction. Since an SR-lock functions as a placeholder, it reserves an object O for (later) use by its owner in one or more (consecutive) (trans)actions. Every subject can ask for an SR-lock at any time. The SR-lock can be granted if no TR-, OR-, or SR-lock is (currently) assigned to some competitor in an incompatible mode. Here, a competitor is either a transaction/application (in case of a TR-lock) or a subject (in case of a concurrent SR-lock) or an object (in case of an OR-lock). The owner of an SR-lock can hold the lock as long as he wants; i.e. an SR-lock is released by an explicit command of its owner. This can be done at any time.

An SR-lock imposes restrictions on the way in which competitors are allowed to work on the locked object. Consequently, the external effect of an SR-lock corresponds to the external effect of a TR-lock. The internal effect determines which TR-lock on the object can be granted to a transaction at most. This means, that an SR-lock does not assign any directly usable rights to its owner. Instead, rights can only become valid if they are supplemented by a TR-lock within a concrete transaction. However, since the SR-lock is a placeholder it is guaranteed that the corresponding TR-lock can immediately be granted, provided that the requested TR-lock is not stronger than the SR-lock. If it is stronger, of course, the TR-lock has to compete with all already granted locks on that object. Each internal effect/external effect-pair which is a valid TR-lock represents also a valid SR-lock.

The additional acquisition of the TR-lock is necessary to ensure that the locked object O can only be manipulated within a transaction. Moreover, it guarantees that the owner of the SR-lock cannot improperly exploit his rights, for example, by using O in an incompatible way within different transactions. The TR-lock ensures that O can only be handled in a correct way. Only after the TR-lock is released, O is once again put at the disposal of the owner of the SR-lock and can, therefore, be employed in another transaction. Of course, since O can only be used if a proper TR-lock is granted, an SR-lock can be released at any time. Either O is currently not used by some transaction or it is still protected by the additional TR-lock.

Example 9

Let us assume that a user P has acquired the SR-lock *U/S* on O (allows P to modify the object, concurrent transactions may still read it). If P wants to modify O in transaction T he can directly supplement the SR-lock by the corresponding TR-lock. This prevents P from acquiring afterwards an incompatible lock mode on O in a concurrent transaction.

7.7 Conclusion

Applications on a Cooperative Information System place sophisticated demands on the control of collaboration. Especially, different styles of (team)work must be supported by such a system (even within the same application). In this chapter we have presented a flexible concurrency control scheme based on the locking approach. However, the set of lock modes and its use was substantially improved so that the resulting approach can even satisfy different levels of synergistic cooperative work. The proposed concepts are not meant to be directly applicable by the user or application. Instead, they can be seen as a set of building blocks for the implementation of semantically richer operations (as, e.g. methods within object-oriented systems).

The emphasis of our work so far, has been on providing the basic building blocks for the coordination and control of access to objects within synchronous and asynchronous teamwork applications, especially design applications. However, much work is still needed to verify the usefulness and applicability of our concepts and to gain a more profound in-depth knowledge about teamwork.

Chapter 8

Enhancing Organizational Intelligence through Cooperative Problem Solving

Stefan Kirn

8.1 Introduction

Most organizational strategies that have been developed to meet current market challenges aim to enhance the flexibility (short term) and adaptability (long term) of enterprises. Current "buzz-words" such as downsizing of organizational structures, increased local autonomy, decentralization, cooperation and team work, business process orientation and workflow management, point to the different concepts that are available today (e.g. see (Guilfoyle and Warner 1994, Davenport 1993, Morton 1991, Nirenberg 1993). Also, most organizational experts agree that the ability of an enterprise to achieve competitive advantages in the market and to continuously survive in dynamic, and even hostile environments largely depend upon its information technology infrastructure, which is required to efficiently support the organizational information processing and problem solving capabilities (Blanning *et al.* 1992, Ishida 1992, Marsden and Pingry 1988).

Consequently, an increasing number of organizational researchers draw their attention to the design of "intellectual" organizational capabilities such as organizational communication, memory (e.g. Favela and Connor 1994, Morrison and Olfman 1994, Paradice 1988), learning (e.g. Elofson and Konsynski 1993, Niwa 1992, Sunita 1992, Watanabe 1992) cognition, and reasoning (Matsuda 1988a). Concurrently they reshape the scope of their analysis by claiming to explicitly integrate computer-based information processing technology into the body of organizational theory (e.g. Blanning *et al.* 1992, Favela and Connor 1994, Huber and McDaniel 1986, Marsden and Pingry 1988, Matsuda 1988a). Both trends unite in a new discipline that has recently begun to emerge, namely that of Organizational Intelligence (OI). According to Matsuda (1988, 1992) OI can be defined as the intellectual capability of an organization, which integrates human and computational problem solving capabilities (see also Malone 1988, Petrie Jr 1992).

Within this context, this chapter develops towards what we call "organizational multiagent systems" which are no longer a more or less passive component of the organizational model. Instead, organizational multiagent systems are supposed to play an active, self-contained role, and to form an organizational body in their own right. This differs from current organization theory in which organizational multiagent systems are supposed to establish an additional organizational subsystem which originates from both the social subsystem and the information processing (or: technology) subsystem of the organization (see also ACM Computing Surveys 1994, Guilfoyle and Warner 1994, Carley and Prietula 1994). Based on the cooperation paradigm that they provide an organizational knowledge processing environment is particularly well suited to support intelligent organizational capabilities (Matsuda 1988a, Warnecke 1993). Organizational multiagent systems are a key technology (Kirn 1995) to support information and knowledge processing activities in cooperative, networked organizations. This, in turn, requires integrating them with the related human organization. Thus, organizational multiagent systems (see Chapter 10).

1. must be able to adapt themselves to the organizational aims and objectives, strategies and operations, and to the organizational structures, procedures, and constraints,
2. they must actively contribute to an organization's "intellectual" capabilities such as organizational cognition, organizational memory and learning, organizational problem solving, and organizational communication skills.

With respect to the inherent distribution of organizations our basic hypothesis is that there are many interactions between Organizational Intelligence (see also Chapter 9) and the field of Distributed AI (Chapters 10, 11 and 12) which urgently need to be investigated. This contribution seeks to initiate such work. To this purpose, and with respect to our interest here in Distributed AI we first introduce the concept of Organizational Intelligence which originates from recent work of organizational researchers in Japan and the US (Section 2). We then ask how Organizational Intelligence can contribute to the design and research of multiagent systems (Section 3). Finally, we discuss how Distributed AI will benefit the design of intelligent organizational skills (Section 4).

8.2 Organizational Intelligence (OI)

Today, organizational experts approach the current market, political and environmental challenges by a set of organizational strategies such as downsizing of hierarchical structures, decentralization of autonomy, business process orientation, networking among more or less mutual independent organizational units, and the implementation of teamwork-like cooperation styles.

These concepts provide the groundwork from which current issues on Organizational Intelligence has evolved. Within this field two major research communities can be identified. The first one has been established around the annual *Hawaii International Conferences on System Sciences* (HICSS), starting from a tutorial on "Intelligent Organizations" presented by G. P. Huber in 1987. The second has its roots in Japan, where T. Matsuda is developing towards a holistic approach of what he calls "Organizational Intelligence" (OI).

The reader may be aware of the great deal of related work carried out in disciplines such as organizational theory, organizational computing, office information systems, and others. However, while all these disciplines have worked out particular facets such as organizational learning, bounded rationality, or self organization, they are not providing an overall concept of intelligence for human-centered organizations.

This deficiency has motivated Matsuda to evolve a model of Organizational Intelligence that integrates human, and machine-based knowledge processing and problem solving capabilities (Matsuda 1988a, 1991, 1992). In contrast to others he stresses that machine intelligence is an integral part of the intelligence of an organization. As Matsuda points out, in conformity with recent work on *user agents* and *personal assistants* in computer science, cooperative organizational work includes both, human beings and machine based problem solving agents.

In Matsuda view, Organizational Intelligence (OI) may provisionally (so long as it is useful for further discussion) be defined as the intellectual capability of an organization as a whole. As such, OI includes two different components: Organizational Intelligence as a process and Organizational Intelligence as a product. While *Organizational Process Intelligence "…* provides theoretical analysis of an organization with a set of subprocesses", *Organizational Product Intelligence "…* supplies the organization with … synthetic policy (and design) guidelines for information system design" (Matsuda 1992). It is clear, and Matsuda outlines it in detail, that these two components are mutually dependent.

Organizational Product Intelligence considers how information systems must be designed with respect to the needs of Organizational Intelligence. This requires to develop OI-orientated information system design guidelines. This raises the question *how can Distributed AI systems be designed* so they effectively support the intellectual capabilities of organizations (section 4). On the other hand, modeling *Organizational Process Intelligence* means to analyze, design, and effectively perform organizational knowledge and information processing and problem solving activities. This raises a further question, *how can Distributed AI benefit Organizational Process Intelligence* (Section 5).

8.2.1 Organizational Process Intelligence

Human intelligence as well as machine intelligence (which includes artificial intelligence) represents certain processes (information processing activities) within an organization. These processes can be characterized by three attributes *interaction, aggregation,* and *coordination.* Hence, *Organizational Process Intelligence* has been defined as "the interactive-aggregative-coordinative complex of human intelligence and machine intelligence of the organization as a whole" (Matsuda 1992).

Interactions within an organizational body involve different types of actors (humans, and machine agents), which serve very different purposes (e.g. transfer of data and knowledge for remote use, coordination of interrelated activities etc.). Within a computerized organization interactions involve

1. human intelligence vs. human intelligence,
2. human intelligence vs. machine intelligence,
3. machine intelligence vs. machine intelligence.

The *aggregation* of intelligence "is observed as the process of collection of members proceeds from an individual to the entire organization via various sizes of groups" (Matsuda 1992). Thus, individual knowledge is iteratively transformed into group level knowledge, and in turn, for instance by negotiation, it is transformed into organizational knowledge.

Mere human or machine intelligence is not enough. Instead, both are to be coordinated towards the respective organizational objectives. *Coordination* provides tools to control interactions as well as the execution of aggregation processes. As such, it involves the human and machine intelligence of an organization, and aims to speed up organizational processes as much as possible.

Organizational process intelligence can be subdivided into five parts.

1. *Organizational memory:* Organizational memory is the basic requirement for any kind of OI. It is the capability to store events, situations both successful and unsuccessful behavior and to remember this if required.
2. *Organizational cognition:* This covers the organizational perceptive and comprehensive capabilities, that enable an organization to concentrate on the essentials and have an influence on, respectively, can adapt future evolutions.
3. *Organizational learning:* This means the capability of an organization to use the knowledge which is stored in the organizational memory at the right time and to learn from the experiences made in the past. The learning refers to the behavior in non-standard situations and the assessment of the (newly) developed way of acting.
4. *Organizational communication:* Communication describes the entire data, information and knowledge exchange between human and machine actors in the organization.

5. *Organizational inference*: Organizational inference not only covers problem solving. It also includes the avoidance, bypassing and encapsulation of a problem.

8.2.2 Organizational Product Intelligence

Organizational Product Intelligence requires the development of design guidelines in order to support the building of organizational information systems. It is one of the most important shortcomings of the work of Matsuda in that it does not provide any suggestions to develop these guidelines. This is also the case if we turn our attention to Distributed AI. We see that there are no design guidelines to help to develop multiagent systems with a particular, predefined profile of "organizational" characteristics.

8.3 Incorporating Organizational Intelligence into Distributed AI Systems

Current Distributed AI is dominated by an "individualistic" approach which mainly focuses on the single member of an agent organization and its local activities. As an immediate consequence Distributed AI is in a position to further develop a sound understanding of what "organizational" intelligence of a multiagent system should be, and what the relevant components are that contribute to the intellectual skills of the system as a whole. Thus, we adopt the approach of Organizational Intelligence as a starting point to extend our research into the design of intelligent group level skills of Distributed AI systems (Chapter 10 adopts a similar goal).

To this purpose, each subsection below (1) first introduces the current state of the art in organizational theory, and (2) secondly introduces related work in Distributed AI, in order to discuss those issues that are relevant for (3) the design of *organizational intelligent* multiagent systems and, finally, (4) we identify important tasks for future research on group level intelligence in multiagent systems.

8.3.1 Organizational Memory

(1) Organizational Theory

Organizational memory enables an enterprise to preserve, remember and utilize its experience (information about successes and failures in the past) and, thus learn from its individual history. Organizational researchers have already spent a great deal of effort on the question how can important organizational knowledge be identified, how it should be represented, and how an organization can make sure that this knowledge can, and will be accessed in the right way in future. Traditionally, organizational knowledge is represented in charts representing the division of labor, as descriptions of predefined organizational processes and procedures, and, in addition, as a large body of written material. Thus, organizational memory is completely different to the individual memory of the members of the organization, and organizational knowledge is distinct from the knowledge of the individuals joining the enterprise.

Since the mid-1980s organizational researchers have learned that recent advances in information technology change the functions, and, thus, the role of organizational memories significantly (Favela and Connor 1994, Morrison and Olfman 1994, Paradice 1988). In future, a broad range of different types of software systems need to be considered:

1. databases and knowledge bases,
2. model bases and case bases, and
3. workflow management systems.

Apparently, these systems differ in that they use different knowledge representation paradigms, and provide distinct tools for the acquisition, storage, maintenance, and retrieval of information, and implement either more passive (databases) or more active (cooperative knowledge bases) modes of behavior etc. However, during the last three to five years we have seen a number of successful attempts to achieve standardization which has demonstrated that very different types of software systems will be able to communicate, and even to cooperate, in the near future. This again will give rise to further enhance the capabilities of organizational memories by knowledge processing technology.

(2) Multiagent Systems – State of the Art

It is commonly agreed in Artificial Intelligence that the existence of a (mostly supposed: long term) memory is a necessary prerequisite for any type of intelligent skills such as learning, reflection, and rationality. We may expect that this also holds for single entities and organizational bodies. Thus, it is quite an interesting point that the question remains to be investigated whether multiagent systems would need any organizational memory and what would such a facility look like. Instead, most multiagent systems have only a short term memory for the single agents involved, without considering any memory function that stands for its own on the multiagent systems' level.

With respect to the organizational memory we stress that there is an important difference between the structure of a human organization (which has been designed top down, and which represents the – predefined –

division of labor), and the structure of a multiagent system which must be derived (more or less dynamically) from the individual competencies of the single agents involved. Thus, it is right so far that this structure *may* represent a subsequent division of labor (e.g. see (Gasser 1992)). However, as the agents in a multiagent system are autonomous, an agent may not agree to be involved in collaboration, even if she is the only one capable of solving a particular task. Thus, the structure of a multiagent system does not represent organizational knowledge concerning the *division* of labor but only the availability of individual competencies, and their distribution across the multiagent system.

(3) Design Issues

The design of an organizational memory for a multiagent system requires a decision to, *where* the respective organizational knowledge should be stored. Subsequently, some additional questions must be addressed. These involve the formal representation of (may be different types of) organizational knowledge, the creation (and maintenance) of indexes which support knowledge retrieval, and the design of knowledge access mechanisms including database-like transaction concepts in order to coordinate conflicting knowledge access operations. Finally, appropriate role concepts need to be developed in order to enable the system to update and maintain its own knowledge.

(4) Research Issues

As a direct consequence of not representing organizational memories, there is no real discussion on how multiagent systems can exhibit higher-level intelligent skills, such as learning or reflection. One may feel that this is particularly surprising since Distributed AI researchers widely agree that any multiagent system may also be interpreted as a single (complex) entity! Thus, it seems that there is still a great difference between the definition of intelligence in mainstream Artificial Intelligence and in Distributed AI which urgently needs to be resolved by future research.

Another important point concerns the maintenance of distributed knowledge bases, and the problem of knowledge base consistency. We may hope that the recently increased collaboration of the database community with researchers in AI and CSCW (for example, see the Cooperative and Intelligent Information Systems Initiative, (Jarke and Ellis 1993)) provides for developing transaction-like consistency-preserving mechanisms for distributed knowledge bases.

Finally, if one implements organizational memory within a multiagent system, this does not only affect the static and dynamic structure of the whole system. It also effects the design of role definitions, and of coordination mechanisms. Thus, global search processes will significantly change. This also gives rise to a number of new questions that haven't been addressed in the recent Distributed AI literature.

8.3.2 Organizational Cognition

(1) Organizational Theory

According to Matsuda, the collective cognition of an organization is essentially composed of four components (Matsuda 1992):

1. *Organizational Perception:* Environmental monitoring and self-monitoring by the organization.
2. *Organizational Comprehension:* This includes auto-evaluation in the environmental setting, evaluation of other organizations, and, in general, the evaluation of the environmental structure.
3. *Attention Focusing (Matsuda: Mastery Perception):* This is the "mind's eye" of an organization, namely the analytic eye for the relevant process, and the transcendental eye for the "unseen" opportunity.
4. *Generation of premises:* These are premises for decision making, i.e. they include both, value premises and factual premises.

Within this context the information processing activities of an enterprise need to be coordinated towards organizational aims and objectives. As the attention focusing capabilities are the real scarce resource of an organization (Blanning *et al.* 1992), it is of particular importance to identify and retrieve all information which is relevant to a problem at hand, and to integrate this information in order to develop towards a satisfactory solution. Especially for large organizations this has proven to be a nearly unsolvable challenge.

(2) Multiagent Systems – State of the Art

Distributed AI still lacks an operational description of what the notion of intelligence could mean to a *group* of interacting agents. There is no explanation of what cognition would mean for a multiagent system. If we apply it to the taxonomy of Matsuda we may feel that, up to now, Distributed AI has mainly concentrated on the ability of comprehension (provisionally defined as ability to analyze and interpret) and on the attention focusing capabilities of multiagent systems. Little work has been carried out on perception which, may not be so important for multiagent systems than for human organizations.

(3) Design Issues

Cognitive abilities are quite well suited to design role concepts and to assign these roles to agents. Depending on the requirements of the respective application one may start from comprehensive, or perceptive capabilities, or may primarily apply to the design of attention focusing capabilities of a multiagent system. By this we expect that multiagent systems might be better adapted to (or even embedded into) their current environment. This, in turn, could significantly improve the chance to implement productive multiagent systems applications, especially in domains like business, robotics, and computer-integrated manufacturing (see Chapter 10).

(4) Research Issues

From the perspective of future research we are convinced that primarily the perceptive abilities of a multiagent system should be addressed. This would also involve the question of how perceived data and information can be evaluated and interpreted internally, in such a way, that it transforms into the organizational knowledge of the multiagent system. We further believe that enhanced perceptive capabilities will significantly improve the self-adaptation capabilities of multiagent systems.

8.3.3 Self Organization, and Organizational Learning Skills

(1) Organizational Theory

Organizational learning refers to an organization's capability to identify and to store knowledge derived from both individual and organizational experiences, and to modify its own behavior according to feedback received from its environment (Teramoto 1992, Tsuchiya 1992). Thus, organizational learning supposes that an organization is able to control its behavior with respect to its own aims and objectives, to perform self monitoring activities, to filter out the relevant information from environmental scanning processes, and to adapt itself to changes in its social, economic, and political environment.

 Organizational learning is performed on three interacting levels. *Individual (human) learning* may contribute to an organization if it is not obstructed by organizational constraints, such as responsibilities or well established information processing procedures. On the *micro-organizational level* (the group level) the members of an organization negotiate and integrate their individual experiences in order to build up group level knowledge. The results of this (permanently evolving) process, i.e. whether the group performs better than the best of its members largely depend upon both the intra-group and the inter-group relationships within an organization. It is important to note that, to a large extent, micro-organizational learning evolves informally, i.e. not primarily determined by fixed organizational rules and procedures. *Macro-organizational learning* evolves on an organization's macro structure, i.e. its performance, successes and failures are largely determined by the structure of its inter-group relationships.

The ability of an organization to learn from individual knowledge and both individual and organizational experiences assumes that:

1. Knowledge to be learned is described in terms of a common ontology.
2. Conflict resolving mechanisms help to decide which knowledge shall be included into the body of organizational knowledge, and which knowledge shall be excluded from it.
3. Knowledge management tools are needed which guarantee, that organizational knowledge is accessible to (and will be accessed by) exactly those members of an organization who need it for doing their work.
4. Pieces of organizational knowledge must be related to each other by a network of relationships in order to provide for organizational reasoning. These are the basic mechanisms within an organization (such as forward or backward chaining in rule-based systems) from which more complex organizational problem solving procedures are created.

(2) Multiagent Systems – State of the Art

Quite similar to organizational theory, Distributed AI distinguishes between short term and long term organizational learning. While the former concerns organizational flexibility, the latter deals with the modification of organizational structures as a result of changes in the environment (Gasser 1992). The most important approaches work towards self-organization skills of multiagent systems (Corkhill 1982, Ishida 1992, Ishida *et al.* 1992, Sugawara and Lesser 1993). Within such work, most researchers are primarily interested in how those systems can be enabled to reorganize themselves in order to meet changing problems or dynamic environments.

However, until 1994 there has not been any significant research effort in Distributed AI addressing the issue of learning in multiagent systems. This situation, however, has changed with an IJCAI-95 workshop on "Adaptation and Learning in Multi-Agent Systems" (Weiß 1996, Weiß and Sen 1996). Since then, a respectable scientific discussion has evolved which lets us hope that this important gap in Distributed AI research will be closed soon.

(3) Design Issues

To implement organizational learning into a Distributed AI system a designer would need to create agents which are responsible for meta-level capabilities such as self-monitoring and self-control. One further needs to develop (explicit, or heuristic) reorganization strategies, and the respective control and coordination knowledge. Two major questions need to be addressed:

1. *What kind of knowledge can, and shall, be learned on the level of the multia-*

gent system? The most important uses are: successes and failures in the past, the usefulness of different pieces of knowledge with respect to different tasks and situations, the competencies and accountability of other agents in the system, and the relationships between the multi-agent system and its environment etc.

2. *What type of learning strategies need to be developed?* We may divide between learning through interaction and learning through introspection, and between inductive and deductive learning.

(4) Research Issues

In organizational theory the distinction between individuals, (formal and informal) groups, and organizations is fundamental for the description and analysis of processes of organizational learning. Up to now, there are no similar three-level architectures available in multiagent systems. However, we are convinced that the concept of partial global planning (Durfee and Lesser 1987), which divides between nodes, acquaintances, and the whole multiagent organization may provide a platform from which one can start to work towards a similar static and dynamic architecture. Further, if we compare the discussion on learning in mainstream Artificial Intelligence and Distributed AI it seems that the body of knowledge on learning within Distributed AI still remains to be integrated within the knowledge already available in mainstream Artificial Intelligence.

8.3.4 Interactions between Multiagent Systems and their Environment

(1) Organizational Theory

Organizational communication refers to the total amount of exchange of data, information and knowledge which evolves among the human and machine-based actors within an organization and between an organization and its environment. Individual and organizational communication differ in that the latter performs as a set of unobservable processes in the human brain only, while the former occurs as observable interactions among machines, humans, groups and divisions of an organization, using classical communication structures such as sender, receiver, messages, and channels (Matsuda 1988a, 1992).

Dynamic environments require an organization to permanently monitor its environment, to filter and assess the informations received, and to distribute the results of this perceptive activity to other members of the organization (Hammer and Champy 1991). Thus, organizational communication is closely related to the status (and its changes over time) of the organizational environment. On the other hand, organizations are supposed to inform their environment about past and future activities, about their internal status (e.g. accounting, profits and losses etc.). This, in turn requires them to represent and to store the respective knowledge in such a way that it can be retrieved and accessed quite easily at any time in the future.

(2) Multiagent Systems – State of the Art

Research in Distributed AI mainly addresses the interactions between the agents of a multiagent system (some examples are included in (Bond and Gasser 1988)). However, very little work has addressed the issue of communication between a multiagent system and its environment. A well known example is the unsolved problem of designing user interfaces for cooperative problem solvers. Another point is that, in general, a multiagent system can be viewed as a community of interacting agents, or as a single (complex) entity, depending on the current focus of interest. However, from the perspective of communication between a multiagent system and its environment only the former of these two views is supported.

It may be expected that the integration of multiagent systems into other disciplines such as Computer Supported Cooperative Work (CSCW) (see Chapter 6), intelligent user agents (personal assistants) and decision support systems may help to address this issue.

(3) Design Issues

First of all, any interactions between a multiagent system and its environment suppose the availability of a canonical interaction language (see Chapter 11). Such an interaction language needs to provide data and knowledge communication facilities, explanation facilities, and fine-grained dialogue management support. Further, if the user of the system is a human expert, he or she might wish to be actively involved in the global reasoning process. Thus, it becomes evident that we need to develop a "well-shaped" role concept for the multiagent system which also needs to be able to assign roles to the actors in the environment of the multiagent system.

(4) Research Issues

The ability of a multiagent system to effectively communicate with its environment is one of the most important issues for developing successful applications. This is particularly true for any applications that aim to support human experts' intellectual work. We can see today that research on interaction architectures and languages already involve standardization issues. Two prominent examples are the CORBA standard of the Object Management Group, and the Knowledge Sharing Effort which has been launched by DARPA in 1991. It has been argued that an integration of the research, development and standardization efforts in the related fields of information technology will significantly increase technological competitiveness (Davidow and Malone 1992, Guilfoyle and Warner 1994, Kirn 1995, Petrie Jr 1992, Warnecke 1993).

8.3.5 Organizational Reasoning

(1) Organizational Theory

Organizational reasoning does not only include organizational problem solving, it also involves strategies such as problem avoidance, problem evasion, and problem encapsulation (Matsuda 1992). Typically, organizational reasoning applies to one of the following basic strategies:

1. *Process-orientated reasoning* is performed on the bases of predefined organizational workflows and well established algorithms etc.
2. *Case-based reasoning* tackles a problem by accessing a solution that has proven useful for a previously solved similar problem.
3. *Heuristic reasoning* is used to approach a problem where the necessary information is not available, uncertain, or possibly false.
4. *Explorative reasoning* includes search strategies (goal driven, data driven), trial-and-error concepts, and creativity generating methods such as brainstorming, scenario technique, and delphi, etc.
5. *Structural reasoning (adaptation)* evolves whenever an organization modifies its internal structure in order to operate better with (identified or anticipated) changes in its environment.

Organizational problem solving supposes a set of basic tools such as problem analysis and the selection of critical success factors, the exploration and identification of well suited organizational competencies and resources, the processes of coordinating these resources with respect to the problem at hand, and the ability to focus the attention on the most relevant processes at a time, is to name a few.

Thus, it is commonly agreed in organizational theory that the ability to design efficient organizational information processing and reasoning capabilities is one of the key characteristics of successful enterprises.

(2) Multiagent Systems – State of the Art

Reasoning processes within a multiagent system can be studied from two different perspectives. The external perspective considers the multiagent system as a single entity, and it gives descriptions of how the system behaves in its environment. In contrast, the internal view focuses on the description and analysis of the internal processes. This perspective represents the mainstream of work on multiagent reasoning processes (Singh 1990b, Stephens and Merx 1989). As a result, we have available today a large body of knowledge on cooperation strategies (Durfee *et al.* 1987), coordination mechanisms (e.g. see Fickas and Helm 1991, Malone 1987, Malone and Crowston 1993, v. Martial 1992, Smith 1979), conflict resolving mechanisms, concepts for modeling intentions and commitment (e.g. see Cohen and Levesque 1987a, Cohen and Levesque 1987b, Jennings and Mamdani 1992, Jennings 1992, Singh 1990a) and, for example, dependency relationships between different agents of a Distributed AI system. However, on the other hand we still lack a sufficient understanding of *how* the design and processing of internal procedures relates to the behavior of the whole system. It is important to realize that this question is of prior importance for any decisions within an enterprise that involve investing money into the development of a Distributed AI system.

(3) Design Issues

From the above considerations we learn that whenever we design a multiagent system we should carefully think about adding an organizational layer to the architecture of the system (Kirn 1994). This organizational layer should include at least the organizational knowledge, the set of available problem solving strategies and the respective mechanisms to control and monitor cooperative processes within the multiagent system. We also see that again this asks for the development of appropriate role concepts. In other words: step by step we discover that role concepts are of prior importance for the design of fine-grained internal structures of multiagent systems. (It should be noted, that the organizational layer need not necessarily be a centralized resource within the system, it can also be decentralized.)

(4) Research Issues

This subsection has demonstrated the importance of an organizational layer together with the respective role concepts for the design and, as one may want to add, for the expected commercial success of multiagent systems. While the demand for an organizational layer is new in multiagent systems research, significant research has already been done (unfortunately, in splendid isolation) on the development of role concepts. But we still lack an integrated, holistic approach to designing an overall model of roles in multiagent systems in order to provide for a systematic, application-driven design and implementation of future Distributed AI systems.

8.4 The Contribution of Distributed AI to the Intelligence of Computerized Enterprises

There is already a large body of literature originating from both, the field of organizational research and management science and also from the community of Distributed AI which argues that a lot of business and organizational problems could be solved quite naturally through a multiagent system approach. Some prominent examples are the virtual enterprise (Davidow and Malone 1992) and the "fractalization" of organizations (Warnecke 1993), the modeling and simulation of enterprises (Fox 1981), the efforts towards an integrated theory of coordination (Malone 1987), support of business processes and workflows (Malone *et al.* 1993), and enterprise integration (Petrie Jr 1992). As this shows, the same holds for some of the components of Organizational Intelligence.

Distributed AI offers interesting advantages to organizational designers who aim to improve the intelligence of their organizations, and who agree to apply agent-oriented information technology. On a more abstract level we may primarily argue that Distributed AI provides technical facilities (coordination protocols) that support interactions among a set of information servers. Secondly, it contributes knowledge discovery tools assisting users to identify, select and access information relevant to their task at hand. Thirdly, many applications require the ability to select data from different nodes of a network and to combine them with respect to a particular "problem profile" (for instance, a set of customer preferences). We will expand on the above discussion in more detail below.

With regard to *organizational memory* we feel that, at the moment, Distributed AI may have little to contribute. However, this may change in future, for example, if one starts to integrate results from case-based reasoning.

Distributed AI can benefit *organizational cognition* in that it provides easy-to-use knowledge exchange facilities and collective reasoning capabilities. This involves the question of how to integrate problem solving at the human level (for example, see Newell 1982) with problem solving procedures at the machine level, or more precisely: Distributed AI technology can be used only if it does not bless the organizational procedures and dependencies that are involved. The reader will remember that this point was the motivation behind our notion of "organizational multiagent systems".

Distributed AI methods can also contribute to *organizational learning* on both the micro-organizational and on the macro-organizational level (Nunamaker *et al.* 1988, Teramoto 1992, Tsuchiya 1992, Yamamoto *et al.* 1992). While, primarily, the latter may be supported by the instantiation and maintenance of inter-group relationships, the former may be supported by single- and multistage negotiation, by the instantiation and maintenance of intra-group relationships, and by the availability of sophisticated conflict resolving mechanisms (see also the contribution of Unland and Kirn in this book).

Further, we would like to stress that computerizing an organization also effects the performance of organizational learning. As far as humans are considered individual learning can be supported by local "personal assistants". Thus, organizational learning within a group of software agents may also contribute to the individual learning of the human users. As organizational learning among software agents is part of (and controlled by) those organizational processes that have been established formally, the transfer of the knowledge back to humans establishes a kind of individual learning which is "supervised" by organizational rules and procedures. This is a major issue also within the new of field of Human–Computer-Teams (Kirn 1995).

Typically, Distributed AI systems exhibit a more or less decentralized organizational structure. Thus, they can also contribute a great deal to *organizational communication*. This holds for conventional, human-centered organizations, but its effectiveness is directly related to the degree of computerization of the enterprise (Ginsberg 1987, Numaoka 1991). Possible low-level communication support services may include retrieval and identification of addresses, knowledge-based intra- and inter-network communication management (for instance, routing), and intelligent communication control facilities. On a semantically higher level, these services include amongst others, group-level information filtering, appointment system applications, tools for distributed interpretation, context modeling, knowledge discovery by which the coherence of interactive activities can be improved. As some of these services can also be provided by conventional software, others would benefit a lot more from Distributed AI methods (for example, knowledge discovery).

With regard to *organizational reasoning*, Distributed AI provides several quite useful tools whenever an organizational problem requires the involvement of distributed expertise, to focus the attention of distinct organizational units on a particular task, or if distributed interpretations are to be supported (for example, see (Ginsberg 1987, Guilfoyle and Warner 1994, Kirn 1995, Kirn *et al.* 1992). All these problems assume efficient coordination by which the various types of unilateral or bilateral dependencies among different tasks, activities, objects, and actors can be detected and managed. We feel that coordination techniques of Distributed AI are particularly well suited in all cases where the system support of the coordination task is required, and workflow management technology is too rigid.

Chapter 9

Organizational Intelligence and Negotiation Based DAI Systems – Theoretical Foundations and Experimental Results

Rainer Unland and Stefan Kirn

9.1 Introduction

Today's organizations are faced with rapidly changing markets, global competition, decreasing cycles of technological innovations, world wide (and just in time) availability of information, and dramatic changes in their cultural, social, and political environments. In such highly dynamic environments, the expertise of many agents, both computational and human, needs to be combined and coordinated, in order to achieve effective and informed decision making. It is our belief that the organization of the twenty first century will not solely take account of the human factors, but will be comprised of human and computational agents and recognized as organizations within their own right. Two perspectives arise from such scenarios: On the one hand, organizational theory needs to much more explicitly incorporate these new computer-based data and information processing tools into its body of knowledge and research. This, in turn, requires computational technologies to be appropriate and amenable to assimilation into the organization.

Recently, different computer-based approaches were analyzed and compared with one another (cf. Kirn 1994, Syring and Hasenkamp 1993) with respect to their ability to support information and knowledge processing activities between humans and computers in cooperative, networked organizations. While the evaluation of (Syring and Hasenkamp 1993) is on a more general level, (Kirn 1994) especially investigates the capability of different computer-based approaches to meet the strong demands of organizational intelligence. All investigations came to the conclusion that DAI offers by far the most promising potential. However, although these results are rather encouraging they also showed that DAI techniques have some shortcomings.

Among others, the integration with the underlying human-centered organization is an open question. However, organizational multiagent systems have to actively contribute to the "intellectual" capabilities of an organization and therefore have to support organizational features such as organizational cognition, organizational memory and learning, organizational problem solving, and organizational communication skills.

Within this context the chapter starts with a brief introduction to organizational intelligence as defined by Matsuda (Section 2) (see also Chapter 8). It will be shown that organizational process intelligence especially relies on an adequate support of intellectual organizational capabilities such as organizational cognition, communication, problem solving, memory, and learning. While the first three features are relatively well covered by DAI the latter two are only covered on a rather rudimentary level. In this chapter we will concentrate on negotiation based multiagent systems, more precisely, on the contract net approach. Section 3 will briefly introduce this technique and present a solution for an extension of this approach by organizational memory and learning capabilities. In Section 4 we will introduce a concrete scenario (the game "Scotland Yard") and show what organizational memory and learning capabilities mean within this scenario. In Section 5 we will present the results of an experimental analysis and evaluation of the basic contract net approach and its extended version. It will be shown, that the increased "intellectual" capabilities of the extended contract net will substantially contribute to the performance as well as the quality of solution processes. Finally, Section 6 will conclude this chapter.

9.2 Theoretical Foundations

As a theoretical concept Matsuda's OI approach is of major importance in organization theory. He calls OI the "collective intellectual capability of an organization [...] in handling its problems" (Matsuda 1992). This points to an integration of human and machine problem solving, for this approach is well suited for the above demands. In this section we will briefly introduce Matsuda's approach of OI and the capability of learning from the point of view of organization theory.

9.2.1 Matsuda's OI Approach – a Brief Introduction

Following Matsuda's approach *organizational intelligence (OI)* can be interpreted as the entire "intellectual" manpower of an organization and, therefore, describes the collective problem solving capability of an organization. More specifically, OI consists of the totality of ordered information, experiences, knowledge and understanding. OI integrates the existing human and machine intelligence of an organization. *Machine intelligence* means the computer-based information and knowledge processing capability of an organization. OI can be viewed from two mutually dependent viewpoints: organizational intelligence as a (dynamic) process (*process intelligence*) and organizational intelligence as a (static) product (*product intelligence*).

Organizational product intelligence is the totality of all structured, synthesized and goal-directed information. It is generated when the information systems of an organization increases its problem solving capability. Three levels of product intelligence can be distinguished: (1) *data* (physical in the nature and formal in its character), (2) *information* (purposeful sort concerning the goals of an organization) and (3) *intelligence* (that is to say actively used information). In order to achieve product intelligence, general rules have to be developed which permit the design of information systems in the OI sense.

Organizational process intelligence is the interactive, aggregative, and coordinative complex of human and machine intelligence within an organization. This implies that any (human and machine) intelligence is orientated towards workflows (processes). *Interaction* takes place not only between human and human but also between human and machine as well as machine and machine. Aggregation of intelligence takes place hierarchically: on the lowest level the knowledge of individual members of an organization is gathered. The next level is the level of groups, while the final one is the level of the organization as a whole. *Coordination* is of central importance, since it refers to both the execution of interactions and the aggregation processes.

Matsuda (1992) divides Organizational Process Intelligence into five components: (1) Organizational Cognition, (2) Organizational Memory, (3) Organizational Learning, (4) Organizational Communication, and (5) Organizational Reasoning. These five sub-processes can provide a set of powerful tools to analyze and improve organizational decision making processes (details are presented by Kirn, Chapter 8 in this book).

9.2.2 The Capability to Learn from the Point of View of Organization Theory

As shown in other research work (Bond and Gasser 1988, Müller and Wittig 1993, Kirn and Unland 1994), multiagent systems (MAS) are well suited to solve complex and interdisciplinary problems in a flexible and autonomous way. From the features of OI discussed above they are especially strong in communication, cognition and inference. Not yet well examined are the questions, of how multiagent systems behave with respect to global memory and learning capability. This will be examined in this chapter with respect to the contract net approach. We will start with a brief introduction into the foundations of organizational learning capability.

The *learning capability* of an organization depends on the individual capabilities of its members as well as on the forms of organizational connection between these members. The definition of the following learning concept originates from Foppa (Foppa 1968). It will be taken as the basis for the further studies: "In the end the question in learning processes [...] is always, how an organism can adapt to the various requirements of its environment. However, the process of adaptability cannot be observed directly as it is possible with the "memory". We, therefore, do not observe the actual learning progress, but behavior and its change. If someone repeatedly performs or omits something in a certain situation, that he omitted or performed in similar situations in the past, or if he reacts quicker or more safely, we will call this a learning process."

With this definition in mind, organizational learning can be observed on three levels.

1. The knowledge of an organization can be improved by individual learning of its members. However, individual learning does not automatically contribute to organizational learning. Duncan and Weiss (Duncan and Weiss 1979) defined three demands, that must be met to make individual learning valuable for an organization:

- Organizational knowledge must be communicable; i.e. it must be expressed in terms that can be understood by the other members of the organization.
- It must also meet with general approval. The members of the organization must accept it as useful knowledge.
- Finally, knowledge must be expressible in if-then relations. The connection of actions and its effects are mandatory for the creation of coordinated actions.

2. Learning within groups (group processes) constitutes the next level. Groups form the micro social unit for organizational learning. They integrate the existing experiences and capabilities of learning of its individual members. Whether a group behaves as efficiently as the best of its members or, to mention another extreme, even better than the sum of the capabilities of its members, depends both on the interconnections within the group and between the groups of the entire organization.

3. The macro structure constitutes the core of organizational learning. While the micro structure describes the interconnections within groups the macro structure concentrates on the interconnections between the groups of an organization. It is responsible for the success of the transformation process from individual and micro social learning to organizational learning.

The addressed levels will be analyzed in more detail in the next sections.

9.2.2.1 Individual Learning

Individual learning is the simplest form of organizational learning. It means that an organization profits from the acquisition of new knowledge by its members if this new knowledge is exploited in the sense of the organization. Individual learning can be subdivided into adaptive and innovative learning. *Adaptive learning* means to learn by imitating observed ways of acting. *Innovative learning* means to learn by models and simulations. However, it can only be applied if the characteristics and features of the model can be presented by symbols. With the help of models frameworks for future behavior can be designed and rehearsed, resulting in an innovative way of acting.

There are a number of (psychological) learning theories in the field of individual learning which we do not want to discuss here. The interested reader is referred, e.g. to Reber (Reber 1989) for a summarized presentation.

9.2.2.2 Micro Organizational Learning

Micro organizational learning describes the next level and means learning on the level of groups. The capabilities and the knowledge of individuals can be exploited to treat and solve more complex problems which exceed the manpower of individuals. The efficiency, respectively, inefficiency of the teamwork essentially depends on group standards like confidence, openness, conformity and antagonism. By a proper choice of the concept of leadership positive influences can be strengthened.

In economic organization theory such social psychological features are second rate. Coordination between the group members and the organization as a whole is of more importance.

9.2.2.3 Macro Organizational Learning

Each organization possesses structural characteristics which were introduced to increase the learning capability of an organization. In this chapter we will only refer to the well established structures of organization theory, e.g. functional, self-constrained, project orientated and matrix structures (Daft and Steers 1986, Khandwalla 1977, Gareis 1991).

The problematic nature of macro structures is caused by the opposite tasks of "distribution of labor" and "coordination of labor". On the one hand, tasks must be standardized to achieve a simplification of the process sequences. On the other hand there must be a continuous development, from which standardized behavior patterns cannot be excluded. Therefore, there will always be tasks that differ from existing patterns and have to be treated individually. On the adaptive level, macro organizational learning is described by the capability of an organization to develop simple, standardized behavior patterns on the level of macro structures. Innovative learning means, for example, the calculated unlearning of obsolete behavior patterns. Knowledge and behavior, prior assumed to be correct, can prove wrong or at least obsolete and, therefore, is no longer of any relevance.

By a change of the macro structure organizational (un)learning processes can be stimulated. Of course both necessary factors – time and resources – must be available because learning processes need both to be able to safely move from one solid state to another.

9.3 Extension of Contract Net-Based Systems by OI Components

Cooperative problem solving is divided into the stages of problem decomposition and distribution, solving of the subproblems and the answer synthesis. If the allocation of the problem happens through negotiations between agents, this is called a negotiation-based multiagent system. The best known representative of those systems is the contract net approach (Smith 1980, Smith and Davis 1981, Davis and Smith 1983). Here the problem is decomposed by a specific agent (the manager) in independent subtasks. These subtasks will be announced for solving to other agents. If an agent believes he can solve an announced subproblem, he sends a bid to the announcing agent. Based on the information in the bids, the manager selects the best suited agents and sends an award message to them.

Stephens and Merx (Stephens and Merx 1989) summarize the performance results of four methods of solution with respect to six different scenarios of the pursuit problem[1]. One of the results of their research work was that negotiation-based systems are superior to autonomous agents. So far no studies have been made with respect to the question, in which way contract net systems are able to learn and to store the learnt things beyond the rudimentary individual level as a whole or at least in parts (learning on the micro and macro level of organizations). This question will be investigated in the following.

Even a brief analysis of the contract net approach shows that its strengths are "flexibility/self organization" and "problem inference". Significant deficits can be found in the areas of "memory" and "learning" capability. An overall memory is neither at hand nor intended. The learning capability suffers enormously by this lack.

Therefore, the next section presents a way of how to extend the contract

---

1. The "pursuit problem" has been discussed by various researchers for several times, see e.g. Bende *et al.* 1988, Gasser and Rouquette 1988, Korf 1992, Stephens and Merx 1989 & 1989, Levy 1991

net approach by an organizational memory.

Figure 9.1 shows a scenario with five agents. The dashed lines indicate the given possibilities for negotiation in the contract net. In the local databases the agents' individual knowledge is stored. To make this individual knowledge useful for the organization, that is to say to store knowledge on the group or organizational level, new structures are necessary. It is proposed to design an organizational memory for the entire MAS or for several groups of agents. The organizational memory can be implemented as an additional "memory agent" (see Figure 9.1). This agent can either be addressed by new message types which have to be introduced or, in the simplest case, the message types "request" and "information", as defined in the contract net protocol (Smith 1980), can be used. In a system like the one in Figure 9.1 organizational learning can be established on the individual level. Through the (semi-) autonomy of the agents each one can have local knowledge, which he does not share with the rest of the system (organization). The knowledge that is made available for the organization is stored in the organizational memory. How the data are stored and how many agents share a common organizational memory is transparent to the individual agents.

To realize the level of micro- and macro-organizational learning within the contract net, a simple memory agent will no longer be sufficient. As mentioned above, among other things the point for micro organizational

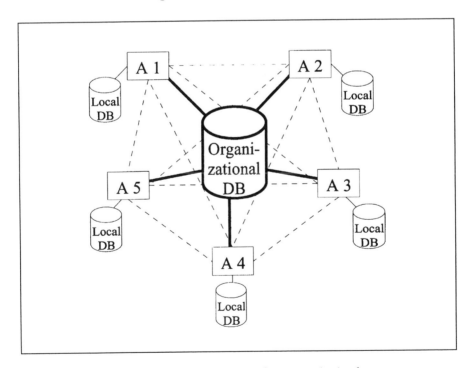

Figure 9.1   Extension of the contract net by an organizational memory

learning is to choose the best suited concept in a given situation. This does
not, or only on a rudimentary basis, exist in the contract net. There is indeed
a message type called "directed award", which was added to the protocol to
avoid the negotiation process by assigning a task directly. To handle fuzzy,
uncertain, non-monotonous knowledge etc. further extension must be made.
Figure 9.2 shows the architecture we propose.

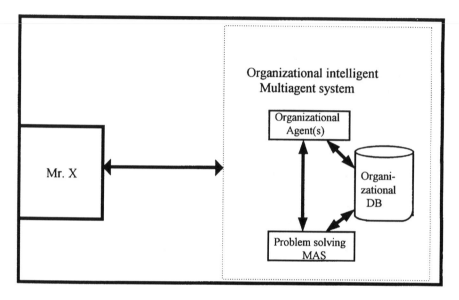

Figure 9.2   Extended multi agent architecture

The original MAS will be extended by a second level, the level of the so-
called organizational agents. This organizational MAS is responsible for finding the coordination strategy best suited for the given situation and for the
control of its realization within the problem solving MAS.

Both multiagent systems have access to the organizational memory (via
the memory agent(s)) so that organizational learning on the individual level
can take place without incorporation of the organizational MAS.
Negotiations take place on two different levels. On the problem solving level
there is no change at all, whereas on the organizational level the strategy for
the solution of the problem is regulated.

The advantages of the chosen architecture are:

● Neither the failure of the organizational memory nor that of the organizational MAS leads to a breakdown of the problem solving MAS
  because the negotiation mechanisms are still available.

- Because of the strict separation of the organizational extensions from the basic system, additional organizational and memory agents can be added later without any problem.
- Existing multiagent systems can be extended with less effort than if the organizational capabilities have to be implemented in each (problem solving) agent. In addition, the overall system has less redundancy.

Currently there is no universally valid answer to the question of how many organizational agents will be needed and how they must be conceived in respect to macro organizational learning, for example. This will be one of the subjects of our future research work. In this context it seems to be interesting to include several organizational agents, which prefer different coordination strategies. These organizational agents would have to decide during a negotiation process, which strategy fits best in the concrete situation.

9.4 Realization in a Scenario

9.4.1 Description of the Scenario

In the following sections the extended contract net, as introduced in Chapter 3, will be examined by a concrete scenario. The main question in this context is, how the efficiency and performance of such a system can be improved by adopting organizational memory and learning.

The implemented scenario is based on the game "Scotland Yard". A group of five agents tries to catch a runaway (called Mr. X) in a given number of moves. A simplified map of London with 199 fields is the playing board. The agents can move by taxi, bus or subway from one field to another, whereby the availability and radius of the different means of conveyance differ from one another (there are, for example, only 14 fields with a connection to the subway). Additional ferryboat connections can only be used by Mr. X. After each of his moves Mr. X has to announce, which method of conveyance he used. After several (individually regulated) moves during the game he has to tell on which field he is. The purpose of the game can only be achieved by a coordinated behavior of the agents.

9.4.2 The Basic Structure of the System

Two scenarios were implemented. One nonlearning reference scenario and the proper OI scenario, in which the concepts of Chapter 3 have been implemented.

The implementation of Mr. X is the same in both scenarios. The multiagent system (MAS) of the nonlearning scenario has been extended within the OI scenario in such a way, that the concept of OI could be realized. The organizational MAS described in the previous chapter consists of exactly one agent who also takes on the function of the organizational memory simultaneously.

9.4.2.1 Implementation of Mr. X

Concerning the implementation of Mr. X it should be remarked that he behaves in a deterministic way. He will always make the same decision in the same situation. This is important for the learning of the MAS and will be assumed in the following sections.

9.4.2.2 Implementation of the Agent System

9.4.2.2.1 The Negotiation Process in the Problem Solving System The agents' negotiation process will be initiated, when one gets the information of Mr. X's last move. This agent, therefore, becomes the manager of the move and calls on his combatants to give him a list of their possible moves. The specific agent should sort this list in such a way, that his favored move is at the top of the list. Based on these lists the manager computes the best position for all agents. The resulting moves are finally passed to the specific agents. In addition Mr. X. will be informed about the agents' new position.

The negotiation mechanism can be found in both the learning and the nonlearning system. In the former it will only appear, if the situation is unknown to the system. In this case the move has to be negotiated, but then the manager is an organizational agent.

9.4.2.2.2 Learning Within the Scenario Within the (OI) scenario learning can be manifested on three levels. On the simplest level there is the learning of the single agents (*individual learning*), that is, an agent can act faster, although he only has the same information. This means for example, that an agent does not need any longer to compute a proposal, but can refer to a prior stored one. The time of his reaction (defined as the difference between the moments of the request and the answer) will on average decrease significantly (point (2) of the learning concept).

Learning on the level of the system is reflected by changing coordination mechanisms (*micro organizational learning*). In this scenario the result of a learning process is, that, if the global state of the system is known, the allocation of the moves to be executed can be made directly, that is without the collection of the proposals.

In this scenario *macro organizational learning* means the calculated unlearning of former reactions to a specific state of the system. The space to be searched, that is to say the fields, on which Mr. X. could be, can for example, be reduced by examining two successive states. The resulting new information can cause the system to deviate from the reaction that was assumed to be "optimal" up to that time.

Example:

Table 9.1a   Hypothetical part of the organizational memory

No. of move	Position of the agents	Possible position of Mr. X	Flag
i	63,78,82,109,131	64,80,81,98,112,114,125	NF
i+1	64,79,81,110,125	not interesting in this context	NF

The data in this example are based on a real part of the playing board.

The abbreviation "NF" in the column "Flag" indicates, that Mr. X was **not** **found** in the states i and i+1. By the choice of moves, that led to state i+1, Mr. X was not found.

This is why the following can be deduced with the help of proper algorithms.

Table 9.1b   Hypothetical part of the organizational memory

No. of move	Position of the agents	Possible position of Mr. X	Flag
i	63,78,82,109,131	64,80,81,98,112,114,125 (limited to 80, 98, 112, 114)	NF
i+1	80,79,101,110,114	not interesting in this context	NF

The change in the agents' behavior can be explained by the failure of the initial version. If the same state of the game is reached again and Mr. X is not found with the agents' new position the space to search can be deduced to two fields (98 and 112).

The following section shows, how the negotiation mechanism works when organizational memory and learning are included in the scenario.

9.4.3   Schematical Run of a Move in the OI Scenario

Figure 9.3 shows the run of a move in our scenario. The agent who receives the information of Mr. X's move creates a *OI task* message which activates the organizational agent. Thereby he becomes the manager of the move. For the choice of the coordination strategy he refers to the organizational memory. If he finds data that are suitable for the current situation the negotiation process can be dropped and the tasks will be directly allocated to the agents. Otherwise the organizational agent initiates the negotiation process.

The boxes with the thick border represent the involved agents, respectively, Mr. X. Boxes with a thin border indicate the actions to be executed by the organizational agent.

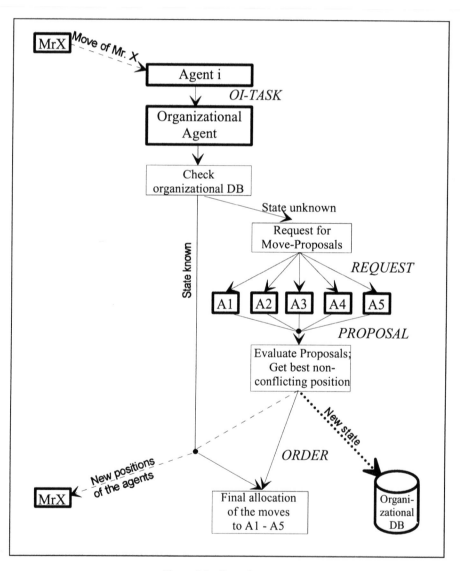

Figure 9.3   Run of a move

9.5 Presentation and Evaluation of the Results

Based on the scenario mentioned above, this chapter will illustrate on how far an extended contract net (eCN) that is extended by organizational memory and learning ability offers a faster and/or improved solution as opposed to the conventional contract net (CN) without learning capability.

Preliminary remarks:

The following considerations on complexity clearly show that the series of tests can cover only a small range of possibilities.

- Starting positions:

According to the rules of the game, there are 20 potential starting fields for the agents and Mr. X. When the possible starting conditions are calculated, $\binom{20}{4}$ = 38.760 different positions are obtained

- Size of state space:

When trying to store in the organizational memory all states of the game, when Mr. X is visible on the board, approximately $8*10^{10}$ records are obtained. Adding those situations when Mr. X is invisible and could stay on exactly two fields, the order of magnitude of $4,6*10^{13}$ records is already achieved. These numbers clarify already that it is impossible to store all of possible states of even such a small scenario in the organizational memory. Instead it is only possible to manage a small part efficiently.

Due to the large amount of possible starting situations, a clever selection of similar positions had to be made to guarantee that the agents could meet with already known system states during the game. This method can be justified considering the fact that generally the space to search in real organizations is definitely smaller. Several series of tests were tried, thereby slightly changing the game parameters (e.g. different number of moves after which Mr. X must reveal himself). Since all series of tests principally led to the same results, only one series of tests will be presented in detail and analyzed in the following. Starting with a system with an empty organizational memory, from a basic set of 50 different starting positions 30 were arbitrarily chosen and played consecutively. The games were not completed, but finished after a fixed number of moves. In the system with memory, new game constellations were stored so that the system became "more intelligent" with increasing numbers of games. It should be mentioned that due to the enormously high number of possible game constellations the organizational memory in our series of tests has always shown a linear increase.

9.5.1 Comparison Conventional ↔ Extended Contract Net

Figure 9.4 shows a comparison of the performance of the eCN with the CN. For this, the moves in the eCN were classified in two categories and the average determined for each category. In the Best Case, the move is already contained in the organizational memory and must, therefore, not be negotiated. The Worst Case means that the move must be negotiated. The Average Case indicates the average time needed to decide a move in the eCN. The dashed line marks how long the negotiation of a move would have taken in average for the CN. The graphic shows that the gain in time for a move that must not be negotiated is considerable. For the measured data, the factor lies at almost 7 (for other series, it nearly approached factor 10). However, despite of favorably chosen starting positions, not even every 12th move was already stored in the organizational memory. For this reason, the average time per move is only about 10% lower than the time needed for negotiated moves. Through the extreme examples "Best Case" and "Worst Case" and the very small organizational memory in the test it is to be expected that the efficiency gains of the eCN can be still increased in further test runs. This holds particularly true, since – owing to the fixed number of moves – our test scenario does not consider the fact that the eCN has the ability to learn and will therefore select increasingly more favorable moves in the course of the time, increasing the probability that Mr. X is to be caught considerably quicker.

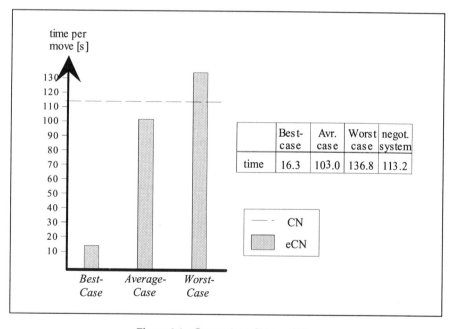

Figure 9.4   Comparison CN ↔ eCN

Furthermore, Figure 9.4 informs about the possible potential of efficiency gains of the eCN compared to the CN. If all moves were already stored in the organizational memory, the "best case" would become the normal case. According to the graphical representation, an efficiency increase by factor 7 would thus become possible. The following analysis, however, shows that this statement should be made with care.

9.5.2 Size of Organizational Memory

Figure 9.5 reflects an analysis on the relation time per move and the size of the organizational memory. This relation is first characterized by clear efficiency gains (shortening of time per move) and a simultaneous increase of the organizational memory (medium gray area). These gains quickly decrease in the light gray area and become zero at the intersection of the light gray and dark gray area of the relation. The dark-gray area is finally characterized by an increasing organizational memory and a simultaneous decrease in efficiency.

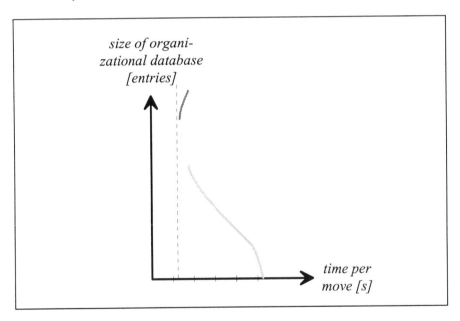

Figure 9.5 Time per move in dependence of the size of the organizational memory

The decrease in efficiency and its final reversion into the negative are caused by the overhead for searching the organizational memory. From a certain size the time needed for searching a position is greater than the time saved. By means of the potential order of magnitude of the organizational memory, which was calculated in the preliminary remarks of this chapter, it can be understood that these are no irrelevant assumptions.

9.5.3 Time Needed for Negotiated Moves

Figure 9.6 shows the range of deviation for the time needed for negotiated moves in the eCN scenario. For representing the deviation range, 10 equidistant intervals with length 15 and one open interval (length of move > 150 s) were selected and the number of moves, which fall in these intervals, were marked.

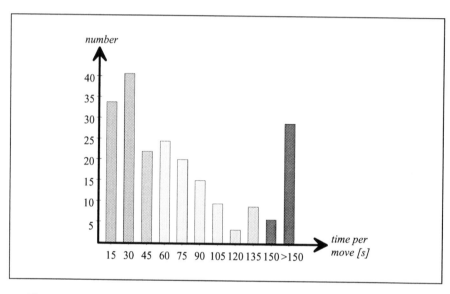

Figure 9.6   Range of deviation for the time needed for negotiated moves in the eCN

It can be deduced from the graphic that there are considerable time differences between moves already stored in the organizational memory and moves which have to be first negotiated. The following causes can be responsible:

1. Unsuccessful search in the organizational memory
Since only after comparison with all data of the organizational memory it has been settled that the searched state is not stored (negative decision), it can be assumed that unsuccessful searching in the organizational memory takes twice as long on average as in the case of a positive decision, provided that the search is linear (as is the case in our scenario).

2. The negotiating mechanism

The time needed for negotiation may be subdivided into time consumed for communication and into time that each agent needs for calculating his proposal. The communication time of the agents for exchanging the order and the resulting data may be neglected due to the software architecture. The time which each agent needs for drawing up his proposal list is of greater interest. This time, in turn, is dependent on the agent's actual position (how many possible successive fields exist?), the number of possible fields of Mr. X and on the distance between his successive fields and the positions of Mr. X. The time required increases in proportion to the number of possible successive positions of Mr. X.

3. Elimination of conflicts

Elimination of conflicts is a factor that is of high importance. A conflict occurs if at least two agents indicate the same field they both want to move to. By eliminating this conflict, new conflicts can arise so that great efforts to eliminate them may be required. The following example illustrates this situation:

Example:

Two starting positions are given.

No.	*Starting position of the agents*	*Position of Mr. X*
1	10, 50, 76, 79, 182	196
2	5, 6, 7, 16, 30	196

For those positions results:

No.	*Number of moves to be checked*	*Time needed*
1	20	54
2	11	78

Although for the first starting position almost twice as many successive fields have to be checked, the time needed amounts to only two-thirds of that of starting position 2. This is due to the fact that starting position 1 is free of conflicts, whereas for starting position 2 many conflicts have to be solved first.

The above considerations suggest a classification of the negotiated moves into three categories. The first category (medium gray) is characterized by a conflict-free position and only few possible fields for Mr. X. In the second category (light gray), either conflicts occur or the number of possible fields for Mr. X is relatively high. The last category (dark-gray) combines both negative properties.

On the whole, the graphic depicts that a really "intelligent" system should not store all game constellations, but only those which at least do not belong to the medium gray category. Thus it is guaranteed that on the one hand, the memory does not increase too much, and on the other hand, in case of a hit a profit as high as possible is obtained.

9.6 Conclusion

This chapter has outlined that a contract net can be extended by organizational memory and learning capabilities in a way that meets the high requirements of computer-aided systems to a high degree. The simulations performed with the help of a game scenario have shown that an extension of the contract net by an organizational memory can considerably improve efficiency and capacity of this approach.

In further research, on the one hand our simulations will be further improved by including other DAI approaches into our series of tests, thus allowing a comparison of different DAI approaches. Simultaneously, we will continue to work on construction and performance of the organization MAS of our extended contract net. In particular the question is concerned on how many and which organization agents can be linked in which way.

The long-term goal of the research work is to design a concept that organizationally intelligent MAS can be productively used within real organizations. Whether this goal can be achieved, depends very much on the success of designing a reference architecture for cooperative (DAI) systems. Such an architecture is necessary in order to enable the integration of different software systems.

Chapter *10*

Incorporating Organizational Design Principles and Experiences into the Design and Implementation of Multi Agent Systems

Shaheena Abbas and Gregory O'Hare

10.1 Introduction

The concept of an "organization" has emerged as central to the structuring of activities of both decentralized industrial and commercial conglomerates and collections of intelligent problem solvers within Distributed Artificial Intelligence (DAI) systems (Gasser 1992). Industrial and commercial organizations, require adequate support from information systems architectures in order they may exhibit cooperative problem solving capabilities. There exists a need in industrial and business applications to intelligently integrate data, information and knowledge from a diverse range of sources, particularly during product design, or policy formation. In order to achieve effective and informed decision making, the expertise of many agents, both computational and human, needs to be combined and coordinated. Highly organized DAI systems are critical in human problem solving environments (Gasser 1992). Organizations of the future demand new technologies and techniques (Gasser 1992, Papazoglou *et al.* 1992).

"It is expected that the next generation of intelligent systems will be based on distributed environments in which each node will communicate with other nodes." (Gasser 1992)

Lately a new discipline has begun to emerge that of Organizational Intelligence (OI) (see also Chapters 8 and 9). Organizational Intelligence demands a greater synthesis between the principles of Organizational Theory (OT) and DAI, by the explicit incorporation of theories of both organizations and DAI into the field of OI. OI can be defined as the intellectual capability of an organization, which integrates human and computational problem solving capabilities (Matsuda 1988, Matsuda 1992). The motivation for a multifaceted approach can be seen in the growth of interdisciplinary research areas, such as Computer Supported Cooperative Work (CSCW), Management and Office Systems and Coordination Science (Gasser 1992, Papazoglou *et al.* 1992).

This chapter investigates the fields of organizational theory and DAI, looking specifically at their respective concept of an organization. It synthesizes this work identifying general design guidelines that ought to be incorporated into the design of Multi Agent Systems (MAS). Section 2 provides a brief introduction to DAI, whilst Section 3 introduces OT. The subsequent section reviews more recent perspectives on organizations adopted by DAI researchers. Section 5 seeks to synthesize these two bodies of research. A particular Multi Agent scenario is considered, that of "Warehouse World", from which an organizational workbench subsequently emerges. The development of this workbench is realized through the use of Agent Oriented Programming techniques (Shoham 1993). Sections 8 and 7 describe these respectively. This workbench has, and is being, used in order to experiment with the form and structure of computational organizations. We strive to export these findings to organizational theory. Section 9 describes the design and experimentation while the final section presents a number of conclusions from this research.

10.2 Distributed Artificial Intelligence (DAI)

Distributed Artificial Intelligence (DAI) represents a departure from the centralized approach advocated by mainstream Artificial Intelligence (AI). It seeks to develop intelligent systems by distributing intelligence (or expertise) across a community of semiautonomous automated intelligent agents (O'Hare and Jennings 1996).

These agents are sometimes referred to as actors, knowledge sources, or processing nodes. They are often physically and logically distinct and are capable of reasoning, planning, communicating and cooperating (Hern 1988). Agents may be robotic and be defined in terms of sensory input, motor control and time pressures, they may perform cognitive functions, react to stimuli, contain symbolic plans, or possess natural language capabilities. Shoham 1993 points out that:

"An agent is an entity whose state is viewed as consisting of mental components such as beliefs, capabilities, choices, and commitments." (Shoham 1993).

An agent is thus regarded as an entity, that functions continuously and

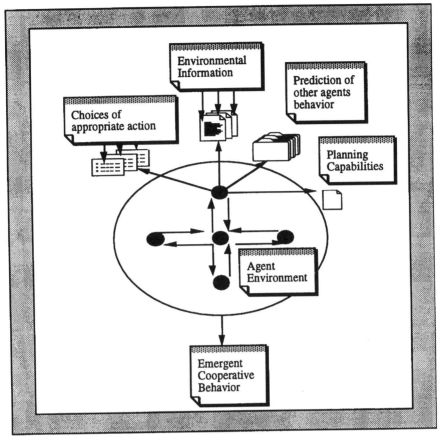

Figure 10.1 Cooperating agent community

largely autonomously, with little guidance or intervention. An agent functions in an environment which is typically highly dynamic and unpredictable, within which other agents coexist and perform.

DAI research endeavors to deal with the problem of integrating and coordinating the activities and expertise of such agent communities (see Chapters 6, 11, 12 and 13). These are similar to the difficulties faced by human organizations (Fox 1979, Fox 1988). DAI addresses the problem of task and resource allocation and interagent communication, in order to provide mutual assistance in the solution of problems (Lesser and Corkill 1981, Lesser and Corkill 1983, Lenat 1988, Lesser 1991). DAI necessitates the interaction of "teams" of agents, equipped with a set of "skills", with the potential to interact with other agents and their environments, in an opportunistic, mutually beneficial manner, in the pursuit of cooperative solutions, to shared problems. These teams evolve, as do the relationships between team members. Figure 10.1 presents a diagrammatic representation of "cooperating agents". No one agent may have sufficient information to solve the entire problem, but be the most appropriate to perform a particular task, or able to supply relevant information (Huhns 1987). Agents must necessarily collaborate, and demand mutual assistance referred to as "collective problem solving". Such collective behavior evolves and generally reflects the development of interagent relationships. Consequently the resultant distributed behavior is often described as being emergent in nature (Anderson and Sharrock 1993).

Traditional research in Artificial Intelligence has often turned to the field of human psychology or cognition as a source of models and metaphors. DAI research, however, draws upon concepts such as group interaction, social organization and society as metaphors for source models (Lenat 1988, Kornfield and Hewitt 1981, Gasser 1992) which have subsequently been commissioned in the design and structuring of DAI systems.

10.3 Organizational Theory (OT)

Organizational theory deals with the internal processes and structures of organizations and their relationship with their environment (see Chapter 1). It is a social science-based theory of how purposive social organizations function and is essentially interdisciplinary in its origins. It draws particularly upon three social science disciplines, those of economics, psychology and sociology (Butler 1992).

The contribution of economics was primarily in the study of individual purposive behavior. This behavior aggregated over a large number of individual decisions, resulted in effective meaningful collective outcomes without the participating individuals ever intending to achieve those outcomes. They added to this the notion of the firm (Cyret and March 1963), which was viewed as a coalition of interests in which agreement among participants over a decision could only be achieved through a social process of bargaining and the making of temporary alliances over specific issues. Major contributors to the field like Cyret and March 1963 also stressed the influence of uncertainty in making it difficult to reach agreement over these goals.

The important contribution made by psychology was in improving our understanding of group behavior within organizations. Roethlisberger and Dickson 1939, for instance, demonstrated that workers in factories could not be treated as an amorphous mass, but rather had to be viewed as individuals forming a social structure out of their interactions, beliefs and values.

Sociologists, concentrated upon the social structural aspects of organizations. Authors like Gouldner 1954 were concerned with the wider issues of social structure outside the factory or organization.

A study of OT reveals that organizations are complex and paradoxical phenomena that can be understood in many different ways. In more recent years, researchers like Scott 1987 have attempted to integrate these various approaches. Generally, an organization emerges whenever there is a shared set of beliefs about a state of affairs to be achieved and that state of affairs requires the efforts of more than a few individuals. An organization is thus a mechanism for accomplishing a great variety of objectives beyond the reach of any individual. An organization may also be subject to a number of changing demands and may exhibit emergent behavior. It synthesizes the different and often conflicting, demands made from inside and outside, in order to define (redefine) its objectives. The organization must induce participants to contribute services, it must provide a medium within which these contributions can subsequently be controlled and coordinated, it must secure resources from the environment and dispense products or services back to the environment and it must support the establishment and maintenance of working relationships. This implies that even when structures that establish patterns of behavior are fixed, an organization will reveal diverse and often conflicting forms of behavior that can be observed at individual or group level.

The term organization also implies a unity of purpose, interdependent activities, a willingness to cooperate and a sense of belonging. A basic definition of an organization, taken from the work of Daft 1989 is described below:

- an organization is a social entity,
- it is established for the collaborative pursuit of specified goals,
- it has a boundary, so that some members are considered inside while others are considered outside,
- and an organization patterns the activities of members into a recognizable structure.

Organizations are also highly influenced by, and conduct exchanges with, their environments. Organizations also receive information about their performance from the environment and have to adapt to changing environmental circumstances, by collecting information about constraints and opportunities in the task environment and to adapt accordingly. Analogies are frequently made to ecosystems where different species are better suited to coping with the demands of particular environments. Within this framework organizations are born, they develop and adapt to changing environments, or they decline and eventually die. Subsequent generations evolve and become increasingly suited to the environment in which they inhabit and occurs through the natural propagation of those species which are more able to survive (Mintzberg 1983, Miller and Friesen 1984).

10.4 A DAI Perspective on Organizations

DAI emphasizes the importance of populations of agents rather than individual agents. Multiple agents modeled within DAI systems can exhibit emergent behavior that is normally associated with cooperating agents in organizations, such as ant colonies and human communities (Lesser and Corkill 1981).

There exists two crude classes of Multi Agent system, those of deliberative or reflective systems and those regarded as reactive systems (Wooldridge and O'Hare 1991). Deliberative Multi Agent systems ascribe roles to their agents, with the appropriate expertise facilitating cooperation between agents. The concept of *role* is cited by Werner 1992, as an important mechanism for building complex social structures, these structures he terms "organizations". According to Werner 1992, in order for agents to be cooperative they must have information about their environment together with some planning capability, or at the lowest level, procedures or programs. Agents are able to make inferences in choosing the most appropriate action, (this can be viewed as *rational* behavior) and are able to predict the behavior of other agents. These agents make "evaluations" or "deliberations", over a choice of action or reaction. When faced with a problem, agents take the appropriate action to arrive at a solution. This manifests itself as emergent social behavior.

Chaib draa *et al.* 1992 state that an agent's ability to engage in social activity requires sophisticated local control, including the ability to reason about the actions of other agents (their goals, plans, interactions and beliefs). Such *social abilities* also require an agent to be able to assess its distributed situation or *perceive* the organization within which they exist.

Generally deliberative systems are more complex and exhibit more sophisticated behavior. Correspondingly, they are obliged to maintain a more complete and accurate model of the world within which they reside. The maintenance of such abstract computational models are computationally demanding and has the associated penalties in terms of response.

The deliberative approach also receives support from the sociology community. Anderson and Sharrock 1993, state that perception is embedded in courses of action. Actions are patterned, learned and shared and can be viewed as cultural practices, or socially organized accomplishments. Having organizational knowledge and becoming socialized, involves acquiring organizational information from the social environment. Familiarity with the organization means having knowledge of the temporal sequencing of activities. Agents come to understand the organization by perceiving the working division of labor by the acquisition of organizational information. This demands that an agent must acquire, organize and abstract information about its environment.

Other researchers prefer the reactive approach. They believe that frequently a swift decision is often better than no decision at all. Within the reactive approach agents are typically more simplistic and offer a much more limited range of capabilities. The system behavior can be considerably more involved but this is merely achieved through the aggregation of the behavior of large numbers of constituent agents. Steel's 1990 case study of cooperative space exploration typifies this reactive approach. He illustrates how the activities of a number of agents reflects their emergent behavior. An individual agent is represented as a distributed robot, which on discovering samples must communicate its findings to other robot agents. The robot agents must efficiently establish a path of crumbs between the sample location and a space vehicle. Communication between robot agents is via this crumb path, which is used as a mechanism around which agents may organize their behavior. According to Steel 1990 the process of "Self Organization" is applicable in modeling reactive agent systems that are capable of responding to their immediate environment in which they happen to be embedded.

The "Organization Self Design" (OSD) (Ishida *et al.* 1992) problem solving model supports the explicit representation of agent knowledge yet strives to provide improved performance. Within this framework problem solvers represent a society of distributed agents with distributed control. These agents can achieve improved real-time performance through the reorganization of their society. This allows agents to manage themselves by adapting to changing environmental demands. Agents need knowledge of their organizational role that explains their necessary interactions. Organizational knowledge represents how a local decision made by one agent, may affect the decisions of a number of agents and the global behavior of the entire organization. This knowledge is formalized as a set of relationships between agents and between agents and their organization.

Organizational Knowledge, Organizational Learning and Organizational Change are important in explaining the complexity of human organizations (see Chapter 8). However, a more detailed study of these is beyond the scope of this chapter. Herein, we concern ourselves merely with one aspect of organizations namely their structure, in an attempt to help manage and control the complexity of Multi Agent systems. The next section attempts to bring together issues that are relevant for our aim.

10.5 Synthesizing DAI & OT

Social metaphors like the "Community of Cooperating Experts" (Lenat 1988), have been imported into DAI and used as prescriptive models upon which to base the social dynamics of the agent community (Lesser and Corkill 1981, Lenat 1988, Pattison *et al.* 1987, Gasser *et al.* 1987, Malone and Smith 1984,

Malone 1988). Researchers have proposed approaches analogous to the way that human organizations coordinate their actions (Malone 1988), organize their resources and improve their performance, by varying the membership and size of their agent groups (Pattison *et al.* 1987, Gasser *et al.* 1987, Ishida *et al.* 1992). Star 1989 believes that the development of DAI systems should be based on such social metaphors. The most influential research in this area, considers mechanisms for implementing market-like organizations, such as the Contract Net Protocol (Davis and Smith 1983) or modeling coordination in organizations and markets (Malone 1988). These models are perceived as structural models (Chaib draa *et al.* 1992) and by definition these models have limited flexibility for adapting their global behavior in the face of change. For this reason it has been argued that more adaptable models are needed for managing control and coherence in DAI systems (Gasser 1992, Chaib draa *et al.* 1992). To create more satisfactory models for DAI systems, researchers must shift their attention away from structural models which are frequently brittle and restrictive in nature. They must understand the fundamental social phenomena that underpin organizational behavior and in turn they must seek to replicate such functionality through the use of sophisticated programming techniques.

Within the field of OT disagreement exists over what perspective and which assumptions should be used in developing the appropriate variables and their relationships in designing organizations (Mintzberg 1983). All organizations are characterized by an assemblage or combination of dependent parts (Scott 1987).

Organizations vary greatly, nevertheless there exists considerable commonality. In our attempts to understand organizations, both human and computational, we have sought to identify a set of *organizational descriptors* which could be used as a medium within which organizations could be described, compared and scrutinized. Such close examination would potentially enable us to characterize certain classes of stereotypical organization in terms of these descriptors. Thereafter we would hope to be able to create an experimental environment or *Organizational Workbench* which would permit the support and creation of virtual computational organizations together with subsequent experimentation within which these descriptors could be customized and the resultant effects observed.

Within this work we regard the most critical aspects of an organization as:

- Social Ability.
- Organizational Coherence.
- Task Decomposition.
- Coordination.
- Authority Relationships.
- Decision Autonomy.
- Communication.

- Groups, Norms and Conformity.
- Membership Role.
- Environment.

Each of these topics will be developed further in the following subsections.

10.5.1 Social Ability

Social ability plays an important role in Multi Agent interactions (Werner 1992). Human organizations can be viewed as specific instances of Multi Agent systems. DAI researchers (Chaib draa *et al.* 1992, Gasser 1992) believe that an organization is a virtual concept embedded in the beliefs, intentions and commitments of constituent agents. Building on this notion an organization is defined in terms of a set of agents with beliefs and mutual and global commitments. This manifests itself as joint intentions when agents act together to achieve a defined goal. They feel that such organizations, exist through cooperation which is achieved, in part, by the exchange of beliefs, intentions and commitments. Organizations are thus viewed as social entities with associated *social ability* which necessitates agent interaction and results in evolving agent relationships.

10.5.2 Organizational Coherence

The modern business organization can be viewed as a large distributed system. Within a distributed system, local agents have control over their own actions, have their own goals and their own functions. Within distributed computer systems, as a task grows larger and increasingly complex, the amount of information available increases and correspondingly the complexity of control increases. It becomes less clear how to achieve a system of global control. The problem arises as to how these locally motivated agents can best be organized to attain global goals.

Global coherence in human organizations is achieved by the setting of appropriate *"structures"* within which decisions can be made and executed. The most obvious manifestations of these structures are procedures and rules that guide the behavior of an organization's members during decision making and provide constraints and opportunities for action.

10.5.3 Task Decomposition

Task decomposition is operationally important for the efficiency of an organization. Task decomposition involves decomposition of an overall task so it can subsequently be distributed among appropriate agents. Purposeful action is thereafter guaranteed by coordinating their computations by means of relevant information exchange of appropriate information.

There are a number of ways to divide a task. In organizational theory, a task can be divided in a manner so these divisions are different rather than similar and each individual is apportioned a small component of the overall task. This has two effects in that it generally results in an equitable distribution of tasks, however, it increases task dependence necessitating a need for coordination among dependent roles. Such a strategy demands that an agent is knowledgeable about selecting an appropriate strategy to decompose the task and matching resources and capabilities of agents. Choosing a decomposition strategy that provides all the resources the agent requires to perform its tasks, is referred to as "self containment" in organizational theory (Galbraith 1977) and has been applied by Lesser and Corkill 1981 in defining a self directed agent which makes the best use of information resource it has available.

10.5.4 Coordination

Attempting to coordinate an organization demands the division of labor, effective communication and the distribution of resources and processing capacity (see Chapters 2 and 11). Within human organizations coordinating the division of labor is achieved through the design of specific "positions". Agents are differentiated on the basis of such factors as expertise, power, status and such notions as reliability, dependency and trust. Typically the authority relationships within such organizations result in a hierarchical structure.

Each agent has access to resources associated with its "position" and is expected to enact certain behaviors. The set of expected behaviors associated with a position will be established by rules and regulations. These rules represent a repetitive procedure worked out in advance of their execution. Rules reduce the need for communication between dependent agents. Within the field of DAI they can be viewed as representing a protocol of interaction (Lenat 1988).

10.5.5 Authority Relationships

We are aware that organizations do not have to manifest themselves in a hierarchical structure, however, it is this form which historically has gained prevalence in human organizations. It remains to be seen if there ought necessarily to be a transference of this structure to computational organizations. Furthermore, we recognize that increasingly intelligent organizations will need to be able to dynamically reconfigure their infrastructure to reflect environmental demands.

The hierarchy establishes authority relationships that introduce the notion that no member should receive directives from more than one superior. Every position except the one at the top is obliged to follow directives from the position superior to it. Positions except those of the very bottom, are expected to issue directives to coordinate the tasks of those subordinate to it. Throughout the hierarchy, information is distributed on a "need to know basis". The top of the hierarchy can be viewed as being composed of *nodes* having a global information perspective which is used to shape and reshape policy, control and coordinate the activities of the lesser informed nodes, by decomposing and allocating tasks. Nodes lower down the hierarchy must accept or comply with any task directives made from above, they possess only local information relating to their task. In order to help maintain global information at the top of the hierarchy, these nodes continually pass information or "decision data" up the hierarchy.

One strategy suggested by Lesser and Corkill 1981, is to structure the hierarchy as a search space with higher levels representing increasingly more abstract representations of the problem. Using this hierarchical structure, a partial solution developed for one aspect of the problem may be used to constrain the search for solutions to other aspects of the same problem.

10.5.6 Decision Autonomy

Coherence is achieved by limiting decision autonomy to reduce the coordination involved in a complex task. However, variation, uncertainty and complexity within a subtask and the demand for a quick response to local conditions, often requires decision making authority to be brought to where it is needed. This can be problematic, in that these fragmented decisions are difficult to coordinate.

Decision autonomy can further cause problems, by individual agents setting goals for themselves, which take precedence over the groups objectives or indeed the total organization's objectives. This may manifest itself through conflict (Gibson *et al.* 1979). Conflict may be "intra group conflict", which results through disagreement over goals, plans and member roles; "*interpersonal conflict*", which is the result of differences in values, beliefs, attitudes between members behavior; and "*intergroup conflict*", which results as a group competes with other groups for scarce resources. What decision powers should be delegated down the chain of authority of prime importance and should relate to: the goals the group is trying to achieve; and the means to which the group will employ to achieve these goals (Thompson and Tuden 1964).

10.5.7 Communication

Communication is a mechanism to coordinate labor and dependent tasks. Organizations establish a minimum of formal communication channels, linking together all dependent groups (see Chapters 3, 4 and 5). Typically these channels may be hierarchical in nature. However, each communication channel has limited capacity, since each individual position or position within a group, can communicate only directly with those above and below or at the same level. Other contacts must be made through one or more intervening nodes. This may prove unnecessarily restrictive and stifle the emergent behavior of an organization.

Attempts to improve communication in human organizations have been made by cutting across the lines of authority in an attempt to increase lateral communication between managers (Mintzberg 1983). This can be achieved by creating what has been termed a *"liaison role"* between departments or positions, creating *"task forces"* and establishing *"matrix structures"* which are temporary project groups (Galbraith 1977). By placing in direct contact processors which share a common problem, or common resources organizations establish work groups. In an attempt to overcome the restrictiveness of formal hierarchical communication a more convenient method of communication, which achieves task coordination by the process of informal communication between two or more people is referred to as "mutual adjustment" (Mintzberg 1983).

10.5.8 Groups, Norms and Conformity

By definition all organizations are in fact groups, groups need to be limited in size in order for meaningful interaction to occur between its members, and groups must meet over a period of time. Groups can be viewed as collectives that evolve naturally and defined as any form of joint action or activity by a collection of individuals who pursue a common goal. Large corporate or multinational organizations can be viewed as being composed of numerous subgroups.

Groups manage the process of local behavior by using implicit rules which govern appropriate and inappropriate ways of acting. These are referred to as *"group norms"*, they represent standards shared by members and tend to develop around issues of central importance. These are referred to a *pivotal norms* and categorized in terms of *task norms* and *maintenance norms* (Cartwright and Zander 1968). Task norms, influence the way in which a group will accomplish its goals. Maintenance norms, emerge in order to assist the group to remain as a cohesive unit.

Group cohesiveness is a measure of the closeness of attitude with regard to behavior and performance which encourages members to remain in a group. The pressure to conform relies upon group norms to structure behavior. As cohesiveness increases the level of conformity to group norms also increases. Two responses exist that challenge group conformity, these are deviancy and independence. There is a tendency to adopt one particular type of response to group norms this, however, is situation dependent and relates to the nature and purpose of the group.

10.5.9 Role

The concept of role refers to the expected behavior patterns an agent must perform. Within Multi Agent systems the adoption of a *role*, with the appropriate expertise facilitates cooperation between agents and is an important mechanism for building organizations. Each agent will have a perceived role which is a set of behaviors they, or the group, believe they should enact. However, different members will have different perceptions of behavior associated with a given role.

Individuals may also perform "multiple roles", known as a "role set" (see Gibson *et al.* 1979), this refers to those members who are expected to exhibit different behavior associated with different roles either in different groups, or in different organizations. The more expectations and role demands placed on an individual member, the more complicated their role set. This can lead ultimately to role conflict.

10.5.10 Environment

The activities of a number of agents is organized around an environmental resource. The survival of the organization often rests upon its ability to make exchanges with environmental elements and its ability to adapt to environmental changes. This may involve applying organizational design techniques to improve its survival chances. Agents thus need to be reactive to be capable of responding to their immediate environment in which they happen to be embedded (Steels 1990).

Strategies for coping with increases in environmental information attempt to reduce the amount of information that needs to be processed. For instance, the "environmental management strategy" (Galbraith 1977) attempts to modify the organizations environment by creating slack resources. This can be achieved by decreasing an organizations level or quality of performance or using additional resources such as increasing the time available to perform a task, or employing more equipment or personnel.

10.6 Design Principles

Within Section 5 we sought to assemble general guidelines that could usefully be incorporated into the design and subsequent implementation of Multi Agent systems. This set of guidelines is enumerated below and encompasses the set of organizational descriptors that were alluded earlier. We categorize these guidelines under three headings those relating to the structure of the organization, group and individual agent.

An Organizational Structure:

- The primary unit of an organization is an agent.
- Each agent performs an operating task(s).
- Each agent achieves a local goal which contributes to a global goal.
- A "strategic agent" is defined that identifies an appropriate agent for any given task.
- In achieving all goals, agents rely on task allocation.
- An agent does not receive directives from more than one agent at the same time.
- An agent is subject to a superior and subordinate relationship.
- Agents are defined either as superiors , for instance "managers", or subordinates, for instance "automated guided vehicles", in a Computer Integrated Manufacturing (CIM) sense.
- An agent's behavior is governed by the programming language.
- Agents pass on relevant information to the appropriate agent to inform them about the state of the world.
- An agent must comply with directives.
- Agent relationships implicitly define communication channels.
- Methods to perform a task are defined within the agent's structure as capabilities.

A Group Structure:

- Agents are structured into work groups that share a common task.
- Groups are of equal position in the organization, only an agent which issues directives exists at the top of the organization.
- Groups size is limited to the size of the task.
- Task information is communicated throughout a group by a manager.
- Agent work groups are organized around a dynamic world.

Agent Structure:

- Agent behavior is determined by the state of a dynamic world.
- Each agent needs to have a view of the world.
- This view may be partial and may be inaccurate. Agents need only be made aware of the minimum amount of information needed to perform their task.
- An agent's view must be maintained.
- Agent behavior is governed at any point in time, by their programmed beliefs and commitments.
- An agent name defines an agent position, each position performs the same role within each work group.
- An agent's "role set" should be minimized in order to support modular design. This suggests that modules should be designed with simplicity and a unique purpose in mind.

10.7 Agent Oriented Programming (AOP)

Having identified those design principles that we sought to incorporate we had to identify an appropriate implementation medium. Earlier we made reference to the need for sophisticated programming metaphors that will provide the necessary primitives from which we can assemble Multi Agent systems. It is recognized that apt software engineering tools must be employed in the commissioning of such systems. Deficient tools will generally result in deficient systems. This however, does not mean that powerful tools will produce powerful systems.

Latterly, MASs have been constructed using three classes of software support: those of Object Oriented Programming Systems (OOPS), Object Based Concurrent Programming (OBCP) which builds on earlier actor based approaches, and those based on Agent Oriented Programming (AOP) techniques.

Gasser and Briot 1992, believe that in order to design and implement DAI systems we should find complementary relations between the theory of social organization chosen for DAI problem solving and the theory of modeling and implementation used for system construction. They propose the use of Object Based Concurrent Programming techniques (OBCP) (Masini *et al.* 1991), to implement their social model of problem solving. OBCP techniques are based upon the notion of active and autonomous objects, which compute concurrently and interact via message exchange.

Object Oriented Programming Systems (OOPS) are based upon the notion that computing systems perform a certain number of actions on a finite number of objects (O'Hare and Wooldridge 1992). Software systems using this paradigm are structured as objects, which are seen as *reacting* to stimuli from the world within which they reside and as such perceive changes that take place.

Attempts have been made to integrate the object oriented paradigm with other programming paradigms. Recent work conducted by Shoham 1993 at Stanford, has proposed the Agent Oriented Programming (AOP) paradigm. This is regarded as a specialization of object oriented programming, which promotes a societal view of computation. Within this platform, multiple "agents" interact with one another and are capable of passing messages to other agents addressable by name (whether they reside in the same processor or in others). Whereas, OBCP techniques rely on representing objects and their physical characteristics, AOP techniques rely on representing mental states to model agent interaction and thus this paradigm is more suitable for modeling organizations. Other methodologies which make use of Agent Oriented Programming paradigms include the testbed MYWORLD (Wooldridge and Vandekerckhove 1993) and Agent Factory (O'Hare and Wooldridge 1992).

The Agent Oriented approach provides an appropriate medium to support the implementation of an organization of interacting intelligent agents. An agent can be viewed as an object with a particular structure imposed upon it, which characterizes its *mental state*. For instance, this includes components like: beliefs, capabilities, commitments and choices. The mental state is represented by epistemic logic where belief and knowledge operators are equipped with some awareness of time. Explicit operators are also introduced to represent, commitment, capability and choice. In addition, agents are each empowered with communication operators which are strongly typed and are based upon Speech Act theory (Austin 1962, Searle 1969, Cohen and Perrault 1979), which includes verbs like *inform, request, unrequest, do and refrain*. Each communication act involves different presuppositions and has different effects (see Chapter 11 for a detailed examination of Speech Acts).

The choice as to which paradigm and language to adopt was constrained somewhat by availability. Within the Computation Department at UMIST, we had access to: ABCL/1 (Yonezawa 1990) developed at Tokyo Institute of Technology and representative of OBCP, Common Lisp Object System (CLOS) an object-based language rooted within a functional framework and Agent0, MYWORLD and Agent Factory which were AOP systems. We selected Agent0 which represents an early attempt at developing a programming language for the paradigm of Agent Oriented Programming. A prototype Agent0 Interpreter has been implemented in Common Lisp and has been ported and installed on to Sun sparcstations. Despite the fact that it is still in its infancy, Agent0 offers an important mechanism for developing agent architectures. Such a tool provides the necessary building blocks and primitives required in the construction of Multi Agent systems. In part, our choice was influenced by a desire to evaluate and gain some insights into the virtues and failings of Agent0.

10.8 Warehouse World

Having selected Agent0 as the implementation medium, we then sought to identify a problem scenario that would be amenable to organizational experimentation. As with all AI research we sought a problem that was well bounded yet sufficiently complex necessitating multiple agents which communicate and cooperate. We did not want the complexity of the problem to be needlessly intrusive, nor did we want its comprehension to demand domain specific expertise. The virtual world that we selected was that of a warehouse world and we christened it accordingly.

This world represents a warehouse scenario, where orders are received and products are dispatched to a loading bay. This is illustrated in Figure 10.2. The environment is essentially composed of two work groups that send products to the loading bay, using an automated guided vehicle (agv). Each work group is represented as a "warehouse unit", which consists of a strategic agent, manager agent, stacker agent and unstacker agent. The strategic agent issues incoming orders to a manager agent. Each manager agent directs instructions to a stacker agent to locate the appropriate product, which is represented as a block, and make it available for transportation by the agv agent to the loading bay. Typically retrieval of a given product can necessitate cooperation between the stacker and unstacker agents. At the loading bay, the products are loaded onto lorries for transport. This process requires communication and cooperation between agents.

The organizations base component is the *agent*. Each agent is required to perform an operating task(s). The method used to perform such tasks is defined within the agent's structure as capabilities. In order to maintain a level of coherence, an agent must comply with directives received, where such directives emanate from no more than one agent at any given time. An agent relationship is implicitly defined in the communication channels used. An agent passes on relevant information to appropriate agent(s), informing them about any revisions to the state of the world to which they are privy.

Within a static world what has been asserted continues to be true forever. Organizations or groups, however, are inherently dynamic, implying continuous change and adjustment of agent mental states and consequently inter agent relationships.

In order to represent a dynamic world, changes in state have to be recorded. Each agent needs to have a view of the world, which may be partial and inaccurate. An agent's behavior is determined by the state of this dynamic world and is governed at any point in time, by their programmed beliefs and commitments. Agents are provided with a minimum amount of information that is needed to perform their task. This view of the world exists within an agent's beliefs database, called a "sub world", which includes an awareness of other group members and the presence of blocks. Any changes that take place in this sub world are mirrored in the beliefs and commitments

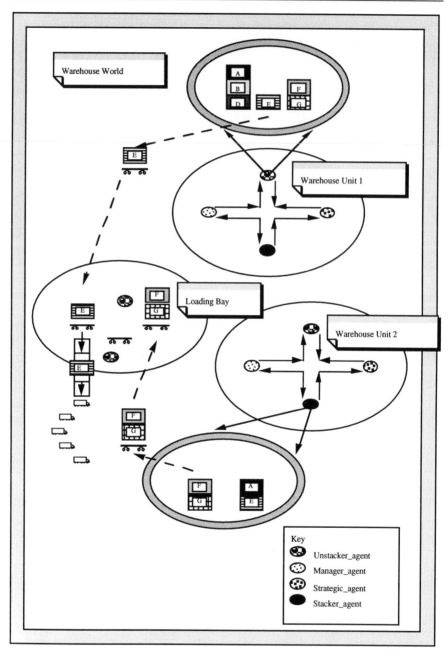

Figure 10.2   Warehouse world

of an agent. Beliefs can be updated in one of two manners: firstly through the receipt of messages informing the agent of revisions to other agent's mental states; alternatively they may be updated through cognitive actions performed within the agent itself.

10.9 Design and Experimental Testing of Emergent Organizations

To date a simple warehouse world has been designed and developed. This design and implementation specifically incorporated the design principles identified within Section 6. The implemented model represents a computational world or environment, inhabited by an organization of agents. These agents are organized into work groups, which carry out local goals, which if invoked appropriately may contribute to the attainment of a global goal. Agents are made aware of their environment through their belief set. Their membership of a work group and its composition for example, represent its sphere of interest and as such are embodied within its belief base. The membership of other groups, or their very existence, may be beyond this, and as such may not be of any relevance to its communicative or cognitive actions.

Each agent within warehouse world is of a particular "type". These types are finite and their enumeration is stacker, unstacker, manager, strategic and agv. Each type has an associated set of generic capabilities. These capabilities are represented within the commitment rules and private actions associated with each agent. Each agent type is instantiated to reflect a specific instance of that type and thus reflect a particular agent. The instantiation involves the population of the belief base to reflect the particular sub world that the agent inhabits. A detailed description of the design of warehouse world is beyond the scope of this chapter however, interested readers are referred elsewhere (Abbas 1993).

The organizational model developed represents a rudimentary dynamic model of multiple agent interaction. The computational agents perform relatively simple tasks, revealing basic authority relationships, cooperation, communication and coordinated activity. These agents perform interdependent tasks, updating their beliefs and exchanging current information. Figure 10.3 illustrates a typical interaction with warehouse world. The interaction depicted simply involves two agents namely manager-agent1 and stacker-agent1. This simplified case is chosen in order to reduce complexity and size of the interaction. The interaction illustrates Agent0 in its interactive mode with agent belief bases and interagent messages being displayed at appropriate points. This mode of operation permits the agent community to be

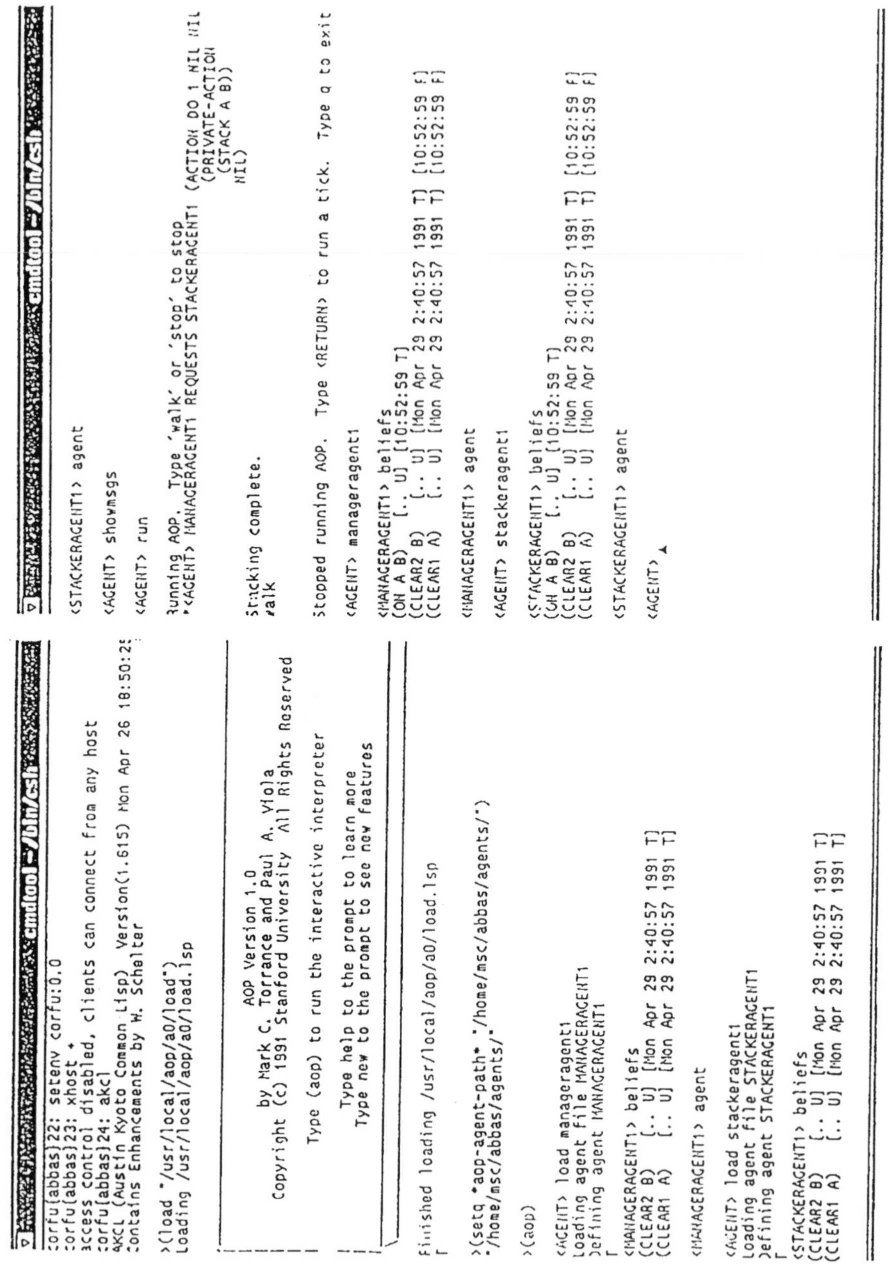

```
corfu(abbas)22: setenv corfu:0.0
corfu(abbas)23: xhost +
access control disabled, clients can connect from any host
corfu(abbas)24: akcl
AKCL (Austin Kyoto Common lisp) Version(1.615) Mon Apr 26 18:50:25
Contains Enhancements by W. Schelter

>(load "/usr/local/aop/a0/load")
Loading /usr/local/aop/a0/load.lsp

                AOP Version 1.0
        by Mark C. Torrance and Paul A. Viola
Copyright (c) 1991 Stanford University All Rights Reserved

Type (aop) to run the interactive interpreter
Type help to run the prompt to learn more
Type new to the prompt to see new features

Finished loading /usr/local/aop/a0/load.lsp

>(setq *aop-agent-path* "/home/msc/abbas/agents/")
"/home/msc/abbas/agents/"
>(aop)

<AGENT> load manageragent1
Loading agent file MANAGERAGENT1
Defining agent MANAGERAGENT1

<MANAGERAGENT1> beliefs
(CLEAR2 B)   [.. U] [Mon Apr 29 2:40:57 1991 T]
(CLEAR1 A)   [.. U] [Mon Apr 29 2:40:57 1991 T]

<MANAGERAGENT1> agent

<AGENT> load stackeragent1
Loading agent file STACKERAGENT1
Defining agent STACKERAGENT1

<STACKERAGENT1> beliefs
(CLEAR2 B)   [.. U] [Mon Apr 29 2:40:57 1991 T]
(CLEAR1 A)   [.. U] [Mon Apr 29 2:40:57 1991 T]
```

```
<STACKERAGENT1> agent

<AGENT> showmsgs

<AGENT> run

Running AOP. Type 'walk' or 'stop' to stop
*<AGENT> MANAGERAGENT1 REQUESTS STACKERAGENT1 (ACTION DO 1 NIL NIL
                                               (PRIVATE-ACTION
                                                (STACK A B))
                                               NIL)

Stacking complete.
walk

Stopped running AOP. Type <RETURN> to run a tick. Type q to exit

<AGENT> manageragent1

<MANAGERAGENT1> beliefs
(ON A B)     [.. U] [10:52:59 T]
(CLEAR2 B)   [.. U] [Mon Apr 29 2:40:57 1991 T]  [10:52:59 F]
(CLEAR1 A)   [.. U] [Mon Apr 29 2:40:57 1991 T]  [10:52:59 F]

<MANAGERAGENT1> agent

<AGENT> stackeragent1

<STACKERAGENT1> beliefs
(ON A B)     [.. U] [10:52:59 T]
(CLEAR2 B)   [.. U] [Mon Apr 29 2:40:57 1991 T]  [10:52:59 F]
(CLEAR1 A)   [.. U] [Mon Apr 29 2:40:57 1991 T]  [10:52:59 F]

<STACKERAGENT1> agent

<AGENT>
```

Figure 10.3   Typical warehouse world interaction

observed while controlling the internal clock and stepping through virtual time. Thus the activation of commitment rules can be observed as can the revision of the beliefs.

In order to achieve flexible design strategies to meet changing situations we adopted an approach of reorganization which supported the dynamic revision of agent relationships, agent knowledge and the agent population. An agents ability to organize and reorganize, is constrained by user defined commitments and beliefs. Agents can only be reassigned to work groups by the appropriate adjustment being made to the commitment rule and belief bases.

The behavior demonstrated by the agent community within warehouse world was such that emergent properties associated with the organization became apparent. Having constructed the initial model of the world we sought to use this as an experimental environment or *Organizational Workbench*. Warehouse world represents a virtual computational organization and one which can be configured in various manners. This configuration involves the conductance of laboratory style experiments whereby various organizational descriptors are customized. A series of such experiments have been performed and more complex experiments are on going. The resultant effects have been, and are being observed, and the results analyzed.

Simple experiments conducted thus far have, in the main, focused upon the size and structure of agent work groups. We have varied the number of certain types of agent in each work group and observed the effect. Intuitive feelings have been supported, in that attempts to increase the number of stacker agents, without increasing the number of unstacker agents, results in a resource bounded problem associated with the unstacker agent(s). Comparable increases in the stacker and unstacker agents merely causes the problem to migrate to the agv resource.

More interesting experiments involve interactions between the different work groups and the possibility of certain resources being shared across work groups. The agv agents already dynamically leave and join two such work groups and on going experiments are investigating the possibility of pooled resources such as stackers and unstackers performing similar migrations. The dynamic construction of work groups would be instigated by the strategic agent, whose contingent upon current order levels, would seek appropriate resources from the pool.

We are interested in maximizing the usage of organizational resources, particularly the more expensive resources like managerial and strategic skills. Further enhancements may provide insights into the most effective organizational composition for given categories of task. Warehouse world is concerned with a specific set of tasks, clearly these are not incidental but nevertheless we regard them as secondary to the generic organizational structure.

Future work will include a more detailed investigation of group dynamics and of the impact changes have on group members. More attention could be directed to the integration of local and group goals, by introducing strategies for conflict resolution between goals and agents. Further developments would include the modeling of a real-world industrial organization and its task objectives, using cooperative problem solving techniques.

10.10   Conclusions

This chapter has investigated the fields of OT and DAI looking specifically at their respective concept of an organization. It synthesizes this work identifying general design guidelines that should be incorporated into the design of MASs. A particular Multi Agent scenario has been addressed, that of warehouse world, from which an organizational workbench has emerged. The development of this workbench has been realized through the use of Agent Oriented Programming techniques (Shoham 1993). This workbench has, and is being used, in order to experiment with the form and structure of computational organizations. We strive to export these findings to organizational theory.

Since warehouse world represents a virtual world, one may question the relevance of such experimental results and indeed the transference of such findings into real-world organizations. The general spirit of this work is that no longer can societies of computational agents and human agents be regarded as separate entities. There needs to be a reengineering of the term Multi Agent system to ensure they embrace the precepts of organizational intelligence. Organizations must effectively integrate human and other technologies and Multi Agent systems must accommodate human and computational agents within the same design methodology.

It is our conjecture that such findings are particularly relevant. Whatever the reader's view, it is clear that the cost, time and the practicalities associated with conducting experiments of this nature, is such that they represent a very attractive alternative to in situ testing. Within this work we have endeavored to harness the findings of organizational theory recognizing that this rich corpus of knowledge is equally applicable to societies of computational agents. Having imported valuable expertise to assist in the design of our organizational workbench, we in turn seek to export valuable findings accrued from laboratory experiments and thus contribute to organizational theory. This bi-directional exchange of expertise is pivotal in order to establish the theoretical foundations for organizational intelligence.

This chapter has provided interesting and valuable insights into modeling computational organizations and *Organizational Intelligence*. It seems clear that this is an important field that needs to be researched and will contribute significantly to the fields of DAI, OT and CSCW. Specifically we seek to investigate further areas such as Organizational Knowledge, Organizational Learning and Organizational Change.

Acknowledgments

This work was funded in part through an SERC Studentship awarded to S. Abbas and through the British Council and the DAAD Anglo German Academic Research Grant (ARC) entitled Multi Agent INtentionality (MAIN) 1993–1995.

Chapter *11*

Coordination Protocols

Kurt Sundermeyer

11.1 Introduction

Any social organization (either natural or artificial) needs forms of coordination and cooperation. Cooperation and coordination is possible with and without explicit communication. "Cooperation without Communication" is indeed a title of a paper (Genesereth *et al.* 1986), describing how agents rationally infer other agent's intentions, instead of querying them. Another case of cooperation without explicit communication is by stimulus-response like reactions of an agent to actions of other agents, for which no common communication language is required.

In this article we solely deal with coordination by communication within artificial organizations, as they are the topic of DAI ("Distributed Artificial Intelligence"). The ideas about communication are inspired by human communication. However, it is obvious that human communication is much too rich to be executed by an artificial agent. On the other hand, to describe communication by the classical model, where a sender uses some channel to transport a message to a receiver, is too poor. What is needed is an extension of simple send and receive operations by some means to structure message exchange. To first settle the context, one should be aware of the various aspects behind a communication act.

Due to Austin (1962), is the distinction of locutionary, illocutionary and perlocutionary aspects in communication. In the words of (Cohen and Perrault, 1979): "A speaker performs a locutionary act by making noises that are the uttering of words in a language satisfying its vocabulary and grammar, and by the uttering sentences with definite meaning (though perhaps having more than one). Such acts are used in the performances of illocutionary acts which are those acts performed in making utterances. For instance, stating, requesting, warning, ordering, apologizing, are claimed to be different types of illocutionary acts, ..." Furthermore: "... perlocutionary act – the act performed by making an utterance. For instance with the illocutionary act of asserting something, I may convince my audience of the truth of the corresponding proposition (or insult or frighten them). Percolutionary acts produce percolutionary effects: convincing produces belief and frightening produces fear."

By this distinction, the simple utterance of a sentence (locutionary) is distinguished from its intended effects (illocutionary) and its actual effects (perlocutionary) on the receiver. Inevitably, the actual securing of the perlocutionary effects is beyond the control of the speaker. The locutionary aspect of a speech act falls within the realm of standard communication theory, where it is well studied. It is of interest therefore, for communication in agent systems, to be illocutionary acts.

It was argued that properties of illocutionary acts can be derived from the speaker's and hearer's mental states, especially from its beliefs and intentions (Cohen and Levesque 1990). This has lead to some interesting results and is definitely the case for human communication. However, since artificial agents have the benefit of using artificial languages, the illocutionary aspects can be explicitly coded in a message through the use of message types.

Very influential to communication in agent systems has been the work of J. R. Searle on illocutionary acts. Although several aspects of his classification do not apply to agent systems, it is the basis for message types used in dialogs. This is described in Section 2. For artificial agents, in order to avoid ambiguities, dialogs must be structured by a fixed set of rules, leading to the idea of protocols. Browsing through the literature one finds various, largely incomparable protocol structures; Section 3. Some of them deal with standard tasks of agent systems (like resource allocation), others are designed for specific applications, and some tend to be generic. In the conclusion (Section 4) the main results so far on cooperation protocols are stated. A quest for standardization is specified as well as requirements on protocols.

11.2   From Speech Acts to Dialogs

A literature survey in "cooperation, coordination and communication" reveals that the majority of authors claim to base their work on speech act theory. There are at least two kinds of uses for this theory. The first is dealing with message types, and the other is considering speech acts as steps in a dialog in action planning. A thorough overview on the theoretical background and historical development of these approaches is given in (Galliers 1988) (see also Chapter 3).

11.2.1 Speech Acts and Message Types

If communication would be described solely in terms of sending and receiving messages, each agent must be able to infer what the sender intended by uttering a message. Natural language has a plethora of communication verbs for expressing this, like "announcing", "asserting", "commanding", "confirming", "demanding", "explaining", "informing", "querying", "notifying", "persuading", "promising", "offending", and "warning". This small set of illocutionary verbs already demonstrates that it is not possible in principle to use these for artificial agent systems. It also demonstrates, that there are semantically related verbs, like "commanding" or "demanding", which only differ in intensity, there are general verbs, which are refined by others, like "notifying" refining "inform", and there are emotional verbs, like "offending", which are of no interest at all for artificial agents.

The obvious is to classify communication verbs. Very influential to DAI is the classification of J. R. Searle. He made a distinction between illocutionary verbs and illocutionary acts. Whereas the list of illocutionary verbs is "endless", there are, according to (Searle 1969) five and only five basic categories of illocutionary acts, namely:

1 assertives: which commit the speaker to something being the case, i.e. to the truth of the assumption expressed, e.g. "Bill opened the door".
2 directives: which attempt to get the hearer to do something; e.g. "Open the door".
3 commisives: which commit the speaker to some future course of action; e.g. "I will open the door".
4 declaratives: which bring about the state of affairs described in the speech act; e.g. "You're fired".
5 expressives: which convey a psychological state of affairs or emotional attitude, e.g. apologizing.

Observe that "questions" are not an independent category, since they can be understood as directives.

Each speech act has the form F(p), where F ("illocutionary force") is one of the five act types, and p is the "propositional content" that specifies what is being requested, ordered or warned about. In (Searle and Vanderveken 1985) seven components of illocutionary force are identified. As one of the components they treat the degree of strength in order to be able to distinguish e.g. "demand" and "command" which are of a same illocutionary force, namely "directive".

From various sides it was criticized, that this theory lacks proper semantics, (Werner 1987), (Singh 1991). E. Werner gave a semantic-pragmatic description of the categories while investigating the relation of communication to the information and intention states of an agent, and M. P. Singh formulated a model-theoretic semantics for speech acts.

Searle's classification also received criticism on the grounds that distinctions are not made on a principled basis. The classification is doubtful in that some communication verbs fall into different classes. For instance "warning" is both assertive and directive. Furthermore, as far as agent systems are concerned, there is no need for declaratives and expressives. The remaining three classes are still too rough for structuring messages.

The classification of illocutionary acts by Searle has given the inspiration to the researchers in DAI for the choice and nature of message types. In (Cohen and Perault 1979) the message types "inform" and "request" were used to model assertives and directives. Since then many message types have been introduced and employed, to name just one example, in the IMAGINE project (Lux *et al.* 1992) the following message types were considered:

- TELL: forwards information to others.
- ORDER: expects some action to be executed by the recipient.
- ASK: asks for information without committing.
- REQUEST: requests expecting acceptance or refusal without further negotiation.
- PROPOSE: begins a negotiation sequence.
- ACCEPT: terminates a negotiation sequence by accepting the last proposal.
- REJECT: rejects a proposal and waits for modification.
- MODIFY: modifies a proposal and sends a counter proposal
- REFINE: refines an already accepted proposal for further negotiation.

Observe that TELL is a directive, the last three message types are commissives, and the remaining ones are directives. These performatives are to be considered halfway between the five categories of Searle and the huge list of communication verbs, and these again tend to be rather large. No one so far has succeeded in finding a structuring principle, and there are good reasons to doubt that such a principle exists. Some authors introduce basic ones and build others from these. So for instance in (Huhns *et al.* 1990) "assertions" and "queries" are considered to be basic, and in (Numaoka and Tokoro 1990) the "conversational actions" "answer", "report" and "forward" are built from "inform", "query" and "request".

Furthermore, even if two authors use the same name for a message type, they in general do not give the same meaning to it. Thus the work on message types is not comparable, and apart from the KQML proposal (KQML 92), no attempt has been made on the standardization of message types.

Although message types are already a valuable means to structure messages they themselves are too weak and should be augmented by some elements of discourse to further assist the message interpretation:

- Work in the IMAGINE Project has led to combine message types with "generic objects" such as GOAL, PLAN, TASK-ASSIGNMENT, RESOURCE-ALLOCATION. Furthermore "interaction atoms" are built as pairs of message types and "generic objects", for instance PROPOSE-GOAL, REQUEST-TASK-ASSIGNMENT. Finally "interaction molecules" (negotiation, order, contract net) are constructed from these "interaction atoms".

In (Huhns *et al.* 1990) message types are characterized by a pair <illocutionary force, expected response>, examples being

- assertion: <inform, acceptance>
- acceptance: <inform, none>
- query: <question, reply>
- reply: <inform, acceptance>
- command: <request, acceptance>.

Apart from the fact that "illocutionary force" is not used in the sense of Searle, this is just another method of structuring, which fails to convey any systematics.

11.2.2 Speech as Planned Action

A dialog can be considered as a plan in the sense of AI planning approaches, where speech acts are considered as operators, defined in terms of the preconditions which must be true for the action to take place, the effects obtained when the action has been performed, and the body of the act, which describes the means by which the effects are achieved. Most of the work in this area is concerned with indirect speech acts (example: "Would you mind opening the door ?") and with inferring the intentions of an agent from its utterances, which in a first approach must not be considered for artificial agents.

Some of the early advocates were (Cohen and Perrault 1979) who define the preconditions, effects and body of a speech act according to the beliefs and wants of the communication partners, for example

INFORM (sender, receiver, prop)
      precondition: sender KNOW prop
      effect: receiver KNOW prop
      body: receiver BELIEVE sender WANT receiver KNOW
                     prop

A further example is "Situated Conversation Theory" (Numaoka and

Tokoro 1990), where the primitive "conversational actions" INFORM, QUERY, and REQUEST are augmented by preconditions and effects in form of epistemic and temporal objects.

It is not at all obvious if conversations can be adequately described by the classical planning approaches because the course of conversation cannot be planned in detail, the other dialog participants follow their own goals and the planner may be forced to follow several different goals, mostly imposed on him by the discourse participants (Bussmann and Müller 1993).

11.2.3 Dialog

As pointed out by various authors, speech acts alone cannot represent a dialog. S. C. Levinson makes a very harsh statement: "... dialogue has no syntax, speech act types are not the relevant categories over which to define the regularities of conversation; there exists no other finite alphabet over which to define the regularities; ..." (Levinson 1981), although he mainly bases this statement on human communication. E. Werner claims that "... real conversation is planned using whole linguistic action strategies or linguistic modules rather than individual speech acts" (Werner 1987).

(Ballmer and Brennenstuhl 1981), after facing enormous difficulties when attempting to classify all English speech act verbs top-down into Searle's classes, they rather employed a bottom-up approach by looking up all the available verbs in a dictionary and grouping verbs that are similar in meaning into semantic categories, and the semantic categories into models. For example the "Struggle Model" contains categories "attack" and "defend". The models also include an ordering of the categories according to their temporal relationship and degree of strength. For instance a "defense" happens only after an "attack", and "threatening" is stronger than "warning". The categories, models and their temporal relationships lead to dialogs and frameworks for structuring dialogs.

The "Dialogue Games" (Levin and Moore, 1977) directly deal with dialog structures themselves, instead of considering the speech acts involved. Examples of dialog games are "helping", "action-seeking", "instruction".

11.3 Protocols

Ultimately, not only messages, but also dialogs should be bound by formal restrictions within some framework, i.e. a protocol (see Chapters 4 and 6). According to ISO/OSI standards "a protocol is a set of previously defined rules and conventions for behavior between two parties" (ISO, 1984). Protocols, in the context of this article describing dialogs as a fixed pattern, can reduce the computational load. As a matter of fact, by their very idea, they make speech act planning obsolete. Within a protocol, the agent has a fixed set of alternatives to react to a message of another agent. What is left, is of course to decide which alternative to take.

A number of researchers have proposed such frameworks, and in the sequel a selection will be given. Some of the proposed protocols were designed to solve different specific tasks arising in the phases of cooperative problem solving as defined by (Smith and Davis 1981), namely problem decomposition, task allocation, task solution, and solution synthesis. Other protocols were designed for specific applications or domains, and some tend to be generic.

11.3.1 Task & Domain Specific Protocols

The most well known protocol in DAI is the Contract Net Protocol (Smith 1980), (Davis and Smith 1983), which exclusively deals with task allocation. The idea is rather simple: If an agent (in this context called the "manager") recognizes a problem it cannot solve on its own, it announces the task for solving this problem and calls for bids, in general with certain eligibility and termination conditions. Other agents who might feel able to solve the problem offer a bid. The manager decides among the bidders and makes a contract with one of them. This contract might include a commitment of the bidder for reports. The Contract Net Protocol specification fixes the syntax of messages. Part of the syntax are communication acts like TASK-ANNOUNCEMENT, BID, AWARD, ACCEPTANCE/REFUSAL, and various types of REPORT. The full protocol also contains procedures of how received messages are processed and a transition net of how steps in the protocols are executed.

Many other negotiation patterns seen in the literature are also called protocols, although no explicit reference is made to communication and message types. They are rather protocols for structured coordination patterns.

PERSUADER (Sycara 1988) deals with conflict resolution by an arbitrating agent. The basic idea is that an initial compromise is proposed by the arbitrator, a rejected proposal becomes modified, and the conflict partners are persuaded to change their evaluation of a proposed compromise. The control of this kind of negotiation is represented as a flow diagram, in which both reasoning and communicative processes are visible.

The "Hierarchical Protocol" (Durfee and Montgomery 1990) is meant for conflict detection and conflict resolution. So it primarily deals with how in interacting with other agents, an agent acquires the necessary amount of knowledge to get optimal support or to avoid hindrance.

A "Negotiation Protocol" for multiagent action planning, proposed by F. von Martial deals with a system of various "planners" and a "coordinator" (Martial 1992). The protocol has three components: (1) the states a conversation can be in, (2) the message types which can be exchanged, and (3) the conversation rules relating states to message types. The conversation rules are represented as state transition diagrams, in which the states are connected by colored directed links representing the message type and the originator of the message. Some of the message types are:

- action: a planner (P) announces a planned action to the coordinator (C).
- proposal: C proposes an action modification to P.
- approval/counter/rejection: possible reactions of P to the proposal.
- resolution/failure: positive or negative confirmation by C.
- disappearance: announces the reason for a negotiation to have vanished.
- back-out request/re-proposal: initiate a re-negotiation either by P or by C.

The "Negotiation Protocol for Conflict Resolution" (Kakehi and Tokoro 1993) deals with conflicts arising from non-shareable resources. By specific kinds of messages it is possible to communicate complete plans, parameters of plans and resources.

(Brandau and Weihmayer 1989) adopt their protocols to network management. They use message types "propose", "deny", "confirm", and "retract", where "deny" and "confirm" are possible reactions to "propose": "deny" has the meaning of "The proposed action is not possible", and 'confirm' means "The proposal can be followed". 'retract' in a certain sense is the negation of 'propose'.

In a number of articles, M. Klein and collaborators dealt with cooperation patterns as they are observed in design teams (Klein 1990). Based on a "Conflict Hierarchy" conflict resolution strategies like "abandon goal", "try alternative way", "add detailing" are described in terms of condition-action rules.

In the context of machine learning, Sian (1991) introduces several operators for communicating hypotheses: ASSERT (non-modifiable assertion), PROPOSE, MODIFY, AGREED (changes the status of a hypothesis from "proposed" to "agreed"), DISAGREE, NOOPINION, CONFIRM (indicates confirmatory evidence for a hypothesis), ACCEPT (causes acceptance for a previously agreed hypothesis), WITHDRAW (withdraws a previously formed hypothesis). The "interaction protocols" are represented as kind of state-transition diagrams showing the possible sequencing of these operators.

11.3.2   Generic Protocols

In the COORDINATOR system (Winograd and Flores 1986) dialogs ("conversations") are represented and analyzed by networks of speech acts.

As far as representation is concerned their graphs are very expressive and easy to follow. However, they miss information required to make them operational.

In (Campbell and D'Inverno 1990) roughly a dozen "tones of communication" are introduced, amongst others: "action requesting", "information seeking", "understanding an unexpected event", "intimidating", "offending", "misleading", "amusing". As seen from this selection, this is a rather random enumeration of communication verbs. These are combined into dialogs in the form of state-transition diagrams, which not only show the communication between two agents, but also – in some pseudo-logical formalization – the reasoning involved in the course of a protocol. Although these graphs may well serve their purpose, the concept of adopting such a notation as a general means of representing protocols is doubtful, since it is questionable if reasoning behind each node is application-independent.

The SANP (Speech Act based Negotiation Protocol) (Chang and Woo 1991) is based on the work of (Ballmer and Brennenstuhl 1981), in that the "Struggle Model" and the "Institutional Model" (for appealing to authority in case two agents alone are unable to compromise) are termed into well defined phases. From its very idea, the SANP is a task specific protocol meant for multilevel negotiation, including the opening of the negotiation and the possible call for authority. But the syntax and semantics of SANP graphs do allow for other dialog situations. Nodes in SANP can be either single states of conversation, or "calls" to other protocols (or what they term "phases"), which gives SANP a modular architecture.

The approach by (Haugeneder and Steiner 1991) combines task specific aspects with generic features, so "cooperation structures" can be composed from "cooperation primitives" and instantiated to cooperation strategies.

The "Cooperation Primitives" are for example:

- NOMINATE (TASK, CONSTR): S nominates R to perform TASK within CONSTRaints.
- ACCEPT (TASK,CONSTR) S accepts (w-commits) to perform TASK within CONSTR.
- ASSIGN (TASK,CONSTR, RPT).
- COMMIT-C (TASK, CONSTR): S c-commits to perform TASK (can do in principle).
- COMMIT-W (TASK, CONSTR).
- CAN (TASK, CONSTR): S c-commits to perform TASK obeying CONSTR.
- REPORT (TASK,PR): S reports TASK progress PR to R.
- WANT (TASK, CONSTR).
- OFFER (TASK, CONSTR)- POST (ITEM): S posts ITEM on global communication area.

- ASKFOR (ITEM): S looks for ITEM in global communication area.

As message types they use the ones from the IMAGINE project (cited above). So an example of a full message is:

send ((S,R), propose (ASSIGN (TASK, CONSTR, RPT) [accept, reject] deadline)).

which includes an information of which reaction is possible in principle. The composition of cooperation primitives to cooperation structures is again visualized graphically.

The KQML (Knowledge Query and Manipulation Language) is part of the ARPA "Knowledge-Sharing-Effort" project. According to (Finin *et al.* 1994) KQML is meant as "... a language that is designed to support interactions among intelligent software agents". During its development KQML underwent various modifications. In one of these (more conceptually clear) versions KQML expressions are considered as consisting of a "content" expression (i.e. an expression in some common knowledge representation language) encapsulated in a "message" wrapper (containing sort of message types) which is in turn encapsulated in a "communication" wrapper (with ingredients needed for physical communication, like sender, receiver, message IDs, synchronization). The message wrapper is itself a layered structure, where on top of a speech act layer there are three kinds of performatives – primitive: being related to adding/deleting pieces of knowledge or adopting/dropping goals – core: "several dozen" operators like ASSERT, RETRACT, ASK, MONITOR - extended: up to contracting and negotiating. Among these performatives are some by which a common language is agreed upon and others setting the boundary of the discourse domain. There are about two dozen reserved performatives in order to distinguish different kinds of questions, control messages, and replies. Although this is rather expressive for the exchange of knowledge, these details hide the core problem of coordination protocols, namely how to describe dialogs by performatives. To make the bookkeeping about messages IDs surely is not sufficient for this purpose. We also doubt that the many details treated in the KQML proposal are semantically clear enough to serve as a standardization.

The GCP ("Generic Configurable Protocols") (Burmeister *et al.* 1993) are generic in the sense that a protocol execution algorithm treats the domain independent parts separately from the application dependent reasoning and decision making processes involved, and that protocols are defined from primitives and recursively from other protocols. GCP have different abstraction levels, namely (1) structure/syntax of messages; (2) message types; (3) procedures for preparing messages to send and for processing received messages; (4) protocols combined from message types and procedures. A GCP message consists of a header and a content. The header contains administrative information such as addresses of the sender and receiver. The semantics of a message is described by the content which includes the fields message type, descriptor, and text.

GCP provides some basic message types which are used by most of the other authors. These are INFORM (with subtypes ANSWER, REJECT, REPORT), QUERY, COMMAND, and OFFER. A descriptor describes whether the proposition is referring to resources, behaviors or intentions, which are the building blocks of the agent description language. The field text is an application dependent syntactic construct for the actual proposition.

Messages are prepared and sent by send-procedures. Each procedure is specialized to prepare messages with a specific message type, and instantiates the required fields of the message. Similarly for each message type there is a process-procedure. A process-procedure's task is to interpret and handle reactions to received messages.

The graphical representation of a GCP (see Figure 11.1) consists of a heading which is the name of the protocol and some parameters, and a labeled tree which represents the possible steps of dialogue in that protocol.

The parameters in the heading are the addresses of the sender and receiver of the first message in the protocol, and two parameter lists. One list is employed by the initial sender and the other by the initial receiver in the protocol. For the initial sender, the list contains at least the content of the message, and for the initial receiver, the message received. These parameters will be given to the send- and process-procedures of the sender and receiver respectively.

The nodes in the tree represent conversation states, links represent transitions from a conversation state to another, and branches represent possible next states where only one branch can be taken from one level to another.

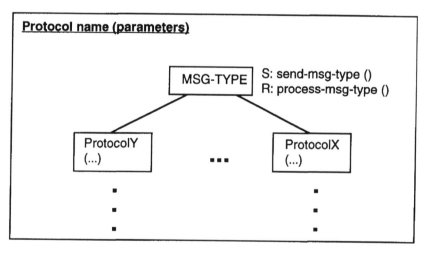

Figure 11.1   A generic protocol

This makes the tree an exclusive OR tree.

For ease of readability and consistency, nodes in a protocol tree are designated as follows:

- The root node characterizes the protocol, it represents the state when the first message is sent by the sender and processed after being received by the receiver. This is represented by denoting the send-procedure after the "S:"-label and the corresponding process-procedure after the "R:"-label.
- Other nodes are calls to other protocols (subprotocols).

Nodes are labeled using color and text:

- The color represents the active agent (i.e. sender of the message) at that node. A white node indicates that the sender of the first message in the protocol is also the sender at this node. A gray node indicates that the receiver of the first message in the protocol is the sender at this node.
- The text label on the root node is the message-type which characterizes the protocol. For every protocol there has to be a unique message type so that the receiver could infer which protocol to follow. The texts on the other nodes are (sub)protocol names with their parameters.

In Figure 11.2, four primitive protocols are presented. The Informing protocol is used to provide information to the receiver. Messages of type

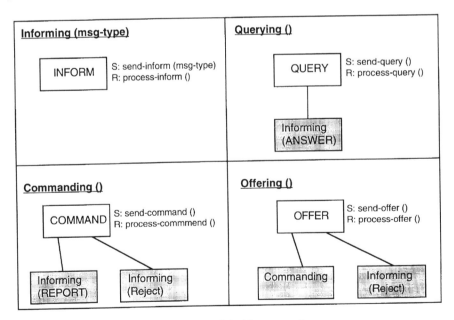

Figure 11.2   Primitive protocols

ANSWER, REJECT, REPORT and the like are also sent using the Informing protocol with the corresponding message type as its parameter. A Querying protocol, of course, is used to inquire some information. The receiver of the first message processes the query, prepares the answer and invokes the Informing protocol (as the subprotocol of Querying) to send the answer. Commanding is used to command an agent (by default the receiver) to execute a behavior. If the receiver does not reject the command, it sends a report to the commander after execution. Finally, Offering is used when an agent offers to execute a behavior for another agent.

If required, other application specific primitives can be defined, or an already defined primitive can be modified. For instance, in a Commanding protocol, one can include appropriate responds after the report is sent or eliminate the option of rejecting the command.

The primitive protocols can be used as building blocks in more complex protocols. For demonstration, two example protocols Requesting and Proposing are described and demonstrated in Figure 11.3.

In a Requesting (used to request another agent to execute a behavior protocol), the possible reactions of the receiver of the request are: (1) reject the request; (2) accept the request by using an Offering protocol, which in turn gives the receiver of the offer (i.e. the sender of the request) options of rejecting the offer (i.e. withdrawing the request), or commanding it; or (3) propose to carry out the requested action with different conditions. The Proposing protocol, used by an agent to propose to execute a behavior for another agent, can similarly be read off the protocol graph.

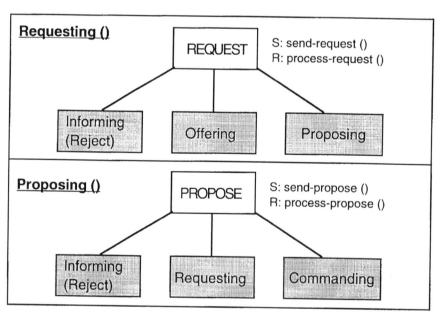

Figure 11.3 Requesting and Proposing protocols

In summary, GCP graphs represent the possible conversation courses, hiding away the reasoning states, as opposed to diagrams of (Campbell and D'Inverno 1990). Since reasoning and decision processes involved in the course of a cooperation are application dependent, they are not present at the representation level, but treated outside the protocol. GCP can be seen as an abstraction from those state transition diagrams where a node denotes either the sender or the receiver of a message. In GCP graphs, the sending, receiving and processing of a message is adhered to a single node and the transition to the next state is made when sending or receiving a new message. In the same lines as (Chang and Woo 1992), the GCP is modular since nodes can also be calls to other protocols.

However, the GCP graphs are not only demonstrative for sketching cooperation methods for analysis, but may be translated to an executable representation. As a matter of fact they are building blocks in the DASEDIS testbed, developed in the COSY project [Sundermeyer 91]. The designers are provided means by which they can convert the graphical representation of a protocol to the equivalent LISP-representation. Message type(s) associated with a protocol can be defined as unique message types, or as subtypes of previously defined message types.

The concepts behind GCP are independent of the message types used. The approach can adopt any standardization of message types the DAI community might agree upon. Since the reasoning and decision making processes involved are kept outside protocols, a designer can take protocols intact and interface them to the application's reasoning needs.

11.4 Conclusion

In summary, the studies of high-level communication within agent systems owe a great deal to the work in speech act theory, specifically, their impact on message types. However, DAI can at most get inspired by linguistic speech act theory and, if dealing with artificial agents, restrict itself to simplified contexts. For instance, there are no problems with indirect speech acts, emotional speech acts are inapplicable, and largely synonymous communication acts can be modeled alike.

Numerous message types have been introduced in the literature, however, each author has his/her own interpretation. To describe communication on a more abstract level, one requires structures which go beyond message types, leading to dialogs and coordination protocols. Individual protocols have been devised for specific tasks and fail to clearly separate the domain independent and domain dependent aspects of coordination. As a matter of fact a literature survey is rather disappointing. The protocols proposed are difficult to compare since in each protocol, low level aspects concerning communication and aspects of a cooperation dialog are related differently.

For generic protocols it is accepted that, in view of the wide span of rather complex cooperation patterns (like "contracting") to primitive communication forms (like "inform") various layers are to be distinguished, for instance

- procedures for preparing messages to be sent and methods for processing received messages.
- message types.
- communication forms: offer, bid, contract, report.
- coordination structures: example contract netbinding protocols to known techniques of coordination, like multistage coordination (Conry et al. 1986), partial global planning (Durfee and Lesser 1989), or constraint-directed negotiation (Sathi and Fox 1989).

This gives rise to the questions (i) How rich should the syntax of a message be, to aid its "fast" interpretation? (ii) Is it possible to define application independent protocols? (iii) Could one find a set of primitives and build protocols from these primitives? or (iv) Is it more appropriate to have separate categories of cooperation primitives to model cooperation forms?

On the other hand, the requirements on protocols are:

- general and simple (graphical) notation.
- explicit representation of a dialog showing both agents involved – representation of message processing.
- modular generic building blocks, such that complex protocols or domain specific ones can be configured from simpler ones.
- operational semantics, in the sense that the representation is directly translatable to the implementable equivalent – ease of design and modification.

It is agreed in the community that communication in DAI is more than communication in traditional distributed systems. But whereas traditional communication already has its standard in terms of the OSI layer model, there is not yet a communication standard in DAI. The KQML proposal so far is not sufficient for multiagent systems, since it is restricted to communication involved with exchanging knowledge and cannot accommodate communication about actions, intentions, and resources other than knowledge.

Acknowledgments

I would like to thank the other members of the COSY team, especially Birgit Burmeister and Afsaneh Haddadi for their collaborative work on GCP, and Stefan Bussmann and Michael Wooldridge for their careful reading of the last version of this article.

Chapter 12

Modeling Distributed Industrial Processes in a Multi-Agent Framework

*Frances M. T. Brazier, Barbara Dunin-Keplicz,
Nick R. Jennings and Jan Treur*

12.1 Introduction

Automation of industrial and business processes has focused primarily on modeling information available within and applicable to an organization. Large quantities of data have become not only available but also easily accessible, to appropriate (groups of) individuals within an organization.

The processes themselves, however, have been given less attention. Different (coordinated) processes within an organization can often be modeled as autonomous distributed processes with known goals. Goal-driven processes can be seen as tasks within an organization. Tasks can often be decomposed into subtasks and most often involve more than one individual. Coordination between individuals, also called agents, is essential, as is interaction and cooperation (see Chapters 2–6 and 11). To model business processes not only the requirements tasks impose upon individual agents within an organization are of importance, but also the requirements tasks impose on coordination and interaction between (groups of) individual agents.

For individual agents the specific expertise required to perform tasks for which the agent is responsible should be made explicit in terms of knowledge and reasoning capabilities. The expertise required to guide interaction, cooperation and coordination between agents is of a slightly different nature. Individual agents should know of the implications of distributed task performance with respect to interaction, cooperation and coordination, and be capable of acting appropriately.

A modeling framework should support explicit specification of both types of expertise. Transparent models of distributed agents and the relevant interaction are essential. The framework DESIRE (framework for DEsign and Specification of Interacting REasoning components; (Langevelde *et al.* 1992, Brazier *et al.* 1994)), supports specification of knowledge, interaction and coordination of complex tasks and reasoning capabilities (see Chapter 13).

Within the framework, complex processes are designed as interacting task-based hierarchically structured components: as compositional architectures. The interaction (and coordination) between components, between components and the external world, and between components and one or more users (Brazier and Treur 1994), is precisely specified. Components can be reasoning components (including a knowledge base), but may also be subsystems which are capable of performing tasks such as calculation, information retrieval, optimization, etc. As the framework inherently supports interaction between components, interaction between agents (modeled as components) is a natural application of the framework, shown in (Brazier *et al.* 1995, Dunin-Keplicz and Treur 1995).

The philosophy behind the DESIRE framework is that it should support knowledge engineers on focusing on the specification of the conceptual design of a system: on both the static and the dynamic aspects to be considered. Implementation generators exist to automatically generate prototype implementations from specifications. DESIRE is currently used by a number of companies and research institutes for the development of compositional systems for complex tasks. A number of these systems are currently operational.

Specifications in DESIRE and their semantics can be made formal (on the basis of temporal logic (Engelfriet and Treur 1994, Gavrila and Treur 1994, Treur 1994)). The formal basis offers the possibility to develop dedicated verification and validation methods for the domain of multi-agent systems. In contrast to general purpose formal specification languages, such as Z and VDM, DESIRE is committed to well structured compositional architectures. Such architectures can be specified in DESIRE at a higher level of conceptualization than specifications in Z or VDM.

This chapter briefly describes the framework DESIRE and its application to a multi-agent organization. One of the few operational real-world distributed artificial intelligence applications, modeling an electricity transportation management task (Jennings *et al.* 1995), is used to illustrate how business processes are modeled within this framework. This domain of application is described below in Section 2. In Section 3 a brief description of the DESIRE framework is presented. The results of modeling and specifying the multi-agent electricity transportation management task are presented in Section 4. Finally, in Section 5 these results are discussed and further perspectives presented.

12.2 The Application Domain

The multi-agent system used as an illustration in this chapter was developed in the ARCHON project (Cockburn and Jennings 1996) and is currently running on-line in a control room in the North of Spain (Jennings *et al.* 1995). An electricity transportation network carries electricity from generation sites to the local networks where it is distributed to customers. Managing this network is a complex activity which involves a number of different subtasks: monitoring the network, diagnosing faults, and planning and carrying out maintenance when such faults occur. Seven agents are distinguished in the running application, of which five are discussed in this chapter.

The Control System Interface Agent (CSI) continuously receives data from the network – e.g. alarm messages on unusual events and status information about the network's components. From this information, the CSI periodically produces a snapshot which describes the entire system state at the current instant in time. It also performs a preliminary analysis on the data it receives from the network to determine whether there may be a fault.

Two diagnosis agents are also considered – an Alarm Analysis Agent (AAA) and a Blackout Area Identifier Agent (BAI). Both of these agents are activated by the receipt of information from CSI which indicates the possibility of a fault. They both use CSI's snapshot information to update their model of the network on which their diagnosis is based. BAI is a fast and relatively unsophisticated diagnostic system which can pinpoint the approximate region of the fault (the initial blackout area) but not the specific element which is at fault. AAA, on the other hand, is a sophisticated model-based diagnosis system which is able to generate and verify the cause of the fault in the network. It does this in a number of different phases. Firstly, it performs an approximate *hypothesis generation task* which produces a large number of potential hypotheses (the knowledge used here guarantees that the actual fault is always contained in this initial list). It then takes each of these hypotheses in turn and performs a time consuming *validation* task to determine the likelihood that the given hypothesis is the cause of the problem.

Cooperation occurs between AAA and BAI in that BAI's initial blackout area can be used to prune the search space of AAA's hypothesis validation task. It can do this because the fault will be contained in the initial blackout area – hence any hypotheses produced by AAA's generation task which are not in the blackout area can be removed from the list to be considered by AAA's validation task. The blackout area can be received by AAA in two different ways. The most usual route is that BAI will volunteer it as unsolicited information – BAI maintains a model of all of the agents in the system (its *acquaintance models*) and its model of AAA will specify AAA's interest in receiving information about the blackout area. Hence, when this information is produced, BAI will automatically send it to AAA. The other route is that AAA will generate a request for information as the initial blackout area – this request will be directed to BAI because AAA's acquaintance model of BAI indicates that BAI has a task which produces the initial blackout area as a result.

The final agent considered is a Service Restoration Agent (SRA) which generates a plan of action to be used to repair the network once the cause and location of the fault have been determined. To this end candidate actions are proposed and examined for feasibility and relevance. Finally, a repair plan is prepared with approved actions. The execution of this plan (guided by the human operator) is monitored cooperatively by CSI, which groups any alarm messages coming from the network, and BAI checks that SRA's predictions about the various intermediate states of its recover plan are reflected in the real network.

12.3 A Specification Framework for Multi-Agent Systems

The architectures upon which specifications for compositional multi-agent systems are based are the result of analysis of the tasks performed by and between agents. Task (de)compositions include specifications of interaction between subtasks at each level within a task (de)composition, making it possible to explicitly model tasks which entail interaction between agents. Task models define the structure of compositional architectures: components in a *compositional architecture* are directly related to (sub)tasks in a task (de)composition. The hierarchical structures of tasks, interaction and knowledge are fully preserved within compositional architectures. Often more than one agent is involved in the performance of a given task. Task coordination between agents then becomes essential. As agents are often capable of performing one or more (sub)tasks, either sequentially or in parallel, task coordination within agents themselves is also essential.

Below a formal compositional framework for modeling multi-agent tasks is introduced, in which

1. a task (de)composition,
2. information exchange,
3. sequencing of (sub)tasks,
4. subtask delegation, and
5. knowledge structures,

are explicitly modeled and specified.

12.3.1 Task (De)composition

To model and specify (de)composition of tasks, knowledge is required of:

- a task hierarchy,

- information a task requires as *input*,
- information a task produces as a *result* of task performance
- *meta-object relations* between (sub)tasks (which (sub)tasks reason about which other (sub)tasks).

Within a task hierarchy *composed* and *primitive* tasks are distinguished: in contrast to primitive tasks, composed tasks are tasks for which subtasks are identified. Subtasks, in turn, can be either composed or primitive. Tasks are directly related to components: composed tasks are specified as composed components and primitive tasks as primitive components.

An example of a *task hierarchy* for the task of electricity transportation management is shown below in Figure 12.1. The hierarchy represents the task structure as a whole, independent of the agents involved. The leaves represent the primitive tasks.

Information required/produced by a (sub)task is defined as *input* and *output signatures* of a component. The signatures used to name the information are defined in a predicate logic with a hierarchically ordered sort structure (order-sorted predicate logic). Units of information are represented by the (ground; i.e. instantiated) *atoms* defined in the signature.

The role information plays within reasoning is indicated by the level of an

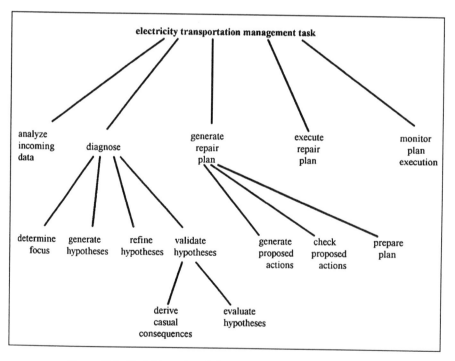

Figure 12.1   Task hierarchy of electricity transportation management

atom within a signature: different (meta)levels may be distinguished. In a two level situation the lowest level is termed *object-level information*, and the second level *meta-level information*. Meta-level information contains information about object-level information and reasoning processes; for example, for which atoms the values are still unknown (*epistemic information*). Similarly *tasks* which include reasoning about other tasks are modeled as meta-level tasks with respect to object-level tasks. Often more than two levels of information and reasoning occur, resulting in meta-meta-... information and reasoning.

12.3.2 Information Exchange Between Tasks

Information exchange between tasks is specified as *information links* between components. Each information link relates output of one component to input of another, by specifying which truth value of a specific output atom is linked with which truth value of a specific input atom. Atoms can be renamed: each component can be specified in its own language, independent of other components. The conditions for activation of information links are explicitly specified as task control information: knowledge of sequencing of tasks.

12.3.3 Sequencing of Tasks

Task sequencing is explicitly modeled within components as *task control knowledge*. Task control knowledge includes not only knowledge of which subtasks should be activated when and how, but also knowledge of the goals associated with task activation and the amount of effort which can be afforded to achieve a goal to a given extent. These aspects are specified as (sub)component and link activation together with sets of targets and requests, exhaustiveness and effort to define the component's goals. Subcomponents are, in principle, black boxes to the task control of an encompassing component: task control is based purely on information about the success and/or failure of component activation. Activation of a component is considered to have been successful, for example, with respect to one of its target sets, (given specifications of the number of goals to be reached (e.g. any or every) and the effort to be afforded) if it has reached the goals specified by this target set.

Task control is limited to global internal control and is independent of the content of the underlying components or knowledge.

12.3.4 Delegation of Tasks

During knowledge acquisition a task as a whole is modeled. In the course of the modeling process decisions are made as to which (sub)tasks are best performed by which *agent*. This process, may also be performed at run-time, results in the delegation of (sub)tasks to the parties involved in task execution.

For electricity transportation management tasks can be divided over the participating agents as shown below in Figure 12.2.

12.3.5 Knowledge Structures

During knowledge acquisition an appropriate structure for domain knowledge must be devised. The meaning of the concepts used to describe a domain and the relations between concepts and groups of concepts, must be determined. Concepts are required to identify objects distinguished in a domain, but also to express the methods and strategies employed to perform a task. Concepts and relations between concepts are defined in *hierarchies* and *rules* (based on order-sorted predicate logic). In a specification document references to appropriate knowledge structures (specified elsewhere) suffice.

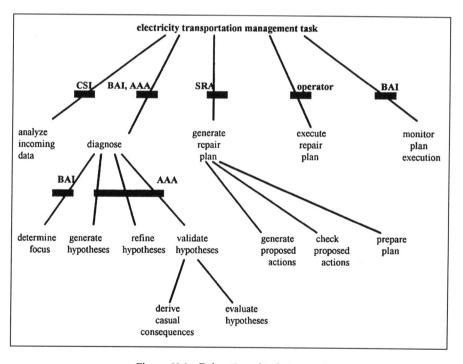

Figure 12.2   Delegation of tasks to agents

12.4 Formal Model and Specification of a Multi-Agent System

A *compositional agent* is a composed component with a number of subcomponents representing the agent's tasks. The types of knowledge distinguished above are described below for the compositional agents involved in the electricity transportation management task.

12.4.1 Task Decomposition and Role Allocation

The task hierarchy presented in Section 3.1 is a task hierarchy for the electricity transportation management task represented as a single composed task. In Section 3.4 subtasks are delegated to individual agents. Agents, however, not only perform tasks directly related to electricity transportation management; but also perform tasks related to their own internal process management and tasks related to interaction with other agents and to interaction with the material world.

The example system described in Section 2 consists of five agents (CSI, AAA, BAI, SRA, operator) and their interactions. The main tasks of each of the agents in this example are similar; they each have the same three generic tasks (own process control, update world state information, preparing communication) and one agent-specific task to perform: e.g. diagnose fault (for the agent AAA), or identify blackout area (for the agent BAI). In Figure 12.3 agent AAA's first level decomposition is depicted. These generic tasks are generic in the sense that they can be (specialized and) instantiated for different agents (reuse).

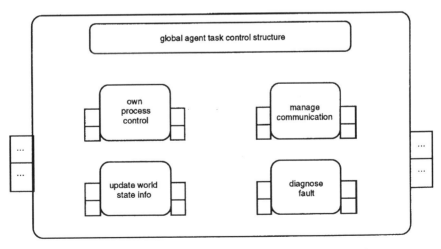

Figure 12.3 Top-level compositional structure of agent AAA

In Figure 12.3 the small boxes on the left- and right-hand side denote the leveled input and output interface, respectively, indicating object-meta distinctions. Agent AAA's complete task hierarchy as described in Section 2 is shown below in Figure 12.4:

1.	Own process control	
	1.1	Monitoring incoming data
	1.2	Evaluating the process state
2.	Update world state information	
3.	Diagnose fault (agent specific task)	
	3.1	Hypothesis generation
	3.2	Hypothesis refinement
	3.3	Hypothesis validation
		3.3.1 Evaluating hypothesis
		3.3.2 Deriving causal consequences
4.	Manage communication	
	4.1	Examining the acquaintance model
	4.2	Generating requests

Figure 12.4   Complete task hierarchy of agent AAA

Task-subtask relations for AAA's top level (as shown in Figure 12.3) are specified as follows:

task structure AAA
    subcomponents own_process_control, update_world_state_info,
                     diagnose_fault, manage_communication;
   ....

12.4.2 Information Flow Within an Agent

Information links are defined to model *information exchange* between components *within an agent*. The information links of AAA's top level are depicted in Figure 12.5. The information links used within a component are specified as part of the task structure; for agent AAA, the specification of AAA's *task structure* is as follows:

task structure AAA
    subcomponents own_process_control, update_world_state_info,
                   diagnose_fault, manage_communication;

links   incoming_snapshot_for_own_process_control,
                             incoming_snapshot_for_world_info_update,
                             grouped_alarms, blackout_area,
                             current_snapshot, request_info, request_to_output,
                             fault_results_to_output, request_out;
end task structure AAA

An example of an *information link specification* (see Sections 3.1.2 and 3.2.2) within AAA is link (5) between the component update_world_state_information and the component diagnose_fault:

private link   current_snapshot: object-object
   domain   update_world_state_information
   output   world_state_info
   codomain   diagnose_fault
   input   world_state_info
   sort links   (World_state,World_state)
   object links   identity
   term links   identity
   atom links   (current_world_state_info(I:World_state),current_
                             world_state_info(I:World_state)):
                             <<true,true>,<false,false>>
endlink

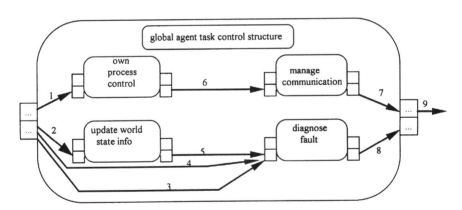

incoming_snapshot_for_own_process_control (1),
incoming_snapshot_for_world_info_update (2),
grouped_alarms (3), blackout_area (4),
current_snapshot (5), request_info (6), request_to_output (7),
fault_results_to_output (8), request_out (9)

Figure 12.5   Information flow of agent AAA's top level

This link relates output of the component update_world_state_information to input of the component diagnose_fault. The truth value (true, resp. false) of the atom   current_world_state_   info(l:World_state)   is   transferred   from update_world_state_information to diagnose_fault.

One level down in AAA's hierarchy, the decomposition and information flow within agent AAA's component diagnose_fault is specified as follows:

task structure diagnose_fault
        subcomponents hypothesis_generation, hypothesis_refinement,
                    hypothesis_validation;
      links   import_disturbances, import_blackout_info,
                    poss_hyps_to_refine,
                    import_snapshot_info, lim_hyps_to_validate,
                    poss_hyps_to_validate, diagnosis_to_output;
end task structure diagnose_fault

This information is depicted in Figure 12.6.

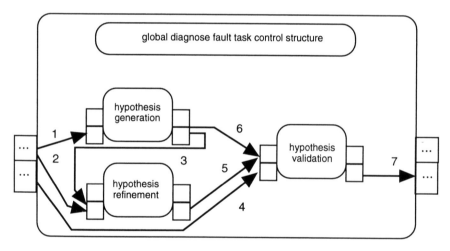

import_disturbances (1), import_blackout_info (2),
poss_hyps_to_refine (3),
import_snapshot_info (4), lim_hyps_to_validate (5),
poss_hyps_to_validate (6), diagnosis_to_output (7)

Figure 12.6   The component diagnose fault of agent AAA

An example of an information link specification within the component diagnose_fault is link (6) between the components hypothesis_generation and hypothesis_validation:

private link	poss_hyps_transfer: object-object
domain	hypothesis_generation
output	poss_hyps
codomain	hypothesis_validation
input	hyps
sort links	(Hyps,Hyps)
object links	identity
term links	identity
atom links	(poss_hyp(H:Hyps), hyp(H:Hyps)):
	<<true,true>,<false,false>>

    endlink

This link relates output of the component hypothesis_generation to input of the component hypothesis_validation, by which the truth value true (resp. false) of an atom of the form poss_hyp(H:Hyps) is translated into the truth value true (resp. false) of an atom of the form hyp(H:Hyps). Note that this link actually renames atoms between components.

The components hypothesis_generation and hypothesis_refinement are meta-level reasoning components (with respect to the object level reasoning about the world). They reason about the reasoning process. Which hypotheses to consider, for example, requires information about which hypotheses have already been examined: whether they have been confirmed, rejected, or are yet unknown, in the current information state of the reasoning process (epistemic information). As this is information about the state of the process itself and not about the world, the meta-level components hypothesis_generation and hypothesis_refinement use meta-information from outside the component diagnose_fault as their input: their input links start one (meta-)level higher in the input interface (see links (1), (2) and (4) in Figure 12.6).

In the specification the information links have names that can be used in the task control knowledge to specify under which conditions to transfer the up-to-date information.

12.4.3 Task Control Within an Agent

Task control knowledge (for complex and primitive tasks alike), specifies an agent's reasoning and acting patterns distributed over the hierarchy of agent components. Within our compositional framework such knowledge is expressed in temporal rules (Engelfriet and Treur 1994, Gavrila and Treur 1994, Treur 1994). Each component is assumed to have a (local, linear) discrete time scale. When and how a component will be activated (and whether activation is continuous or not) is specified explicitly. This often includes the specification of at least:

- the *interactions* required to provide the necessary input facts,

- the set of facts for which truth values are sought (*target set*).

Evaluation of the status of other components is often required to determine when a specific component is to be activated. A component is considered to have been successful with respect to one of its target sets if it has reached its goal, specified by this target set (given default specifications of the number of targets to be reached (e.g. any, or every) and the effort to be afforded). If not, it is considered to have failed.

Below, AAA's task control knowledge (Section 4.3.1) and its subcomponent diagnose_fault (Section 4.3.2) are discussed.

12.4.3.1 Agent AAA's Task Control

Control over AAA's four subtasks is limited: the seven rules presented in this section express the knowledge required to specify interaction between the four subcomponents. Activation of components does not always depend on the completion of a specific component. In some cases receipt of input causes a component to become active. The specification of the fact that a component is to be continually capable of performing its subtask during task execution (in parallel with other components), depending on the availability of new input, is expressed by the keyword awake. From the start both AAA's component own_process_control and the information link incoming_snapshot_for_own_process_control have to become and remain awake. This is expressed by:

if   start
then   next-component-state(own_process_control, awake)
   and next-target-set(own_process_control, all_targets)
   and next-link-state(incoming_snapshot_for_own_process_control, awake)

A typical example of a component's task control knowledge rule in which the success of one component is required (whether or not incoming snapshot data have been monitored by the component own_process_control) before a following component (update_world_state_info) can be activated with the required information, is the following:

if   evaluation(own_process_control, ts_update, succeeded)
then next-component-state(update_world_state_info, active)
   and next-target-set(own_process_control, ts_poss_hyps)
   and next-link-state(incoming_snapshot_for_world_info_update,
      up_to_date)

This knowledge rule states that

if   the component own_process_control has succeeded in accomplishing

the targets defined by its target set ts_update,
then the component own_process_control is assigned a new set of targets to accomplish, and the next component to be activated is specified, namely the component update_world_state_info, given information which has been recently updated by activation of the link incoming_snapshot_for_world_info_update.

Note that next-link-state(incoming_snapshot_for_world_info_update, up_to_date) indicates that the link incoming_snapshot_for_world_info_update has been activated in order to transfer the information required for the next component, update_world_state_info. This is not a guarantee that the information itself is new: it is only a guarantee that the link has been activated.

The component diagnose_fault is activated if the component own_process_control determines that a fault should be diagnosed (because alarms are monitored); input information is provided on grouped alarms, the current snapshot and (if available) on the blackout area:

if state(diagnose_fault, idle)
    and evaluation(own_process_control, diagnose_target_set, succeeded)
then next-component-state(diagnose_fault, active)
    and next-target-set(diagnose_fault, faults)
    and next-link-state(grouped_alarms, up_to_date)
    and next-link-state(current_snapshot, up_to_date)
    and next-link-state(blackout_area, up_to_date)

The component manage_communication is activated if the component own_process_control determines that a request for blackout area information is needed (because this information is still lacking):

if evaluation(own_process_control, ts_requests, succeeded)
then next-component-state(manage_communication, active)
    and next-target-set(manage_communication, outgoing_requests)
    and next-link-state(request_info, up_to_date)

The actual communication is performed if the component manage_communication succeeds in generating outgoing requests; note that no component states are changed, but only two links are activated in sequence: one to AAA's output interface, and, subsequently, one from the output interface of AAA to the input interface of the agent BAI (note that the order of activation of links is expressed by the list notation):

if evaluation(manage_communication, outgoing_requests, succeeded)
then next-link-state([request_to_output, request_out], up_to_date)

If fault results are found, these are transferred to AAA's output interface:

if   evaluation(diagnose_fault, fault_results, succeeded)
then   next-link-state(fault_results_to_output, up_to_date)

If blackout information has arrived, then the diagnose fault task should be activated, with the extra information that blackout information is available:

if   evaluation(own process control, ts_blackout_area, succeeded)
then   next-link-state(blackout_area, up_to_date)
   and next-component-state(diagnose_fault, active)
   and next-target-set(diagnose_fault, faults)
   and extra_info(diagnose_fault, blackout_info_available)

12.4.3.2 Task Control Knowledge for Diagnose Fault

Task control knowledge in a lower-level component is expressed in precisely the same way as task control knowledge of a higher-level component. The control of the three subcomponents of the component diagnose_fault (hypothesis_generation, hypothesis_refinement and hypothesis_validation) begins after the activation of the component diagnose_fault:

if   component-state(diagnose_fault, start)
then   next-component-state(hypothesis_generation, active)
   and next-target-set(hypothesis_generation, ts_poss_hyps)
   and next-link-state(import_disturbances, up_to_date)

This rule states that once the component diagnose_fault has been activated, the component hypothesis_generation is to be activated with target set ts_poss_hyps and up-to-date information about disturbances.

If blackout information is available and hypotheses have been successfully generated, hypothesis_refinement has to be activated, and information on the blackout area and the generated hypotheses has to be provided.

if   evaluation(hypothesis_generation, ts_poss_hyps, succeeded)
   and extra_control_info(diagnose_fault, blackout_info_available)
then   next-component-state(hypothesis_refinement, active)
   and next-target-set(hypothesis_refinement, ts_ref_hyps)
   and next-link-state(import_blackout_info, up_to_date)
   and next-link-state(poss_hyps_to_refine, up_to_date)

If no blackout information is available, the component hypothesis_validation has to be activated, using updated snapshot information and the generated hypotheses:

if   evaluation(hypothesis_generation, ts_poss_hyps, succeeded)
    and   not extra_info(diagnose_fault, blackout_info_available)
then   next-component-state(hypothesis_validation, active)
    and   next-target-set(hypothesis_validation, ts_faults)
    and   next-link-state(import_snapshot_info, up_to_date)
    and   next-link-state(poss_hyps_to_validate, up_to_date)

The next rule expresses that if blackout information becomes available while the component hypothesis_validation is active, it has to be interrupted and cleared (to be able to first refine the generated hypotheses).

if   evaluation(hypothesis_generation, ts_poss_hyps, succeeded)
    and   extra_info(diagnose_fault, blackout_info_available)
    and   component-state(hypothesis_validation, active)
then   next-component-state(hypothesis_validation, idle)
    and   next-info-state(hypothesis_validation, clear)

After hypothesis_refinement has succeeded, hypothesis_validation has to be activated (again), using input information on the snapshot and the limited set of hypotheses obtained by the refinement:

if   evaluation(hypothesis_refinement, ts_lim_hyps, succeeded)
then   next-component-state(hypothesis_validation, active)
    and   next-target-set(hypothesis_validation, ts_faults)
    and   next-link-state(import_snapshot_info, up_to_date)
    and   next-link-state(lim_hyps_to_validate, up_to_date)

12.4.4 Control and Communication Between Agents

In addition to task control within agents, limited *global task control* is required to initially awaken all agents involved in task performance. Once agents are active, their agent task control knowledge determines the sequencing of task execution. Therefore, task control at the highest (central) level, between agents, is minimal. Only very simple start rules are specified to awaken the agents. For example:

if   start
then next-component-state(AAA, awake)

Communication between agents is modeled by activation of information links. Specific types of interaction can be modeled explicitly. For example, in a given situation an agent may require specific information to complete a reasoning task. The agent transfers this request as meta-information to one or more other agents through information links. The information requested may, as a result, be transferred back to the agent through other information links. This mechanism is an essential element in modeling communication between agents.

Interaction between an agent and the external world is modeled almost identically from the agent's point of view. For example: an *observation of the external world* may be modeled as an agent's specific request for information about the external world, transferred as meta-information to the external world through an information link. As a result of the request, information may be transferred through another link, back to the requesting agent. The external world includes information on the current state of the world.

Another form of interaction between an agent and the external world is the *performance of a specific action*. An agent performs an action by transferring information to this purpose to the external world, upon which the external world state changes.

An example of agent communication between AAA and BAI is the request AAA issues to BAI for blackout area information. The information link request_out from AAA to BAI exists for this purpose: to transfer meta-information stating that blackout area information is needed:

```
private link          request_out: object-object
    domain            AAA
    output            request_output
    codomain          BAI
    input             request_input
    atom links        (boa_info_needed, boa_info_needed): <<true,true>>
endlink
```

The control of this information link is specified in the task control knowledge of the sending agent (see the fifth rule in Section 4.3 for the control of request_out). From BAI to AAA there is an information link blackout_area_transfer to provide AAA with blackout area information; this link is controlled by BAI's task control knowledge.

12.5 Discussion

Industrial and business processes most often entail interaction between multiple autonomous agents. Modeling such processes is essential from the perspective of both knowledge management and knowledge engineering. To be able to provide support to organizations in which distributed processes are inherent, distributed models of parts and their interaction are essential. Declarative distributed models, models in which strategic, procedural and factual knowledge of the participating agents and their interaction are explicitly represented, provide a basis for such support.

The declarative compositional framework DESIRE (Langevelde *et al.* 1992, Brazier *et al.* 1994) supports the specification of multiple agents and of interaction and coordination between agents, as presented in this chapter. The cooperative interaction between agents in the example domain of electricity transportation management, used to illustrate our approach, was well defined. The framework provided the expressiveness required to model the agents and their interaction. Knowledge of other agents, coordination of parallel processes and event-driven processing, for example, are aspect characteristics to multi-agent systems, which have been explicitly modeled for this example. Other aspects, such as different states of awareness, willingness to communicate, and different (sets of) goals (for a more extensive list of agent characteristics, see, e.g. (Dieng *et al.* 1994) were not relevant to the example at hand. Current joint research focuses on a number of such aspects.

To verify and validate DESIRE models (Treur and Willems 1995), not only have formal semantics devised on the basis of temporal logic (Brazier *et al.* 1994), but also automated implementation generators have been constructed. The implication of both synchronous and asynchronous activation of agents is currently another topic of research.

Acknowledgments

This research was partly supported by the ESPRIT III Basic Research project 6156 DRUMS II on Defeasible Reasoning and Uncertainty Management Systems.

Chapter 13

Utilitarian Coalition Formation Between Autonomous Agents for Cooperative Information Gathering

Matthias Klusch

13.1 Introduction

The approach of the FCSI is motivated by the idea of following the recently introduced paradigm of Intelligent Cooperative Information Systems (ICIS) (Papazoglou *et al.* 1992) for solving one essential problem in the research area of interoperability of database systems: *a context-based recognition of InterDatabase Dependencies (IDD) between heterogeneous, autonomous database systems.*

An IDD describes the relationship between related data of different database schemas by an integrity constraint (Elmagarid and Zhang 1992). Any approach of declarative or functional specification of IDDs like in (Sheth *et al.* 1991a, Ceri and Widom 1992, Elmagarid and Zhang 1992) presumes knowledge about where to find which kind of semantically related data. The related problem of tackling semantic heterogeneity (Sheth and Kashyap 1992) is aggravated by the need to respect in particular the association autonomy (Sheth and Larson 1990) of all respective database systems. In other words, the problem is how to find in a completely decentralized environment some semantically related non-local schema data having no prior possibility to browse through all respective exportable schema structures. Recent criticism (Bouguettaya 1992) on Federated Database Systems (FDBS) (Sheth and Larson 1990) state in particular their lack of support with respect to this *object discovery problem* (Hammer *et al.* 1993) and the recognition and maintenance of IDDs (Papazoglou *et al.* 1992).

The FCSI is the first approach towards a federative system (Müller 1993) which aims for such an intelligent support of a context-based recognition of interrelated data in autonomous databases. For this purpose the FCSI uses in particular, methods from the different research areas of terminological knowledge representation and reasoning (Nebel 1990a) as well as distributed artificial intelligence (DAI) (Müller 1993).

Local construction of a terminological information model on top of the local database schema and appropriate linking of some externally available schema objects into the local ontology enables the agent to find semantically related data already at information type, i.e. terminological level. This is done by sending some aspect terms each describing one semantic aspect of a schema object terminologically and their formal classification into the local terminological information models by the receiving agents. Proposed inter-schema assertions are compositions of locally attached state constraints on related schema objects with respect to the type of detected terminological relationship between both schema objects. Such recognition of some inter-database dependencies and respective data sharing is done without any efforts in partial or global schema integration. In order to organize a *cooperative search for semantically related data* methods for *utilitarian coalition building among the autonomous agents of the FCSI* are currently being investigated. Thus, no global information agent (Barbuceanu and Fox 1994) or central mediator agent (Behrendt *et al.* 1993) exists. In order to implement the FCSI agents we recently developed an interactive development environment for the specification and simulation of agent systems IDEAS-1 on a set of networked SUN-workstations.

The remainder of this chapter is organized as follows. Section 2 contains an introductory overview of the related research areas of federated databases and terminological knowledge representation. It is further assumed that the reader is basically familiar with the area of Distributed Artificial Intelligence (DAI) (see Chapters 10–12). A good survey of the DAI area can be found in (Müller 1993, Bond and Gasser 1988, O'Hare and Jennings 1996) or (Wooldridge and Jennings 1995). Section 3 presents the functionality and architecture of each FCSI agent while the utilitarian coalition formation between the information agents is described in Section 4. This is followed by an overview of our development toolkit for agent systems IDEAS as an implementation platform for the FCSI in Section 5. Section 6 concludes and gives an outlook on future research on the FCSI.

13.2 A Brief Introduction to some Related Research Areas

In the following two sections a short introductory overview of some of the research areas related to the FCSI approach is given: *federated database systems* and *terminological knowledge representation*. Concerning the main purpose of the FCSI, namely the cooperative, decentralized search for semantically related data in a set of autonomous databases, existing approaches for specifying interdatabase dependencies and the respective recognition problem are also outlined.

13.2.1 Federated Database Systems

The following short introduction is based on the work of (Sheth and Larson 1990).

Classification and Architecture
A Federated Database System (FDBS) is a collection of cooperating but autonomous component databases. In contrast to a Distributed DataBase System (DDBS) an FDBS is created in a top-down fashion, means by a partial integration of already pre-existing databases while respecting particularly their association autonomy and solving semantic heterogeneity between them. Semantic heterogeneity occurs when there is a disagreement about the meaning or intended use of the same or related data, like homonyms, synonyms, value or domain conflicts as presented, e.g. in (Sheth and Kashyap 1992). Association autonomy implies that each component database decides itself which kind of private schema data in the local conceptual schema it is willing to share. There is no centralized control for data sharing in a federated architecture.

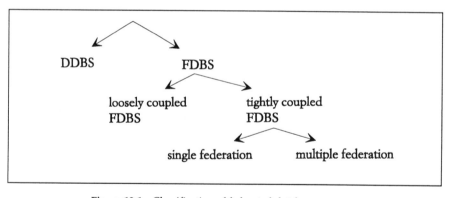

Figure 13.1   Classification of federated database systems

The development of an FDBS includes the equivalent translation of the given local schemas into homogeneous *component schemas* using a canonical data model, the definition of the available parts of these component schemas as *export schemas* and finally their integration into a *federated schema* of a federation, is shown in the five-level schema architecture in Figure 13.2. An *external schema* defines a schema or view customized for each user. The *federal data dictionary or directory* is for auxiliary purposes. It includes for example,

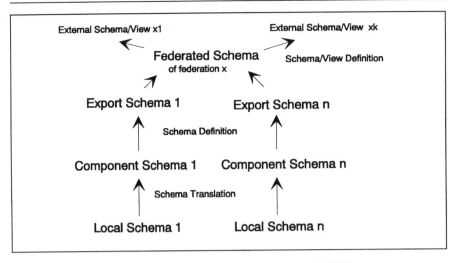

Figure 13.2   5-Level-schema architecture of a FDBS

information about the translations, mappings and the addresses of the federation participants.

Federated databases can be further classified with respect to who creates and manages the federation and how the component databases are integrated. A *tightly coupled* FDBS provides location, replication, and distribution transparency. This is accomplished by developing a federated schema that integrates multiple export schemas (Figure 13.2). The transparencies are provided by the mappings between the federated and the export schemas, so the user can pose a query against one single or multiple federation schemas, without knowing where the requested data is located. A federation administrator defines and manages the federated schema and the external schemas related to it. There may exist a single or multiple federated schemas within one FDBS.

In contrast to that, in *loosely coupled* systems no static global or partial schema integration takes place and provides no transparency. Instead of a central federation administrator the user has to be sophisticated to find appropriate export schemas to provide the required data to define the respective mapping operations. Systems which are based on such a dynamically integration of export schema by the use of an extended query language are called Multidatabase-Language Systems (Bright and Hurson 1991).

The federated dictionary of each component database and the respective export schema provides the information needed for defining a set of transactions stored locally for the access of the non-local and available importable data. This is realized in (Elmagarid and Zhang 1992) by their concept of quasi-views, i.e. views of data, derived from other importable data with possible non-immediate consistency, allowing transparent distributed data access. They use an extended SQL-based query language similar to MSQL in the work of (Litwin 1985) for the creation of such global views by the user. The necessary mapping and administrative information, means that the description of exportable schema data and its importer verifies consistency criteria as well as, e.g. time constraints used for processing queries, must be maintained by both, the importer and exporter, to provide support for interdependent data. After the user has determined the data on which the quasi-view will depend, such information is used for negotiation between exporter and importer.

However, the fact that each component database is autonomous leads to the inherent problem of enforcing *global concurrency control* in order to ensure data consistency in the federation. In the literature many approaches exist to deal with pragmatical efforts to limit the functionality of such control in favor of preserving the local site autonomy. This is done, for example, by the introduction of weaker consistency criteria and respective methods for multidatabase transaction processing. Because of space limitation we omit going into such detail.

Specification of interdatabase dependencies
Following (Elmagarid and Zhang 1992) interdependent data are data which are related by an integrity constraint specifying their mutual dependency. Kinds of semantic heterogeneity determine respective interdatabase dependencies. Examples of interdependent data include replicated data, partially replicated data or summary data. Existing approaches for a declarative or functional specification of such dependencies between related data in different databases are listed below:

- Data Dependency Descriptors D3 (Sheth and Karabatis 1991)
- Existence and Value Dependencies (Ceri and Widom 1992)
- Semantic Proximities (Sheth and Kashyap 1992)
- Inter-Schema Correspondence Assertions ISCA (Naiman and Ouksel 1993)

The approach of (Sheth *et al.* 1991a) denotes directed data dependencies by a logical predicate using relational algebra while (Ceri and Widom 1992) a SQL-based language is used for this purpose. We omit to describe all approaches here. For example, the *data dependency descriptor* (D3) in (Sheth *et al.* 1991a) between so-called source and target data objects is defined by the following expression

$$D3 = (S, U, P, C, A)$$

S   *source data objects*
U   *target data objects*

P   *Boolean-valued dependency predicate using relational algebra operators on S, U;*

C   *Boolean-valued consistency predicate;*

specifying when P has to be satisfied: uses temporal and data state events, i.e. after t, before t, every t, at t, during t and #updates on, #versions of, respectively,

A set of procedures for consistency restoration; invocation iff C=true and P=false

Thus, as an example, the following D3 describes a kind of interdatabase dependency (P), namely the replication of a relation E_1 in database db_1 as E_2 in db_2, together with the desired consistency requirement (C), means checking this dependency every 15 updates of $db_1.E_1$, and the respective simple restoration procedure duplicate-E which copies $db_1.E_1$ into $db_2.E_2$:

($DB_1.E_1$, $DB_2.E_2$, $E_1 = E_2$, $c_1 :=$ (15 updates on $DB_1.E_1$), **when** c_1 duplicate-E)

The Object Discovery Problem in FDBS:
All of the above mentioned approaches, have in common the so-called object discovery problem. In order to specify any kind of interdatabase dependency there must be knowledge given on where to find the kind of related data. This means, how to acquire the relevant knowledge and how to automate the underlying decentralized search for such intensional relationships.

Some criticism on federated database systems like in (Bouguettaya 1992) and (Papazoglou *et al.* 1992) state in particular their lack of support with respect to the recognition and maintenance of interdatabase dependencies. (Larson 1989) emphasizes that in loosely coupled federated databases no global integrity constraints can be expressed across sites, because no global control exists to detect the underlying data relationships to enforce them. Even in tightly coupled FDBS where the local export schemas are integrated into a fixed federated schema by the responsible central federation administrator, there must be some way to give information *a prior* about the local semantics of the available data. The recognition of this intensionally related data respecting the association autonomy of each component database can be done without any effort at static schema integration or any necessity for the user to browse through known export schemas to find relevant schema data which is in contrast to the tightly coupled and loosely coupled FDBS. One main drawback of browsing through export schemas is that the local interpretation of importable, non-local schema structures is heavily burdened to the potential importer and relies on the unique mutual understanding of the semantic descriptions attached to these schema data by the exporter. Besides, all parts of one export schema are visible in the same degree for all participants in the federation as are the others. Discovery of relationships between data in different databases is obviously needed, for example, for specifying a query for relevant non-local data "on-the-fly" in a view for a negotiation with the exporter (Elmagarid and Zhang 1992).

The FCSI provides an approach for cooperatively discovering intensionally related data in a decentralized and autonomous environment by utilizing particular techniques from terminological knowledge representation and reasoning.

13.2.2 Terminological Knowledge Representation

Within the research area of terminological knowledge representation and reasoning, during the last decade many so-called *description logics* were investigated. Nearly all of them are decidable fragments of first-order predicate logic and much more expressive than prepositional logic. They are based on the work of Brachman and Schmolze, the KL-ONE System (Brachman and Schmolze 1985). Such terminological or concept languages provide a structured formalism to axiomatically describe the relevant *concepts* of an application domain and the interactions between these concepts using *roles*. Concepts and roles can be seen as unary and binary predicates, respectively. Complex concepts will be inductively build from primitive components or atomic concepts and roles by given *term-forming operators*. A *terminology* (Tbox) is a set of such complete or partial definitions, i.e. *terminological axioms*, of named concepts and roles. Unlike in other conceptual or semantic data models it is possible to describe concepts and roles using intensional descriptions phrased in terms of necessary but not sufficient properties that must be satisfied by their instances. The first kind of concepts are so-called primitive while the latter are so-called defined concepts. Usual term-forming operators are among others conjunction and complement for concepts, and number and value restrictions for roles. In addition, concrete domain objects can be explicitly asserted as concept instances and related to other objects via roles by a set of so-called *assertional axioms* (Abox). This is similar to the classical distinction between the schema and state level in the database area. The terminological and the assertional formalism together constitute a so-called *hybrid knowledge representation language*. Its set-theoretically semantic is defined by an extension or interpretation function which maps the respective concepts, roles and objects to elements of the underlying domain. In contrast to databases in the area of terminological knowledge representation the open world assumption holds. This means that since there can be more objects in the universe of domain than those designated by constants in the terminological knowledge base there can be true facts that are not actually contained unless a respective given constraint prevents this. The well known unique name assumption is also valid in such systems.

Classification of some concept into a given terminology bases on the notion of *subsumption*. One concept subsumes another one if in a perfect world, the set of instances is contained in that of the other. It is possible to determine subsumption between concepts as well as roles by only considering their given terminological definitions and a structural comparison of respective terms. This leads to a *subsumption hierarchy* of named terms, the concept and the role taxonomy.

Although for almost all expressive description logics term subsumption is decidable, as it is e.g. for ALC (Smolka and Schmidt-Schauß 1991) while in (Schmidt-Schauß 1989) it is proven to be undecidable for KL-ONE, its computation is inherently intractable (Nebel 1990b, Smolka and Nebel 1989). So for pragmatic reasons most terminological systems use an incomplete but polynomial subsumption algorithm. Available systems are, e.g. CLASSIC (Borgida *et al.* 1989), KRIS (Baader and Hollunder 1991) or BACK (Luck 1989).

Each system is for terminological representation and reasoning. They provide the following main inference services:

- *Classification*:
  Determine the exact position of a given concept definition in a known concept taxonomy by calculating the respective subsumption relationships.
- *Consistency of the terminological knowledge base*:
  Check if the set of assertions respects all axioms of the terminology, so all instantiations in the Abox are consistent with the given vocabulary.
- *Terminological realization of an object*:
  Compute the set of the most specialized concepts of the terminology; a given object is an instance of.
- *Instantiation*:
  Check if a particular assertion is valid with respect to the terminological knowledge base.
- *Retrieval*:
  Retrieve all known instances of a given concept description.

Because of space limitation a more detailed introduction to hybrid terminological knowledge representation and reasoning is given in (Nebel 1990a).

13.3 The FCSI-Agent: Functionality and Architecture

13.3.1 Local Construction of Information Models

As already reported in (Klusch 1995b) according to a set of user-specified *aspect scripts* or views on some exportable own schema objects a local *Domain Information Terminology* (DIT) and its actually instantiated meta-object world

(W) on top of the conceptual database schema is built at each agent independently from each other. Such terminological knowledge bases constitute the so-called *local information models* at intensional level. For this purpose an *Information Terminological Formalism* (ITF) as well as a *Schema Aspect Assertional formalism* (SAF) as its conservative extension (Nebel 1990a) is used at each local site. The ITF provides most usual term-forming operators like conjunction of concepts, number, value and existential restriction for roles as well as atomic concept negation. Both formalisms constitute together the hybrid terminological description language (ITL). The choice of ITL does not influence the functionality of the FCSI agents in principle. Obviously, there exists several alternatives for hybrid terminological reasoning within each agent like the more expressive ALC (Smolka and Schmidt-Schauß 1991, Hollunder and Nutt 1990) or ALCF(D) (Baader and Hanschke 1992). In (Smolka and Schmidt-Schauß 1991) term subsumption in ALC is proven to be PSPACE-complete and in time co-NP-hard (Smolka and Nebel 1989) decidable. This also holds for its sublanguage ITL. As mentioned in Section 2.2 for reasons of efficiency the used subsumption algorithm is polynomial but incomplete as is the case in most practical terminological systems. The expressivity of ITF restricts the more natural-language based description of semantic aspects of schema objects that the user intends to represent. Note that it is not intended to restrict the use of such terminological description formalism on just an equivalent translation of the given schema like in (Beck *et al.* 1989, Sheth *et al.* 1993, Catarci and Lenzerini 1993b) or in particular (Blanco *et al.* 1994). Only in order to achieve homogeneous interschema assertions by a rule-based composition of local integrity constraints into global ones (Section 3.2.3), do we currently presume an extended entity-relationship (EER) data model to include a respective query language (Kandzia and Klein 1993) as a canonical data model for each local schema (Sheth and Larson 1990). But this assumption is unnecessary for the first phase of finding related data at the intensional, meaning terminological information level.

The main steps for the construction of a local information model DIT/W on top of a local database schema are as follows.

- **by user:**

  for each semantic aspect i_x of available schema object $o_k \in SObj$ specify one so-called *aspect script* with two following kinds of entries

1. *terminological aspect description*:

- term introductions of relevant information reference concepts c (initial)
- set of appropriate, consistent assertions about object o_k considered as an instance of c
  Terms of named information concepts are formulated in ITF, consistent term restrictions for asserted instances in SAF.

2. *aspect valuation over database schema* σ:

- (part of) relevant schema object structure: CP^{ix}
- at database state level (DML): JC^{ix}

The so-called justification constraint JC^{ix} is a qualification constraint, derived function or self denotation, means that a local integrity constraint at database state level is specified by the user. Each such *aspect valuation* can be seen as a schema view definition identified by i_x for the schema object o_k formulated in the local DML. The *aspect description* is comparable to a linguistic representation of this view definition at terminological level.

- **by FCSI Agent**: *Construction of Local Information Model and Schema Object Linking*

1. Read all given aspect scripts;

2. **Build** or extend the local terminology `DIT`:

- Collect all term introductions of concepts and roles

3. **Determine** directed, acyclic information concept hierarchy:

- Compute term subsumption hierarchy;

4. **Build** actual aspect world W of reference objects $intob \in RObj$:

- Create for each schema aspect (o_k, i_x) one reference object $intob_{k,ix}$
- Collect all assertions, substitute occurrences of o_k by $intob_{k,ix}$

5. **Check** consistency of assertions in W wrt. the terminology `DIT`;

6. **Store** one computed *Aspect Term* for each Schema Aspect (o_k, i_x):

- build conjunction of expanded terms by constraint propagation on all given assertions for unique reference object $intob_{k,ix}$ in W, i.e. terminological abstraction of the reference object wrt. `DIT/W`. It contains *only primitive term components* (`concept`$_p$, `role`$_p$).

Linking a schema object o_k into the agent's local terminological knowledge base like in (Behrendt *et al.* 1993) is formally done by interpreting the respective reference objects *intob* as one semantic aspect of o_k:

$$
\begin{array}{lll}
\text{DIT} & c_1 \doteq c_1 - term & \dots \quad c_m \doteq c_m - term \\[2pt]
           & \mid & \mid \\[2pt]
\text{W}   & (c_1\ intob_{k,i_1}) & (c_m\ intob_{k,i_n}) \quad (c_l\ intob_f) \\[2pt]
           & \updownarrow & \updownarrow \\[2pt]
           & (o_k, i_1) & (o_k, i_n) \\[2pt]
\sigma   & & o_k \\[2pt]
           & < CP^{i_1}, JC^{i_1} > & < CP^{i_n}, JC^{i_n} >
\end{array}
$$

Similar to the classical view definitions this allows to attach the same schema object to several information concepts where each is relevant for a terminological description of one of the object's particular semantic aspect. Roughly speaking, this enables to negotiate each other's conceptual schema at information type level (Bouguettaya 1992) *without* having the need and possibility to access the respective, fixed schema data structures. It is possible for each agent user to change the actual terminological representation of some aspect of an schema object without the need to change the valuation at the schema or state level and vice versa.

Example 1: Parts of a simple local information modeling for two FCSI agents are shown below. Because of space limitation the presentation of the comprehensive local DITs is omitted.

▷ FCSI agent a_1:

$$
\begin{array}{lll}
\text{DIT}_1 & Man \doteq (\underline{and}\ \text{Human Man}_p) & \dots \quad Woman \doteq (\underline{and}\ \text{Human}\ (\underline{not}\ \text{Man}) \\
 & & \qquad (\underline{atleast}\ \text{has-child}\ 1)\ (\underline{all}\ \text{has-child Child})) \\[2pt]
\text{W}_1 & (Man\ intob_{1,i_1}) & (Woman\ intob_{1,i_2}),\ (\text{has-child}\ intob_{1,i_2}\ \underline{atmost}\ 3) \\[2pt]
 & \downarrow & \downarrow \\[2pt]
\sigma_1 & (Student, i_1) & (Student, i_2) \\[2pt]
 & \mid & o_1 = Student \qquad \mid \\[2pt]
 & < \{Sex\}, \forall s_{Student} : s.Sex =' male' > & \dots \quad < \{Sex\}, \forall s_{Student} : s.Sex =' fem' >
\end{array}
$$

Part of the respective interpretation domain for a local information model: $intob_{1,i1} \in RObj_1\ (\mapsto)$ $(Student, i_1) \in SObj_1 \times Int_1$; $intob_{1,i2} \in RObj_1\ (\mapsto)$ $(Student, i_2) \in SObj_1 \times Int_1$ etc.

For example the **aspect term** for "female students" is

(and Human$_p$ Woman$_p$ (not Man$_p$) (all has—child$_p$ Child$_p$) (atleast has—child$_p$ 1) atmost has—child$_p$ 3))

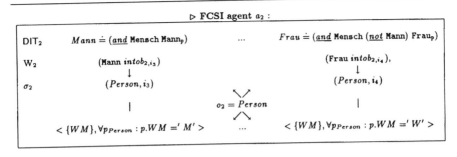

The **aspect term** for "female persons" is ($\underline{and}$ Mensch$_p$ Frau$_p$ ($\underline{not}$ Mann$_p$)). $\square$

13.3.2 Local Recognition of Interdatabase Dependencies

13.3.2.1 Terminological Interdatabase Dependencies

It is now possible for the agents to automatically detect a set of terminological relationships between two objects o_1, o_2 in different schemas with respect to some or all of their semantic aspects, the so-called *intensional interdatabase dependencies* i-IDD:

Let tsub(t_2,t_1) compute *term-subsumption* $t_2 \geq t_1$, intabst(o_1,i_x) denotes the computed *aspect term* of (o_1,i_x) and intset$_1$ set of *aspect identifier* of schema object o_1, then:

p − **intsub**(o_1, o_2, M, N) :⇔
($\forall i_x \in M \subseteq intset_1 \exists i_y \in N \subseteq intset_2$:
$tsub(intabst(o_2, i_y), intabst(o_1, i_x))$)∧
($\forall i_y \in N \exists i_x \in M$:
$tsub(intabst(o_2, i_y), intabst(o_1, i_x))$)

c − **intsub**(o_1, o_2, M, N) :⇔ p-intsub with M =$intset_1$
inteq(o_1, o_2) :⇔ $c − inteq(o_1, o_2, intset_1, intset_2)$
intdis(o_1, o_2) :⇔ $c − intdis(o_1, o_2, intset_1, intset_2)$
intsub(o_1, o_2) :⇔ $c − intsub(o_1, o_2, intset_1, intset_2)$

For example, **p-intsub(o_1,o_2,M,N)** means that the schema object o_1 is partially, intensionally subsumed by o_2 exactly wrt. the (sub-)sets M, N of their semantic aspects. The complete set of these terminological relationships can be found in (Klusch 1996). In accordance with (Sabbath 1993), to enable mutual understanding of received foreign terms a set $CPC_{1,2}$ of corresponding local primitive components is used between communicating agents a_1,a_2 to avoid linguistic ambiguity at the lowest level.

The *recognition process of terminological dependencies I-IDDs* executed at each agent locally bases them on classifying a received aspect term into the local terminological information model, finding relevant reference objects and projecting them down to the attached local schema data (Klusch 1994b, Klusch 1994a).

EXAMPLE 2:

Assume FCSI agent a_2 receives the aspect term $intabst(Student, \{i_2\})$ from FCSI agent a_1 Let the relevant subset of corresponding primitive components in $CPC_{i,j}$ for both agents be as follows :

for concepts: (Human$_p$, Mensch$_p$), (Man$_p$, Mann$_p$), (Woman$_p$, Frau$_p$), (Child$_p$, Kind$_p$)
for roles: (has − child$_p$, hat − Kind$_p$), etc.

Then, for example one of the following three cases can be detected by agent a_2:

$\{i_2\} \subset intset_1, \{i_4\} \subseteq intset_2$:   p − intsub$(Student, Person, \{i_2\}, \{i_4\})$, or
$\{i_2\} = intset_1$:   c − intsub$(Student, Person, \{i_2\}, \{i_4\})$, or
$\{i_2\} = intset_1, \{i_4\} = intset_2$:   intsub$(Student, Person)$. $\square$

13.3.2.2   Tasks and Productions

Having the ability to recognize such dependencies, each FCSI agent possesses the following two kinds of tasks. The FIND-task is for finding some terminological interdatabase dependencies with respect to a given local schema aspect. Each FIND-task frame contains an aspect term, and the desired type of term dependency as task goal with some additional execution information for the receiver. A task is satisfied if its task goal is satisfied. Local execution of such received tasks results in sets of term dependencies produced with respect to the task terms, i.e. task-related productions of an agent. Specification of a REQUEST-FOR-task depends on the result of some FIND-task: and contains an agent-directed, contextual data request (Section 3.2.4).

EXAMPLE 3:

FIND-Tasks $t_x^{a_1}$

Task-Term tt :	Aspect Term of $(Student, i_2)$
Task-Goal TG : p − $intsub(Student, ?, \{i_2\}, \{?\})$	
...	: ...

$t_y^{a_2}$

Task-Term tt :	Aspect Term of $(Person, i_4)$
Task-Goal TG : p − $intsub(?, Person, \{?\}, \{i_4\})$	
...	: ...

FIND-Task-related Production of a_2 having received $t_x^{a_1}$:   p − $intsub(Student, Person, \{i_2\}, \{i_4\})$ $\square$

13.3.2.3   Interdatabase Schema Assertions

The agent's ability to propose some *interdatabase schema assertion (IDSA)* is realized by using integration rules for composing the local state constraints JC on attached schema objects into global integrity constraints, with respect to the type of the detected terminological object relationship:

if p − $inteq(o_k, o_j, \{i_x\}, \{i_y\})$ then propose $[JC'_x \Leftrightarrow JC'_y]$;
if p − $intsub(o_k, o_j, \{i_x\}, \{i_y\})$ then propose $[JC'_x \Rightarrow JC'_y]$; a.o.

Example for a composition by propose:

Let p − $intsub(o_k, o_j, \{i_x\}, \{i_y\})$ be recognized with
  $o_k = E_1 \in E_{\sigma_1}, o_j = E_2 \in E_{\sigma_2}$ of $EER - Schemas \sigma_1, \sigma_2$;
  $CP'_x \subseteq attr(E_1)$, $CP'_y \subseteq attr(E_2)$;
  $JC'_x := \forall e1_{E_1} : < ic_1 - qual_{e_1} >$, $JC'_y := \forall e2_{E_2} : < ic_2 - qual_{e_2} >$
propose: $\forall e1_{E_1}, e2_{E_2} : (e1.key(E_1) = e2.key(E_2)) \Rightarrow (< ic_1 - qual_{e_1} > \Rightarrow < ic_2 - qual_{e_2} >)$

EXAMPLE 4:

Suppose that agent a_2 has detected the terminological IDD p − $intsub(Student, Person, \{i_2\}, \{i_4\})$ (cf. Example 2). Then, the corresponding IDSA proposal is $\forall s_{Student}, p_{Person} : (s.key(Student) = p.key(Person)) \Rightarrow (s.Sex =' female' \Rightarrow p.WM =' W') \square$

Each set of IDSA proposals gives hints for possible object domain mappings and can be extended as the agent's dependency knowledge grows. Note that this automated recognition of such kinds of interdatabase schema assertions is only possible if the respective intensional, i.e. terminological interdatabase dependencies are previously cooperatively recognized.

13.3.2.4 Context-Based Data Selection

Context-based data sharing is possible by any request of the agent a_j on a remote schema object o_2 to a_i yet known to be related wrt. some aspects. The receiver of an agent's intensional data request like [**request-for** structure part **from** schema object **wrt** aspect] will first check the respective aspect identifier, select the corresponding state constraint and compile the intensional query into a local database query.

EXAMPLE 5:
▷ FCSI-Agent a_2: (o_j, i_y) in relation to (o_k, i_x) owned by a_1; $o_k = E_1 \in E_{\sigma_1}$, $A \in \text{avail}(E_1, i_x, a_2)$:
                                   request-for A from E_1 wrt i_x
▷ FCSI-Agent a_1: (E_1, i_x) valuation includes $JC^{i_x} = \forall \text{el}_{E_1} : < ic - qual_{e1} >$
                                   retrieve $e1.A$ from E_1 where $< ic - qual_{e1} >$;   (EER-DML)

Now, summarizing the continued simple example for both FCSI agents wrt. contextual data requests:

FCSI Agent a_1:   **FCSI Agent a_2:**

FIND-Task on $(Student, i_2)$ FIND-Task on $(Person, i_4)$

process tasks: produce i-IDDs (cf. section 3.2.2), determine utility and coalition offer (cf. section 4) coalition commitment: information availability and maintenance

                                   $\text{avail}(Person, i_4, a_2)$: incl. $Name \in attr(Person)$

REQUEST-FOR-Task (context-based agent query): *'Names of Persons related to female Students'* $(i_2 : i_4)$
request-for $Name$ from $Person$ wrt i_4
                                   - check $(Person, i_4)$: get $JC^{i_4} = (p.WM =' W')$;
                                   - compile into local EER-DML query:
                                      retrieve $p.Name$ from $Person$ where $p.WM =' W'$

13.3.2.5 Modular Structure of an FCSI Agent

Each FCSI agent is coarsely structured as shown in Figure 13.3.

The main task of each autonomous FCSI agent is to support its local users in discovering the available information space, with respect to its own local domain of interest. This can be followed by the agent, through cooperatively detecting some i-IDDs requested by the user as one of the agent's FIND-tasks within its own task set. The *Agent User Interface* (AUI) enables the local user to use task specification and to access all internal modules of an agent. A central *nucleus* module is responsible for internal action scheduling with respect to the execution of some task received from a local user or other agents. Local own and received tasks are maintained by the *Task manager* (TM). All user-specified descriptions of schema object aspects are maintained by the *script manager* (SM). The terminological knowledge DIT/W on the local schema is constructed and maintained by the *terminological knowledge*

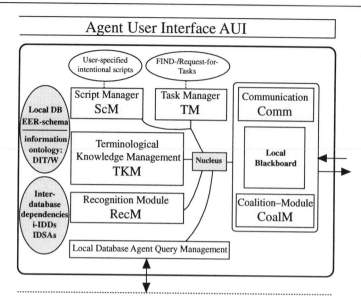

Figure 13.3   Macrostructure of a FCSI agent

management module (TKM). The used description language ITL mentioned in Section 3, TKM will be the currently implemented TEWIS system (Gao 1996). A *recognition module* (RecM) infers i-IDDs by joining the TKM and projects on respective valuations stored at the SM. It is also responsible for maintaining these detected i-IDD in its *belief base* including in particular all logically deduced i-IDD facts (PROLOG facts). IDSA proposals are reported by a RecM's submodule.

The *coalition module* (CoalM) is responsible for determining the agent's interest in participation in coalition with other FCSI agents. We will discuss this topic in Section 4. An appropriately partitioned local blackboard at each agent is used for agent's tasks announcements, coalition offers and constrained local knowledge propagation between actually committed agents.

13.4   Coalitions of FCSI Agents

In order to deal in particular with the required association autonomy while searching for some relevant data, the aspect of rational agency is essential for the FCSI approach. The main aim of *utilitarian coalition building* is to find partitions of rationally cooperating agents based on the calculation of their local utility resulting from the execution of some actions for own or received tasks. Such partitions or coalitions will form, if each member can see that by joining such a coalition he will gain rather than being by himself. There are several ways of creating such coalitions and dividing the joint payoff among the members. For coalition formation within the FCSI we adapted Shechory's production-orientated approach (Shechory and Kraus 1994). It relies on a real valued *agent utility function* calculating the agent's utility on known knowledge-based productions obtained by execution of received or own FIND-tasks. The *self value* denotes the utility an agent obtains when he exclusively satisfies his own tasks. The *coalition value* is the sum of these utilities of all its potential coalition members. Considering the *marginal contributions* of agents to all possible coalitions and computing their averaged sum leads to a fair division of the coalition value on all members by each agent's *Shapley value* (Kahan and Rapoport 1984). For bilateral coalition negotiation we obtain a more simple term for its calculation. *Individual rationality* is described as the relationship between agent's expected Shapley-value and his self value. It is assumed that the agents have common knowledge of this coalition value function of the respective coalition game and to agree on this particular utility division method. The currently used coalition negotiation algorithm for building approximate stable coalition configurations based on (Ketchpel 1993) (see Section 3.2).

Let $\mathcal{A}$ set of n FCSI agents, $a_i \in \mathcal{A}, C \subseteq \mathcal{A}$

Agent Utility Function	$U_{agent_{id}}^{type}(p(t_{tid_x,a_j}^{a_k}))$, with production $p(t_{tid_x,a_j}^{a_k})$
Coalition Value	$v(C)$: $\mathcal{P}(\mathcal{A}) \mapsto \mathbb{R}^+$, $v(C) := \sum_{a_k \in C, \, p \in Prod_{a_k}} U_k(p)$
Self-Value of Agent a_i	$v(\{a_i\})$
Marginal Contribution of Agent a_i to Coalition $C_i, a_i \notin C_i$	$v(C_i \cup \{a_i\}) - v(C_i)$
Shapley-Value of agent a_i	$sv_C(a_i) := \frac{1}{n!} \sum_{\pi} (v(C_i^{\pi} \cup \{a_i\}) - v(C_i^{\pi}))$
Restriction on *pairs of agent entities* for coalition formation:	$sv_{\{a_i,a_j\}}(a_i) = \frac{1}{2}v(\{a_i\} + \frac{1}{2}(v(\{a_j,a_i\}) - v(\{a_i\}))$
Individual Rationality	$sv_C(a_i) \geq v(\{a_i\})$

Different types of agent utility functions lead to respectively different coalition types.

13.4.1 FCSI Coalition Types

One FCSI coalition type, is the so-called *task interaction coalition type* (C_{ti}) based on the notion of FIND-task interaction. This means that one terminological dependency was found which satisfied the goal of the received as well as an own find-task. The amount of such task interactions determines the agent's utility on his task-orientated productions, i.e. the terminological dependencies, for this special type of coalition.

FIND-*task interaction*	$t^{a_i}_{tid_1,a_j} \xrightarrow{<intrel>(o_k,o_j,M,N)} t^{a_i}_{tid_2} :\Leftrightarrow$
	i-IDD $< intrel >$ satisfies the Task-Goal Part tg of <u>both</u> FIND-Tasks
C_{ti}-*utility function* U^{ti}_k	$U^{ti}_k(p(t^{a_k}_{tid_x,a_j})) := \| \{t^{a_k}_{tid_x,a_j} \xrightarrow{<ir>(o_k,o_j,M,N)} t^{a_k}_{tid_y}\} \| \in \mathbb{N}_0$
C_{ti}-*coalition value*	$v_{ti}(C) = \sum_{a_k \in C, p \in \mathcal{P}_{a_k}} U^{ti}_k(p)$

Each rational FCSI agent tries to coalesce with other FCSI agents to maximize its own utility in satisfying its FIND-tasks as much as possible. The detailed algorithm for local determination of task interactions between two FCSI-agents can be found in (Klusch 1996).

EXAMPLE 6:

Consider the FCSI agents $\{a_1, a_2\} = \mathcal{A}$ as in the examples above, and suppose both aspect terms $intabst(Student, i_2)$, $intabst(Person, i_4)$ as task terms of mutually exchanged and thus respectively received FIND-tasks $t^{a_1}_{y,a_2}, t^{a_2}_{x,a_1}$. Then, according to their respective local knowledge about each other, both agents are able to determine FIND-*task interactions*, e.g. $t^{a_1}_{y,a_2} \xrightarrow{p-intsub(Student,Person,\{i_2\},\{i_4\})} t^{a_1}_x$ by agent a_1.

Concerning the decentralized coalition value calculations, assume that $v_{ti}(\{a_1\}) = 0$ and $v_{ti}(\{a_2\}) = 3$, i.e. only agent a_2 can satisfy 3 of its own FIND-tasks exclusively by itself through considering all reflexive task-interactions induced by dependencies relating local objects. This yields $v_{ti}(\{a_1, a_2\}) =$

$v_{ti}(\{a_1\}) + v_{ti}(\{a_2\}) + U^{ti}_1(\{p-intsub(Student, Person, \{i_2\}, \{i_4\})\}) + U^{ti}_2(\{p-intsub(Student, Person, \{i_2\}, \{i_4\})\}) = 0 + 3 + 1 + 1 = 5$, thus for the marginal contribution of a_1 to $\{a_2\}: 5 - 3 = 2$ and in turn for $a_2: 5 - 0 = 5$, which leads to the agents' Shapley-values $sv_{\{a_1,a_2\}}(a_1) = 1$, $sv_{\{a_1,a_2\}}(a_2) = 4$. Since their individual rationality is fulfilled and since no better offer from other agents exists, both agents try to coalesce with each other. They are then mutually committed to get access to all respective schema aspect valuations by some now executable REQUEST-FOR tasks. □

Other coalition types exist within the FCSI which do not restrict the productions utility on such mutual task satisfaction. For example, the C_{tsat} coalition type relies exclusively on the amount of satisfied own FIND-tasks, and another "benevolent" agent utility function for C_{tserv}-coalitions considers only the satisfaction of received tasks as a server while independent from the fact that if any own FIND-task for the locally found objects exists. At the physical level one could imagine utility functions based, for example, on transportation costs, including the amount of visited agent nodes and probable sizes of potentially requested relevant schema data etc. Because of space limitation we omit to go into more detail. We currently investigate several calculable types of FCSI coalition utilities.

13.4.2 Decentralized Coalition Formation Between FCSI Agents

The method for coalition formation between FCSI agents is based on the decentralized, bilateral coalition formation algorithm in (Ketchpel 1993) which is adapted for the cooperative recognition process within the FCSI (Klusch 1996). A brief summary of the main steps in the FCSI coalition process follows.

1. **communication** for task announcements and/or information exchange.
2. **local calculation** of utilities on coalition participation.
   ```
   for each agent:
   ```

- task-orientated, terminological interdatabase dependency recognition;
  ```
  for each coalition type:
  ```

- compute agent utility for these productions and respective coalition values
- determine an individually rational *preference list of agents*: ordered list of agent's Shapley-Values for particular coalitions.

3. **bilateral negotiation about coalition offer**
   ```
   for each of both negotiation entities:
   for each coalition type:
   ```

- offer coalition to other agents wrt. the own internal preference order;
- if maximum of already received offers: accept as current partner

4. **coalition commitment**
   ```
   for each coalition type:
   ```
   - if mutually preferred as current partner:

   preliminary (proto-coalition) commitment between both agents entities, repeat step 1 (next round), or
   - if no new coalition is built in previous round: fix coalition commitments.

Since for our autonomous, distributed application environment there is in particular no possibility to centralize the calculations in one selected agent as it is proposed, e.g. in (Shechory and Kraus 1994), the above greedy algorithm's complexity is cubic (Ketchpel 1993). Each agent can participate in several coalitions of different types by concurrent coalition negotiations for each different type of a FCSI coalition utility to enable a fine-grained mutual utilitarian assessment between the information agents.

Several distributed coalition domain information terminologies (C-DIT) are implicitly built during coalition formations. Each member of a fixed coalition is committed to maintain the respectively known interdatabase dependency within a coalition, by providing immediate notification on any relevant local modification of domain aspect representation, and executing local database queries generated from received REQUEST-FOR-tasks.

Cooperation dialog can be modeled by using a set of cooperation primitives, objects and constraints (Müller 1993) in compliance with the KQML standard performatives (Genesereth *et al.* 1994) as it is possible with IDEAS.

13.5 IDEAS – an Environment for the Implementation of FCSI Agents

The *interactive development environment for agent systems* (IDEAS) has been primarily built within the FCSI project in order to provide the facilities for implementing the agents of the FCSI. Following Shoham's paradigm of *agent-oriented programming* (AOP) (Shoham 1990, (Shoham 1993) (see Chapter 10) the beliefs and actions of each agent and his message-orientated reactive behavior has to be specified by using a given *agent specification language* (ASL) (see Appendix A.1) (see Chapter 12) like AGENT-0 (Shoham 1993) or PLACA (Thomas 1993). The theoretical basics of IDEAS, in particular is the underlying agent model and ASL, can be found in (Grossmann 1995), a more detailed description concerning implementation issues of IDEAS in (Scheew 1995). For an informal survey of other available environments for building agent-based systems we refer to (Byrne and Edward 1994) and (Scheew 1995).

13.5.1 A Brief Overview of IDEAS

IDEAS is implemented in J. Ousterhout's (Ousterhout 1994) *Tool Command Language* Tcl with the Tk Toolkit for the X Windows System running on UNIX platforms. The base of the IDEAS system is the so-called *User Agent Manager* (UAM). At each local site where IDEAS has been installed the initial local UAM provides the user with facilities to create the agents and to supervise their activities. An agent in IDEAS runs as a separate process in UNIX (Bach 1986) under the control of his local UAM[1]. The internal links between the UAM and the local agents are realized via UNIX pipes (Bach 1986) while the agents establish their communication with other known agents at remote sites for cooperative work on TCP-sockets via the Internet. No global agent or central mediator exists. Each agent in IDEAS is autonomous and works in a completely decentralized environment. For *belief representation and reasoning* each agent maintains his own Prolog process using P. Taraus' (Tarau 1994) BinProlog. Unlike AGENT-0 or PLACA in the current version of IDEAS it is not possible to specify temporal beliefs or commitment rules and facts in the agent's *ASL* scripts although this will be the case in the next version of IDEAS-2. Agent *plans* can be specified by the appropriate developed rules for message evaluation. *Actions* can be defined in Tcl as well as in C, while the latter possibility is based on the extension facility of Tcl/Tk for embedding functions written in C in respectively named Tcl commands. IDEAS provides some predefined standard actions for communication, while managing the

---

1 Note that even if the overall UAM process breaks down all locally created agent processes keep on working only to be killed by the user if required.

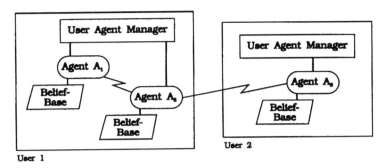

Figure 13.4 Simplified structure of an agent system in IDEAS

agents belief base etc. Figure 13.4 gives an example for the connectivity within an agent system. It consists of two agents A_1, A_2 together with their UAM at one local site of *User$_1$* and an agent A_3 created by his UAM at the other local site of *User$_2$*. In this scenario communication is established between A_1 and A_2 and also between A_2 and A_3.

13.5.2 Working with IDEAS

The appearance of IDEAS in the X Windows System is given by the window of the UAM and several observation windows, i.e. one for each of the agents created by the user from the UAM. Figure 13.5 shows the windows of the UAM and both agents A_1, A_2 created by User$_1$ in Figure 13.4.

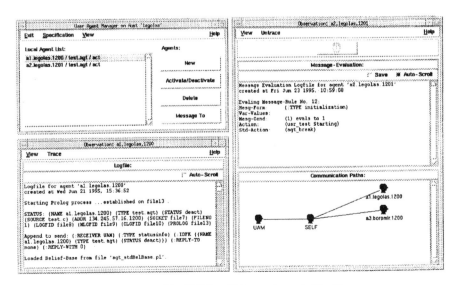

Figure 13.5 The UAM and his agents created by User$_1$

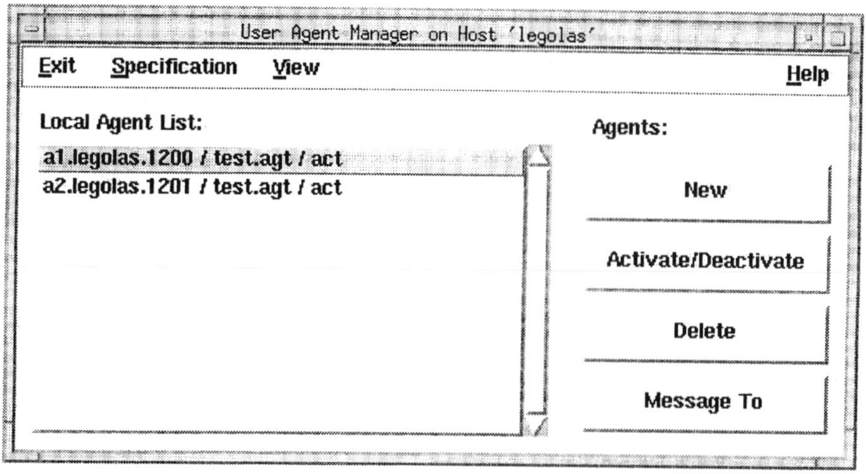

Figure 13.5a

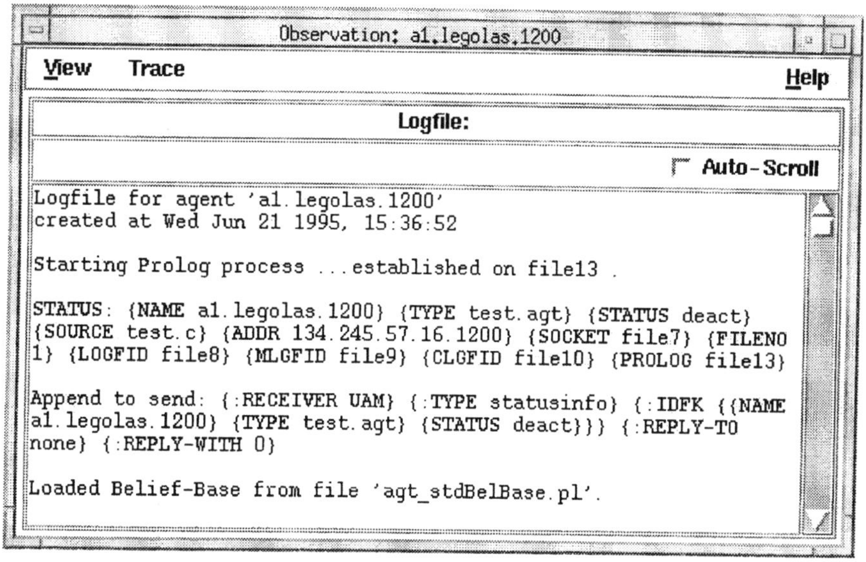

Figure 13.5b

The window of the UAM is dominated by the *Local Agent List* which includes all agents at the local site the UAM which it currently supervises. Each entry in this list contains the name of an agent, the respective user-specified *ASL agent description file* and its current status, which can be active or deactive. The item Specification in the UAM main menu leads to facilities for specifying new or modifying already existing agents descriptions

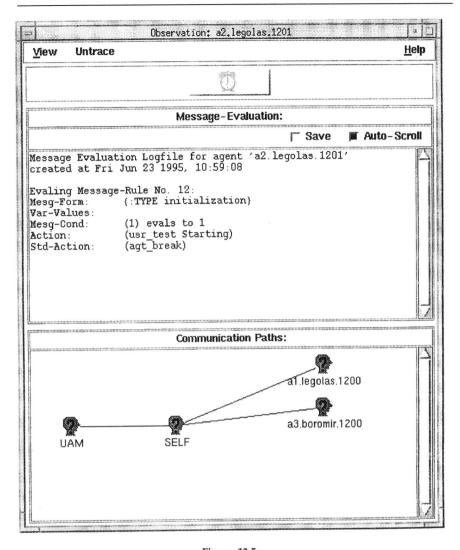

Figure 13.5c

with respect to the language ASL. If a set of agents together with their connectivity is specified, not only one agent but the respective *multi-agent system* will be created after pressing the New button beside the Local Agent List. Since the status of each initialized agent is deactive the user has to activate it as required by using the Activate/Deactivate button. Moreover, the UAM provides deletion of some agents by the Delete button. In order to control the message-orientated reactive behavior of an agent the user sends messages with respective contents (Message To button). After being activated, each agent opens his own *Observation window*. All activities within

IDEAS, causes the initialization of the UAM and the communication via agents as well as the complete activities of each separate agent, which are stored in several kinds of *logfiles* to be selectively inspected by the user's View button to allow flexible observation. The display of the initial content of one such agent *standard logfile* is shown in Figure 13.5 for agent A_1. Another type of logfile stores a rule-based reaction on received messages, shown in the observation window of agent A_2. The View menu provides a simple graphic overview of the set of agents while the considered agent is actually connected, as shown in Figure 13.5 for agent A_2 offering the possibility to browse through the actual content of the belief base of the agent. Moreover, the user can select a subset of agents for observing their activities with respect to one special agent. All messages exchanged between this set of agents and the designated agent will be stored in the respective *communication logfile*. In addition, a Trace item in the agent's observer menu enables the user to set some *trace-points* in the agent's action sequence, described in his *ASL* description. Such a trace mode supports agent debugging in the sense that whenever the agent execution reaches such a tracepoint he immediately freezes all his activities and goes into standby mode. This is indicated by the alarm clock sign button which has to be pressed by the user to awake the agent to continue his work. Finally, the Help item leads to the *built-in help* of IDEAS.

13.5.3 Agent Execution

After starting, the agent goes through initialization. He opens his observation window, reads his own ASL script file and builds the initial Prolog belief base. The interpretation of the agent's *ASL* script leads to an infinite *message evaluation* loop until it is deactivated or deleted by the user from the UAM. As mentioned above each agent behavior is a message-orientated reactive one. The respective *execution cycle of an agent* in IDEAS is shown in Figure 13.6.

insert Figure 13.6 about here

After entering the main loop the agent waits for incoming messages. The format of the messages in IDEAS is similar to that of the KQML language (Genesereth *et al.* 1994). Each *message* has a message type, in KQML the so-called performatives, are divided in to several slots each of them named with a unique keyword. A message contains at least the following keys:

:TYPE	type of message;
:SENDER	sender of the message;
:RECEIVER	receiver of the message, maybe a list of receiver;
:REPLY-TO	number of the message this message responds to,

maybe "none" if no reference exists;
:REPLY-WITH   number of this message,
can be used to reply to this message.

Each arriving message will be evaluated by the agent by applying a set of rules which are predefined in his *ASL* script (see Appendix A.13.1). A *message-rule* in IDEAS has the form

```
((<mesg-form>), (<mesg-cond>), (<if-action>), (<else-
action>), (<std-action>))
```

Based on these messages evaluation rules, each agent decides on how to react to the received message, i.e. which actions he has to execute next. Besides, an *evaluation priority* can be given to each message in the slot :PRIOR-ITY. IDEAS in providing four priority classes, which determine the order of message evaluation (Figure 13.6).

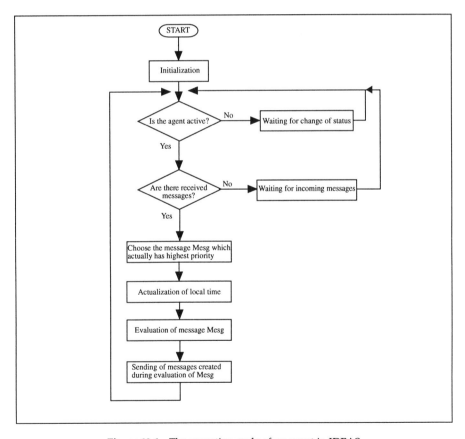

Figure 13.6   The execution cycle of an agent in IDEAS

Having received a message the agent checks the `<mesg-form>` part of the first rule in his message-evaluation rule set. If this test is successful he tries to further match the message with the logical *evaluation condition* `<mesg-cond>` which can contain any form of expression and status checks, especially the requests to an agent with respect to his actual belief base. The Boolean valued result of this condition evaluation determines which action has to be executed next by the agent. If the condition is true the `<if-action>` is executed, if not the `<else-action>` is taken. In each case the `<std-action>` is executed, if no special break command has been specified in one of the previous action types. After evaluating the `<std-action>` the agent tries to match the next message-rule in sequential order until the last rule is checked or evaluation of the actual message is stopped by a break command.

13.6 Conclusion and Discussion

The shortly proposed FCSI realizes a cooperative, decentralized search for semantically related data in heterogeneous and autonomous databases by the use of:

- **Local, Terminological Information Models** on top of local conceptual database schema σ
- Recognition of *terminological dependencies* i-IDD and respectively induced *interdatabase schema assertions* IDSA;
- **Utilitarian Coalition Formation** between FCSI Agents;
- *Context-based requests* for semantically related data.

This enables the user to discover some intensionally relevant data without the need to browse through all available schema structures first without any help. In particular, it is impossible to get access to the local schema or state level before any utilitarian coalition commitment with other rational agents is fixed. Context-based recognition is exclusively done by the FCSI agents at information type level, i.e. by formal terminological classification of some considered aspect term independent from its actually attached and protected data structures. This is similar to the idea of incrementally building and using some shared ontology for contextual interchange (Behrendt *et al.* 1993) respecting association autonomy (Sheth and Larson 1990). Thus, possible data sharing and proposing IDSAs is determined by the necessary prior success and mutual aspect term classification and restriction on the respective aspect valuations specified by user. The agent provides the user with all locally deducted i-IDDs and reports on respective possible IDSAs. These can be used for final decisions in specification of IDDs by the human (Sheth *et al.* 1991b).

There has been little research related on using formal terminological classification for the object discovery problem (Catarci and Lenzerini 1993). Recent work on system approaches which have influenced the FCSI approach are in particular (Bouguettaya 1992), Behrendt *et al.* 1993 and Hammer *et al.* 1993). Other partially related works are (Beck *et al.* 1989) and (Barbuceanu and Fox 1994). In contrast to our work, (Sheth *et al.* 1991b) aims for schema integration. Since cooperation and the acquisition and propagation of knowledge about data relevance between autonomous FCSI agents rely on decentralized, utilitarian coalition building, there exists no global information agent (Barbuceanu and Fox 1994) or central mediator agent (Behrendt *et al.* 1993). Terminological representation and corresponding classification enables in particular a formal treatment and automated, local processing. For a more detailed discussion of related works see (Klusch 1996).

The approach of the FCSI is unique in supporting the recognition of interdatabase dependencies in decentralized, autonomous environments. As mentioned in the last section we will use the *Interactive Development Environment for the specification and simulation of Agent Systems* (IDEAS-1) on a network of SUN-workstations for the implementation of FCSI agents. Ongoing research on the FCSI includes the following main distinguishing topics:

- investigations on *formal FCSI agent description* (Wooldridge 1993, Wooldridge and Jennings 1995) and implementation in IDEAS-1;
- further investigations on the application of *utilitarian coalition building* for organizing cooperation within the FCSI (Shechory and Kraus 1994, Ketchpel 1993);
- possibilities for using uncertain representation and inference for *deducing uncertain (plausible) intensional object relations* (i-IDD).

Acknowledgments

I would like to thank Prof. Dr. D. Klusch and Prof. Dr. P. Kandzia for reviewing an earlier draft of this chapter and giving many helpful hints and advice.

13.7 Appendix

A.13.1: Syntax of the `Agent Specification Language ASL`
It follows the definition of the Agent Specification Language ASL in an extended BNF where the following notations are used:

        `< >`   Non-Terminal-Symbols
        `::=`   Definition-Symbol
        `|`   Alternative-Symbol
        `[ ]`   Optional-Symbols
        `*`   n-times Repetition of the previous expression; n = 0, 1, 2, ...
      `"` "Comments

All other characters are Terminal-Symbols.

```
<program> ::=  [<action-C-source>]
               [<initial-beliefs>]
               [<belief-rules>]
               [<mesg-rules>]
               [<action-decl>]

<action-C-source> ::= ACTION-C-SOURCE {[<filename>]}

<initial-belief> ::= BELIEFS {(<belief>)*}

<belief> ::=  <prolog-fact> |
              (<prolog-fact>), <from-time-expr> [,
              <till-time-expr>]

<from-time-expr> ::= <time-expr>

<till-time-expr> ::= <time-expr>

<time-expr> ::= "time specification as described in
                IDEAS Help-Index"

<prolog-fact> ::= "regular Prolog fact not including ':-
'                  and without a '.' at the end"

<belief-rules> ::= BELIEF-RULES {(<prolog-rule>)*}

<prolog-rule> ::= "regular Prolog rule with ':-',
                   but without a '.' at the end"

<mesg-rules> ::= MESSAGE-RULES {(<m-rule>)*}
```

```
<m-rule> ::= (<mesg-form>), (<mesg-cond>), ([<if-
             action>]),
             ([<else-action>]), ([<std-action>])

<mesg-form> ::= {:<key-string> <match-expr>}*

<key-string> ::= "string of capital letters"

<match-expr> ::= "string of characters, may include
                 <variable>;
                 if it should contain spaces you have
                 to set double-quotes around it!"

<variable> ::= "character string starting with a
               capital letter"
  <mesg-cond> ::= "Tcl-expression"

  <if-action> ::= <action>
  <else-action> ::= <action>
  <std-action> ::= <action>

  <action> ::= "Tcl-commandblock"

  <action-decl> ::= ACTIONS {("Tcl-proc-declaration")*}
```

For the syntax of the Prolog and Tcl parts we refer to the respective literature for PROLOG e.g. (Clocksin and Mellish 1981), and for Tcl/Tk (Ousterhout 1994).

Epilogue

Computers, Networks and the Corporation

Thomas W. Malone and John F. Rockart

About 150 years ago the economy in the U.S. and Europe began to undergo a period of change more profound than any experienced since the end of the Middle Ages. We call that change the Industrial Revolution. The industrial economies are now in the early stages of another transformation that may ultimately be at least as significant.

There is a critical difference this time, however. Changes in the economies of production and transportation drove the revolution of the last century. The revolution under way today will be driven not by changes in production but by changes in coordination. Whenever people work together, they must somehow communicate, make decisions, allocate resources and get products and services to the right place at the right time. Managers, clerks, salespeople, buyers, brokers, accountants - in fact, almost everyone who works - must perform coordination activities.

It is in these heavily information-based activities that information technologies have some of their most important uses, and it is here that they will have their most profound effects. By dramatically reducing the costs of coordination and increasing its speed and quality, these new technologies will enable people to coordinate more effectively, to do much more coordination and to form new, coordination-intensive business structures.

The core of the new technologies is the networked computer. The very name "computer" suggests how one usually thinks of the device - as a machine for computing, that is, for taking in information, performing calculations and then presenting the results. But this image of computing does not capture the essence of how computers are used now and how they will be used even more in the future. Many of the most important uses of computers today are for coordination tasks, such as keeping track of orders, inventory and accounts. Furthermore, as computers become increasingly connected to one another, people will find many more ways to coordinate their work. In short, computers and computer networks may well be remembered not as technology used primarily to compute but as coordination technology.

To understand what is likely to happen as information technology improves and its costs decline, consider an analogy with a different technology: transportation. A first-order effect of transportation technology was simply the substitution of new transportation technologies for the old. People began to ride in trains and automobiles rather than on horses and in horse-drawn carriages.

As transportation technology continued to improve, people did not use it just to substitute for the transportation they had been using all along. Instead a second-order effect emerged: people began to travel more. They commuted farther to work each day. They were more likely to attend distant business meetings and to visit faraway friends and relatives.

Then, as people used more and more transportation, a third-order effect eventually occurred: the emergence of new "transportation-intensive" social and economic structures. These structures, such as suburbs and shopping malls, would not have been possible without the wide availability of cheap and convenient transportation.

Improved coordination technology has analogous effects. A first-order effect of reducing coordination costs is the substitution of information technology for human coordination. For example, data-processing systems helped to eliminate thousands of clerks from the back offices of insurance companies and banks. Similarly, computer-based systems have replaced scores of factory "expediters." Today computers track the priority of each job in the factory and indicate the most critical ones at each workstation. More generally, the long-standing prediction that computers will lead to the demise of middle management finally seems to be coming true. In the 1980s many companies flattened their managerial hierarchies by eliminating layers of middle managers.

A second-order effect of reducing coordination costs is an increase in the overall amount of coordination used. For instance, contemporary airline reservation systems enable travel agents to consider more flight possibilities for a given customer more easily. These systems have led to an explosion of special fares and price adjustments. American Airlines and United Air Lines, which provide the largest systems, have benefited significantly from the fees they charge for this service. For instance, in 1988 American made about $134 million from its reservation system - almost 15 percent of its total income. In addition, access to up-to-the-minute information about ticket sales on all airlines enables American and United to adjust their fare schedules to maximize profits.

Otis Elevator Company also increased the amount of its coordination - primarily to improve maintenance service for its customers. With its Otisline system, highly trained multilingual operators receive trouble calls through a national toll-free number. The operators record the problems in a computer data base and then electronically dispatch local repair people.

This real-time availability of data has vastly improved the management of repair activities. For instance, if a particular type of part has failed during the past week on eight of 100 elevators, Otis can preemptively replace that part on the other 92 elevators. Although this kind of nationwide correlation of data was possible before, the degree of communication and coordination required was impractical. These capabilities have played a major role in reducing maintenance calls by nearly 20 percent.

In some instances, the second-order effect of an increase in demand may overwhelm the first-order effect of substitution. For example, in one case we studied, a computer conferencing system helped to remove a layer of middle managers. Several years later, however, almost the same number of new positions (for different people at the same grade level) had been created. According to people in the company, the new specialists took on projects not considered before. Evidently, managerial resources no longer needed for simple communication could now be focused on more complex coordination tasks.

A third-order effect of reducing coordination costs is a shift toward the use of more coordination-intensive structures. A prime example is Frito-Lay, Inc., studied by Lynda M. Applegate of Harvard Business School and others. At Frito-Lay, some 10,000 route salespeople record all sales of each of 200 grocery products on hand-held computers as they deliver goods to customers on their route. Each night, the stored information is transmitted to a central computer. In turn, the central computer sends information on changes in pricing and product promotions to the hand-held computers for use the next day. Each week, the main computer summarizes the centrally stored information and combines it with external data about the sales of competitive brands. Some 40 senior executives and others can then gain access to this information through an executive information system (EIS).

The availability of these data has enabled Frito-Lay to push key decisions down from corporate headquarters to four area heads and several dozen district managers. The managers can use the data not only to compare actual sales to sales targets but also to recommend changes in sales strategy to top management. This entire coordination-intensive structure has become possible only in the past few years because of the improved capability and reduced costs of hand-held computers, EIS software, computer cycles and telecommunications equipment.

Coordination-intensive structures do not just link different people in the same companies. Many of the most interesting new structures involve links among different companies. For example, the U.S. textile industry has begun implementing a series of electronic connections among companies as part of the Quick Response program. As described by Janice H. Hammond of Harvard Business School and others, these electronic connections link companies all along the production chain, from suppliers of fibers (such as wool and cotton) to the mills that weave these fibers into fabric, to the factories that sew garments and, ultimately, to the stores that sell the garments to consumers.

When such networks are fully implemented, they will help companies respond quickly to demand. For instance, when a sweater is sold in New York City, a scanner reading the bar-coded label may automatically trigger ordering, shipping and production activities all the way back to the wool warehouse in South Carolina. This new, multiorganizational structure will reduce inventory costs throughout the value chain. The textile-apparel retail industry spends about $25 billion in inventory costs every year; the Quick Response approach may save half that amount.

Wal-Mart has already established parts of a similar system that links the retailer to Procter & Gamble Company and several of its other major suppliers. In doing so, Wal-Mart has eliminated significant parts of its own purchasing groups and contracted with its suppliers to replace products as they are sold. In one such experiment, both unit sales and inventory turnover increased by about 30 percent.

Sometimes technology helps to create interorganizational networks - not just among buyers and suppliers but also among potential competitors. For example, Eric K. Clemons of the University of Pennsylvania has studied the Rosenbluth International Alliance, a consortium of travel agencies around the world that share customer records, services and software. The alliance also provides clients with toll-free English-language help lines in every major country. This consortium of independent agencies, led by Rosenbluth Travel in Philadelphia, can therefore manage all travel arrangements for international trips and for meetings of people from many parts of the globe.

The textile firms near Prato, Italy, illustrate a related kind of interorganizational alliance. As described by Michael J. Piore and Charles F. Sabel of the Massachusetts Institute of Technology, the operation of a few large textile mills was broken into many small firms, coordinated in part by electronic connections among them. This network can flexibly adjust to changes in demand, sometimes shifting orders from an overloaded mill to one with spare capacity. The structure also takes advantage of the entrepreneurial motivation of the owners: in small mills, the owners' rewards are more closely linked to their own efforts than is the case in large ones.

As these examples show, information technology is already facilitating the emergence of new, coordination-intensive structures. What do these changes mean for the organizations of the near future?

A surprising result of our research is a prediction that information technology should lead to an overall shift from internal decisions within firms toward the use of markets to coordinate economic activity. To see why, consider that all organizations must choose between making the goods or services they need and buying them from outside suppliers. For instance, General Motors Corporation must decide whether to make tires internally or purchase them from a tire manufacturer.

Each of these two forms of coordination - internal and external - has advantages and disadvantages. As Oliver Williamson of the University of California at Berkeley and others have argued, buying things from an outside supplier often requires more coordination than making them internally. To buy tires, General Motors may need to compare many potential suppliers, negotiate contracts and do formal accounting for the money that changes hands. Coordinating the production of tires internally, on the other hand, can often be done less formally and at lower cost, with telephone calls and meetings.

But improved information technology should reduce the costs of both internal and external coordination, much as transportation technology lowered the expense of traveling. When trains and automobiles reduced the difficulty of traveling, more people chose to live in the suburbs rather than in the cities to reap such benefits as extra living space. Similarly, when information technology reduces the costs of a given amount of coordination, companies will choose to buy more and make less. The additional coordination required in buying will no longer be as expensive, and buying has certain advantages. For instance, when General Motors buys tires, it can take advantage of the supplier's economies of scale and pick the best tires currently available from any supplier whenever its needs change. Thus, we expect networks to lead to less vertical integration - more buying rather than making - and to the proliferation of smaller firms. More electronically mediated alliances (such as the Rosenbluth International Alliance) and an increased use of electronic markets to pick suppliers (such as the airline reservation system) will result.

This argument implies that information technology will help make markets more efficient. Buyers will no longer have to exert great effort to compare products and prices from many different suppliers. Instead an electronic market can easily and inexpensively collect and distribute such information.

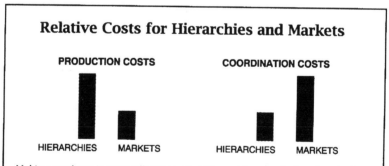

Relative Costs for Hierarchies and Markets

PRODUCTION COSTS

HIERARCHIES   MARKETS

COORDINATION COSTS

HIERARCHIES   MARKETS

Making products in vertically integrated hierarchies usually involves higher production costs than buying them in the market. Buying from an outside supplier allows a company to exploit economies of scale and other production cost advantages. But buying usually requires higher coordination costs; a firm must find a supplier, negotiate contracts and account for payments.

These more efficient markets threaten firms whose strategic advantages rest on market inefficiencies. For instance, as Clemons described, when the London International Stock Exchange installed an electronic trading system, the trading floor became virtually deserted within weeks. Trading moved to electronic terminals around the world. The system greatly reduced the costs of matching buyers and sellers. This change, in turn, dramatically reduced the profits of brokers and trading specialists, who previously had had a monopoly on performing this function. The potential decline in profit may explain why many other exchanges still resist electronic trading.

Many other kinds of intermediaries, such as distributors and retailers, are becoming vulnerable as well. For example, consumers can now bypass retail stores entirely by using computer-based systems such as Comp-U-Card and Comp-u-store to buy household goods and services at substantial savings. Electronic markets can also make evaluating product quality easier; we expect that it is only a matter of time before networks contain extensive comments and evaluations from previous buyers, becoming a kind of instantaneous, on-line Consumer Reports.

Increasing market efficiency also implies that firms should focus more carefully on the few core competencies that give them strategic advantages in the marketplace. They should buy the additional, more peripheral products and services they need instead of making them. For instance, in the past few years, Ford Motor Company and Chrysler Corporation have significantly increased their proportion of externally purchased components, such as tires and batteries.

Even though information technology can be strategically important, single innovations in information technology are seldom in themselves a source of continuing competitive advantage. For example, American Hospital Supply (now Baxter Healthcare Corporation) won high praise for its early system that let customers place orders electronically without requiring a salesperson. This system made ordering from American Hospital easier than doing so from competitors and reduced the time salespeople had to spend on the clerical aspects of taking an order. But contrary to original expectations, systems like these do not "lock in" customers in the long run. Instead customers eventually seem to prefer electronic systems that provide a choice among several vendors. Similarly, an automatic teller machine system that may once have been a competitive advantage for a bank is now largely a competitive necessity.

One way to maintain an upper hand is to keep innovating so rapidly that other firms always lag a step behind. Another way, as Clemons has noted, is to use information technology to leverage some other structural advantage. For instance, Barclay deZoete Wedd, a British brokerage firm, continues to benefit from an electronic stock-trading system because the company already controlled the trading of far more stocks than did any of their competitors.

In addition to markets, another coordination-intensive organizational structure likely to become much more common is what some management

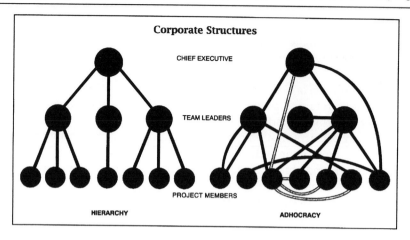

theorists call a networked organization, or, more picturesquely, an "adhocracy," a term Alvin Toffler popularized in his book Future Shock. This form is already common in organizations such as law firms, consulting companies and research universities. Such organizations and institutions must continually readjust to a changing array of projects, each requiring a somewhat different combination of skills and other resources. These organizations depend on many rapidly shifting project teams and much lateral communication among these relatively autonomous, entrepreneurial groups.

The adhocracy contrasts with the conventional business of today: the hierarchy. Hierarchies are common partly because they provide a very economical way of coordinating large numbers of people. In principle, decision makers in a hierarchy can consider all the information known to anyone in the group with much less communication than would be needed if each person communicated with everyone else.

In practice however, hierarchies have severe limitations. Central decision makers can become overloaded and therefore unable to cope effectively with rapidly change in environments or to consider enough information about complex issues. Furthermore, people at the bottom may feel left out of the decision making and as a result be less motivated to contribute their efforts.

As information technology reduces communication costs, the nonhierarchical structures (such as markets and adhocracies) may help overcome the limitations of hierarchies. For example, because of the large amount of unpredictable lateral communication, the adhocracy is extremely coordination intensive. New media, such as electronic mail, computer conferencing and electronic bulletin boards, can make the coordination easier and, therefore, enable the adhocracy to work much more effectively. Computer networks can help find and coordinate people with diverse knowledge and skills from many parts of an organization.

Moreover, computer-based technologies can transfer information not only faster and more cheaply but also more selectively. These capabilities help to mitigate information overload. Systems now exist to help people find, filter and sort their electronic mail based on topic, sender and other characteristics. Together these new coordination technologies can speed up the "information metabolism" of organizations - the rate at which firms can take in, move, digest and respond to data.

Abundant information poses two potential difficulties for organizational power. Some people worry that managers may become "Big Brothers" who use the information to exert stronger centralized control over those who work for them. Others fear that if power is decentralized throughout the organization, workers might use their newfound power to serve their own narrow interests, leading to organizational chaos.

In fact, neither dark vision has been realized. Instead what appears to be happening is a paradoxical combination of centralization and decentralization. Because information can be distributed more easily, people lower in the organization can now become well enough informed to make more decisions more effectively. At the same time, upper-level managers can more easily review decisions made at lower levels. Thus, because lower-level decision makers know they are subject to spot-checking, senior managers can retain or even increase their central control over decisions.

The changes at Phillips Petroleum Company illustrate this process. Previously, senior managers decided what price to set for petroleum products. These critical decisions depended on the recommendations of staff analysts several levels down. When Phillips Petroleum developed an executive information system, senior managers began to make some of these decisions more directly based on the global information provided by the system. The senior executives soon realized, however, that they could pass on this global information directly to local terminal managers, who could take into account information such as competitors' prices. By decentralizing the pricing decision in this way, the company made sounder, more profitable pricing strategies in each area of the country.

Another way of understanding this paradoxical effect is to realize that new technology does not just redistribute power. It can provide a sense of more power for everyone. For example, the agents of several insurance companies currently carry laptop computers when they visit the homes of customers. The agents use the computer to fill out applications and to project premiums and benefits. But typically, underwriters at the corporate headquarters require several weeks to review the applications and to issue new policies.

Soon the underwriting rules for certain routine policies will be included in the laptop computer itself. The agent will be able to issue these policies immediately in the customers' homes.

These systems will thus "empower" the agents, who will control the time and place of the policy-acceptance decisions and can make sales immediately. The authority of the central underwriters will increase as well, because the rules they have created will be applied consistently. The underwriters will also be able to devote more time to analyzing interesting and potentially more profitable nonroutine cases.

Information technology not only changes power; it also changes time. On the one hand, time has expanded. Electronic mail, voice mail and facsimile transmissions can be sent or received at any time of day or night, almost anywhere around the globe. Similarly, customers of automatic teller machines and some stock markets can make transactions around the clock. The "work day" has much less meaning, and companies can compete by expanding the times their services are available.

On the other hand, time has contracted. Companies can also compete on speed. For instance, effective coordination can reduce the time needed to develop new products, deliver orders or react to customer requests. Management teams, such as the one at Phillips Petroleum, have information available throughout the management hierarchy, which enables them to react to market conditions much more quickly. Decisions that might have taken days in the past can now be made within hours or minutes.

The changes discussed so far require no great predictive leaps; they are already happening. What will happen as information technology improves even more? What other kinds of organizations might emerge in the globally interconnected world that the technologies make feasible?

One possibility is the increasing importance of "answer networks", networks of experts available to answer questions in different areas. One might go to these services with questions such as "How many bars of soap were sold in Guatemala last year?" or "What are the prospects of room-temperature superconductivity in consumer products by 1995?" The services would include massive data bases and layers of human experts in many different topic areas. Some questions will be easily answerable from infor-mation in a data base. Others will be referred to progressively more knowl-edgeable human experts. Depending on how much one is willing to spend and how quickly one wants the answer, the response might range from a newspaper clipping to a personal reply from a Nobel laureate scientist. Similar but limited services exist today - product hot lines and library refer-ence desks are examples - but computer networks and data bases will make such services much less expensive, much more valuable and, therefore, much more widely used.

Electronically mediated markets can also assemble armies of "intellectual mercenaries" virtually overnight. For instance, there may be a large number of consultants who make their living doing short-term projects over the network. If a manager has a job to be done, such as evaluating a loan or designing a lawnmower, he or she could quickly assemble a team by adver-tising electronically or by consulting a data base of available people. The data base might contain not only the skills and billing rates of prospective work-ers but also unedited comments from others who had used their services before. Although consulting firms and advertising agencies sometimes work like this now, pervasive networks will allow teams to be assembled much more quickly, for shorter projects and from many different organizations.

This kind of market for services might be used inside an organization as well. Instead of always relying on supervisors to allocate the time of people who work for them, extensive internal markets for the services of people and groups may exist. Murray Turoff of the New Jersey Institute of Technology has suggested how such a system might work. Someone with a short programming project to be done, for instance, might advertise internally for a programmer. Bids and payments for this internal market could be in real dollars or some kind of point system. The bids from programmers would indicate their skill and availability. The payments that programmers receive would reflect how valuable they had been to other parts of the organization.

Improved technology can also help create decision-making structures that integrate qualitative input from many people. For instance, in making complex decisions, such as where to locate a new plant, the amassing of many facts and opinions is critical. Today companies often make such decisions after incomplete discussions with only a few of the people whose knowledge or point of view might be valuable. In the future, companies may use computer networks to organize and record the issues, alternatives, arguments and counterarguments in graphical form. Then many different people can review and critique the parts of the argument about which they know or care.

For instance, someone in a remote part of the firm might know about the plans for a new highway that completely changes the desirability of a proposed plant location. As such information accumulates, people can vote on the plausibility of different claims. Then, using all the information displayed in the system, a single person or group can ultimately make the decision.

What will happen as the globally networked society leads to a world in which vast amounts of information are freely available or easily purchased? Clearly, this world will require services, both automated and human, to filter the tremendous amount of information available. In general, as the amount of information increases, people who can creatively analyze, edit and act on information in ways that cannot be automated will become even more valuable.

But what else people will do will depend on the values that are important to them. When trains and automobiles reduced the constraints of travel time, other values became more significant in determining working and living patterns. As Kenneth T. Jackson of Columbia University has documented, for example, American values about the importance of owning one's home and the moral superiority of rural life played a large role in determining the nature of suburbs in the U.S.

Similarly, when the costs of information and coordination are not a barrier to fulfilling people's needs and wants, other values may emerge to shape the workplace and society. The new information technologies will almost certainly help gratify some obvious wants, such as the desire for money. Some of the emerging corporate structures may be especially good at satisfying nonmaterial needs, such as those for challenge and autonomy.

But perhaps these desires are themselves manifestations of some still deeper needs. Psychologists sometimes refer to a need for self-actualization. Others might call this a desire for spiritual fulfillment. To use the new technologies wisely, we will need to think more carefully about what we truly value and how the technology can help us reach our deeper goals.

Further reading:

Electronic Markets and Electronic Hierarchies. Thomas W. Malone, Joanne Yates and Robert I. Benjamin in Communications of the ACM, Vol. 30, No. 6, pages 484-497; June 1987.

Beyond Vertical Integration: The Rise of the Value-Adding Partnership. Russell Johnston and Paul R. Lawrence in Harvard Business Review, Vol. 66, No. 4, pages 94-104; July-August 1988.

Evaluation of Strategic Investments in Information Technology. Eric K. Clemons in Communications of the ACM, Vol. 34, No. 1, pages 22-36; January 1991.

Global Competition and Telecommunications: Proceedings of a Symposium held at Harvard Business School, May 2-3, 1991. Edited by Stephen Bradley, Richard Noland and Jerry Hausman (in press).

References

Abbas S (1993) Organisational Theory and Multi Agent Systems: A Synergistic Study, MSc Dissertation, Department of Computation, UMIST, UK.

Ackerman M and Malone Th (1990) Answer Garden: A Tool for Growing Organizational Memory. In: Lochovsky FH, Allen RB (eds) Conference on Office Information Systems. April 25–27, 1990. ACM SIGOIS Bulletin, 11(2,3), 1990, pp. 31–39.

ACM (1994) Communications of the ACM, Special Issue on Intelligent Agents, 37(8) August 1994.

Ader M and Tueni M (1987) An Office Assistant Prototype – Using a Knowledge-Based Office Model on a Personal Workstation. In: ESPRIT '87. Achievements and Impact. Proceedings of the 4th Annual ESPRIT Conference, Amsterdam, 1987, pp. 1205–1225.

Anderson R and Sharrock W (1993) Can Organisations Afford Knowledge? Computer Supported Cooperative Work (CSCW) , 1: pp. 143–161.

Applegate L, Ellis C, Holsapple CW, Radermacher FJ and Whinston AB (1991) Organizational Computing: Definition and Issues (Editorial), Journal of Organizational Computing, 1, pp. 1–10.

Austin JL (1962) How to do things with words, Oxford Univ. Press, Oxford.

Axelrod . (1984) The Evolution of Cooperation. Basic Books, New York.

Baader F and Hanschke P (1992) Extensions of concept languages for a mechanical engineering application, in: LNAI 671, Springer, pp. 132–143.

Baader F and Hollunder B (1991) A Terminological Knowledge Representation System with complete inference algorithms, LNAI 567, Springer, pp. 67–86.

Bach MJ (1986) The design of the UNIX operating system, Prentice-Hall.

Bakken B, Gould J and Kim D (1991) Experimentation in Learning Organizations: A Management Flight Simulator Approach. MIT Industrial Liaison Program Report, Sloan School of Management Working Paper SSWP-3247-91-BPS, Cambridge, MA.

Balck H and Kreibich R (ed) (1991) Evolutionäre Wege in die Zukunft. Wie lassen sich komplexe Systeme managen? Beltz, Weinheim et al.

Ballmer T and Brennenstuhl W (1981) Speech Act Classification: A Study in the Lexical Analysis of English Speech Activity Verbs, Springer, Berlin, Heidelberg.

Barber G (1982) Office Semantics. PhD Dissertation MIT. Cambridge, 1982.

Barber G (1983) Supporting Organizational Problem Solving with a Workstation. In: ACM Transactions on Office Information Systems, 1(1), 1983, pp. 45–67.

Barbuceanu M and Fox MS (1994) The information agent: an infrastructure for collaboration in the integrated enterprise, Proc. CKBS-94, Keele (UK).

Barrett E (ed) (1992) Sociomedia, MIT Press, Cambridge, Mass.

Beck HW et al. (1989) Classification as a query processing technique in the CANDIDE SDM, IEEE Computer, pp. 572–581.

Beer S (1981) Brain of the Firm, Wiley, Chichester.

Beeri C, Schek H-J and Weikum, G (1988), Multi-Level Transaction Management: Theoretical Art or Practical Need, Proc. Intl. Conference Extending Data Base Technology (EDBT), Lecture Notes in Computer Science 303, Schmidt JW, Ceri S, Missikoff M (eds) Springer Publishing Company.

Behrendt W et al. (1993) Using an intelligent agent to mediate multibase information access, Proc. CKBS-93, Keele (UK), pp. 27–43.

Bena C, Montini G and Sirovich F (1987) Planning and Executing Office Procedures in Project Aspera. In: Proceedings of the 10th International Joint Conference on Artificial Intelligence (IJCAI '87), 1987, pp. 576–583.

Benda M, Jagannathan V and Dodhiawalla R (1988) On Optimal Control of Knowledge Sources, in: Gasser L (ed) Proceedings of the 1988 Workshop on Distributed Artificial Intelligence, May 1988.

Bentley R, Rodden T, Sawey P and Sommerville I (1992) An architecture for tailoring cooperative multi-user displays, in: Turner J and Kraut R (ed) Proceedings of the ACM CSCW'92 Conference on Computer Supported Cooperative Work: Emerging Technologies for Cooperative Work, ACM, POB 64145, Baltimore, MD 21264, pp. 187–194.

Bhandaru N and Croft W (1990) An Architecture for Supporting Goal-Based Cooperative Work. In: Gibbs S, Verrijn-Stuart AA (Hrsg): IFIP WG8.4 Conference on Multi-User Interfaces and Applications. Heraklion, Crete, Sept. 24–26, 1990, Amsterdam, 1990, pp. 337–354.

Blanco JM et al. (1994) Building a federated relational database system: an approach using a knowledge-based system, International Journal on Intelligent & Cooperative Information Systems 3(4), pp. 415–455.

Blanning RW (1992) Knowledge, Metaknowledge, and Explanation in Intelligent Organizational Models. In Masuch M and Warglin M (eds) pp. 65–86.

Blanning RW, King DR, Marden JR and Seror AC (1992) Intelligent Models of Human Organizations: The State of the Art. Journal of Organizational Computing, 2 (1992), pp. 123–130.

Bocionek S (1994) Software Secretary Kernel: An Extendable Architecture for Learning and Negotiating Personal Assistants. ai communications 7 (3/4) 1994, pp. 147–160.

Bogen M and Weiss K (1988) Group Coordination in a Distributed Environment. In: Speth R (ed) European Teleinformatics Conference – EUTECO 88 on Research into Networks and Distributed Applications, Vienna, April 20–27, 1988, Amsterdam et al., 1988, pp. 111–128.

Bond A and Gasser L (1988) Readings in Distributed Artificial Intelligence. Morgan Kaufmann Publishers, San Mateo, CA., 1988.

Bond A H and Gasser L (1988) An Analysis of Problem and Research in DAI, in: Readings in DAI, Bond A H and Gasser L (eds), Morgan Kaufmann Publishers, San Mateo, CA, pp. 3–35, 1988.

Borgida A et al. (1989) CLASSIC: a structural data model for objects, ACM SIGMOD pp. 59–87.

Bouguettaya A (1992) A dynamic framework for interoperability in large MDB, PhD thesis, University of British Columbia, USA.

Bowers J and Churcher J (1988), Local and Global Structuring of Computer-Mediated Communication: Developing Linguistic Perspectives on CSCW in COSMOS. In: Proceedings of the Conference on Computer-Supported Cooperative Work. Sept 26–28, 1988, Portland., New York, 1988, pp. 125–139.

Bowers J, Churcher J and Roberts T (1988) Structured Computer-Mediated Communication in COSMOS. In: Speth R (ed) European Teleinformatics Conference – EUTECO '88 on Research into Networks and Distributed Applications, Vienna, April 20–22, 1988, Amsterdam et al., 1988, pp. 195–209.

Brachman, R.J. and Schmolze, J.G. (1985), An overview of the KL-ONE knowledge representation system, Cognitive Science, pp. 421-431

Brandau R and Weihmayer R (1989) Heterogeneous Multiagent Cooperative Problem Solving in a Telecommunication Network Management Domain, Proc. Workshop DAI-89, Eastwood, WA, 41–57.

Brauer W and Hernandez D (ed) (1991) Verteilte Künstliche Intelligenz und kooperatives Arbeiten. 4. Internationaler GI-Kongreß "Wissensbasierte Systeme". München, 23.–24.10.1991. Springer, Berlin.

Brazier FMT and Treur J (1994) User centered knowledge-based system design: a formal modelling approach. In: Steels L, Schreiber G and Van de Velde W (eds) A future for knowledge acquisition, Proceedings of the 8th European Knowledge Acquisition Workshop, EKAW '94. Springer Verlag, Lecture Notes in Artificial Intelligence 867, pp. 283–300.

Brazier FMT and Ruttkay ZS (1993) Modelling collective user satisfaction, Proc. of HCI International '93, Elsevier, Amsterdam, 1993, pp. 672–677.

Brazier FMT, Dunin-Keplicz B, Jennings NR and Treur J (1995) Formal Specification of Multi-Agent Systems: a Real World Case. In: V. Lesser (ed) Proc. of the First International Conference on Multi-Agent Systems, ICMAS-95, MIT Press, 1995, pp. 25–32.

Brazier FMT, Treur J, Wijngaards NJ. and Willems M (1994) Temporal semantics and specification of complex tasks. Technical Report IR-375, Vrije Universiteit Amsterdam, Department of Mathematics and Computer Science. Shorter version in: Bioch JC, Tan YH (eds) Proc. Seventh Dutch AI Conference, NAIC '95, 1995, pp. 307–316. Preliminary version in: D. Fensel (ed) Proceedings of the ECAI '94 Workshop on Formal Specification Methods for Knowledge-Based Systems, 1994, pp. 97–112.

Brazier FMT, van Eck PAT and Treur J (1995), Modelling Exclusive Access to Limited Resources within a Multi-Agent Environment: Formal Specification. Technical Report, Vrije Universiteit Amsterdam, Department of Mathematics and Computer Science

Bright MW and Hurson AR (1991) Multidatabase systems: an advanced concept in handling distributed data, Advances in Computers, pp. 149–200.

Brooks RA (1991) Intelligence Without Representation. In: Meyer AR a.o. (eds) Research Directions in Computer Science. An MIT Perspective, MIT Press, Cambridge, Mass.

Bui TX (1987) Co-oP. A Group Decision Support System for Cooperative Multiple Criteria Group Decision Making. Berlin *et al.*, 1987.

Bunge M (1977, 1979), Treatise on Basic Philosophy, 3(4) (Ontology I, II), Reidel, Dordrecht.

Burmeister B, Haddadi A and Sundermeyer K (1993) Generic Configurable Cooperation Protocols for Multi-Agent Systems, Proc. MAAMAW-93, Neuchâtel.

Busch E *et al.* (1991) Issues and Obstacles in the Development of Team Support Systems. In: Journal of Organizational Computing, 1(2), 1991, pp. 161–186.

Bussmann S and Müller J (1993) A Communication Architecture for Cooperating Agents, Computers and AI, 1.

Butler R (1992) Designing Organisations: A Decision Making Perspective, Routledge.

Buxton B and Moran T (1990) EuroParc's Integrated Interactive Intermedia Facility (IIIF): Early Experiences. In: Gibbs S and Verrijn-Stuart AA (eds) IFIP WG8.4 Conference on Multi-User Interfaces and Applications. Heraklion, Crete, Sept. 24–26, 1990, Amsterdam, 1990, pp. 11–34.

Byrne C and Edward P (1994) Building Agent-Based Systems, Tech. Report AUCS/TR9405, University of Aberdeen, Scotland UK.

Campbell JA and D'Inverno MP (1990) Knowledge Interchange Protocols, Demazeau, Y, Müller JP, Decentralized AI, Elsevier/North-Holland, Amsterdam, 63–80.

Canning RG (1985) More Uses for Computer Conferencing. In: EDP Analyzer, 23(8), 1985, pp. 1–12.

Carley KM and Prietula M. (eds) 1994) Computational Organization Theory. Lawrence Erlbaum Ass., Publishers, Hillsdale, New Jersey 1994.

Cartwright D and Zander A (eds) (1968) Group Dynamics, Third Edition, Tavistock.

Catarci T and Lenzerini M (1993a), Interschema knowledge in cooperative IS, Proc. ICICIS-93, Rotterdam, pp. 55–62.

Catarci T and Lenzerini M (1993b), Representing and using interschema knowledge in cooperative Information Systems, International Journal on Intelligent & Cooperative Information Systems 2(4), pp. 375–389.

CECOIA 3 (1992) – Proceedings of the Conférence Internationale sur l'Économique et l'Intelligence Artificielle. Tokio, Japan, August 31 – September 4, 1992. Published by The Japan Society for Management Information.

CEMIT92 (1992) – Proceedings of the International Conference on Economics/Management and Information Technology 92. Tokio, Japan, August 31 – September 4, 1992. Published by The Japan Society for Management Information.

Ceri S and Widom J (1992) Managing semantic heterogeneity with production rules and persistent queues, Politecnico Milano TR 92-078.

Chaib draa B, Moulin B, Mandiau R and Millot RP (1992) Trends in Distributed Artificial Intelligence, Artificial Intelligence Review, 6, pp. 35–66.

Chang MK and Woo CC (1992) SANP: A Communication Level Protocol for Negotiations, Werner E and Demazeau Y (eds) Decentralized AI 3, Elsevier/North-Holland, Amsterdam, 31–54.

Chen M and Liou Y (1991) The Design of an Integrated Group Support Environment. In: Nunamaker JF and Sprague RH(eds) Proceedings of the 24th Hawaii International Conference on system Sciences. Kauai, Hawii, Jan. 8–11, 1991. Vol. IV, Los Alamitos, 1991, pp. 333–342.

Chrysanthis P, Raghuram S and Ramamrithan K (1991) Extracting Concurrency from Objects: A Methodology, Proc. ACM-SIGMOD Int. Conf. on Management of Data, Denver, Colorado, May 1991.

Clark DD (1991) The Changing Nature of Computer Networks. In: Meyer AR a.o. (eds) Research

Directions in Computer Science. An MIT Perspective, MIT Press, Cambridge, Mass.

Clemons EK (1991) Evaluation of Strategic Investments in Information Technology, Communications of the ACM, 34(1) January 1991, pp. 22–36.

Clocksin WF and Mellish CS (1981) Programming in PROLOG, Springer-Verlag.

Cockburn D and Jennings NR (1996) ARCHON: A Distributed Artificial Intelligence System for Industrial Applications. In: Foundations of Distributed Artificial Intelligence (eds O'Hare GMP and Jennings NR), Wiley & Sons.

Coenen F (1992) TSL User Guide, Department of Computer Science, The University of Liverpool, Liverpool.

Coenen F, Finch I, Bench-Capon T, Shave M and Barlow J (1992a) Building Intelligence into the Aide de Camp System, Graham I, Proceedings of the Applications Track Expert Systems '92, BCS, Cambridge.

Coenen F, Finch I, Bench-Capon T, Shave M and Barlow J (1992b) Task Scripting for an Intelligent Aide de Camp System, Niku-Lari A Proceedings Expersys-92, iitt International, Gournay sur Marne, 191–196.

Cohen PR and Levesque HJ (1990) Rational Interaction as the Basis for Communication, Cohen PR, Morgan J, Pollack ME, Intentions in Communication, MIT Press, Cambridge, MA, 221–255.

Cohen PR and Levesque HJ (1988) On Acting Together: Joint Intentions for Collective Actions. In Workshop on Distributed AI 1988.

Cohen PR and Perrault CR (1981) Elements of a Plan-Based Theory of Speech Acts. In Nilsson, NJ and Webber BL (eds) Readings in Artificial Intelligence. Morgan Kaufman. Also in: Bond AH and Gasser L (eds) (1988) Readings in Distributed Artificial Intelligence, Morgan Kaufman, San Mateo, CA, 169–186.

Cohen PR and Levesque HJ (1987a), Persistence, Intention, and Commitment. Technical Report CSLI-87-88, Center for the Study of Language and Information, Stanford University, Stanford, CA. March 1987.

Cohen PR, Levesque HJ (1987b) Intention = Choice + Commitment. Proceedings of the 6th National Conference on AI (AAAI-87), pp. 410–415.

Conklin J and Begeman M (1988) gIBIS: A Tool for all Reasons. MCC Technology Report STP-252–88, 1988.

Conry SE, Meyer, R.A. and Lesser, V.R. (1986), Multistage Negotiation in Distributed Planning. COINTS Technical Report 86-67, Amherst, MA. December 1986. Also in: Bond, A.H. and Gasser L. (eds.) (1988), Readings in Distributed Artificial Intelligence, Morgan Kaufman, San Mateo, CA, 367-384

Cook P *et al.* (1987) Project Nick: Meeting Augmentation and Analysis. In: ACM Transactions on Office Information Systems, 5(2), 1987, pp. 132–146.

Corkill D (1982) A Framework for Organizational Self-Design in Distributed Problem Solving Networks. PhD Thesis. Department of Computer and Information Science, Univ. of Massachusetts at Amherst, MA. COINS-TR-82-33. Dec. 1982.

Coy W and Bonsiepen L (1989) Erfahrung und Berechnung. Kritik der Expertensystemtechnik, Springer, Berlin.

CRC Project Team (1993) Cooperative Requirements Capture, IED Project No: 1130, Final Report, ICL, UMIST, Human Technology, Brameur Ltd, UK.

Crocker DH (1982) Standard for the Format of ARPA Internet Text Messages, Tech. Rep. RFC822, DARPA.

Croft W and Lefkowitz L (1988) Using a Planner to Support Office Work. In: Allen RB (ed) Conference on Office Information Systems. Palo Alto, March 1988. ACM SIGOIS Bulletin, 2(3), New York, 1988, pp. 52–62.

Crowley T *et al.* (1990) MMConf: An Infrastructure for Building Shared Applications. In: Proceedings of the Conference on Computer Supported Cooperative Work. Los Angeles, CA, Oct. 7-10, 1990, New York, 1990, pp. 329–342.

Cyert RM and March JG (1964) The Behavioral Theory of the Firm – A Behavioral Science-Economics Amalgam. In: New Perspectives in Organizational Reasearch, New York 1964, pp. 289–299.

Daft R L (1989) Organisational Theory and Design, Third Edition, West Publishing Company.

Daft RL, Steers RM (1986) Organizations: A Micro/Macro Approach, Glenview (Illinois), London.

Davenport TH (1993) Process Innovation: Reengineering Work through Information Technology. Harvard Business School Press, Boston, Mass., 1993.

Davidow WH and Malone MS (1992) The Virtual Corporation. Structuring and Revitalizing the Corporation for the 21st Century. Harper Collins Publishers.

Davis R and Smith RG (1983), Negotiation as a Metaphor for Distributed Problem Solving, Artificial Intelligence, Vol. 20, No.1, pp. 63–109.

Dayal U, Buchmann A and McCarthy D (1988) Rules are Objects too: A Knowledge Model for an Active, Object-Oriented Database Management System, Proc. 2nd Int. Workshop on Object-Oriented Database Systems, Bad Münster, Germany, Sept. 1988.

DeCindio F et al. (1988) CHAOS: A Knowledge-Based System for Conversing within Offices. In: Lamersdorf W (ed) IFIP TC 8 / WG8.4 International Workshop on Office Knowledge, Representation, Management and Utilization, Amsterdam, 1988, pp. 257–276.

de Greef P, Mahling D, Neerincx M and Wyatts (1991) Analysis of Human-Computer Cooperative Work. Imagine Technical Report Series, Technical Report No. 4, Munich 1991.

de Jong P (1991) A Framework for the Development of Distributed Organizations. Proceedings of the IJCAI-91 Workshop on Intelligent and Cooperative Information Systems: Bringing AI and Information Systems Technology Together, Darling Harbour, Sydney, Australia, August 25, 1991, pp. 1.

Decker K and Lesser V (1992) Generalizing the Partial Global Planning Algorithm. International Journal of Intelligent & Cooperative Information Systems, 1(2) June 1992, pp. 319–346.

Desanctis G and Gallupe B (1985) Group Decision Support Systems: A New Frontier. In: Data Base, Winter, 1985, pp. 3–10.

Dieng R, Corby O and Labidi S (1994) Agent-based knowledge acquisition. In: Steels L, Schreiber G and Van de Velde W (eds) (1994) A future for knowledge acquisition, Proceedings of the 8th European Knowledge Acquisition Workshop, EKAW '94. Springer-Verlag, Lecture Notes in Artificial Intelligence 867, pp. 63–82.

Dollimore J and Wilbur S (1991) Experiences in building a configurable CSCW system, in: Bowers JM and Benford SD (eds) Studies in Computer Supported Cooperative Work, Elsevier Science Publishers B.V. (North-Holland), pp. 173–181.

Duncan R and Weiss A (1979) Organizational learning: Implication for Organizational Design, Staw V (ed) Research in Organizational Behavior, Vol. 1, pp. 75–123, 1979.

Dunham R (1991) Business Design Technology – Software Development for Customer Satisfaction. In: Nunamaker JF (ed) Proceedings of the 24th International Conference on System Sciences. Kanai, Hawaii, Jan. 8–11, 1991. Vol. III, Los Alamitos, 1991, pp. 792–798.

Dunin-Keplicz B and Treur J (1995) Compositional formal specification of multi-agent systems. In: Wooldridge M and Jennings N (eds) Intelligent Agents, Proc. of the ECAI '94 Workshop on Agent Theories, Architectures and Languages, Lecture Notes in AI, Vol. 890, Springer Verlag, 1995, pp. 102–117.

Durfee EH and Lesser VR (1987) Using Partial Global Plans to Coordinate Distributed Problem Solvers. IJCAI-87, pp. 875.

Durfee EH and Lesser VR (1989) Negotiating Task Decomposition and Allocation Using Partial Global Planning, Gasser L and Huhns M Distributed Artificial Intelligence II, Morgan Kaufmann, San Mateo, CA, 229–243.

Durfee EH and Montgomery TA (1990) A Hierarchical Protocol for Coordinating Multiagent Behavior, Proc. AAAI-90, 86–93.

Durfee EH, Lesser VL and Corkill D (1987), Coherent Cooperation Among Communicating Problem Solvers. IEEE Transaction on Computers, C-36, 1987, pp. 1275. Also in: Bond A and Gasser L (eds) Readings in Distributed Artificial Intelligence. Morgan Kaufmann Publishers, San Mateo, CA., 1988, pp. 268.

Egido C (1988) Videoconferencing as a Technology to Support Group Work: A Review of its Failures. In: Proceedings of the Conference on Computer-Supported Cooperative Work. Sept. 26–28, 1988, Portland, New York, 1988.

Ellis C and Bernal M (1982) Officetalk-D. An Experimental Office Information System. In: Limb JO (ed) SIGOA Conference on Office Automation Systems. Philadelphia June 21–23, 1982, pp. 131–140.

Ellis C, Gibbs S and Rein GL (1991) Groupware – Some Issues and Experiences. In: Communications of the ACM, 34(1), 1991, pp. 38–58.

Ellis C, Gibbs S and Rein G (1990) Design and Use of a Group Editor, in: Engineering for Human–Computer Interaction, Cockton G (ed) North-Holland, Amsterdam.

Elmagarmid E and Zhang A (1992) Enforceable interdatabase constraints in combining multiple autonomous databases, Purdue Tech. Rep. CSD-TR-92-008.

Elmargarmid E (ed) (1992) Database Transaction Models for Advanced Applications, Morgan

Kaufmann Publishers.

Elofson GS and Konsynski BR (1993) Performing Organisational Learning with Machine Apprentices. Decision Support Systems 10 (1993), pp. 109–119.

Engelfriet J and Treur J (1994) Temporal Theories of Reasoning. In: MacNish C, Pearce D, Pereira LM (eds) Logics in Artificial Intelligence, Proc. of the 4th European Workshop on Logics in Artificial Intelligence, JELIA '94. Springer-Verlag, pp. 279–299. Also in: Journal of Applied Non-Classical Logics, Special Issue with selected papers from JELIA '94, 1995, in print.

Farhoodi F, Proffitt J, Woodman P and Tunnicliffe A (1991) Design of Organisations in Distributed Decision Systems. AAAI-Workshop on Cooperation Among Heterogeneous Intelligent Systems, 1991.

Favela J and Connor JJ (1994) Accessing Corporate Memory in Networked Organizations. Proceedings of the 27th Hawaii International Conferences on System Sciences, 1994, pp. 181–190.

Fickas S and Helm R (1991) Acting Responsibly: Reasoning about Agents in a Multi-Agent System. Technical Report CIS-TR-91-02. Department of Computer and Information Science, University of Oregon, Eugene, OR 87403, 1991.

Fikes R and Henderson D (1980) On Supporting the Use of Procedures in Office Work. In: AAAI 1980 Conference, Aug. 18–21, 1980, Menlo Park, 1980, pp. 202–207.

Finch I (1993) Adcmail User Guide, Department of Computer Science, The University of Liverpool, Liverpool.

Finch I, Coenen F, Bench-Capon T and Shave M (1994) A Knowledge-Based Adviser's Assistant, Milne R and Montgomery A, Applications and Innovations in Expert Systems, Proceedings of Expert Systems '94, Information Press, Oxford, 71–85.

Finch I, Coenen F, Bench-Capon T, Shave M, and Barlow J (1992) Applying CKBS Techniques to Electronic Mail, Deen SM, CKBS-SIG Proceedings 1992, DAKE Centre, University of Keele, Keele, 101–118.

Finin T, Fritzon R, McKay D and McEntire R (1994) KQML as an Agent Communication Language, Proc. Third International Conference on Information and Knowledge Management, ACM Press.

Fish R et al. (1988) Quilt (1988) A Collaborative Tool for Cooperative Writing. In: Allen RB (ed) Conference on Office Information Systems, March 23–25, 1988, Palo Alto, CA., ACM SIGOIS Bulletin, 9(2,3), pp. 30–37.

Flores F and Ludlow J (1980) 1 Doing and Speaking in the Office. In: Fick G, Sprague RH (eds) Decision Support Systems: Issues and Challenges, Oxford, pp. 95–118.

Flores F et al. (1988) Computer Systems and the Design of Organizational Interaction. In: ACM Transaction of Office Information Systems, 6(2), 1988, pp. 153–172.

Flores F, Graves M, Hartfield B and Winograd T (1988) Computer Systems and the Design of Organisational Interaction, ACM Transactions on Office Information Systems, 6, 2, 153–172.

Foppa K (1968) Lernen, Gedächtnis, Verhalten, Köln/Germany.

Foroughi A and Jelassi M (1990) 1 NSS Solutions to Major Negotiation Stumbling Blocks. In: Sprague RH (ed) Proceedings of the 23rd Hawaii International Conference on System Sciences. Kailua-Kona, Hawaii, Jan. 2–5, 1990. Vol. IV, Los Alamitos, 1990, pp. 2–11.

Fox MS (1979) Organisational Structuring: Designing Large Complex Software, Technical Report CMU-CS-79-155, Department of Computer Science, Carnegie Mellon University, Pittsburgh, PA.

Fox MS (1981) An Organizational View of Distributed Systems. IEEE Transactions on Systems, Man and Cybernetics, SMC-11, 1981, pp. 70–80.

Fox MS (1988) An Organisational View of Distributed Systems, In Readings in Distributed Artificial Intelligence, Morgan Kaufmann Publishers, San Mateo, California, pp. 140–150.

Fox MS (1992) The TOVE project: Towards a Common Sense Model of the Enterprise, Proc. of the 5th International Conference, IEA/AIE-92 on Industrial and Engineering Applications of Artificial Intelligence and Expert Systems, Paderborn, June 1992, Springer-Verlag, LNAI 604, p. 25.

Frese E (1972) Koordination, ZfO vol. 41, pp. 404–411.

Gaitanides M (1983) Prozeßorganisation. Verlag Vahlen, München.

Galbraith J (1977) Organisation Design, Addison-Wesley Publishing Company.

Galliers JR (1988) A Theoretical Framework for Computer Models of Cooperative Dialogue, acknowledging Multiagent Conflict, Diss. Oxford.

Gao H (1996) Entwicklung und Implementierung eines terminologischen Wissensrepräsentations- und Inferenzsystems TEWIS, MSc. Thesis, University of Kiel (in preparation).

Gareis R (1991) Management by Projects: The Management Strategy of the 'New' Project-Oriented Company, International Journal of Project Management, 9(2) pp. 71–76, 1991.

Gasser L (1991) Social conceptions of knowledge and action: DAI foundations and open systems semantics. Artificial Intelligence, Vol. 47, January 1991, pp. 107–138.

Gasser L (1992) An Overview of DAI, In Avouri, NM and Gasser L (eds) Distributed Artificial Intelligence : Theory and Praxis, Computer and Information Science Vol 5, Kulwar Academic Publishers, for the Commission of the European Communities, The Netherlands, pp, 9–30.

Gasser L (1992) DAI Approaches to Coordination. In: Avouris NM and Gasser L (eds) Distributed Artificial Intelligence: Theory and Practice. Kluwer Academic Publishers, 1992, pp. 31–52.

Gasser L, Braganza C and Herman N (1987) MACE: A Flexible Testbed for Distributed A I Research, In Huhns M Distributed Artificial Intelligence, Morgan Kaufmann Publishers, Los Altos, California, pp. 119–153.

Gasser L and Briot J-P (1992) Object-Based Concurrent Programming, In Avouris NM and Gasser L (eds) Distributed Artificial Intelligence: Theory and Praxis, Computer and Information Science Vo. 1 5, Kulwar Academic Publishers, for the Commission of the European Communities, The Netherlands, pp. 81–107.

Gasser L and Rouquette N (1988) Representing and Using Organizational Knowledge in Distributed AI Systems, In: Gasser L (ed) Proceedings of the 1988 Workshop on Distributed Artificial Intelligence, California, May 1988.

Gavrila IS and Treur J (1994) A formal model for the dynamics of compositional reasoning systems. In: Cohn AG (ed) Proc. 11th European Conference on Artificial Intelligence, ECAI'94, Wiley and Sons, pp. 307–311.

Genesereth M et al. (1993) Specification of the KQML Agent-Communication Language, Draft Spec. Rep. 6/1993, DARPA Knowledge Sharing Initiative EIWG.

Genesereth MR, Ginsberg, ML and Rosenschein JS (1986) Cooperation without Communication, Proc. AAAI-86, 51–57.

George J (1991) The Conceptualization and Development of Organizational Decision Support Systems. In: Nunamaker JF, Sprague RH (eds) Proceedings of the 24th Hawaii International Conference on System Sciences. Kanuai, Hawaii, Jan. 8–11, 1991. Vol. IV, Los Alamitos, 1991, pp. 57–64.

Gibson JL, Ivancevich JM and Donelly JH (1979) Organisations, Behaviour, Structure, Processes, Third Edition, Business Press.

Ginsberg M (1987) 1 Decision Procedures. In: Huhns M (ed) Distributed Artificial Intelligence. Morgan Kaufman Publishers, 1987, pp. 3–28.

Gioia DA (1992) Common Ground? The Intersection of Artificial Intelligence and Organization and Management Theory. In Masuch M. and Warglin, M. (eds.), pp. 295-309.

Glance N, Hogg T and Huberman BA (1991) Computational Ecosystems in a Changing Environment. Technical Report P91-00012. Dynamics of Computation Group, Xerox Palo Alto Research Center, Palo Alto, CA 94304, 1991.

Gouldner AW (1954) Patterns of Industrial Democracy, Collier Macmillan, New York.

Gray JN et al. (1976) Granularity of Locks and degrees of Consistency in Shared Data Base Management Systems. Nijssen GM (ed), North Holland 1976.

Greenberg S (1991) Computer-Supported Cooperative Work and Groupware: An Introduction to the Special Issue, International Journal of Man-Machine Studies, 34, 2, 133–141.

Greenberg S (1991a) Computer supported cooperative work and groupware. In: Greenberg S (ed) Computer supported cooperative Work and Groupware, Academic Press, Cambridge, pp. 1–8.

Greif I and Sarin S (1988) Data Sharing in Group Work, in: Greif, I. (ed) Computer-Supported Cooperative Work: A Book of Readings, Morgan Kaufmann, San Mateo, CA, 1988.

Grossmann B (1995) Spezifikation von Agentensystemen in der interaktiven Entwicklungsumgebung IDEAS, MSc. Thesis, University of Kiel, Kiel

Guilfoyle, C. and Warner, E. (1994), Intelligent Agents: the New Revolution in Software. Ovum Ltd. London, 1994

Gutenberg, E. (1951) Grundlagen der Betriebswirtschaftslehre. Erster Band: Die Produktion. Springer-Verlag Berlin, Heidelberg, New York.

Haghjoo M, Papazoglou M and Schmidt H (1993) A Semantic-based Nested Transaction Model for Intelligent and Cooperative Information Systems, Proc. Int. Conf. on Intelligent and Cooperative Information Systems, IEEE Computer Society Press, Rotterdam, The

Netherlands, May 1993.

Hales K and Lavery M (1991) Workflow Management Software: the Business Opportunity. Ovum Report. London.

Halonen D *et al.* (1990) Shared Hardware: A Novel Technology for Computer Support of Face-to-Face Meetings. In: Lochovsky FH and Allen RB (eds) Conference on Office Information Systems. ACM SIGOIS Bulletin, 11(2,3), 1990, pp. 163–168.

Hammainen H, Eloranta E and Alasuvanto J (1990) Distributed form management. ACM Transactions on Office Information Systems, 8(1) pp. 50–76.

Hammer J *et al.* (1993) Object discovery and unification in FDBS, Proc. DBTA-Workshop on Interoperability of Databases and DB Applications, 10/1993, Fribourg.

Hammer M and Champy J (1991) Reengineering the Corporation. Harper Collins Publisher, New York.

Hansen RA and Kern W (1992) (eds) Integrationsmanagement für neue Produkte, Verlagsgruppe Handelsblatt, Düsseldorf, Frankfurt a. M., ZFBF Sonderheft 30.

Hastings C (1993) The New Organization: Growing the Culture of Organizational Networking. McGraw Hill, London *et.al.*, 1993.

Haugeneder H and Steiner D (1991) Cooperation Structures in Multi-Agent Systems, Brauer W and Hernandez D, Verteilte Künstliche Intelligenz und kooperatives Arbeiten, Informatik Fachberichte 291, Springer-Verlag, Berlin, Heidelberg, 160–171.

Herlihy M and Weihl W (1988) Hybrid Concurrency Control for Abstract Data Types, Proc. ACM Symposium on Principles of Database Systems.

Hern LEC (1988) On Distributed Artificial Intelligence, The Knowledge Engineering Review, Cambridge University Press.

Hewitt C (1986) Offices are Open Systems. In: ACM Transactions on Office Information Systems, 4(3), pp. 271–287.

Hiltz SR and Turoff M (1991) Computer Networking Among Executives: A Case Study, Journal of Organizational Computing, 1(4), pp. 357–376.

Hogg J (1985b) Intelligent Message Systems. In: Tsichritzis D (ed) Office Automation – Concepts and Tools, Berlin *et al.*, 1985, pp. 113–133.

Hogg J, Nierstrasz O and Tsichritzis D (1985a) Office Procedures. In: Tsichritzis D (ed) Office Automation. Concepts and Tools, Berlin *et al.*, 1985, pp. 137–165.

Hollunder B and Nutt W (1990) Subsumption algorithms for concept languages, DFKI-Res. Rep. RR-90-04.

Hoschka P (1991) Assisting Computer – A New Generation of Support Systems. In: Brauer W. and Hernández, D. (Hrsg.), Verteilte Künstliche Intelligenz und Kooperatives Arbeiten, Proceedings 4. Intern. GI-Kongresses Wissensbasierte Systeme, München, Oktober 1991, S. 219-230

Huber GP and McDaniel RR (1986) The Decision-Making Paradigm of Organizational Design. Management Science Vol. 32, 1986, pp. 572–589.

Huberman BA (ed) (1988) The Ecology of Computation, North Holland, Amsterdam.

Huberman BA (1992) The Value of Cooperation, In: Masuch M and Warglien M (eds) (1992), S. 235–244.

Huhns M (1987) Distributed Artificial Intelligence, Morgan Kaufmann Publishers, Los Altos, California.

Huhns MN, Bridgeland DM and Arni NV (1990) A DAI Communicative Aide, in Proc. Workshop DAI-90, Bandera, TX

Ishida, T. (1992), The Tower of Babel: Towards Organization-Centered Problem-Solving. In: Working Papers of the 11th International Workshop on Distributed Artificial Intelligence, Glen Arbor, Michigan. February 25–29, 1992, pp. 141–153.

Ishida T, Gasser L and Yokoo M (1992) Organisation Self Design of Distributed Production Systems. IEEE Transactions on Data and Knowledge Engineering. 4(2) 1992, pp. 123–134.

Ishii H and Kubota K (1988) Office Procedure Knowledge Base for Organizational Office Work Support. In: Gibbs S and Verrijn-Stuart AA (eds) IFIP WG8.4 Conference on Office Information Systems: The Design Process. Linz, Austria, Aug. 15–17, 1988, Amsterdam, 1989, pp. 55–72.

Ishii H and Ohkubo M (1990) Design of TeamWorkStation: A Realtime Shared Workspace Fusing Desktop and Computer Screens. In: Gibbs S and Verrijn-Stuart AA (eds) IFIP WG8.4 Conference on Multi-User Interfaces and Applications. Heraklion, Crete, Sept. 24-26, 1990, Amsterdam, 1990, pp. 131–142.

ISO (1984) International Standard Organization (ISO), Information Processing Systems – Open

Systems Interconnections: Basic Reference Model, International Standard 7498.

Jarke M and Ellis CA (1993) Distributed Cooperation in Integrated Information Systems. International Journal of Intelligent and Cooperative Information Systems 2(1) 1993, pp. 85–103.

Jarke M, Maltzahn C and Rose T (1992) Sharing Processes: Team Coordination in Design Repositories, Int. Journal of Intelligent and Cooperative Information Systems, 1(1) 1992.

Jelassi MT and Foroughi A (1989) Negotiation Support Systems: An Overview of Design Issues and Existing Software. In: Decision Support Systems: The International Journal. 5, 1989, pp. 167–181.

Jennings N (1992) Joint Intentions as a Model of Multi-Agent Cooperation. PhD Thesis. Queen Mary and Westfield College, Department of Electronic Engineering, University of London, UK. August 1992.

Jennings N and Mamdani EH (1992) Using Joint Responsibility to Coordinate Collaborative Problem Solving in Dynamic Environments. Proceedings of the 10th National Conference on AI (AAAI-92), San Jose, CA, pp. 269–275.

Jennings NR, Corera J, Laresgoiti I, Mamdani EH, Perriolat F, Skarek P and Varga LZ (1995) Using ARCHON to develop real-word DAI applications for electricity transportation management and particle accelerator control, IEEE Expert – Special Issue on Real World Applications of DAI.

Johansen R (1987) User Approaches to Computer Supported Teams. In: Technological Support for Work Group Collaboration, NYU Symposium, May 21–22, 1987, New York, 1987.

Johnson RE (1992) Documenting frameworks using patterns, ACM SIGPLAN Notices, 27(10) pp. 63–76.

Johnston R and Lawrence PR (1988) Beyond Vertical Integration: The Rise of the Value-Adding Partnership, Harvard Business Review, 66(4) July–August 1988, pp. 94–104.

Kahan JP and Rapoport A (1984) Theories of coalition formation, Lawrence Erlbaum Assoc. Publ., London.

Kakehi R and Tokoro M (1993) A Negotiation Protocol for Conflict Resolution in Multi-Agent Environments, Proc. ICICIS-93.

Kandzia P and Klein H-J (1993) Theoretische Grundlagen relationaler Datenbanken, BI Wissenschaftsverlag Mannheim, Leipzig, Wien, Zürich.

Kaplan S et al. (1992) Flexible, Active Support for collaborative Work with ConversationBuilder. In: Proceedings of the ACM 1992 Conference on Computer-Supported Cooperative Work, New York, 1992, pp. 378385.

Kaplan S, Carrol A and Macgregor KJ (1991) Supporting Collaborative Processes with ConversationBuilder. In: De Jong, Peter (ed) Conference on Organizational Computing Systems, November 5–8, 1991 Atlanta, Gorgia. SIGOIS Bulletin, 12(2u.3), New York, 1991, p. 69.

Karbe B and Ramsberger N (1991) Concepts and Implementation of Migrating Office Processes. In: Brauer W, Hernández D (eds) Verteilte Künstliche Intelligenz und kooperatives Arbeiten. 4. Internationaler GI-Kongreß Wissensbasierte Systeme. München, 23–24.Oktober 1991, Berlin et al., 1991.

Kaye A and Karam G (1987) Cooperating Knowledge-Based Assistants for the Office. In: ACM Transactions on Office Information Systems, 5(4), 1987, pp. 297–326.

Keen PGW (1991) Shaping the Future – Business Design through Information Technology. Harvard Business School Press, 1991.

Kerr E and Hiltz S (1982) Computer-Mediated Communication Systems: Status and Evaluation, Academic Press, New York.

Ketchpel S (1993) Coalition formation among autonomous agents, Proc. MAAMAW-93.

Khandwalla (1977) Design of Organizations, New York, Chicago, San Francisco, Atlanta.

Kieser A (ed) (1993) Organisationstheorien, Kohlhammer, Stuttgart.

Kirn S and Klöfer A (1993) Organisational Intelligence in Multiagentensystemen: State of the Art und Forschungsansätze. In: Müller J (ed) Beiträge zum Gründungsworkshop der Fachgruppe Verteilte Künstliche Intelligenz. Saarbrücken 29–30. April 1993. DFKI Document D-93-06, Kaiserslautern und Saarbrücken.

Kirn St (1994) Supporting Human Experts Collaborative Work: Modelling Organizational Context Knowledge in Cooperative Information Systems. In: Connolly JH and Edmonds E (eds) CSCW and AI. Springer Series on Computer Supported Cooperative Work. Springer-Verlag Berlin, Heidelberg, New York et al. 1994, pp. 217–139.

Kirn St (1995) Cooperative Knowledge Processing: The Key Technology for the New

Organisation. In: Cooperative Knowledge Processing: The Competitive Edge in Banking IT. Special Issue of the International Journal of Intelligent Systems in Accounting, Finance and Management. John Wiley & Sons, 4(4) December 1995 (in print).

Kirn St and Schlageter G (1991) Intelligent Agents in Federative Expert Systems: Concepts and Implementation. In Deen M (ed) Cooperating Knowledge Based Systems. Springer. Berlin, Heidelberg, New York *et al.*, pp. 53–78.

Kirn St and Unland R (1994) Zur Verbundintelligenz integrierter Mensch-Computer-Teams: Ein Organisationstheoretischer Ansatz, Arbeitsbericht Nr. 29, Institut für Wirtschaftsinformatik, Westfälische Wilhelms-Universität Münster, March.

Kirn St (1992) Cooperative Ability of Intelligent Agents in Federative Environments. PhD thesis, FernUniversität Hagen, 1992 (in German).

Kirn St (1993) Organisationale Intelligenz durch kooperative Mensch-Computer-Systeme. In: Thome R (Hrsg) Kommunikation und Oberflächen bei Banken, Bausparkassen und Versicherungen. compuTeam Würzburg, 1993, S. 231–245.

Kirn St, Scherer A and Schlageter G (1992) Problem Solving in Federative Environments: The Fresco Concept of Cooperative Agents. In: Papazoglou M, Zeleznikow J (eds) The Next Generation of Information Systems: From Data to Knowledge. Springer-Verlag. Berlin, Heidelberg, New York *et al.*, Lecture Notes in Artificial Intelligence Vol. 611, 1992, S. 185–203.

Kirn St (1994) Supporting Human Experts Collaborative Work: Modelling Organizational Context Knowledge in Cooperative Information Systems. In Connolly JH and Edmonds E (eds) CSCW and AI. Springer-Verlag. CSCW Series. Spring 1994, pp. 127–140.

Kirn St, Unland R and Wanka U (1994) MAMBA: Automatic Customization of Computerized Business Processes. Information Systems, 19(8), pp. 661–682, December 1994.

Kirn St (1994) Supporting Human Experts Collaborative Work: Modelling Organizational Context Knowledge in Cooperative Information Systems, In: Connolly JH and Edmonds E (eds) CSCW and AI, Springer Series on CSCW.

Klahold P, Schlageter G, Unland R and Wilkes W (1985) A Transaction Model Supporting Complex Applications in Information Systems: Proc. ACM SIGMOD, Austin TX.

Klein M (1990) Supporting Conflict Resolution in Cooperative Design Systems, IEEE Systems, Man, Cybernetics, 21(6), 1379–1390.

Klusch M (1994a) Ein föderatives Agentensystem FCSI zur Erkennung von Interdatenbankabhängigkeiten, Ph.D. thesis, University of Kiel (in preparation).

Klusch M (1994b) Towards a Federative System FCSI for a context-based recognition of plausible Interdatabase Dependencies, Proc. 6. GI-Workshop on Foundations of Databases, Bad Helmstedt.

Klusch M (1994c) Using a cooperative agent system for a context-based recognition of interdatabase dependencies, Proc. CIKM-94 Workshop on "Intelligent Information Agents", Gaithersburg (USA).

Klusch M (1995a) Towards a Federative Cell System FCSI for a context-based discovery of Interdatabase Dependencies, Proc. ETCE-95, Knowledge-based Systems in Engineering Applications, ASME PD-Vol. 67, Houston (USA), pp. 233–240.

Klusch M (1995b) Cooperative Recognition of Interdatabase Dependencies, Proc. Intern. Workshop on Description Logics DL-95, 2.-3.6.1995, Rom. Short version is in: ACM SIGMOD Proc. 2. Intern. Workshop on Advances in Databases and Information Systems ADBIS-95, 27.-30.6.1995, Moskau

Klusch M (1995c) Coalition-based cooperation between intelligent agents for a contextual recognition of interdatabase dependencies, Proc. 1. Intern. Conference on Multi-Agent Systems ICMAS-95, San Francisco.

Klusch M and Shehory O (1996) Coalition formation among rational information agents, Proc. 7. European Workshop on Modelling Autonomous Agents in a Multi-agent World MAAMAW-96, 22.-25.1.96, Eindhoven (Netherlands), van de Velde W and Perram J (eds) Lecture Notes in Artificial Intelligence LNAI Series Vol. 1038 pp 204–217, Springer-Verlag.

Knolle H, Unland R, Schlageter G and Welker E (1992) TOPAZ: A Tool Kit for the Construction of Application-Specific Transaction Managers, In: Objektbanken für Experten, Bayer R, Härder T and Lockemann P (eds) Springer-Verlag, Informatik aktuell, 1992.

König W, Kurbel K, Mertens P and Pressmar D (eds) (1995) Distributed Information Systems in Business and Management (in print).

Koo C (1987) A Distributed Model for Performance Systems – Synchronizing Plans among Intelligent Agents via Communication. PhD Dissertation. Stanford, 1987.

Koo C, Wiederhold G (1988) A Commitment-Based Communication Model for Distributed

Office Environments. In: Allen RB(ed) Conference on Office Information Systems, March 23–25, 1988, Palo Alto, CA. ACM SIGOIS Bulletin, 9(2,3), 1988, pp. 291–298.

Korf R (1992) A Simple Solution to Pursuit Games, Proceedings 11th International Workshop on Distributed Artificial Intelligence, Michigan, February 1992.

Kornfield W and Hewitt C (1981) The Scientific Community Metaphor, IEEE Transactions on Systems, Man and Cybernetics SMC-11(1) pp. 24–33.

KQML (1992) ARPA Knowledge Sharing Initiative, Specification of the KQML agent-communication language, External Interfaces Working Group. Available as http://www.cs.umbc.edu/kqml/papers/kqml-spec.ps.

Kraemer K and King J (1988) Computer-based Systems for Cooperative Work and Group Decision Making: Status of Use and Problems in Development. In: ACM Computing Surveys, 20(2), 1988, pp. 115–146.

Kreifelts Th *et al.* (1991a) Experiences with the Domino Office Procedure System. In: Bannon L, Robinson M and Schmidt K (eds) Proceedings of the Second European Conference on Computer-Supported Work, Sept. 25–27, 1991, Amsterdam, Dodrecht, Boston, London, 1991, pp. 117–130.

Kreifelts Th (1991b) Coordination of Distributed Work: From Office Procedures to Customizable Activities. In: Brauer W, Hernández D (eds) Verteilte Künstliche Intelligenz und kooperatives Arbeiten. 4. Internationaler GI-Kongreß Wissensbasierte Systeme. München, 23.-24.Oktober 1991, Berlin *et al.*, 1991.

Kreifelts Th, Pankoke-Babatz U and Victor F (1991c) A Model for the Coordination of Cooperative Activities. In: Gohrling K and Sattler C (eds) International Workshop on CSCW, Berlin, April 9–11, 1991. Informatik Berlin 7 (1991) 4. Institut für Informatik und Rechentechnik der AdW, Berlin, 1991, pp. 85–100.

Kuwabara K and Lesser VR (1990) Extended Protocol for Multi-Stage Negotiation. Proceedings of the 9th International Workshop on Distributed AI. Bandera, Texas. October 23–27, 1990.

Lai K Y, Malone TW and Yu KC (1988) Object Lens: A "spreadsheet" for cooperative work, ACM Transactions on Office Information Systems, 6(4), pp. 332–353.

Lai KY and Malone Th (1988) Object Lens: A "Spreadsheet" for Cooperative Work. In: ACM Transactions on Office Information Systems, 6(4), 1988, pp. 332-353.

Langevelde IA van Philipsen AW and Treur J (1992) Formal specification of compositional architectures, in Neumann B (ed) Proceedings of the 10th European Conference on Artificial Intelligence, ECAI'92, John Wiley & Sons, Chichester, pp. 272–276.

Larson J (1989) Four reference architectures for distributed DBMS, Computer Standards and Interfaces, Elsevier, Vol. 8, pp. 209–221.

Laßmann A (1992) Organisatorische Koordination: Konzepte und Prinzipien zur Einordnung von Teilaufgaben, Neue betriebswirtschaftliche Forschung, 98, Dissertation Uni Köln, Gabler, Wiesbaden.

Lauriston R (1990) Work-Group Software Worth Waiting For. In: PC World, June, 1990, pp. 122–137.

Lee KC, Mansfield WH Jr, and Sheth AP (1993) A framework for controlling cooperative agents, IEEE Computer, 26(7), pp. 8–15.

Lee J (1990) SIBYL: A Tool for Sharing Knowledge in Group Decision Making. In: Proceedings of the Conference on Computer Supported Cooperative Work. Los Angeles, CA., Oct. 7–10, 1990., New York, 1990, pp. 79–92.

Lee RM (1988) Bureaucracies as deontic systems, ACM Transactions on Office Information Systems, 6(2), pp. 87–108.

Lefkowitz L and Croft W (1989) Planning and Execution of Tasks in Cooperative Work Environments. In: IEEE Conference on Artificial Intelligence Applications., Maimi, 1989.

Lenat D (1988) BEINGs: Knowledge as Interacting Experts, In Bond A H and Gasser L Readings in Distributed Artificial Intelligence, Morgan Kaufmann Publishers, San Mateo, California , pp. 161–168.

Lesser VR (1991) A Retrospective View of FA/C Distributed Problem Solving, IEEE Transactions on Systems, Man, and Cybernetics, 21(6), pp. 1347–1362.

Lesser VR and Corkill DD (1981) Functionally Accurate, Cooperative Distributed Systems, IEEE Transactions on Systems, Man and Cybernetics SMC-11(1) pp. 81–96.

Lesser VR and Corkill DD (1983) The Distributed Vehicle Monitoring Testbed: A Tool for Investigating Distributed Problem Solving Networks, AI Magazine, pp. 15–33.

Levin JA and Moore JA (1977) Dialogue-Games: Metacommunication Structures for Natural Language Interaction, Cogn. Science, 1, 395–420.

Levinson SC (1981) The Essential Inadequacies of Speech Act Models of Dialogue, Parrett H Possibilities and Limitations of Pragmatics, J.Benjamin, Amsterdam.

Levy R (1991) A Game Theoretic Approach to Distributed Artificial Intelligence and the Pursuit Problem, Master thesis, Hebrew University.

Lewe H and Krcmar H (1990) The CATeam Meeting Room Environment as a Human-Computer Interface. In: Gibbs S, Verrijn-Stuart AA (eds) IFIP WG8.4 Conference on Multi-User Interfaces and Applications, Amsterdam, 1990, pp. 143–158.

Lewe H and Krcmar . (1991) The Design Process for a CSCW Research Lab – The Hohenheim CATeam Room Example. In: Nunamaker JF (ed) Proceedings of the 24th Hawaii International Conference on System Sciences. Kanuai, Hawaii, Jan. 8–11, 1991. Vol. III, Los Alamitos, 1991, pp. 668–677.

Lewis B and Hodges J.D. (1988), Shared Books: Collaborative Publication Management for an Office Information System. In: Allen RB (ed) Conference on Office Information Systems, March 23–25, 1988, Palo Alto, CA. ACM SIGOIS Bulletin, 9(2&3), pp. 197–204.

Litwin W (1985) An overview of the Multidatabase System MRDSM, Proc. ACM National Conf., pp. 495–504.

Lutz E, Kleist-Retzow H, and Hoernig K (1990) MAFIA – An Active Mail-Filter-Agent for Intelligent Document Processing Support. In: ACM SIGOIS Bulletin. 1990, 11(4), pp. 16-32.

Lutze R (1988) Customizing Cooperative Office Procedures by Planning. In: Allen RB (ed) Conference on Office Information Systems. Palo Alto, March 1988. ACM SIGOIS Bulletin, 2(3), New York, 1988, pp. 63–77.

Lux A, Bomarius F Steiner, D (1992) A Model for Supporting Human Computer Cooperation, Proc. AAAI-92 Workshop Cooperation Among Heterogeneous Intelligent Systems.

Macaulay LA (1993) Requirements Capture as a Cooperative Activity, In Re'93 IEEE International Symposium on Requirements Engineering, Jan 4–6 1993, San Diego, California, IEEE Computer Press.

Macauley LA, Fowler CJH, Kirby M and Hutt ATF (1990) USTM: A New Approach to Requirements Specification, Interacting With Computers, 2(1), pp. 92–117.

Macaulay L M, O'Hare GMP, Dongha P and Viller S (1994) Cooperative Requirements Capture: Prototype Evaluation, Proceedings of CASE '94, (eds) Spurr K and Layzell P, Published by Wiley Press.

Macaulay L, O'Hare G, Viller S and Dongha P (1993) Cooperative Requirements Capture, In: Ward TO *et al.* (ed) (1993) JFIT Technical Conference Digest, DTI, SERC, pp. 331–338.

Malone T (1987) Modeling Coordination in Organizations and Markets. Management Science, 33 (1987) 10, pp. 1317–1332.

Malone TW (1988) Modelling Coordination in Organisations and Markets, In Bond A H and Gasser L In Readings in Distributed Artificial Intelligence, pp. 151–158, Morgan Kaufmann Publishers, San Mateo, California.

Malone T (1988) Organizing Information Processing Systems: Parallels Between Human Organizations and Computer Systems. In Zachary W, Robertson S Black J (eds) Cognition, Cooperation, and Computation. Ablex Publishing Corporation, Norwood, NJ, 1988.

Malone T and Crowston K (1993) The Interdisciplinary Study of Coordination. CCS WP #157, Sloan School WP #3630-93. Massachusetts Institute of Technology, Sloan School of Management, Cambridge, Mass., November 1993.

Malone TW and Crowston K (1990) What is coordination theory and how can it help design cooperative work systems? In: Halasz F (ed) Proceedings of the ACM CSCW'90 Conference on Computer Supported Cooperative Work, ACM, POB 64145, Baltimore, MD 21264, pp. 357–370.

Malone T, Crowston K, Lee J and Pentland B (1993) Tools for inventing organizations: Toward a handbook of organizational processes. CCS WP #141, Sloan School WP #3562-93. Massachusetts Institute of Technology, Sloan School of Management, Cambridge, Mass., May 1993.

Malone T, Grant K, Lai K, Rao R and Rosenblitt D (1988) Semistructured Messages are Surprisingly Useful for Computer Supported Coordination. In: ACM Transactions on Office Information Systems, 5(2), 1987, pp. 115–131.Also in: Greif I Computer Supported Cooperative Work: A Book of Readings, Morgan Kaufmann, San Mateo, CA., 311–331.

Malone T, Lai KY and Fry Ch (1992) Experiments with Oval: A Radically Tailorable Tool for Cooperative Work. In: Turner J and Kraut R (eds) Proceedings of the ACM 1992 Conference on Computer-Supported Cooperative Work, New York, 1992, pp. 289–297.

Malone T (1988) Organizing Information Processing Systems Parallels Between Human

Organizations and Computer Systems. In Zachary W Robertson S and Black J (eds) Cognition, Cooperation, and Computation. Ablex Publishing Corporation, Norwood, NJ, 1988.

Malone TW (1992) Analogies between Human Organizations and Artificial Intelligence Systems: Two Examples and some Reflections. In Masuch M and Warglin M (eds), pp. 21–40.

Malone TW and Crowston K (1991) Toward an interdisciplinary theory of coordination, Technical Report, Center for Coordination Science, CCS TR# 120, SS WP# 3294-91-MSA, Cambridge, Mass.

Malone TW, Grant KR, Lai KY, Rao R and Rosenblitt DA (1989) The Information Lens: an intelligent system for information sharing and coordination. In: Olson MH (ed) Technological Support for Work Group Collaboration, Lawrence Erlbaum, Hillsdale, NJ.

Malone TW and Smith SA (1984) Tradeoffs in Designing Organisations: Implications for New Forms of Human Organisations and Computer Systems,Technical Report CISR WP 112, Centre for Information Systems Research, Sloan School of Management, Massachusetts Institute of Technology.

Malone Th, Yates J and Benjamin I (1987) Electronic Markets and Electronic Hierarchies, Communications of the ACM, 30(6), June 1987, pp. 484–497.

Mäntylä R, Alasuvanto J and Hämmäinen H (1990) PAGES: A Testbed for Groupware Applications. In: Gibbs S and Verrijn-Stuart AA (eds) IFIP WG8.4 Conference on Multi-User Interfaces and Applications. Heraklion, Crete, Sept. 24–26, 1990, Amsterdam, 1990, pp. 37–47.

March JG and Simon HA (1958) Organizations. New York.

Marsden JR and Pingry DE (1988) The Intelligent Organization: Some Observations and Alternative Views. Proceedings of the 21st Annual Hawaii Conference on System Sciences, 1988, pp. 19–24.

Martens C and Lochovsky FH (1991) OASIS: A programming environment for implementing distributed organizational support systems, in: de Jong P (ed) Conference on Organizational Computing Systems, ACM., 11 West 42nd Street, New York, NY 10036, Published as ACM SIGOIS Bulletin, 12(2 and 3), pp. 29–42.

Martial F and Victor F (1987) An Interactive Planner for Open Systems. Forschungsbericht FB-GMD-87-35. St. Augustin, 1987.

Martial FW (1992) Coordination by Negotiation based on a Connection of Dialogue States with Actions, in Proc. Workshop DAI-92, Glen Harbor, MI.

Marwell G and Schmitt DR (1975) Cooperation, Academic Press, New York.

Masini G, Napoli A, Colnet D, Leonard D and Tombre K (1991) Object Oriented Languages, The APIC Series, Harcourt Brace Jovanovich, Publishers.

Masuch M and Warglien M (eds) (1992) Artificial Intelligence in Organization and Management Theory. Models of Distributed Activity, North Holland, Amsterdam.

Matsuda T (1988) Enhancing Organizational Intelligence Through Effective Information Systems Management. The EDP Auditor Journal Vol. 4, 1988, pp. 17–42.

Matsuda T (1988a) OR/MS, its Interaction with and Benefit from Japanese Organizational Intelligence. OMEGA International Journal of Management Science, Vol 16(3), 1988, pp. 233–241.

Matsuda T (1988b) OR/MS and Information Technology for Higher Organizational Intelligence. Opsearch, 25(1), 1988, pp. 3–27.

Matsuda T (1990) S3-Integration of Human and Machine for Advanced Organizational Intelligence. In: Noro K and Brown O Jr (eds) Human Factors in Organizational Design and Development. Elsevier Science Publishers, North Holland, 1990, pp. 381–384.

Matsuda T (1991) Organizational Intelligence: Coordination of Human Intelligence and Machine Intelligence. In: Bourgine P, Walliser B (eds) Economics and Cognitive Science. Selected Papers from CECOIA 2, July 1990, Paris. Pergamon Press, 1991, pp. 171–180.

Matsuda T (1992) Organizational Intelligence: Its Significance as a Process and as a Product. In: Proceedings of the International Conference on Economics/Management and Information Technology 92. Tokio, Japan, August 31– September 4, 1992. Published by The Japan Society for Management Information. Tokio 1992, pp. 219–222.

Maturana HR and Varela FJ (1987, 1992, rev. edition), The tree of Knowledge. The Biological Roots of Human Understanding, Shambhala, Boston and London.

Mazer M (1987) Exploring the Use of Distributed Problem Solving in Office Support Systems. In: Proceedings of the IEEE Computer Society Office Automation Symposium, Gaithersburg, MD, April 27–29, 1987, Washington, 1987, pp. 217–225.

Medina-Mora R et al. (1992) The Action Workflow Approach to Workflow Management Technology. In: Proceedings of the ACM 1992 Conference on Computer-Supported

Cooperative Work, New York, 1992, pp. 281–288.

Mehandjiev N, Bottaci L and Phillips R (1994) User enhanceability for fast response to changing office needs, in: Nunamaker JF Jr and Sprague RH Jr (eds) Proceedings of the 27th Hawaii International Conference on Systems Sciences: Vol. IV,. IEEE CS Press, pp. 673–682.

Mehlmann OF (1993) Ein aktives computergestütztes Medium zur Verteilten Planung im Unternehmen, Dissertation TU Berlin.

Mertens P (1991) Integrierte Informationssysteme. Bd.I, Administrations- und Dispositionssysteme, 8. Aufl. Wiesbaden.

Mesarovic MD Macko D and Takahara Y (1970) Theory of Hierarchical, Multilevel, Systems, Academic Press, New York.

Miller D, Friesen PH (1984) Organisations A Quantum View, Prentice-Hall, Inc., Englewood Cliffs, New Jersey 07632.

Minsky M (1985) The Society of Mind, Simon & Schuster, New York.

Mintzberg H (1979) The Structuring of Organizations, Prentice-Hall, Englewood Cliffs, NJ.

Mintzberg H (1983) Structure In Fives: Designing Effective Organisations, Prentice-Hall International Editions.

Mooney JD (1947) The Coordination Principle. Reprinted in: Koontz H and O'Donnell C (eds) (1959) Readings in Management, McGraw Hill, New York.

Morrison J and Olfman L (1994) Organizational Memory. Proceedings of the 27th Hawaii International Conferences on System Sciences, 1994, p. 169.

Morton MSS (ed) (1991) The Corporation of the 1990s. Oxford University Press, New York, N.Y., 1991.

Moss JEB (1981) Nested Transactions: An Approach to Reliable Computing, MIT Report MIT-LCS-TR-260, Massachusetts Institute of Technology, Laboratory of Computer Science, 1981 and Nested Transactions: An Approach to Reliable Distributed Computing, The MIT Press, Research Reports and Notes, Information Systems Series, M. Lesk (ed), 1985.

Motiwalla L and Nunamaker J (1992) MAIL-MAN: A Knowledge-Based MAIL Assistant for MANagers. In: Journal of Organizational Computing, 2(2), 1992, pp. 131–154.

Müller J (ed) (1993) Verteilte Künstliche Intelligenz, BI Wissenschaftsverlag Mannheim, Leipzig, Wien, Zürich.

Müller HJ and Wittig T (1993) Anwendungen von Multi-Agenten Systemen, in: Verteilte Künstliche Intelligenz: Methoden und Anwendungen, in: Müller J (ed) (1993), BI Wissenschaftsverlag Mannheim, Leipzig, Wien, Zürich.

Müller RA (1988) Systeme verteilter Intelligenz im Unternehmen. Internes Programmpapier der Forschung der Daimler-Benz AG, Berlin.

Müller RA (1993) Quantitative Reasoning – A new method of simulation with uncertainties, Systems Analysis Modelling Simulation, 11(1), pp. 17–29.

Müller RA (1994) Verteilte Intelligenz. Eine Kritik an der Künstlichen Intelligenz aus Unternehmenssicht. In: Krämer S (ed) Geist – Gehirn – Künstliche Intelligenz. Zeitgenössische Modelle des Denkens, de Gruyter, Berlin and New York.

Nagasundaram M (1990) Style and Substance in Communication: Implications for Message Structuring Systems. In: ACM SIGOIS Bulletin, 11(4), 1990, pp. 33–41.

Nebel B (1990a) Reasoning and revision in hybrid representation systems, LNAI 422, Springer.

Nebel B (1990b) Terminological reasoning is inherently intractable, AI 43, pp. 235–249.

Newell A and Simon HA (1972) Human Problem Solving. Englewood Cliffs NY, 1972.

Newell A (1982) The Knowledge Level. AI 18, 1982, p. 86.

Newman W (1980) Office Models and Office Systems Design. In: Naffah N (ed) Integrated Office Systems – Burotics. Proc. of the IFIP TC-6 Workshop on Integrated Office Systems – Burotics, Versailles, France, Nov. 6–9, 1979, Amsterdam, New York, Oxford, 1980, pp. 3–12.

Nierenburg S and Lesser V (1986) Providing Intelligent Assistant in Distributed Office Environments. In: Proceedings of the 3rd ACM SIGOIS Conference on Office Information Systems, Providence, RI, Oct. 6–8, 1986, pp. 104–112.

Nirenberg J (1993) The Living Organization – Transforming Teams into Workplace Communities. Business One Irwin, Homewood, Ill., 1993.

Niwa K (1922) Knowledge Sharing Systems for Organizational Intelligence. In: Proceedings of the International Conference on Economics/Management and Information Technology 92. Tokio, Japan, August 31 – September 4, 1992. Published by The Japan Society for Management Information. Tokio 1992, pp. 227–230.

Numaoka C and Tokoro M (1990) Conversation Among Situated Agents. In Proceedings of the 10th Workshop on Distributed AI, Chapter 13, Bandera, Texas, October 23–27, 1990.

Numaoka C (1991) A Conceptual Framework for Modeling Conversation in Open Distributed Systems. PhD thesis. Keio University, Department of Electrical Engineering. Yokohama, Japan.

Nunamaker J et al. (1991) Electronic Meeting Systems to Support Group Work. In: Communications of the ACM, 34(7), pp. 41–60.

Nunamaker JF et al. (1988] Nunamaker JF Jr, Weber, , Smith, CAP.: Crises Planning Systems: Tools for Intelligent Action. In: Proceedings of the Twenty-First Annual Hawaii Conference on System Sciences, 1988, p. 25.

Nunamaker JF Jr, Weber ES and Smith CAP (1991) Crises Planning Systems: Tools for Intelligent Action. In: Proceedings of the 21st Annual Hawaii Conference on System Sciences, 1988, pp. 25–34.

O'Hare GMP (1995) Commitment Manipulation within Agent Factory, Proceedings of Decentralised Intelligent and Multi-Agent Systems, DIMAS '95, 22-24 Nov. 1995, Cracow Poland.

O'Hare GMP and Abbas S (1994) Agent Oriented Programming: Communicating Intentional Processes, In KI-94 Workshops, (eds) J. Kunze and H. Stoyan, 18th German Artificial Intelligence Conference KI-94, Saarbruken, 18th–23rd Sept. 1994.

O'Hare GMP, Dongha RP, Macaulay LA and Viller SA (1992) Agency within CSCW: Towards the Development of Active Cooperative Working Environments, In AI, Autonomous Agents and CSCW, (DTI , London, 1992], Springer-Verlag 1994.

O'Hare GMP and Jennings N (1996) (eds), Foundations of Distributed Artificial Intelligence, 6th Generation Computer Technology Series, Wiley Inter-Science, 1996.

O'Hare GMP and Wooldridge M (1992) A Software Engineering Perspective on Multi Agent System Design: Experience in the Development of MADE, In Avouris NM and Gasser L (eds) Distributed Artificial Intelligence: Theory and Praxis, Computer and Information Science Vol. 5, Kulwar Academic Publishers, for the Commission of the European Communities, The Netherlands, pp. 81–107.

Oberquelle H (ed) (1991) Cooperative Arbeit und Computerunterstützung. Stand und Perspektiven, Verlag für Angewandte Psychologie, Göttingen.

Ousterhout JK (1994) Tcl and the Tk Toolkit, Addison-Wesley.

Panko R and Sprague R (1982) Towards a Framework for Office Support. In: Proceedings of the ACM SIGOA Conference. Philadelphia, June 21–23, 1982, New York, 1982.

Papazoglou MP et al. (1992) An organizational framework for intelligent cooperative IS, International Journal on Intelligent & Cooperative Information Systems 1(1) 1992, pp. 169–202.

Paradice DB (1988) The Role of Memory in Intelligent Information Systems. In: Proceedings of the 21st Annual Hawaii Conference on System Sciences, 1988, pp. 2–9.

Pattison HE, Corkill GG and Lesser VR (1987) Instantiating Descriptions of Organizational Structures. In Huhns M (ed) Distributed AI, 1987, p. 311.

Payes P and Brun P (1987) Crmm – a Distributed Bulletin Board, Schicker PS and Speth R Message Handling Systems, IFIP 6.5 Working Conference 1987, Elsevier, Munich.

Pedersen E (1992) Issues of Openness in the Tivoli Project. In: ACM SIGOIS Bulletin, No.2, pp.30–31.

Petrie Jr, CJ (1992) Enterprise Integration Modeling. Proceedings of the 1st International Conference, MIT Press, Cambridge, Mass.

Picot A and Reichwald R (1987) Bürokommunikation. Leitsätze für den Anwender. 3.Aufl. Hallbergmoos.

Pinneseault A and Kraemer K (1989) The Impact of Technological Support on Groups: An Assessment of the Empirical Research. In: Decision Support Systems, 5, 1989, pp. 197–216.

Poensgen OH (1980) Koordination. In Grochla E (ed) Handwörterbuch der Organisation, Poeschel, Stuttgart, 2nd ed., pp. 1130–1141.

Pollok S (1988) A Rule-Based Message Filtering System. In: ACM Transactions on Office Information Systems, 6(3), 1988, pp. 232–254.

Pondy LR, Frost PJ, Morgan G and Dandrigde TC (1983) Organizational Symbolism. Greenwich London 1983.

Porter ME and Millar VE (1985) How Information Gives You Competitive Advantage. In: Havard Business Review, (4), 1985, pp. 149–160.

Porter ME (1985) Competitive Advantage: Creating and Sustaining Superior Performance. New York, Free Press.

Prinz W (1989) Survey of Group Communication Models and Systems. In: Pankoke-Babatz U (ed), Computer-Based Communication. The AMIGO Activity Model, Chichester, 1989, pp. 127–180.

Ram A (1992) Natural Language Understanding for Information-Filtering Systems. In: Communications of the ACM, 35(12), 1992, pp. 80–81.

Reber G (1989) Lernen und Planung, in: HWPlan Szyperski N (ed) pp. 960–972, 1989.

Rein G and Ellis C (1990) rIBIS: A Real-time Group Hypertext System. MCC Technical Report STP-095-90, 1990.

Robinson M (1991) Through a Lens Smartly. In: Byte, 16(5), 1991, pp. 177–187.

Rodden T (1992) ECSCW '91 Developers Workshop. In: ACM SIGOIS Bulletin, No. 2, pp. 3–5.

Roethlisberger FJ and Dickson WJ (1939) Management and the Worker, Harvard University Press, Cambridge, Mass.

Rühli E (1992) Koordination. In Fres E (ed), Handwörterbuch der Organisation, Poeschel, Stuttgart, third ed., pp. 1164–1175.

Sabbath, G. (1993), Knowledge Representation and Natural Language Understanding, AICOM 6(3/4), pp. 155-186

Sandholzer U (1990), Informationstechnik und innerbetriebliche Kooperation. Anforderungen an Informationstechniken aus der Perspektive organisierter innerbetrieblicher Kooperation. Diss. Uni Bayreuth, REA-Verlag, Hummeltal.

Sathi A and Fox MS (1988) Constraint-Directed Negotiation of Resource Reallocations, Gasser L and Huhns M, Distributed Artificial Intelligence II, Morgan Kaufmann, San Mateo, CA, 163–19.

Scheer A-W (1994) Wirtschaftsinformatik: Referenzmodelle für industrielle Geschäftsprozesse. Springer-Verlag Berlin, Heidelberg, New York.

Scheew O (1995) Entwicklung einer interaktiven Entwicklungsumgebung für Agentensysteme IDEAS, MSc. thesis (incl. IDEAS Users Guide), University of Kiel, Kiel.

Schmidt B (1979) Bilanzmodelle. Simulationsverfahren zur Verarbeitung unscharfer Teilinformationen, Bericht des ORL-Instituts der ETH, Nr. 40, Zürich.

Schmidt B (ed) (1988) Information on Complex Systems – Representation and Inference. Five Papers Presented at the 4th International Symposium on Forecasting, London 1984, Verlag der Fachvereine, Zürich.

Schmidt K (1991) Riding a Tiger, or Computer Supported Cooperative Work. In: Bannon L, Robinson M and Schmidt K (eds) Proceedings of the Second European Conference on Computer-Supported Cooperative Work (ECSCW91). Dordrecht, Boston, London 1991, pp. 1–16.

Schmidt K and Bannon L (1992) Taking CSCW Seriously – Supporting Articulation Work. In: Computer Supported Cooperative Work (CSCW), 1(1), 1992, pp. 7–40.

Schmidt-Schauss M (1989) Subsumption in KL-ONE is undecidable, Proc. 1. Int. Conf. on Principles of Knowledge Repr. \& Reason., Toronto, pp. 421–431.

Schooler E, Casner S and Postel L (1991) Multimedia Conferencing: Has it Come of Age? In: Nunamaker JF (ed) Proceedings of the 24th Hawaii International Conference on System Sciences. Kanuai, Hawaii, Jan. 8–11, 1991. Vol. III, Los Alamitos, 1991, pp. 707–716.

Schwarz P and Spector A (1984) Synchronizing Shared Abstract Types, ACM Transactions on Computer Systems, 2(3), August 1984.

Scott WR (1987) Organisations: Rational, Natural, and Open Systems, Second Edition, Prentice-Hall International Editions.

Searle JR (1969) Speech Acts, Cambridge Univ. Press, Cambridge, UK.

Searle JR and Vanderveken D (1985) Foundations of Illocutionary Logic, Cambridge Univ. Press, Cambridge, UK.

Shechory O and Kraus S (1994) Coalition formation among autonomous agents (preliminary report).

Shepherd A, Mayer N and Kuchinsky A (1990) Strudel – An Extensible Electronic Toolkit. In: Proceedings of the ACM 1990 Conference on Computer-Supported Cooperative Work, New York, 1990, pp. 93–104.

Sheth A et al. (1991a), Specifying interdatabase dependencies in a MDB environment, IEEE Computer, pp. 46-52 (also Bellcore TM-STS-018609/1).

Sheth A et al. (1991b) On applying classification to schema integration, Proc. IEEE 1.Wshp Interop. MDBS, Kyoto (Japan).

Sheth A et al. (1993) On automatic reasoning for schema integration, International Journal on Intelligent & Cooperative Information Systems , 2(1), pp. 23–40.

Sheth A and KashyapV (1992) So far schematically yet so near semantically, Proc. IFIP TC2/WG

2.6, pp. 1–29.

Sheth AP and Larson JA (1990) Federated Database Management Systems for Managing Distributed, Heterogeneous, and Autonomous Databases. ACM Computing Surveys, 22(3), September 1990, pp. 183–236.

Shoham Y (1990) Agent-oriented programming, Technical Report, Department of Computer Science, Stanford University.

Shoham Y (1993) Agent-oriented programming, Artificial Intelligence, 60, pp. 5192.

Sian SS (1990) Adaptation Based on Cooperative Learning in Multi-Agent Systems, Demazeau Y, Müller JP, Decentralized AI, Elsevier/North-Holland, Amsterdam, 257–272.

Simon HA (1969) The Science of the Artificial. Cambridge MA, 1969.

Simoudis E and Adler M (1992) Integrating Distributed Expertise. International Journal of Intelligent and Cooperative Information Systems, 1(3&4), 1992, pp. 393–410.

Singh M (1990a) Group Intentions. Proceedings of the 10th International Workshop on Distributed Artificial Intelligence, Bandera, Texas, October 23–27, 1990. MCC Techn. Report, ACT-AI-355-90. Chapter 12.

Singh M (1990b) Group Ability and Structure. In: Preproceedings of the Second European Workshop on Modelizing Autonomous Agents and Multiagent Worlds (MAAMAW-90), Saint-Quentin en Yvelines, France, 1990, pp. 85–100.

Singh MP (1991) Towards a Formal Theory of Communication for Multi-Agent Systems, Proc. IJCAI-91, 69–74.

Smith H (1988) The Requirements for Group Communication Services. In: Speth R (ed) European Teleinformatics Conference – EUTECO '88 on Research into Networks and Distributed Applications, Vienna, April 20–22, 1988, Amsterdam et al., 1988, pp. 89–95.

Smith H, Weiss K-H and Bogen M (1989) An Introduction to Group Communication Service Requirements. In: Smith H, Onions J and Benford St (eds) Ditributed Group Communication. The AMIGO Information Model, Chichester, 1989, pp. 1–11.

Smith R and Davis (1981) Frameworks for Cooperation in Distributed Problem Solving. IEEE Transactions on Systems, Man and Cybernetics, SMC-11/1, 1981, pp. 61–70.

Smith RG (1980) The Contract-Net Protocol: High-Level Communication and Control in a Distributed Problem Solver, IEEE Transaction on Computers, 29(12), pp. 1104–1113, 1980.

Smith RG (1979) A Framework for Distributed Problem Solving. Proceedings of the Joint International Conference on AI (IJCAI-79), pp. 836–841.

Smolka G and Nebel B (1989) Representation and Reasoning with attributive descriptions, IWBS Report 81, IBM Germany.

Smolka G and Schmidt-Schauß M (1991) Attributive concept description with complements, AI 48, pp. 1–26.

Smyth M and Clarke AA (1990) Human–Human Cooperation and the Design of Cooperative Machines. ICL Technical Journal, 7(1) 1990, pp. 110–127.

Smyth M (1994) Towards a Cooperative Agent. In Connolly JH, Edmonds E (eds) CSCW and AI. Springer-Verlag. CSCW Series. Spring 1994, pp. 1–12.

Sridharan NS (1987) 1986 Workshop on Distributed AI. AI Magazine, Fall 1987, p. 75.

Staehle WH (1987) Management, Vahlen, München.

Star SL (1989) The Structure of Ill-suited Solutions: Boundary Objects and Heterogeneous Distributed Problem Solving, In Gasser L and Huhns MN (eds) Distributed Artificial Intelligence, Vol. II, Morgan Kaufmann Publishers, pp. 37–54.

Stary C (1993) Model-Based Design Bases for Task-Oriented Applications. International Conference on Data Engineering (ICDE-93), Wien, Austria, 21–23. April 1993.

Steels L (1985) Expert Systems and Beyond: Community Memories. In: Berold T (ed) Proceedings of the Technology Assessment and Management Conference of the Gottlieb Duttweiler Institute. Zurich, April 25–26, 1985, Amsterdam, 1986, pp. 17–29.

Steels L (1990) Cooperation Between Distributed Agents Through Self-Organisation, In Decentralised AI, Demazeau Y and Muller J-P (eds), Elsevier Science Publishers B.V., North-Holland, pp. 175–196.

Stefik M et al. (1987a) Beyond the Chalkboard: Computer Support for Collaboration and Problem Solving Meetings. In: Communications of the ACM, 30(1), 1987, pp. 32–47.

Stefik M et al. (1987b), WISIWYS Revised: Early Experiences with Multiuser Interfaces. In: ACM Transactions on Office Information Systems, 5(2), 1987, pp. 147–167.

Stefik MJ (1986), The Next Knowledge Medium. In: Huberman (ed) (1988) The Ecology of Computation, pp. 315–342, Elsevier Science Publishers, North-Holland.

Steiner D Mahling D and Haugeneder H (1990a), Human Computer Cooperative Work. In:

Proceedings of the 10th International Workshop on Distributed Artificial Intelligence Bandera, Tx., Oct. 23–27, 1990. MCC Technical Report Number ACT-AI-355-90, MCC, Austin, Tx., 1990.

Steiner D, Mahling D and Haugeneder H (1990b) Collaboration of Knowledge Bases via Knowledge Based Coordination. In: Deen SM (ed), CKBS'90, Proceedings of the International Working Conference on Cooperating Knowledge Based System. University of Keele, England, Oct. 3-5, 1990, Berlin *et al.*, 1991, pp. 113–144.

Stephens L and Merx M (1989) Agent Organization as an Effector of DAI System Performance. 9th Workshop on Distributed Artificial Intelligence, Rosario Resort, Eastsound, Washington, September 12–14, 1989, S. 263–292.

Stephens LM and Merx MB (1990) The Effect of Agent Control Strategy on the Performance of a DAI Pursuit Problem, Proceedings of the 10th Workshop on Distributed Artificial Intelligence, Texas.

Stolze M (1991) Task Level Framework for Cooperative Expert Systems Design. ai communications, Vol. 4 (1991) No. 2/3, p. 98.

Striening H-D (1988) Prozeß-Management, Versuch eines Integrierten Konzepts situationsadäquater Gestaltung von Verwaltungsprozessen – dargestellt am Beispiel in einem multinationalen Unternehmen – IBM Deutschland GmbH, Europäische Hochschulschriften, Reihe V, Volks- und Betriebswirtschaft, Vol. 92, Verlag Peter Lang, Frankfurt a. M.

Suchman L (1983) Office Procedure as Practical Action: Models of Work and System Design. In: ACM Transactions on Office Information Systems, 1(4), 1983, pp. 320–328.

Suchman L (1987) Plans and situated actions. The problem of human–machine communication. Cambridge *et al.*, 1987.

Sugawara T and Lesser V (1993) On-Line Learning of Coordination Plans. In: Proceedings of the 12th International Workshop on Distributed Artificial Intelligence, Hidden Valley, Pennsylvania, May 19–21, 1993, pp. 335–355.

Sundermeyer K (1991) A Development and Simulation Environment for Cooperating Knowledge-Based Systems, Verteilte Künstliche Intelligenz und kooperatives Arbeiten, Informatik Fachberichte 291, Springer-Verlag, Berlin, Heidelberg, 102–112.

Sunita T (1992) A Study on Measurement of Organizational Intelligence. In: Proceedings of CEMIT92/CECOIA 3 – International Conference on Economics, Management and Information Technology, Tokio 1992, pp. 207–210.

Sycara K (1988) Resolving Goal-Conflicts via Negotiation, Proc. AAAI-88, 245–250.

Sycara KP (1989) Argumentation: Planning other Agents' Plans. Proceedings 1989 International Joint Conference on Artificial Intelligence (IJCAI-89), pp. 517–523.

Sycara KP (1985) Arguments of Persuasion in Labor Mediation. Proceedings 1985 International Joint Conference on Artificial Intelligence (IJCAI-85).

Syring M and Hasenkamp U (1993) Communication-Oriented Approaches to Support Multi-User Processes in Office Work, Research Report, University of Marburg, 1993.

Tapscott D and Caston A (1993) Paradigm Shift – The New Promise of Information Technology. McGraw-Hill, Inc., New York *et al.*, 1993.

Tarau P (1994) BinProlog 3.0, User Guide, Universite de Moncton, Moncton, Canada.

Taylor FW (1919) Die Grundsätze wissenschaftlicher Betriebsführung, München.

Teramoto Y, Iwaski N and Richter F-J (1992) Inter-Organizational Learning through Strategic Alliances – Evolutionary Process of Corporate Networking. In: Proceedings of the International Conference on Economics/Management and Information Technology 92. Tokio, Japan, August 31–September 4, 1992. Published by The Japan Society for Management Information. Tokio 1992, pp. 239–242.

The MOCCA Group (1992) Mocca: An Environment for CSCW Applications. In: ACM SIGOIS Bulletin, 2, 1992, pp. 21–23.

Thomas SR (1993) PLACA – an agent-oriented programming language, PhD thesis, Stanford Report STAN-CS-93-1487.

Thompson H (1991) Natural Language Processing: An Overview. In: Brauer W, Hernández D (eds) Verteilte Künstliche Intelligenz und kooperatives Arbeiten. 4. Internationaler GI-Kongreß Wissensbasierte Systeme. München, 23–24.Oktober 1991, Berlin *et al.*, 1991.

Thompson JE and Tuden A (1964) Strategies, Structures and Processes of Organisational Decision, In Leavitt, H. J., and Pondy, L. R., (eds), Readings in Managerial Psychology, University of Chicago Press.

Thurow LC (1991) Foreword. In Morton S (ed.) The Corporation of the 1990s. Oxford University Press. New York, Oxford 1991.

Treur J (1994) Temporal Semantics of Meta-Level Architectures for Dynamic Control of Reasoning. In: Turini F (ed), Proceedings of the 4th International Workshop on Meta-Programming in Logic, META '94. Lecture Notes in Computer Science, Vol. 883, Springer-Verlag, pp. 353–376.

Treur J and Willems M (1995) Formal Notions for Verification of Dynamics of Knowledge-Based Systems. In: Rousset MC and Ayel M (eds) Proc. European Symposium on Validation and Verification of KBSs, EUROVAV'95, Chambery, pp. 189–199.

Treur J and Wetter Th (eds) (1993), Formal Specification of Complex Reasoning Systems, Ellis Horwood, p. 282.

Tsichritzis D (1982) Form Management. In: Communications of the ACM, 25(7), 1982, pp. 453–478.

Tsichritzis D and Gibbs S (1987) Messages, Messengers and Objects. In: Symposium on Office Automation of the IEEE Computer Society, Gaithersburg, MD, April 27–29, 1987, pp. 118–127.

Tsuchiya S (1992) Organizational Learning and Information Technology: Information Technology Improving Strategy Formation Process in a Loosely Coupled System. In: Proceedings of the International Conference on Economics/Management and Information Technology 92. Tokio, Japan, August 31–September 4, 1992. Published by The Japan Society for Management Information. Tokio 1992, pp. 249–252.

Turoff M (1991a) Computer-Mediated Communication Requirements for Group Support. In: Journal of Organizational Computing, 1(1), 1991, pp. 85–113.

Turoff M et.al., (1989) Computer mediated Communications and Tailorability. In: Proceedings of the 22nd Hawaii International Conference on System Sciences. Vol. III, Los Alamitos, 1989, pp. 403–411.

Turoff M, Rao U and Hiltz SR (1991b) Collaborative Hypertext in Computer Mediated Communication. In: Nunamaker JF and Sprague RH (eds) Proceedings of the 24th Hawaii International Conference on System Sciences. Kanuai, Hawaii, Jan. 8–11, 1991. Vol. IV, Los Alamitos, 1991, pp. 357–366.

Unland R and Schlageter G (1992) A Transaction Manager Development Facility for Non-Standard Database Systems, in: Elmagarid (ed) (1992).

Unland R (1990) A Flexible and Adaptable Tool Kit Approach for Concurrency Control in Non Standard Database Systems, Proc. 3rd Int. Conf. on Database Theory (ICDT), Paris, France, Dec. 1990

Unland R (1991) TOPAZ: A Tool Kit for the Construction of Application Specific Transaction Managers, Research-Report MIP-9113, University of Passau, Department of Computer Science, Oct. 1991.

v Martial F (1992) Coordinating Plans of Autonomous Agents. Lecture Notes in Artificial Intelligence, No. 610. Springer. Berlin, Heidelberg. Germany 1992.

v Martial F (1992) Coordinating Plans of Autonomous Agents. Lecture Notes in Artificial Intelligence, No. 610. Springer-Verlag, Berlin, Heidelberg. Germany 1992.

Varela FJ (1990) Kognitionswissenschaft – Kognitionstechnik, Suhrkamp, Frankfurt a.M.

Viller SA (1991) The Group Facilitator: a CSCW Perspective, in Bowers J (ed): ECSCW'91. The Second European Conference on Computer Support for Cooperative Work, Amsterdam, Holland.

von Luck K (1989) Repräsentation assertionalen Wissens im BACK-System – eine Fallstudie, KIT Report 72, TU Berlin/FB Informatik.

Wächter H and Reuter A (1992) The ConTract Model, in: Elmagarid (ed) (1992).

Warnecke H-J (1993) Revolution der Unternehmenskultur – Das Fraktale Unternehmen. Springer-Verlag Berlin et.al., 2. Auflage.

Warnecke H-J (1991) Die Fraktale Fabrik – Revolution der Unternehmenskultur, Springer-Verlag.

Watanabe YA (1992) The Role of Intra-Organization Network (ION) for Organizational Learning. In: Proceedings of the International Conference on Economics/Management and Information Technology 92. Tokio, Japan, August 31–September 4, 1992. Published by The Japan Society for Management Information. Tokio 1992, pp. 277–280.

Watson R (1990) A Design for an Infrastructure to Support Organizational Decision Making. In: Nunamaker JF (ed) Proceedings of the 23rd Annual Hawaii Internal Conference on System Sciences.Kanuai, Hawaii, Jan. 8–11, 1991. Vol. III, Los Alamitos, 1990, pp. 111–119.

Weihl W (1988) Commutativity-Based Concurrency Control for Abstract Data Types, Proc. IEEE 21st Annual Hawaii Int. Conf. on System Sciences (HICSS), Hawaii, Jan. 1988.

Weiß G (1996) Adaptation and Learning in Multi-Agent Systems. Some Remarks and a

Bibliography. In Weit3, G.; Sen, S. (eds) Adaptation and Learning in Multi-Agent Systems. Proceedings of the IJCAI-95 Workshop. Montreal, Canada, August 1995. Lecture Notes in Artificial Intelligence No. 1042, Springer-Verlag, Berlin *et al.* 1996, pp. 1–21.

Weiß G and Sen S (1996) (eds) Adaptation and Learning in MultiAgent Systems. Proceedings of the IJCAI-95 Workshop. Montreal, Canada, August 1995. Lecture Notes in Artificial Intelligence No. 1042, Springer Verlag, Berlin *et al.* 1996.

Weltz F and Ortmann RG (1992) Das Softwareprojekt. Projektmanagement in der Praxis, Campus, Frankfurt a.M.

Werkman K (1991) Using Negotiation and Coordination in Multiple Agent Systems. Proceedings of the IJCAI-91 Workshop on Intelligent and Cooperative Information Systems: Bringing AI and Information Systems Technology Together, Darling Harbour, Sydney, Australia, August 25, 1991.

Werner E (1987) Toward a Theory of Communication and Cooperation for Multiagent Planning, Vardi MY, Theoretical Aspects of Reasoning about Knowledge, Morgan Kaufmann , San Mateo, CA, 129–143.

Werner E (1992) The Design of Multi-Agent Systems, In Werner E and Demazeau Y(eds), Decentralised A.I.3, Elsevier Science Publishers, North-Holland, pp. 3-28.

Westley, F and Waters JA (1988) Group Facilitation Skills for Managers, In Management Education and Development, 19(20, pp. 134–143.

Wilbur S and Yuong R (1988) The COSMOS Project: A Multi-Disciplinary Approach to Design for Computer-Supported Group Working. In: Speth R (ed), European Teleinformatics Conference – EUTECO '88 on Research into Networks and Distributed Applications, Vienna, April 20–22, 1988, Amsterdam *et al.*, 1988, pp. 147–155.

Winograd T (1987a) A Language/Action Perspective on the Design of Cooperative Work. Center for the Study of Language and Information. Report CSLI-87-98. Stanford, CA.

Winograd T and Flores F (1987b) Understanding Computers and Cognition: A New Foundation for Design. Reading.

Woitass M (1990) Coordination of Intelligent Office Agents – Applied to Meeting Scheduling. In: Gibbs S and Verrijn-Stuart AA (eds), IFIP WG8.4 Conference on Multi-User Interfaces and Applications. Heraklion, Crete, Sept. 24–26, 1990, Amsterdam, 1990, pp. 371–387.

Wolf M (1995) New Technologies for Customer Rating: Integration of Knowledge-Based Systems and Human Judgement. International Journal of Intelligent Systems in Accounting, Finance and Management 4(4), December 1995.

Woo C and Lochovsky FH (1987) Integrating Procedure Automation and Problem Solving Approaches to Support Office Work. In: Bracchi G and Tsichritzis D (eds) IFIP WG 8.4 Working Conference on Methods and Tools for Office Systems, Pisa, October 1986, Elsevier, Amsterdam 1987, pp. 17–32.

Woo C (1990) SACT: A Tool for Automating Semi-Structured Organizational Communication. In: Lochovsky FH and Allen RB (eds) Conference on Office Information Systems. April 25–27, 1990, Cambridge, MA. ACM SIGOIS Bulletin, 11(2,3), 1990, pp. 89–98.

Wooldridge M and Jennings N (1995) Intelligent Agents: Theory and Practice, Knowledge Engineering Review.

Wooldridge MJ and O'Hare GMP (1991) Deliberate Social Agents, Proc. 10th UK. Planning Workshop, University of Cambridge.

Wooldridge M and Vandekerckhove D (1993) MY WORLD: An Agent-Oriented Programming Testbed for Distributed Artificial Intelligence, Pre-Proceedings in Cooperative Knowledge Based Systems, University of Keele.

Yamamoto B, Nakano B and Matsuda T (1992) System, Information, Organizational Intelligence and Self-Dynamics. In: Proceedings of the International Conference on Economics/Management and Information Technology 92. Tokio, Japan, August 31–September 4, 1992. Published by The Japan Society for Management Information. Tokio 1992, pp. 211–214.

Yonezawa A (1990) (ed) ABCL An Object-Oriented Concurrent System, MIT Press, Cambridge, Mass.

Yourdon E (1989) Modern Structured Analysis. Prentice-Hall, Englewood Cliffs, NJ.

Zisman M (1977) Representation, Specification and Automation of Office Procedures. Dissertation. Ann Arbor, Michigan.

Zuboff S (1988) In the Age of the Smart Machine: The Future of Work and Power. New York, Basic Books.

Name Index

Abbas S 30, 101, 191
Ackerman M 59
Ader M 58, 59
Adler M 11
Anderson R 176, 178
Applegate L 31, 33, 43
Austin JL 188, 196
Axelrod 15

Baader F 237–8
Ballmer T 201
Barber G 54, 58
Barbuceanu M 255
Barrett E 31
Beck HW 238, 255
Beeri C 118
Behrendt W 238, 254
Bena C 58
Bende M 160
Bentley R 94
Bhandara N 58
Blanco JM 238
Blanning RW 13, 17, 36, 139,
  146
Bogen M 50
Bond AH 2, 15, 150, 157, 231
Bonsiepen L 35
Borgida A 237
Bouguettaya A 230, 240, 255
Bowers J 55, 56, 59
Brachman RJ 236
Brandau R 203
Brazier FMT 212–3, 229
Brauer W 31
Brennenstuhl W 201
Bright MW 233
Briot J-P 187
Brooks RA 33
Bui TX 50
Bunge M 28
Burmeister B 205
Busch E 59
Bussmann S 201
Butler R 176
Buxton B 51
Byrne C 248

Campbell JA 204
Canning RG 52
Carley KM 14, 140
Cartwright D 184
Caston A 9
Cataraci T 238, 255
Ceri S 230, 234
Chaib draa B 178, 180-1
Champy J 149
Chang MK 204, 209
Chrysanthis P 133
Clarke DD 14, 34
Cockburn D 213
Coenen F 66, 69, 70, 71, 78
Cohen PR 15, 152, 188,
  196–7, 199–200
Connor JJ 139, 144
Cook P 50
Corkill D 24, 148, 175, 178–9,
  182–3
Conklin J 59
Conry SE 210
Coy W 35
CRC Project Team 88, 93
Crocker DH 68
Croft W 58
Crowley T 51
Crowston K 7, 29, 31, 37, 152
Cyret RM 176

de Greef P 14, 15
de Jong P 14
Daft RL 159, 177
Davenport TH 8, 139
Davidow WH 19, 151, 153
Davis R 160, 180, 202
Dayal U 130
Desantis G 48
DeCindio F 56
Decker K 23
Dieng R 229
D'Inverno MP 204
Dollimore J 94
Duncan R 158
Dunham R 55
Dunin-Keplicz B 213
Durfee EH 149, 152, 202, 210

Edward P 248
Egido C 51
Ellis C 54, 59, 117, 118, 145
Elofson GS 139
Elmagarid E 230, 233, 236
Engelfriet J 223

Favela, J 139, 144
Fickas S 152
Fikes R 54
Finch I 69, 70, 74, 78
Finnin T 205
Fish R 59
Flores F 26, 28, 29, 31, 33, 34,
  55, 64, 203
Foppa K 158
Foroughi A 49
Fox MS 19, 153, 175, 210,
  231, 255
Friesen D 177

Gaitanides M 21
Gallbraith J 182, 184, 186
Galliers JR 197
Gareis R 159
Gasser L 7, 12, 14, 15, 94,
  145, 148, 150, 157, 160,
  173–4, 176, 179–81, 187
Gavrila IS 223, 231
Gao H 244
George J 49
Genereseth MR 196, 247, 252
Gibson JL 183, 186
Ginsberg M 14, 154
Gioia DA 30, 37
Greenberg S 31, 33, 64
Gray JN 125
Grief I 118
Grossmann B 248
Guilfoyle C 139, 140, 151,
  154
Gutenberg E 3

Haghjoo M 117
Hales K 54

Halonen D 50
Hammainen H 94
Hammer M 10, 149
Hammer J 230, 255
Hansen RA 28
Hasenkamp U 155
Hastings C 10
Haugeneder H 204
Helm R 152
Herlihy M 133
Hernandez D 31
Hewitt C 14, 54, 176
Hiltz SR 33
Hogg J 54
Hollunder B 237–8
Huber GP 3, 139, 141
Hubermann BA 33, 37
Huhns M 176, 199
Hurson AR 233

Ishida T 24, 139, 148, 179–80
Ishii H 51, 58, 59

Jarke M 118, 145, 152
Jelassu M 49
Jennings NR 101, 152, 213–4, 231, 255
Johansen R 59

Kakehi R 203
Kandzia P 238
Kaplan S 55
Karbe B 54
Kashyap V 230, 232, 234
Kaye A 58
Keiser A 27, 31
Kerr E 64
Ketchpel S 245, 247, 255
Khandwalla 159
Kirn St 7, 10, 12, 13, 14, 16, 18, 20, 22, 24, 30, 140, 151, 152, 154, 155, 157
Klahold P 121
Klien M 203, 238
Klöfer A 30
Klusch M 237, 241, 246
Koo C 58
König W 14
Konsynski BR 139
Korf R 160
Kornfield W 176
KQML 199
Kraemer K 49, 50
Kraus S 245, 247, 255
Kreifelts Th 54, 56
Kuwabara K 22

Laßmann, A 30
Lai KY 56, 93
Langevelde IA 212
Larson JA 230, 232, 235, 254
Lauriston R 59
Lee KC 94
Lee J 59
Lee RM 79
Lenat D 175–6, 179, 182
Lenzerini M 238, 255
Lesser VR 22, 23, 24, 148, 149, 175, 178–9, 182–3, 210
Levesque HJ 152, 197
Levin JA 15, 201
Levinson SC 201
Levy R 160
Lewis B 59
Litwin W 234
Lutz E 57
Lutze R 58
Lux A 199

Macauley LM 93, 99
Malone TW 7, 19, 26, 29, 30, 31, 37, 56, 66, 72, 79, 80, 82, 88, 89, 139, 151, 152, 153, 180
Mamdani A 152
Mäntylä R 54, 58
March JG 3, 28, 30, 176
Marsden JR 139
Martens C 94
Marwell G 27
Masini G 187
Masuch M 14, 31, 36
Maturana HR 36
Matsuda T 7, 14, 139, 140, 141, 142, 146, 149, 151, 156, 157, 174
Mazer M 54
McDaniel RR 3, 139
Medina-Mora R 55
Mehandjiev N 92
Mehlmann OF 39
Mertens P 52
Merx MB 152, 160
Mesarovic 26
Miller D 177
Minsky M 33
Mintzberg H 15, 79, 81, 93, 177, 180, 184
Montgomery TA 202
Mooney JD 27
Moore JA 15, 201
Morrison J 144
Morton MSS 4, 5, 10, 14, 139
Moss JEB 118
Motiwalla L 57
Müller J 201

Müller RA 35, 39, 157, 231, 247

Nagasundaram M 56, 57
Nebel B 231, 237, 238
Newell A 153
Nierenburg S 58
Nirenberg J 139
Niwa K 139
Numaoka C 154, 199–200
Nunamaker JF 50, 153
Nutt W 238

O'Hare GMP 28, 30, 95, 101, 102, 178, 187–8, 231
Oberquelle H 31
Olfman L 139, 144
Ortmann RG 35
Ousterhout JK 248

Papazoglou MP 173–4, 230
Panko R 44
Paradice DB 139, 144
Pattison HE 179–80
Payes P 64
Pedersen E 47
Perrault CR 15, 188, 196
Petrie Jr 19, 139, 151, 153, 199–200
Pingry DE 139
Pinneseault A 49
Pollok S 57
Porter ME 8, 45
Prietula KM 140
Prinz W 59

Ram A 56
Reber G 159
Rein G 59
Reuter A 136
Rodden T 47
Rühli E 30, 31

Sabbath G 241
Sandholzer U 31, 35
Sarin S 118
Sathi A 210
Scheer A-W 8, 14
Scheew O 248
Schlageter G 18
Schmidt B 39
Schmidt K 45, 47
Schmidt-Schauß M 237–8
Schmitt DR 27
Schooler E 51

Schmolze JG 236
Schwarz P 133
Scott WR 180
Searle JR 197–8
Sen S 148
Seth A 230, 232, 234, 238, 254–5
Sharrock W 176, 178
Shechory O 245, 247, 255
Shepherd A 55
Shoham Y 174, 188, 194, 248
Sian SS 203
Simon HA 3, 30, 31, 58
Simoudis E 11
Singh MP 151, 152, 198
Smith H 50
Smith RG 152, 160, 161, 180, 202
Smith SA 179
Smolka G 237–8
Smyth M 14
Spector A 133
Sprague R 44
Staehle WH 28, 31
Stefik M 31, 33, 50
Steels L 59, 179, 185
Steers RM 159
Steiner D 7, 12, 14, 58, 204
Stephens LM 151, 160
Striening H-D 28
Suchman L 45
Sugawara T 24, 148
Sundermeyer K 14, 209
Sunita T 139

Sycara K 14, 22, 23, 202
Syring M 155

Tapscott D 9, 14
Tarau P 248
Taylor FW 3
Teramoto Y 147, 153
The MOCCA Group 59
Thomas R 248
Thompson H 56
Thompson JE 183
Thurow LC 4
Tokoro M 199–200, 203
Treur J 213, 223, 229
Tuden A 183
Turoff M 31, 33, 52, 59
Tsichritzis D 49, 54
Tsuchiya S 147, 153

Unland R 154, 157

v Martial F 14, 22, 23, 58, 152, 202
Vandekerckhove D 188
Vanderveken D 198
Varela FJ 33, 36
Viller SA 108, 113

Wächter H 136
Warglien M 31, 36

Warnecke H-J 19, 23, 140, 151, 153
Warner E 139, 140, 151, 154
Watanabe YA 139
Waters JA 100, 112, 113
Watson R 48
Weiß G 148
Weltz RG 35
Weihl W 133
Weihmayer R 203
Weiss A 158
Werner E 178, 180, 198, 201
Westley F 100, 112, 113
Widon J 230, 234
Wilbur S 55, 59
Willems M 229
Winnograd T 26, 28, 29, 31, 33, 34, 203
Wittig T 157
Woitass M 59
Woo CC 46, 58, 204, 209
Wooldridge M 178, 187–8, 231, 255

Yamamoto B 153
Yonezawa A 188
Yourdon E 15

Zander A 184
Zhang A 230, 233, 236
Zisman M 54
Zuboff S 6

Subject Index

acquaintances 149, 214
actions 55, 69
actors 142
adaptation 151
adcmail 65, 69–70
Agent0 188
Agent Factory 188
Agent-Oriented Design (AOD) 101
agent-oriented information technology 153
Agent Oriented Programming (AOP) 174, 187–8
agent structure 186–7
agents, automomous/computational/intelligent 7, 11, 20, 58, 65–8, 70, 81, 93–4, 102–3, 117, 174–6, 179–180, 198, 212–3, 215–228, 231
agents, coalitions of 244–247
agents, human 72
Aide de Camp Project 65, 71
ALC 237
Alvey Initiative Human-Computer-Cooperation project 14
AMIGO 50, 59
ARCHON 213–4
ASPERA 58
assistant, intelligent 12
automate stage 6
authority 180, 182–3
autonomy 180, 183

BPR, see business process orientation
brainstorming 99, 106
business process integration 34
business process orientation 8, 10, 19
business processes, customization of 20

canonical interaction language 150
capabilities, attention focusing 17
capabilities, intellectual organizational 139
capabilities, meta-level 148
capabilities, organizational information processing 139
capabilities, organizational problem solving 139
Capture Lab 50
CATeam 50
CHAOS 56
CFL (Cooperative Filtering Language) 69–70, 74–5
CLOS 101, 188
CMC see Computer Mediated Communication
CN, see contract net
co-authoring 59
cognition, organizational 139, 142, 146, 153, 156
cognitive abilities 146
coherence 180
coherence, organizational 180–1
COKES 58
Colab 50
collaboration 117
collaborative work 82–8
collaborative search 19
collective cognition 146
collective intellectual capabilities 156
commitments 55
communication 32, 41–2, 117, 180, 184, 196, 227–8
communication, asynchronous 52, 56, 64
communication, organizational 139, 142, 149, 154, 156
communication orientated approach 48

communication, structured 49, 52–8
communication structures 55–6
communication, synchronous 50–1, 90
comprehension, organizational 146
Computer Mediated Communication (CMC) 33
computerization of the enterprise 154
COMTRAC/CAP 58
concurrency control/access 119, 120–138
concurrent updates 123
conflict management 42
conflict resolution 118, 203
conformity 181, 184–5
contract net 160, 166
Contract Net Protocol (CNP) 161, 180
conversation model 55, 203–4
COOKBOOK 58
Cooperative Requirements Capture (CRC) see CRC
cooperation strategies 152, 196
cooperative knowledge processing 1, 2, 10, 11, 12
cooperative problem solver 150
cooperative information system 117
coordination 26–34, 117–8, 142, 180, 182, 212, 259–62
coordination, concepts of 27–30
coordination, types of 30–2
coordination mechanisms 71–2, 88–93, 152
coordination systems 47

293

coordination, theory of 33, 153
CORBA 150
COORDINATOR *see* The Coordinator
COSMOS 55, 59, 94
COSY 209
coupled
  lightly 233
  tightly 233
CRC 88, 93, 98–114
CSCW 33, 43

DARPA 11, 150
decision orientated approach 48
Decision Support Systems (DSS) 48
DESIRE 212–3, 229
dialog 201
Distributed Intelligence (DI) 26
Distributed AI systems 143, 180
Distributed Artificial Intelligence (DAI) 12, 174–5, 180, 196, 209–210, 231
division of labor 145
DOMINO 54, 56
D-POLYMER 58
DSS *see* Decision Support Systems (DSS)

ECHOES 80–95
eCN, *see* extended contract net, 81 mail (email) 49, 54
emergence 191, 193
enabling technology 13
enterprise integration 153
enterprise, computerized 153
ESPRIT 11, 229
EuroCoOp Project 54
events 91
expertise, integrating distributed 11
extended contract net 166
external effects 122–134

facilitator 93, 107–8, 114
facilitation 106
Federated Database Systems (FDBS) 230–6
filtering 68, 74–5
filters, active 65–8

filters, intelligent 56–7
filters, message 56–7, 65–6
flexibility, organizational 22, 148
fractalization 7, 9, 153
fractals, organizational 21

GDSS *see* Group Decision Support Systems (GDSS)
global search 145
group(s) 54, 146, 181, 184–5
Group Decision Making 32, 42
Group Decision Support Systems (GDSS) 48, 49
group level 161
group level skills 143
group process 158
GroupSystems 50
groupware 12, 50, 65

Human Computer Cooperative Work 12, 14, 20
human intelligence 142
human knowledge processing 141
human learning 147
Human-Computer Team 154

IDEAS 248–254
illocutionary act 196–9
illocutionary force 198, 200
IMAGINE 15, 199
informate stage 6
information filtering 17, 56–7
information filtering agents 18
Information Lens 56–8, 79
information overload 65, 78
information processing, organizational 139
Information Terminological Formalism (ITF) 238–244
Intelligent Cooperative Information Systems (ICIS) 230
Intelligent Manufacturing Systems initiative 11
interactions 223
interacting agents, community of 150
InterDatabase Dependencies (IDD) 230, 241–244

internal effects 124–135
Internet 18
ISCREEN 57

KIK/TEAMWARE 58
KL-ONE 237
knowledge discovery 16, 18
knowledge discovery agent 18
knowledge, group level 142
knowledge, individual 142
knowledge management tools 148
knowledge, organizational 142, 144, 145, 148, 158, 179
knowledge processing, machine-based 141
knowledge representation 236–237
Knowledge Sharing effort 150
knowledge structures 218
KQML 199, 205, 210

language/action perspective 55
lean processes 21
learning capability of an organization 158
learning strategies 149
learning, adaptive 159
learning, individual 147, 159, 164
learning, innovative 159
learning, macro-organizational 147, 159, 161, 164
learning, micro-organizational 147, 159, 161, 164
learning, organizational 139, 141, 142, 147, 153, 156, 158, 161, 179
lock modes 121–2
locks 118–138
locks, browse 121–6
locks, derivation 121–9
locks, exclusive 121–7
locks, notify 118
locks, object related 133–136
locks, shared 120–133
locks, subject related 136–7
locks, update 121–133
locutionary act 196
LUPINO 58

machine intelligence 141, 142
macro-organizational level
153
Mail-Man 57
Management of the 1990s
Research Program 2,
4, 5, 6
MCConf 51
meeting systems 51
memory, macro-organiza-
tional 159, 161, 164
memory, organizational 59,
139, 142, 143, 144, 145,
153, 156, 161, 162, 169
Message Handling System
(MHS) 49
message types 57, 199
messages, semi-structured 57
messages, structured 55
MHS *see* Message Handling
System
MHS+ 50
micro-organizational level
147, 153
MMC 51
multiagent decision support
systems 12, 18
multiagent reasoning 151
multiagent system, organizational intelligent 162
multiagent systems 140, 144,
146, 148, 150, 151,
178–9, 187–191,
215–228
MYWORLD 188

Natural Language
Processing Systems
56
Negotiation Support Systems
(NSS) 49
Norms 181, 184–5
NSS *see* Negotiation Support
Systems

OASIS 94
Object Based Concurrent
Programming (OBCP)
187
object discovery problem
230, 235–6
Object Lens 56, 58
Object Oriented
Programming
Systems (OOPS) 187
Object Management Group
(OMG) 150
ODSS *see* Organizational

Decision Support
System (ODSS)
OFFICE 58
office information systems
53–55, 141, 80–96
OfficeTalk-D 54
office work 45, 48, 53–5,
80–81
office work, types of 44
OI *see* organizational intelligence
OMEGA 58
ontology 148
open systems 54
organization theory, computational 14
organization, administrative
subsystem of the 3
organization, computerized
14
organization, information
processing subsystem
of the 3
organization, intelligent 141
organization, physical
subsystem of the 3
organization, social subsystem of the 3
organization, subsystem of
aims and objectives of
the 3
organizational agent 162, 166
organizational aims and
objectives 146
organizational attention
focusing 146
organizational change 179
organizational computing
33, 43, 141
organizational coordination
27
organizational DB 162
Organizational Decision
Support System
(ODSS) 48
organizational inference 143
organizational information
processing and reason-
ing capabilites 151
organizational intelligence
14, 37, 139, 140, 141,
153, 155, 173, 194
organizational layer 152
organizational level 161
organizational model 2, 3,
191
organizational model, black
box-orientated 2
organizational model, decision-orientated 2

organizational model,
production-orientated
2, 3
organizational multiagent
system 140, 153, 156
organizational process intelligence 141, 142
organizational processes,
effectiveness of 4
organizational product intelligence 141
Organizational Self Design
(OSD) 179
organizational skills, intelligent 140
organizational structure,
static 19
organizational theory 141,
143, 147, 149, 151, 173,
176-7
Organizational Workbench
180, 193
organizations, computational
7, 193
organizations, intellectual
capability of 141
Oval 56, 58, 81, 93

PAGES 54, 58, 94
Partial Global Planning
(PGP) 149
participatory design 38
perception 32
perception, organizational
146
performatives 199
perlocutionary act 196
personal assistance 12, 18,
20, 141, 150
PERSUADER 202
PGP *see* Partial Global
Planning
PLEXIS 50
planned action 200–1
POLYMER 58
problem inference 160
problem solving, organizational 139, 151, 156
process configuration 21
process customization 21
process management
systems 22
process management, smart
21
process providers 23
Project Nick 50
protocols 201–9
Generic Configurable
Protocols (GCP) 205–9

hierarchical 202
negotiation 202–3
pursuit problem 160

Quantative Reasoning (QR)
    39–41

rationality 178
rationality, bounded 9, 141
reasoning, case-based 151
reasoning, explorative 151
reasoning, heuristic 151
reasoning, organizational
    139, 151, 154
reasoning, process-
    orientated 151
reasoning, structural 151
relationships, inter-group
    148
requirements 45–8, 59–63, 98
role concept 152, 178, 181,
    185
role allocation 219–220

schema(s) 232, 237

SCOOP 54
Scotland Yard 163
script 70
self control 148
self monitoring 148
self organization 9, 23, 47,
    141, 147, 160
social ability 180–1
social behavior 178–9
social meters 112
social syndromes 109, 112–3
social templates 113
Society of Mind 33
software agents 154
specification, framework
    215–8
specification, of multi-agent
    systems 219–228
Speech Acts 55
Speech Act based
    Negotiation Protocol
    (SANP) 204
Speech Act Theory 55–6,
    197–200
stakeholders 98–9, 109
strategies, organizational 7
structured messages 54
Structure Definition
    language (SDL) 55
Strudel 55

task control 223–8
task decomposition 180–3,
    215–7
task delegation 217–8
task hierarchy 216
task sequencing 217
Task Scripting Language
    (TSL) 70–1, 75–6
terminology 236–7
The Coordinator 55, 203
TLA 54

user agent 141
user assistant, intelligent 150
users 65, 77–8

value chain 5
Video Wall 51
virtual enterprise 12, 19, 153

Warehouse World 174,
    189–91
WISDOM 57
workflows 10, 81, 83
workflow management 22

Xerox PARC 50–1